W9-CEX-548

Foundations for Your Faith

Other Books by D. James Kennedy

Abortion: Cry of Reality
Beginning Again
Chain Reaction
Character and Destiny: A Nation in Search of Its Soul
Defending the First Amendment
Delighting God: How to Live at the Center of God's Will
Education: Public Problems, Private Solutions
Evangelism Explosion
The God of Great Surprises
The Great Deception
Help God, I Hurt!
Highway to Holiness
Knowing God's Will
Learning to Live with the People You Love
Messiah: Prophecies Fulfilled
Nation in Shame
Real Meaning of the Zodiac
Reconstruction
Spiritual Renewal
This Is the Life
Truth and Education
Truths That Transform
Turn It to Gold
What If Jesus Had Never Been Born?
Why I Believe
Wolves Among Us
Your Prodigal Child: Help for Hurting Parents

Foundations for Your Faith

D. James Kennedy

Fleming H. Revell
A Division of Baker Book House
Grand Rapids, Michigan 49516

© 1994 by D. James Kennedy

Published by Fleming H. Revell
a division of Baker Book House Company
P.O. Box 6287, Grand Rapids, MI 49516-6287

Printed in the United States of America

Unless otherwise noted, all Scripture is from the King James Version of the Bible.

Library of Congress Cataloging-in-Publication Data

Kennedy, D. James (Dennis James), 1930–
   Foundations for Your Faith / D. James Kennedy.
          p.   cm.
        1. Theology, Doctrinal—Popular works. 2. Christian life. 3.
   Westminster Confession of Faith. 4. Fundamentalist churches—
   Doctrines. I. Title.
      [BT 77.K2767   1995]
      230'.044—dc20
   94-179918

Contents

Part 1: Created for Glory

Introduction to Part 1   9

Who am I?
1. Quest for Life   20

How can I know any ultimate truth for certain?
2. The Only Rule   36

Is there a Source of ultimate truth?
3. A God Suppressed   56

Who or What is the Source of ultimate truth?
4. God Who Grows   72
5. The Absurd Trinity   92

Is anyone in control out there?
6. The God Revolution   110
7. Plan, Power, and Providence   126

If there is a good God, why . . . ?
8. The Sorcerer's Apprentice   142

Part 2: Saved by Grace

Introduction to Part 2   161

How did Jesus Christ make a way to God?
9. All Things Are Made New   170

How can someone come to Christ?
10. The Hound of Heaven   186

What do we do about guilt?
11. Forgiveness to the Uttermost   202

What does it mean that Christians are adopted?
   12. *Abba*, Daddy   222

What is a sanctified life?
   13. The Glint of Gold   238

What is saving faith?
   14. Three-Dimensional Faith   256

What does it mean to repent?
   15. The Gift of a Broken Heart   274

What assurances does the Christian have in death?
   16. The Stinger Is Gone   290

Part 3: Purposed for Good Works
   Introduction to Part 3   307

What makes an ethical standard "Christian"?
   17. The Cut-Flower Generation   316
   18. Good Advice and Good News   334

How is life made free in Christ?
   19. "Give Me Liberty!"   352

How is life made rich in Christ?
   20. A Day Saved for Eternity   370

What makes relationships whole in Christ?
   21. Sand in the Shoes   386
   22. Holy, Catholic Church   404

What does the future hold in Christ?
   23. "I Will Not Be Shaken"   422

The Westminster *pattern*
   24. Transforming Truths   442

   Scripture Index   463
   Subject Index   467

Part 1

Created for Glory

Introduction to Part 1

It had been "one of those days" for the nine disciples. Peter, James, and John had gone off for a mountaintop experience with the Lord. They were seeing Jesus' glory as God partly unveiled, an experience offered to few human beings on this earth. If I had been one of the other disciples I would have felt left out and put-upon, for they were left to look after all the crowd who followed Jesus wherever he went. The disciples were slogging it out in the trenches of ministry.

To make matters worse, they were doing none too well. The immediate problem was a distraught man who had come to them, leading or carrying a little boy. "It is my son. He is troubled by a demonic spirit. Please help me!"

And they had tried. They had seen Jesus heal countless people. They knew his authority over spirits. They had used that authority when he sent them out on a preaching mission. But their commands had no effect whatsoever against the force that obviously afflicted this child.

Finally Jesus returned. Through Mark 9 we can almost see Jesus as he reached the bottom of the mountain. He surveyed the frustrated disciples, the milling people, and the boy's father—who by now was losing all hope.

"O faithless generation," Jesus told them. "How long shall I suffer you? Bring him unto me."

The father eagerly approached and told the sad story of his son's misery, asking that Jesus take pity, "if you can do anything."

The father received a rebuking challenge in reply: "All things are possible to him that believeth."

"I believe," the father responded, then added in honesty, "help thou mine unbelief."

Do you ever feel like that man? I do. As a minister I often feel empathy for those disciples who had their own problems with unbelief. They experienced many wonders as followers of Jesus. Love and power were exhibited in the sandaled rabbi who walked beside them. But they couldn't grasp who Jesus was. As they slowly understood more they were able to say with new consciousness: "I believe."

I believe, but help!

Only after the cross had unveiled God's plan, after Jesus had broken the bonds of death, after he had ascended to his eternal glory, after the Spirit of God had taken permanent dwelling inside of them—did the apostles truly turn the world upside-down. But even then these transformed witnesses to the glory of God echoed that father's humble prayer: "I believe; help thou mine unbelief." And lest we forget, one of those disciples—a sad fellow named Judas—saw Jesus' power and love expressed. He refused to embrace him, save as a traitor.

If you cannot say the first part of that prayer, "I believe," or if you aren't sure, then please read on. I was thinking of you when I wrote the following chapters. If you have rejected God you owe it to yourself to know whom and what you are rejecting. I firmly believe these truths can be a turning point that will revolutionize your life.

But if you stand with the trembling, believing father, this book also is addressed directly to you, for this series of three studies contains the *credo* of life as a disciple. The word *credo* is a venerably ancient Latin verb. It means "I believe." If you know Christ personally, I want to suggest a couple of things to you.

First, your proper goal has become the lifelong spiritual quest toward "credo."

In Christ you are a "new creation," one whose life has been transformed into the lifestyle of a pilgrim who is on a quest to know and love God more profoundly. When you say, "I believe," it ought to mean something fuller, deeper, and richer in your thinking than those same words meant last year or last month or yesterday. The apostle Paul knew Christ as intimately as has any mortal. Do you know what his goal in life was? "That I may know him, and the power of his resurrection, and the fellowship of his sufferings, being made conformable unto his death; If by any means I might attain unto the resurrection of the dead" (Philippians 3:10–11).

Second, intellectual knowledge does not make "credo" belief, but real belief never exists without a factual foundation of knowledge.

A Baptist friend illustrated for me how superficially we often approach what we believe. A southern church met down at the river to baptize new members. One elderly woman was particularly excited about the experience, and when the pastor raised her up from the water she shouted, "I believe!"

Now this young pastor was nervous. He was officiating at his first baptism, so he was overjoyed by such enthusiasm. So he put her under the water again.

This time she shouted all the louder: "I believe!"

Wonderful, warm excitement swept through those gathered at the water's edge. Caught up in the emotion of the moment, the pastor lowered the lady under the water a third time.

"I BELIEVE!" she screamed.

"Now, sister Mabel," the pastor shouted, "I want you to tell us what you believe!"

"I BELIEVE this stinker's tryin' to drown me!"

A great many people are running around looking for something—anything—to get excited about. They want something to believe in, a central focus for life. But when you try to pin them down about exactly why they are so enthusiastic about some cause, their factual foundation seems thin and cracked, not much deeper than that of this water-logged believer.

Mind and heart *credo*

Two interesting tendencies exist side by side in our society. One is the opinion that a proposition must be "reasonable" before it deserves to be hung in the hall of truth. In other words, my mind is the measure of truth. Faith must be rational; it isn't truth if I can't comprehend it or analyze it in a laboratory. The other trend is to think it doesn't matter, really, what you believe, so long as you are sincere and emotionally committed in your beliefs. In other words, the measure of truth is emotion—the warm fuzzies of hope and comfort.

These two ideas are not logically compatible, but they have been blended in truly extraordinary ways. For example, some people consider themselves far too sophisticated to believe in anything so ridiculous as a personal, holy, infinite God. Yet they feel most uncomfortable living without belief. Therefore, they customize their own *credo* foundation, building a sort of warm, cozy cabin from the logs of humanism, Eastern philosophy, and other self-actualizing affirmations. This cabin nestles safely away, deep in the woods of prideful doubt.

Others place their faith in the claims of science, proud to have overcome the old superstitions of the Bible. But still they believe the Bible has some value. It gives identity. Or the Bible "becomes" God's words as it causes some indefinable, emotional "truth" to well up in the consciousness. Jesus may or may not have been a real person. It doesn't really matter, for he "becomes" God to me as I follow his example and live for others.

As I write, the memory is still fresh of the disaster in Waco, Texas, in which members of the Branch Davidian sect burned to death. The fire that took their lives ignited when law enforcement officers invaded their fortress compound. But just as tragic are the untold numbers of lives shattered by cultists of various persuasions. We are invited to sample from a veritable smorgasbord of messiahs and belief systems. Studies show that people who choose to give over their savings and their lives to bizarre cultic doctrines tend to be well-educated, highly intelligent, and creatively gifted. I wonder if this is true because such people reflect with more depth on the meaninglessness of their lives and become all the more starved for something in which to believe and to belong—someone who bids them reach for an emotion-fulfilling purpose beyond themselves.

I may offend some of you by suggesting that another outgrowth of these tendencies sometimes attaches to the popular statements: "I have no creed but Christ" or "I want a *relationship* with Jesus, not a *religion*." You may say this with the caveat that you do believe certain things *about* Jesus quite strongly, and your relationship with Jesus truly assumes his friendship and lordship as God and Savior over your life. If that is the case you have a creed and a religion, whatever you may wish to call it, for your faith is founded on truth statements from Scripture. You may react against the word *creed* because creedal traditions sometimes come to supersede biblical authority. In that mistrust I fervently concur. And you react against the word *religion*, because "religious" people often replace true spirituality with dead orthodoxy. I share that dislike.

But a word of caution must be injected, because there are those who truly do reject creed and religion. Their objective is contentless faith, *love* for Christ that never journeys beyond emotional catharsis. They relate to a Jesus that I have difficulty recognizing in Scripture or personal experience. So please bear with me if I bring up creedal suppositions quite regularly. I use the term *creed* unashamedly to mean *a statement, subordinate to Scripture, of those things the Bible says are true*.

The journey of transforming truth

With those understandings binding us, I propose that we undertake together the quest to know and worship God better, or as Jesus said in John 4:23–24, to worship God "in spirit and in truth." This is a quest for transformation, because its aim is not simply to learn interesting, helpful facts about God, but to be forever transformed by God in how we think and live. For that reason I divide our journey into three parts, corresponding to three areas of transforming knowledge from a never-changing God.

This first part considers how we know God and why I have the temerity to say that what I believe about God *is truth*, and what the world believes is untrue, wrong-headed, sinful, unsatisfying, and deadly. We will strain our mental eyes to see the person of God. This has to do with *theology*, an unpopular subject in an era when feelings about God take precedence over knowledge of him. *Theology* means "the study of God," and I believe that people are transformed only as they study the God they love. We also need to evaluate the three types of relationship between human beings and their God: (1) as he created them to be; (2) as they became in rebellion to him; (3) as they can be in Jesus Christ.

This third relationship will be the subject of part 2. You may have memorized John 3:16: "For God so loved the world that he gave his only begotten Son, that whosoever believeth in him should not perish, but have everlasting life." There is a way—one way—to escape the traps of empty rationalism, humanism, and emotionalism. We call this way "good news," the gospel of salvation through the life, sacrificial death, and bodily resurrection of One who was God and man. Part 2 will look at parts of what John 3:16 means. It will seek to lift the veil from the most mysteriously magnificent plan of all eternity—God's plan of salvation. Theologians call this study *soteriology*.

Philosopher Francis Schaeffer entitled one of his books on the Christian life, *How Should We Then Live?* That question is a good way to phrase the focus of part 3: If we are creatures of the sort of God that our God has revealed himself to be, how should we live? If we have been saved from utter despair and death by the sheer love and mercy of that God, and if we are commissioned by that God to be salt and light in a world that badly needs both, then how should we live? What kind of parents, children, spouses, neighbors, and citizens should we be? What is the shape of a God-centered life? If the world seems to be out-of-control, and if things seem to be a mess, what is the attitude that builds peace and joy for a child of God?

These and other questions covered in part 3 fall under what is sometimes called the study of Christian *ethics*.

Packing for the trip

As they prepare to go forth on a quest, pilgrims are well advised to pack light. They will not want to be burdened with excess baggage, but they must take essentials they will not be able to purchase along the way. This is especially wise advice on the pilgrimage we now undertake. The Epistle to the Hebrews reminds us of all the men and women who have taken this trip before and then relates in 12:1–2: "Wherefore seeing we also are compassed about with so great a cloud of witnesses, let us lay aside every weight, and the sin which doth so easily beset us, and let us run with patience the race that is set before us, Looking unto Jesus the author and finisher of our faith. . . . " For a Christian, the study of God, of salvation, and of living, is a study of what we can see with eyes fixed upon Jesus. Further, the only way to see what hinders and what sins entangle—the excess baggage of our past and present—is to look upon Jesus, rather than upon ourselves.

If we must plan to get rid of misconceived ideas and thoughts, the most important tool in our kit must be the Bible. One young maintenance man for a large hotel had the habit of keeping a Bible in his locker at work and pulling it out for a short study on his lunch break. This, of course, did not escape the notice of the fellow who shared his shift. Over time they became friends, and at last the coworker could no longer hold back the question that had been growing in his mind.

"Do you have a problem reading things?" he asked one day.

"No, I don't think so. Why?"

"It's just that you've been here about eighteen months now, and you still haven't finished that book."

Paul told a young pastor named Timothy: "All scripture is given by inspiration of God, and is profitable for doctrine, for reproof, for correction, for instruction in righteousness: That the man of God may be perfect, thoroughly furnished unto all good works" (2 Timothy 3:16–17). Those seem good reasons never to finish reading this particular book. It contains God's breathed-out truth. Its presence on this trip is of vital importance.

Finally, we will take some written creedal and confessional statements with us, not because they add anything to the Bible, but because they explain what Scripture teaches. I particularly will organize my thoughts around one set of statements, the *Westminster Confession of Faith* and *Larger* and *Shorter* catechisms.

There are a few reasons I prefer this creedal statement. One obvious reason is that I am most familiar with it, and when I look at Scripture I find the same transforming truths its writers found during years of exacting study. A second reason is that the Westminster statements have figured prominently in the teachings of a wide cross-section of Protestant churches, particularly those in the Baptist and Presbyterian or Reformed traditions. If you are part of a Bible-believing church your tradition has strong creeds to look back on. Your church may not refer to those creeds often, but they stand as a part of a heritage you should understand. These confessions and catechisms are not mere historical curiosities. The Westminster documents are an especially helpful summary of what Scripture teaches, framed with care by Christian leaders who met together over a period of years to witness to the Bible. At some points you may interpret the Bible a bit differently than did those men. Such differences contribute to the various denominations across the land. But in every word these leaders mightily strived to pen nothing but what they saw the Bible teaching, and we would be hard-put to field a like number who approached them in godliness and sacrifice.

I also prefer to use the Westminster documents because they stress things about God, salvation, and our lives that we particularly need to hear at this point in history. Their birth was in 1640s England, at an uncertain, bloody time that was at least as tension-filled as our own day. People have not changed fundamentally since God breathed his truth through the human writers of the Bible, and we share most of our problems with those who gathered in London to write a confession for the ages, dedicated to the glory of God, the edification of the church, and the quest to know God.

Who am I?

What is the chief end of man?
Man's chief end is to glorify God and to enjoy him for ever.
[Westminster Shorter Catechism, question 1]

1

Quest for Life

In the introduction I said that you and I will now undertake a quest. But think back on your life to this point. You can probably see signs that your quest began long ago—a quest for *Life*—*Life* with a capital *L*. Has anyone who has any understanding of life at all not begun that quest? Is there anyone who has looked up at the stars in a night sky, or down at the delicate features of a newborn baby's face and not wrestled with life's fundamental questions?

Who am I?
Where did I come from?
Why am I here?
How should I live?
Where am I going?

Those are quest questions, and if you have never wrestled with them, then apparently a brain has been wasted on you. If a person doesn't examine such questions as these, what is he or she living for at all?

Many years ago I came across the source of answers to those questions. Since then I have been testing out the answers in my own life, and I have seen the answers at work in the lives of others. They work. They are true. They come with the only real guarantee. It isn't a money-back guarantee, because the ultimate answers to life don't cost money. They cost your life.

Notice that I don't guarantee that *my* personal answers carry any great wisdom; these are not my answers. I would never have reasoned them out myself. They are a gift. Further, there are only two sets of answers to these questions, only two directions to take in the quest for life. One set of answers is true, and all others are false; one direction takes you somewhere worth going to; the rest go nowhere. Most people in this world are going diametrically in the wrong direction, the opposite direction from the way in which their true quest lies. That is very sad because they obviously will not find that which they seek. What is worse, the nowhere they are going toward does lead somewhere. It leads unerringly toward death.

> *There is a way which seemeth right unto a man, but the end thereof are the ways of death.* [Proverbs 14:12]

All of that sounds dogmatic, and the politically correct path Western culture now follows does not accept dogmatism about final verities. This came home forcefully in a recent news story about the appointment of a new district head for the churches of a mainline denomination. The district was in turmoil because the former bishop had presided over the marriage ceremony of two homosexual men. Such a furor was raised that he decided to step aside so that peace could be restored. A "moderate" with the reputation for wisdom and diplomacy was elevated to lead the troubled churches and was interviewed for a newspaper article.

Would he sanction practicing homosexuals in the pulpit of his churches? No, he would not, he told the reporter firmly. Neither would he participate in legitimizing a homosexual union. The church had made it clear that it was not ready for such boldness.

"But are you personally opposed to gays in the church?" the reporter followed up.

"Oh, no, not personally. I think we are making a big mistake by not embracing this lifestyle option. And I'm sure it won't be long until their lifestyle is considered as acceptable as any other."

This must have confused the reporter just a little. "But doesn't the Bible reject homosexuality as a Christian lifestyle?"

"Well, yes. But you see, we have three guides as a church: the Bible, our traditions as a religious people, and the decisions our leaders make. The Bible is primary, but it doesn't have primacy."

This is the jist of the account of the interview, and I found that last statement fascinating. The new bishop has well stated the spirit of our age, though each person might fill in the blank with those documents or truth claims that are "primary" but have not "primacy." Authorities are handy things to have around: They give us pragmatic direction. They can help bind a people together. But, according to this leader, we must not take them too seriously. He chose three primary authorities he was willing to follow as long as it served the needs of church stability. What he believed to be true made little difference. No one right direction excluded all other ways—certainly not a direction based on the authority of a culturally-bound Bible that took such a narrow view of things.

The way that seems right . . .

To say that there is one single right direction, and all others are wrong, returns to the old Christian habit of proclaiming the existence of one exclusive truth. Wasn't that what caused the Crusades and the Inquisition? Isn't such a view unloving, prejudiced, and out-of-date?

Those are serious charges if it truly makes no difference which direction we take. But what if it does? The Bible quotation that begins this chapter is a proverb written nearly three thousand years ago by Solomon, a king of Israel. Old King Solomon makes a strong statement: "There is a way which seemeth right unto a man, but the end thereof are the ways of death" (Proverbs 14:12). I have cause for concern if Solomon is right, for he is saying that my inner compass is defective and needs to be recalled. What seems the proper course may not be. I am reminded of the fateful around-the-world flight of Amelia Earhart and navigator Frederick Noonan. In those days before satellites and tracking radar, Earhart's plane took off over the South Pacific and then disappeared forever. For decades, expedition after expedition searched for clues of where they went down and why. Finally some badly rusted wreckage was discovered on a tiny atoll, along with a boot like those the aviators wore. If this was, indeed, the site of the tragic end of Earhart and Noonan, they had drifted badly off course. One researcher reasoned that they may have become disoriented and changed their heading just slightly to follow a commercial radio signal toward what promised to be land and safety. If so, that signal became a siren song of death. It wouldn't have taken long over that trackless ocean to stray far off course. As soon as they missed their island markers they were doomed.

I fear for the churches led by such a leader as that bishop. He has a compass—Scripture—and he is checking it as one of the "primary" instruments he uses to chart the course. But he has secretly brought along a second compass of tradition and a third compass of current church politics. These can be relatively reliable, but only if they are constantly recalibrated to a reliable standard. For these compasses can be pulled off course by the radio signals of culture. The poor bishop may have enough trouble simply keeping an eye on these three compasses, but he has secretly snuck aboard a fourth compass he didn't mention to the reporter. There is a way that seems right to him personally, a way that doesn't follow any of the other compasses. This compass is set to the way he personally wants to go. He is just waiting until the rest of us come around to his more all-inclusive truth. What is the authority that this compass is tuned to detect? The desires of God? I'm afraid he only listens for the tunes of his emotional feelings.

What seems right leads off in strange directions. We are warned by Solomon that the end of those directions is disaster. The stakes are high if Solomon is correct. What if there is one purpose for which you truly have been made, one and only one direction toward meaning in life, one and only one way to experience what life is all about? What if there is truth that leads to life and so is worth living and dying for?

Ultimate answers

Truths worth living and dying for: that was precisely what a group of Christians were called to Westminster Chapel in London to ponder just three and one-half centuries ago. The year was 1643—a moment of supreme national crisis. Theirs was no polite philosophical communing of theologians. England's Parliament had decided to tolerate no longer the despotic King Charles I. Parliament declared war on their own king and began raising an army under the crusty veteran Oliver Cromwell to face the king's army. It was Englishman against Englishman, and people were forced to take sides in a bloody civil war. How could Parliament justify such an act of treason, particularly since one of the most divisive issues that precipitated the conflict was the desire for religious freedom?

In one of their first acts as leaders of the rebellion, Parliament voted to call a conference, not of generals and statesmen, but of pastors. In effect their invitation read:

Please come to London to help us! Study God's Word. Write a document that will bear witness if we are doing right or wrong! Tell the people what we are fighting for. Declare whether there is truth by which we must live and for which we are willing to die!

Between 1643 and 1648 these men, some of the most astute and pious Christians the church has known, met as the "Westminster Assembly": 121 ministers, ten members of the House of Lords, twenty members of the House of Commons, and eight advisors from the Church of Scotland. They were fallible men who sometimes argued passionately among themselves. But each day they devoted part of their time to listening to the proclamation of the Word, part of their time to prayer, and part of their time to deliberation.

In the end they forged three remarkable statements that came to be known as the *Westminster Confession of Faith*, the *Larger Catechism* (originally written for Christian ministers to memorize), and the *Shorter Catechism* (for laypeople to memorize). The English Parliament eventually won the war but lost the peace, for their own abilities to govern didn't live up to their convictions. Soon another king was on the throne, their noble experiment to found a theocratic commonwealth a dismal failure. Christians learned the valuable lesson that they need more than a political agenda or godly leaders in power to transform a culture. But they left us those Westminster documents as seeds that can transform people.

There are other worthy statements of Christian faith, and to be sure not every Christian agrees with all that is contained in these writings. But on most matters considered by the *Westminster Confession* and catechisms we can glory in our unity. We must do so, for these are the central foundation stones on which our hope and our message must stand. Here are ultimate answers worth living and dying for. Let us look at some quest questions, and parts of the *Westminster Confession* that were written from Scripture to answer them. In order, those questions and answers are:

How can I know any ultimate truth for certain?
"Of the Holy Scripture"

Is there a Source of ultimate truth?
"Of God, and of the Holy Trinity"

Is anyone in control out there?
"Of God's Eternal Decrees"
"Of Creation"
"Of Providence"

If there is a good God, why . . . ?
"Of the Fall of Man, of Sin, and of the Punishment Thereof"

Is there any hope?
"Of God's Covenant with Man"
"Of Christ the Mediator"
"Of Free Will"
"Of Effectual Calling"
"Of Justification"
"Of Adoption"
"Of Sanctification"
"Of Saving Faith"
"Of Repentance Unto Life"
"Of Good Works"
"Of the Perseverance of the Saints"
"Of the Assurance of Grace and Salvation"

Then how should I live?
"Of the Law of God"
"Of Christian Liberty, and Liberty of Conscience"
"Of Religious Worship and the Sabbath-Day"
"Of Lawful Oaths and Vows"

What is my relationship to others?
"Of the Civil Magistrate"
"Of Marriage and Divorce"
"Of the Church"
"Of the Communion of Saints"

How does God lead his people today?
"Of the Sacraments"
"Of Baptism"
"Of the Lord's Supper"
"Of Church Censures"
"Of Synods and Councils"

Where am I going?
"Of the State of Man after Death, and of the Resurrection
  of the Dead"
"Of the Last Judgment"

In these three parts we will look at each of these questions and examine the Bible's answers.

The search for significance

With that introductory explanation, look at the quotation that begins this chapter. Actually it is a question and an answer. The question begins the *Shorter Catechism*. It asks: *What is the chief end of man?*

Is there a reason why I exist? What is it all about? That is *the* question, the one everyone wants answered. The answer is stunning in its simplicity and dazzling in its profundity: *My most important purpose for existence is to give glory to God and to enjoy him—to serve and live in communing fellowship with him forever!* I believe that behind this answer stands every word of Scripture. Does life have significance? Do I have any significance? The creed's answer is most fascinating:

My chief purpose for being is "to glorify God and to enjoy him forever."

But wait a minute. This answer actually robs me of significance. I become nothing more than a slave to some grand Potentate in the great beyond. If I must continually give away importance to some God, how is that very enjoyable? Desiring to glorify and enjoy God is not the direction with which most people have aligned their compass. Whether they realize it or not, they have framed their own answer to that question:

My chief purpose is to glorify me and to be my own person.

But there are costs to a self-glorifying philosophy as well. For example, men and women refuse to give themselves fully to a marriage relationship. They fear the loss of importance and self-satisfaction and control over their destiny. But how much satisfaction do the lonely survivors of broken marriages and casual affairs possess? Television image to the contrary, are those who enjoy the whole hedonistic singles scene truly so free and happy? Talk with the woman being treated for post-abortion syndrome, or the young man with an HIV time bomb ticking silently in his body about the glories of the good time.

Even inside the churches of our land are many who would gladly enjoy God, but only if that means God can be counted on to give them all of their desires. Unfortunately—or rather fortunately indeed—that isn't what our spiritual fathers saw in their Bibles. No, the men at Westminster found a far superior principle at work.

The blessing of open hands

Once upon a time, longer ago than I might care to admit, I was a newlywed husband charged in my marriage vows to give of myself fully, completely, and without reservation to the young woman I had married. Giving away of self didn't come easily. But ever so slowly, and after many mistakes, I came to realize that my enjoyment of the moments spent with this person I loved became more precious as I came to her with my hands outstretched and open, clutching nothing for self. There seemed to be an exact correlation: The more freely I gave of myself, the more I received for myself. What I demanded for self turned out to be no blessing at all; rather selfishness was a thief that stole from me the enjoyment that was freely mine.

The same thing is true when I come before my Father. When I live before him with my hands closed, grasping some area of my life that I don't want to share, life is neither enjoyable nor meaningful. But when I extend open hands and call him my Lord over some long-grasped tarnished treasure, the treasure is renewed and returned in a far more fulfilling form. Have I withheld time I should be spending in prayer? When I return to God and give that time over to him, I come away refreshed and fulfilled. For this is what I was created to do. Do I withhold some possession, thinking that I have given quite enough in other areas of life? I find it becomes a meaningless toy that gives no pleasure. When I extend it to the Lord, sometimes he blesses it and gives it back to bless me. Or perhaps he takes it away and gives some greater joy in its place. Am I sullenly refusing to forgive someone, desiring mercy for myself but justice for the one who has offended my dignity? I find my dignity is lowered far more by my anger and pride than it ever was by what the other person did to me. And when I open my hand and let go, I am lifted and cleansed.

A passage that often is applied only to giving our financial blessings to the Lord illustrates the blessing of the open hand in all areas of life:

> He which soweth sparingly shall reap also sparingly; and he which soweth bountifully shall reap also bountifully. Every man according as he purposeth in his heart, so let him give; not grudgingly, or of necessity: for God loveth a cheerful giver. And God is able to make all grace abound toward you; that ye, always having all sufficiency in all things, may abound to every good work. [2 Corinthians 9:6–8]

The open, outstretched hand is a blessing because we were made to give glory to God. First Corinthians 10:31 says that "whether therefore ye eat, or drink, or whatsoever ye do, do all to the glory of God." The soul shouts with the apostle Paul that "of him, and through him, and to him, are all things: to whom be glory for ever" (Romans 11:36). And what do we enjoy forever? Will we suddenly become "healthy, wealthy, and wise" because we have extended our open hands? One might think so from hearing some statements that are made by those who promise prosperity for following Christ. God never promises that kind of blessing, and it might not be such a blessing if he gave it to us. Read 2 Corinthians 9:6–8 again. We will have all that we need to "abound to every good work." That may not seem like such a grand deal, but it is if we were made to glorify God and enjoy him forever. Paul is saying that we have all that we need to fulfil our greatest purpose for being. How many lottery winners can say that?

If you are a Christian and are feeling very unblessed in life every morning, great medicine awaits in Ephesians 1:3–14. Read through these verses with a paper and pencil in hand. Make a list of what is yours in Jesus Christ: gift upon gift upon gift, lavished on utterly undeserving rebels, now chosen, adopted as children of the Father, redeemed in Jesus Christ, and sealed by the Holy Spirit. Why? The last phrase of Ephesians 1:14 says the Christian is God's "purchased possession, unto the praise of his glory."

The two paths of faith

That sounds all well and good. But just as my early quest in marriage was full of trials and errors, so I often fail in my quest to give glory to God and to enjoy him. Loving God takes time and practice. I need help. Some of you who are married will suggest that your husband or wife has always been quite ready to point out needed improvements. As much as I hate to hear it, I need to know where improvement is most needed.

But where can I get the feedback I need to continue on in my quest for life with God? The *Westminster Shorter Catechism* makes the answer crystal clear:

> The Word of God, which is contained in the scriptures of the Old and New Testaments, is the only rule to direct us how we may glorify and enjoy him.

As we explore the Christian faith we will not be relying on some 350-year-old confession. The men who first wrote it would have been appalled at the very idea. They wrote about what they saw revealed in God-breathed explanations about himself and directions for the quest. Alongside those fellow searchers we lace up our hiking boots, pick up our backpack, and set forth on the adventure of a lifetime—and more.

With all this in mind let us return to the ultimate quest questions with which we began this chapter. I am most happy to tell you that I have learned the answers, and they are marvelous:

Who am I? I am a child of the King, a prince of the realm (Romans 8:15–25).

Where did I come from? I came from the heart and mind of the Almighty and Omnipotent and Omniscient God. I have been made a little lower than the angels (Psalm 8).

Why am I here? I am here to serve and glorify the Almighty and to enjoy him forever (Romans 12:1–2; Revelation 5:9–13).

How should I live? I should live according to the commandments he has given to me in his Word, which are designed for my good and my advancement (Hebrews 12).

Where am I going? I am going to paradise, which is beyond my comprehension, for "Eye hath not seen, nor ear heard, neither have entered into the heart of man, the things which God hath prepared for them that love him" (1 Corinthians 2:9).

I mentioned that there are other directions beside the one the Bible recommends, and to be perfectly fair I should give a little time to the other side. A student who attends a college in Minnesota recently told me that his biology teacher said at the very beginning of a semester's class that his purpose was to show students that evolution is the way things happened and evolving species is the way things should be.

He was going to do his very best to persuade Christians to abandon their faith and to adopt the faith of evolution.

That teacher is right about one thing: It is faith that we are talking about. You can't avoid making a faith choice when you set out on the life quest. The best known evolutionists have, for their part, often admitted that they walk "by faith and not by sight." Dr. L. Harrison Matthews, a noted evolutionist who wrote the introduction to the 1971 edition of Darwin's *Origin of the Species*, said:

> The fact of evolution is the backbone of biology, and biology is thus in the peculiar position of being a science founded on an unproved theory—is it then a science or faith? Belief in the theory of evolution is thus exactly parallel to belief in special creation—both are concepts which believers know to be true but neither, up to the present, has been capable of proof.

The evolutionist, the secularist, the person who rejects the direction in which we plan to quest has a very different set of answers to the quest questions. Bertrand Russell, one of this century's leading atheist philosophers, wrote a book entitled *Why I Am Not a Christian*. In the book his answer to the ultimate questions of life was: "We started somewhere, we don't know where; we are here, we don't know why; we are going to some great oblivion, we know not whither."

That sounds rather depressing, to put it mildly. Others with a similar viewpoint abound. Here are but a few of their answers to the question, "Who am I?"

"A mere insect, an ant." (Richard Church)

"A fungus on the surface of one of the minor planets." (George du Maurier)

"A rope stretched over an abyss." (Friedrich Nietzsche)

"Small potatoes and few." (Rudyard Kipling)

"A jest, a dream, a show, bubble, air." (George Walter Thornbury)

"A hairless ape." (Arnold Schoenberg)

I would only add the comment of one more witness who has followed the other direction. "There is but one truly serious philosophical problem [in the twentieth century]," said the French author Albert Camus.

Only one? Only one question that you should be directing your mind toward? What is this singular problem at the pinnacle of the whole atheistic, evolutionary view of life?

Answered Camus, "It is suicide."

The danger of a blind quest

Against such profound despair, hear one more voice that calls all of humanity to turn to a new direction, toward a distant horizon: "For whosoever will save his life shall lose it; but whosoever shall lose his life for my sake and the gospel's, the same shall save it," Christ said (Mark 8:35). He was addressing, not only the despair of Albert Camus and the fatalism of Bertrand Russell. He also calls to those who are frantically trying to save their lives by heaping up around them all comforts and pleasures, delights and securities, not realizing that everything they are doing is destroying the very thing they are trying to save.

The great eighteenth-century preacher George Whitefield spoke before most of England's nobility. One day the famous Lord Chesterfield came to hear him and became enthralled in a story he told.

A blind man left his house and with the help of his faithful dog and his iron-shod cane was making his way through the edge of a forest to the home of his daughter. He had made the trip hundreds of times. He knew it by heart.

Suddenly there was an explosion of fur. A rabbit sprang out of the underbrush and disappeared into the forest. The hound yielded to ancient instincts and sprang after him, in spite of the pleas of his master. The man called and called before he finally gave up. But by then he could no longer feel the familiar path beneath his feet. He had wandered away from the path. He tried to retrace his steps and finally came to familiar feeling ground. Everything felt right so he started out again. There would be no problem as he had many times found his way to his daughter's house.

Only he was not on the path at all but was making his way ever closer toward the edge of a precipice that dropped off two thousand feet to rocks below. The blind man drew closer and closer, tapping with his cane, until finally his cane slipped out of his hand and disappeared into the silence below.

Hearing nothing he supposed his cane had simply dropped into the grass. He bent over to find it but felt nothing. This must simply be a slight drop in the ground below him. He leaned forward again. Now his whole trunk and shoulders and head were over the edge. If suddenly sight could have been given to those sightless orbs, he would have beheld a spectacle that would have sent his head spinning, as he was looking straight down into two thousand feet of nothingness.

But he could not see that sight and so he continued feeling for his cane. Surely this decline was deeper than he surmised. He reached farther down. His heels left the ground! He teetered back and forth! He reached for the ground to brace himself lest he fall, but there was nothing in front to steady him. Suddenly, with his arms flailing in the air and a scream of terror issuing from his lips, the blind man hurtled headlong into the abyss that gaped before him!

By this time Lord Chesterfield was so engrossed in this story that he pictured the blind man hurtling downward and leaped to his feet, forgetting where he was.

"Great God, he's gone!" he cried.

There is a way which seemeth right. . . .

How can I know any ultimate truth for certain?

What rule hath God given to direct us how we may glorify and enjoy him?
The Word of God, which is contained in the scriptures of the Old and New Testaments, is the only rule to direct us how we may glorify and enjoy him.
[Westminster Shorter Catechism, question 2]

2

The Only Rule

When Coral Ridge Presbyterian Church first developed a radio ministry we searched for a name that would guide us in this splendid opportunity to tell others about Christ. We wanted to share how important we felt the message of the gospel to be in an individual's life. "Truths That Transform" became our radio and then our television banner. In the quest for life we are changed, and our lives transformed, only by truth—the truth of a never-changing God. The truth of God is living, vital, and transforming in a day of confusion and ignorance. At no time in history has it been more important that people be established in the truth of God's Word.

Jesus Christ said, "Sanctify [change or transform] them through thy truth: thy word is truth" (John 17:17).

One young woman told me she believed the Bible to be the Word of God, so I asked her, "What would you say to people who asked you to *prove* that the Bible is the Word of God? What would you tell them?"

She thought for a moment in silence. "I wouldn't know what to say to them," she admitted.

You who say you believe that the Bible is the Word of God: Is this conviction simply a wish? A blind leap in the dark? The quotation at the beginning of this chapter is from the *Westminster Shorter Catechism*. It comes right after the question and answer we looked at in chapter 1. The writers quickly anticipated the logical question that question 1 begs that we answer. Let us assume the ultimate purpose of each person is to glorify God and to enjoy him forever. Someone answers: "Hey, that is great! I'm going to

> *All scripture is given by inspiration of God, and is profitable for doctrine, for reproof, for correction, for instruction in righteousness: That the man of God may be perfect, thoroughly furnished unto all good works.*
> [2 Timothy 3:16–17]

run right out and sacrifice my first-born to God. What would give him more glory than that? No, better yet, I will assemble $100 million and build the world's largest church. Stained glass everywhere! That will give God glory. Or maybe what God needs is a more glorifying government. A couple of well-placed bombs in the capitol building should be a big step in that direction.

"No? None of those things is what God wants from me? Then you have been no help to me at all if you tell me what I should be doing, but you never tell me how." The men who wrote the *Shorter Catechism* were quick to lay the necessary ground—if there is *only one* rule to direct us how we may experience and reflect the glory and enjoyment of God, we had better know what it is.

The *Westminster Confession* relates:

Although the light of nature, and the works of creation and providence, do so far manifest the goodness, wisdom, and power of God, as to leave men inexcusable, yet are they not sufficient to give that knowledge of God, and of his will, which is necessary unto salvation; therefore it pleased the Lord, at sundry times, and in divers manners, to reveal himself, and to declare that his will unto his church. . . .

The point made here is important. Creation shows God so clearly that not a single person who has reached the age of understanding will stand up before God and say, "I had no way to know you were out there." Yet salvation has not reached one person because nature displayed God before them. We will see later that the sin problem runs too deep. So God bent down to speak all that we need to know in words that we can understand, and that we can translate so others can hear and understand and be directed.

There is, however, a more basic question we must look at closely. How do we know the Bible is that "only rule"? Because 2 Timothy 3:16 and 2 Peter 1:19–21 and other passages tell us so? Why should we believe it? Many books are held out as true. Many claim that their truths are divinely inspired revelation. Why is this one different from theirs? How can I declare without a moment's hesitation that the Bible is the *only* rule of truth and is uniquely God's revelation?

Six facts, I am persuaded, conclusively prove that the Bible is God's Word to anyone who considers them thoroughly and objectively. In fact, those facts are so central to our Christian life and witness that if you get nothing more from this book than the fact that the *Shorter Catechism*'s answer is true, the effort will be worthwhile. If you approach the holy Scripture with confidence it will direct you to all other truth. That is, after all, why God gave it to us.

Here are those six facts:

1. The Bible stakes its own authority on its claim to be the Word of God. If it lies to us at this point it is altogether worthless.
2. The Bible at no point contradicts itself. Scripture is internally consistent.
3. The Bible's batting average for predicting future events—what we call prophecy—is 1.000. When Scripture says something will happen, it happens, though not always in the way we think.

4. The Bible's description of its contemporary world is accurate. Archeologists and historians have looked for that single finding that proves the historical data of Scripture to be inaccurate. In every single case where we have found the proofs, they vindicate the biblical content.

5. The Bible does not contradict the proven truths of science. No, the Bible is not a science book, but scientific findings agree with the fact statements that are in Scripture.

6. The Bible has been kept from error over history. Hundreds of hand-copied ancient manuscripts of Scripture have been uncovered. Some date back almost to the original documents. These manuscripts vary from one another in details. But not one of those differences in reading significantly alters a teaching.

The Bible's claims

The Bible explicitly and repeatedly claims to be the revelation from God Almighty to humankind. I would point out that most of the scriptures of various great religions make no such claims at all.

There is not the slightest hint in the writings of Confucius that they are a divine revelation. The ancient Japanese collected their tribal myths into the *Kojiki* and the *Nihongi*. These are the sacred writings of the Shinto religion, but no thinking Shintoist would call them divinely revealed. The sacred writings of Buddhism, Taoism, and Hinduism are "writings of the enlightened." The faithful believe that sages of old discerned these divine truths, not from a personal deity, but from the higher spheres of the universe. While Hindus disagree among themselves about the authority of the vedic writings, few would regard them as direct revelation.

The Muslims' reverence for the Qur'an is complex and comes closest to our understanding of the Bible, but our conceptions still stand far apart. Muslims believe there is a divine book, directly written by Allah, but it is in heaven and quite unavailable to us. Allah revealed bits and pieces to human prophets, and the angel Gabriel gave God's "last word" directly to Muhammad, who wrote it down in much the way a secretary takes dictation. The *ultimate* Bible is in heaven, so the next best thing, the supreme authority to which Muslims look, is found only in the *Arabic words* of the Qur'an—the actual transcript of the dictation. An English-speaking Muslim who wants to read the true Qur'an must learn Arabic. The authority is in the words themselves more than the thoughts they convey, and orthodox Muslims scoff at the very idea of an English or French Qur'an.

By contrast, Christians look on the thoughts conveyed by the Bible as "inspired." Directed but not dictated by the Holy Spirit, people wrote in their own words, expressing through their own cultures and personalities, the truth content that God revealed to them: "Above all, you must understand that no prophecy of Scripture came about by the prophet's own interpretation. For prophecy never had its origin in the will of man, but men spoke from God as they were carried along by the Holy Spirit" (2 Peter 1:20–21 NIV). Paul tells Timothy that God has "breathed" or "inspired" all Scripture. For *that reason* it "is useful for teaching, rebuking, correcting and training in righteousness" (2 Timothy 3:16 NIV).

In his book *The Inspiration and Authority of the Bible*, theologian Benjamin B. Warfield offered the definition that: "Inspiration is that extraordinary, supernatural influence . . . exerted by the Holy Ghost on the writers of our Sacred Books, by which their words were rendered also the words of God, and, therefore, perfectly infallible." He goes on to make two explanations vital to our understanding: First, *the influence is different from the inspiration of a poet or novelist in literature*. A writer may win the Pulitzer Prize and still be in error. We may not totally understand a Scripture. We may misunderstand. We may take it literally when it is speaking in metaphor. But when we hear it properly it is infallibly true. Second, *the influence acts upon human beings who are expressing as they write their own emotions, language, and culture.* The words are those of people. Yet extraordinarily, supernaturally, the Holy Spirit guides those thoughts, ideas, and language so that they express God's direct revelation to all people at all places and times. I can say without apology that the Epistle to the Ephesians was written by a man named Paul and that its words are the very words of God.

More than 2000 times the Old Testament alone demands attention with the words: "Thus says the LORD . . . then the word of the LORD came unto Jeremiah the prophet. . . . " Jesus stood before his followers and said, "I speak just what the Father has taught me." These are utterly unique and fantastic claims. More than that, I can stand as a preacher before a congregation and read out of my English Bible and say, "Thus says the LORD," for the Bible claims to speak God's thoughts to all, regardless of time or nationality or language.

Making a claim and substantiating it are two entirely different matters. But if the claim were not even made then some would no doubt say, "The Christians are claiming for the Bible that which it never claims for itself, namely, that it is a revelation from God." Bible scholar and teacher J. I. Packer observes in his book *Knowing God*: "Two facts about the Triune Jehovah are assumed, if not actually stated, in every single biblical passage. The first is that He is *king*—absolute monarch of the universe, ordering all its affairs, working out His will in all that happens within it. The second fact is that He *speaks*—uttering words that express His will in order to cause it to be done."

Contradictions and errors?

"Everyone knows the Bible is full of contradictions and errors."

When I hear that I simply pull the New Testament out of my coat pocket and say, "That is very interesting. I've been studying the Bible for years, and I haven't been able to find one. Would you be so kind as to show me where they are?" I'm still waiting to be shown. No, the Bible is not full of contradictions and errors, and those who say so have usually not read it even once.

We might remind them that A. T. Robinson, whose massive work entitled *Greek Grammar in Light of Historical Research* is the greatest work on Greek grammar that has ever been written, believed in the absolute infallibility of the Scriptures. Dr. Robert Dick Wilson of Princeton, who knew forty-six languages and was perhaps the greatest linguist who ever lived, was convinced that the Old Testament is absolutely trustworthy. W. F. Arndt and F. W. Gingrich, authors of the standard Greek lexicon that examines every word of Scripture and virtually all of ancient Greek literature, provide the most microscopic examination of the full meaning of the words in the Greek New Testament. Yet these scholars believed that the Bible is infallibly true and without contradiction. Arndt even wrote a book entitled *Does the Bible Contradict Itself?*, in which he looks at a number of supposed contradictions and shows that they are, indeed, not contradictions at all. The Bible is full of errors? The greatest skeptic minds have sought them. Their arguments, however, have failed and been forgotten, yet the Bible stands unscathed.

A window on the future

It is amusing, if very sad, to read the efforts to redate the writing of the books of the Old Testament. The object of this passion for changing dates is to argue that the stories are actually myths collected long centuries after the events they allegedly recount took place. One tactic is to look at the predictions made by the prophets. The reasoning runs: "Aha! Here is a prophecy in Isaiah that came true during the reign of King Nebuchadnezzar in Babylon. Therefore, this section is *obviously* post-exilic." Has it occurred to these scholars that God might have revealed to the prophets what would happen? Among some Bible scholars that possibility would not even make a hit-and-run appearance in their mind.

The people of the Old Testament world were not nearly so gullible as these scholars assume. In fact, they had in the law of Deuteronomy a simple test for proving whether a prophet had been sent from God: "When a prophet speaketh in the name of the LORD, if the thing follow not, nor come to pass, that is the thing which the LORD hath not spoken, but the prophet hath spoken it presumptuously: thou shalt not be afraid of him" (Deuteronomy 18:22). The penalty when such a prediction did not come true was death. That surely tended to discourage the making of predictions in the name of the Lord. And if the matter was taken so seriously, would writers be inclined to manufacture prophecies after the fact? There is much prejudice, but no proof, that the prophecies from God are anything other than what they say they are.

If that is true, then we have a rather strong authentication of Scripture. Again, this foretelling of the future in the name of the Lord is strikingly absent from all other religious writings. The writings of Buddha and Confucius offer no hint of prediction. The Qur'an prophesies only once, predicting that Muhammad would return to Mecca. This, of course, he proceeded to do—a rather unimpressive fulfillment of his own prediction. This is quite different from the prophecy of Christ, that he would rise from the dead. Literally hundreds of prophecies in the Scripture are concrete and stated with definite specifics.

In 1 Thessalonians 5:20–21 the Bible says, "Despise not prophesyings. Prove all things; hold fast that which is good." These verses deal with the two reactions to prophecy. One part deals with the contempt that has been instilled by our Enlightenment culture toward the idea that God would intrude in our affairs. The other reaction may very well reject Scripture, yet flips immediately to the daily horoscope in the newspaper or listens with rapt awe as a modern-day guru predicts next Thursday's apocalypse. Do people prophesy today? Jeane Dixon, we are told, has made amazing prophecies with astounding accuracy. I lack an overall box score, but during the 1950s she bravely prophesied all of the candidates of the major political parties and the winner in the national presidential elections in 1952, 1956, and 1960. We can safely assume she did not flip a coin, or she would have done better. Not one was correct. A vast leap separates the predictions of every modern soothsayer from the unfailing prophecies of Scripture. They have all come to pass as they were supposed to. Someone has counted 333 specific prophecies in the Old Testament concerning the Christ. Each of them was fulfilled in Jesus Christ.

Tyre

Almost every city and virtually every nation within a thousand miles of Israel were mentioned in biblical prophecy. Most of these are so definite that a high school student with an encyclopedia could check them, yet most people are not even aware that these prophecies exist. Take, for example, the cities of Tyre and Sidon, prominently mentioned by Isaiah and Ezekiel. Tyre was the capital of the world for 2000 years. It became to the sea what Babylon was to the land. Ezekiel uttered God's sentence against her in quite detailed language: "They shall destroy the walls of Tyrus, and break down her towers: I will also scrape her dust from her, and make her like the top of a rock. It shall be a place for the spreading of nets in the midst of the sea: for I have spoken it, saith the Lord GOD. . . . They shall make a spoil of thy riches, and make a prey of thy merchandise: and they shall break down thy walls, and destroy thy pleasant houses: and they shall lay thy stones and thy timber and thy dust in the midst of the water. . . . And I will make thee like the top of a rock: thou shalt be a place to spread nets upon; thou shalt be built no more: for I the LORD have spoken it" (Ezekiel 26:4–5, 12, 14).

So what happened? Nebuchadnezzar, the mighty monarch of Babylon, invaded the coastal regions and besieged Tyre for thirteen years before breaching the walls. The horses of Nebuchadnezzar rode into the streets of Tyre and the entire population was put to the sword. The city was sacked, a few of the towers were destroyed, a few holes were made in the walls, the city was burned, and Nebuchadnezzar returned to Babylon. Was the prophecy fulfilled? Certainly in part (Ezekiel 26:7). The city was destroyed. But there, jutting up into the horizon over the bleak Mediterranean, could be seen the remains of walls and mighty towers. Great piles of stones, timbers, and dust bore eloquent testimony that prophecies were not fulfilled. Who would come and take the huge stones and timbers of this city and dump them in the sea and even scrape the dust until this great mound of rubble would be a bare rock, a place for the spreading of nets? Who would guarantee that this city would be built and inhabited no more?

Ezekiel certainly did not prophesy this after the fact. A quarter of a millennium after Ezekiel died the prophecy had not yet been completely fulfilled. Then came a thrill of terror out of the north—a mighty conqueror clad in silver with armor of gold, plumed helmet, and astride his mighty horse Bucephalus. Alexander the Great appeared with the phalanxes of Macedonia and Greece. At Issus in 333 B.C. he dealt Darius III, the monarch of Persia, the first crushing blow. Darius fled to the east. Before Alexander followed him inland, however, he decided to nullify the force of the great Persian navy by sealing off its seaports. The ports surrendered quickly until Alexander reached Tyre. The new Tyre was heavily fortified and built on an island, half a mile out in the Mediterranean Sea. The Persians laughed at the demand that they surrender. They felt impregnable in their ocean fortress.

Alexander conceived one of the most brilliant schemes in the history of warfare. He would build a causeway across that one-half mile of water. Where would such a vast amount of fill be found for this undertaking? From the rubble of old Tyre, of course.

"Tear down those ancient towers!

"Destroy the walls!

"Cast the huge stones and the timbers into the sea!"

What had been the revelation of God to Ezekiel? "They shall break down thy walls, and destroy thy pleasant houses: and they shall lay thy stones and thy timber and thy dust in the midst of the water" (Ezekiel 26:12).

I myself have seen pictures showing the nets of fishermen spread on the rock of Tyre.

Sidon

Now compare the prophecies in Isaiah 23 and Jeremiah 27:3, 6 and 47:4 concerning Sidon, a few miles north of Tyre. God said that famine and pestilence would come, and he would send the sword. The city, however, would continue (see Ezekiel 28:23). Sidon has been sacked and pillaged many times, but it never has been completely destroyed. It stands today. What do you suppose our stand on the Scriptures would be today if Ezekiel had gotten his prophecies mixed up?

Samaria and Jerusalem

Jerusalem was the capital of the kingdom of Judah, and Samaria was capital of the kingdom of Israel. Concerning Jerusalem, God said he would destroy the city and tear down its mighty walls by the hand of Nebuchadnezzar (Jeremiah 24:9; 29:21; 35:17). But God also said that the walls would be built again, and the city would be re-inhabited (Isaiah 4:3–6). Of course, we know all of that is true. The walls around the old city of Jerusalem stand today as an awesome sight; but what about the great walls of mighty Samaria, built high upon a mountain? Of those walls God said that he would cast down the rocks into the valley below, that he would destroy the city, that he would make it into a vineyard, and that he would uncover the foundations of that city (Micah 1:5–6). I have visited Samaria. Without even being aware of these particular prophecies, I remember looking over the cliff to see huge boulders that had once been city walls. Olive trees and vineyards were pointed out by our guide. Then I saw the great depths of excavations where all of the walls of other centuries, one dynasty after another, had been exposed. The very foundations of Samaria were laid bare.

Edom

These are but a few of the prophecies concerning cities. All of the cities of Edom were to be destroyed. The prophecies are striking and very specific. Jeremiah 49:17–18 says, "Edom [or Idumea as it was known in Roman times] shall be a desolation: every one that goeth by it shall be astonished, and shall hiss at all the plagues thereof. As in the overthrow of Sodom and Gomorrah and the neighbour cities thereof, saith the LORD, no man shall abide there, neither shall a son of man dwell in it." Ezekiel 35:3–4, 9 is more emphatic; the prophet declares that, because Edom (or Mount Seir, the mountain of Edom) had fought the Israelites in the time of their calamity, God would utterly destroy them. No one would ever build cities there again. Ezekiel 25:13 states, "I will stretch out mine hand upon Edom, and will cut off man and beast from it; and I will make it desolate from Teman; and they of Dedan shall fall by the sword."

These startling prophecies are exceedingly specific: No one would live in these cities; no son would be born in them. The cities shall never return. The extent of the desolation, both geographically and chronologically, is described. Here a bold gauntlet is thrown down before unbelievers. Have these spectacular prophecies come to pass? Listen to Constantin Volney, whose writings influenced Abraham Lincoln to skepticism in his early years. Volney visited Edom and saw the traces of many towns and villages, but "at present all this country is a desert" (*Volney's Travels*, vol. 2, p. 338). In Jeremiah 49:9–10 God declares that he would lay Edom bare. John L. Burckhardt (*Burckhardt's Travels in Syria*, p. 442) reported that the whole plain was "an expanse of shifting sands," and "the depth of sand precludes all vegetation of herbage." On Mount

Seir the skeptic Burckhardt found only the ruined cities of Kalaab, Djirba, Eyl, Ferdakh, Anyk, Birel-Beytar, Shemakh, and Syk (*Travels in Syria*, pp. 443, 444).

Nineveh

As capital of the great Assyrian Empire, Nineveh conquered the world of its day, yet Nahum 1:8, 14 declares that "with an overrunning flood he will make an utter end" of Nineveh. "I will make thy grave; for thou art vile." All of the Book of Nahum prophesies doom for a city of idolatry and blood. Nineveh today is utterly gone. Nahum 1:8, 2:5–6, and 3:13 told that the Ninevites would flee in haste to the great defensive walls of their city, but the gates of the rivers would be opened and dissolve the palace. The gates of the land would be set wide open to the enemies and fire would devour the city.

The only detailed historical account of the fall of Nineveh is by Ctesias and is preserved in *Diodorus Siculus*. According to that account, Cyaxares, the Median monarch, aided by the Babylonians under Nabopolassar, laid siege to the city in vain. He was more than once repulsed and was obliged to take refuge in the mountains of the Zagros Range. Then, receiving reinforcements, he drove the Assyrian army back to the walls of the city. A blockade was unsuccessful for two years, until he received unexpected assistance from the flooding Tigris River. An extraordinarily swollen Tigris undermined the very walls of Nineveh, and the Medes entered through the breech. Saracus, the Assyrian ruler, burned himself in his own palace in despair. The city was laid waste, its monuments destroyed, and its inhabitants scattered or taken into captivity.

The total disappearance of Nineveh is confirmed by history. E. A. Rowell wrote that never had the world seen such a city. Its great rampart walls towered 200 feet, and on top chariots could race abreast. Gleaming in the sun, its lofty palaces and temple thrilled the traveler who was yet miles away. Yet in A.D. 627 the Byzantine emperor Heraclius fought a battle on the very site of the ancient city and was not even aware it was there. As recently as 1840 Bible critics assured the world that the city of Nineveh and its great Assyrian kings Sargon and Ashurbanipal were mythical. Little did these writers realize that their very words were confirming Scripture. Nahum 1:14 had warned the Ninevites that no descendants would bear their name. Nahum compared the men on the city walls to swarms of locusts that would disappear in the heat of the sun (3:17). Knowing all that we do today about Nineveh, it seems humorous. When a brick was discovered near the Tigris in 1840, bearing the name of Sargon, experts at the Paris Museum declared it a fraud. It had to be, since Sargon and Nineveh were just products of ancient imagination. Unfortunately for the experts, one of the earliest scientific archeological digs in 1845 uncovered the palace, the library, and finally the whole city.

Babylon

Babylon was probably the greatest city of the ancient world. Here was the magnificent temple of Belus and the wondrous hanging gardens. Babylonians invented an alphabet and developed a system of mathematics. They invented implements for measuring time and engineered enormous structures built from clay, the poorest of all building materials. They discovered the art of polishing, boring, and engraving gems, studied the motions of the heavenly bodies, conceived of grammar as a science, elaborated a system of law, and saw the value of an exact chronology. In almost every branch of science Babylon made a beginning. Much of the art and learning of Greece was born in Babylonia.

More than 100 Bible prophecies concern this city and empire. They cannot have been written after the event, because many of the details of the prophecy were not fulfilled until centuries after the Septuagint translation of the Hebrew Old Testament into Greek in 150 B.C. They cannot be said not to have been fulfilled. The facts are too well known. It cannot be said that they are simply lucky guesses. They have been minutely fulfilled. Nor can anyone claim that such events were likely to take place. Some were so incredible that, although history confirms them, we still stagger at the audacity of the prophets' boldness.

Herodotus tells us that the walls of Babylon had towers that extended above the 200-foot walls to a height of 300 feet. The triple walls of Babylon were 187 feet thick at their base, the mightiest ever built around any city. It is concerning the futility of these fantastic defenses that God says in Jeremiah 51:26, 58: "They shall not take of thee a stone for a corner, nor a stone for foundations; but thou shalt be desolate for ever. . . . The broad walls of Babylon shall be utterly broken, and her high gates shall be burned with fire; and the people shall labour in vain, and the folk in the fire, and they shall be weary."

Jeremiah says: (1) the wall will be broken down; (2) the wall will be broken down utterly; (3) the wall will be broken down permanently.

The walls were not suddenly destroyed. The city was taken by stealth by the Medes and Persians, and the walls still existed when Alexander the Great died there in 323 B.C. Their ruins still jutted into the sky on the day Christ hung on the cross, a reminder that not all prophecies had been fulfilled. The walls stood even into the fourth century A.D. Then an astounding event took place. Emperor Julian, usually called "Julian the Apostate" because of his desire to rid the Roman Empire of Christianity, desired to do everything in his power to destroy belief in the Scriptures. While engaged in a war with the Persians near the remains of Babylon, Julian completely destroyed remnants of the old walls, lest they afford protection to a future Persian army. Had he known of the prophecy he was fulfilling, he might have rethought this great undertaking.

When Babylon was mistress of the world, containing within its mighty walls 196 square miles of the most magnificently developed city of all time, with beautiful parks, lakes, aqueducts, and hanging gardens, Jeremiah 50:13, 39 made this further prophecy: "Because of the wrath of the LORD it shall not be inhabited, but it shall be wholly desolate: every one that goeth by Babylon shall be astonished, and hiss at all her plagues. . . . The wild beasts of the desert with the wild beasts of the islands shall dwell there, and the owls shall dwell therein: and it shall be no more inhabited for ever; neither shall it be dwelt in from generation to generation."

Imagine the reaction if I made such a prophecy about London and expected to be taken seriously. I'm sure that is how the people of Babylon would have treated this crazy prophet had they heard his warning.

Archeologists have uncovered remains of twenty or thirty cities on this site, which was most excellently situated on the Euphrates. The location offered fine possibilities of commerce. Militarily it was almost invincible. Its fields were so fertile that Herodotus was afraid to describe what he had seen there, lest he be thought insane.

Yet a sixteenth-century travel account recorded that not one house was to be seen there (*Ray's Collection of Travels*, p. 234). In the twentieth century only ruins remained to be shown to tourists. Even when the government of Syria re-created a gate and some other features of the city, they did not do it on the site. Will a city ever be built there? Ruins composed, like Babylon, of heaps of rubbish are impregnated with niter and sterilize the soil. The very vastness of the building materials of the ancient city doom the earth so that no gardens, hanging or otherwise, can be established.

There are other amazingly specific details in this prophecy. Isaiah's prophecy predicts that "neither shall the Arabian pitch tent there; neither shall the shepherds make their fold there" (13:20). Travel accounts speak of the common belief through all the country that the tel of Babylon is inhabited by evil spirits, and there has traditionally been a great fear of the place, especially after dark.

Consider two specific, apparently contradictory, prophecies in Jeremiah 51:42–43:

1. "The sea is come up upon Babylon: she is covered with the multitude of the waves thereof."
2. "Her cities are a desolation, a dry land, and a wilderness, a land wherein no man dwelleth, neither doth any son of man pass thereby."

Is this just a prophetic mixed metaphor? Perhaps, but consider that the ancient city now lies on the flood plain of the Euphrates, and two months each year the ruins are inundated by the annual overflow. After the waters subside, the area returns to its normal state, a dry waste like other cities of ancient Chaldea.

These are only representative of specific prophecies relating to the city of Babylon. The wrath of the Lord was poured out upon this wicked ancient city because that was his purpose (Isaiah 48:12–15). One traveler to the ruins of Babylon many years ago, a Captain Mignan, summed up the feeling all should have as we consider the retribution foretold and accomplished at that place: "I cannot portray the overpowering sensation of reverential awe that possessed my mind while contemplating the event and magnitude of ruin and devastation on every side" (*Mignan's Travels*, p. 117).

Do you want to disprove the truth of Scripture? Simply rebuild Babylon. But I should warn you of one man who even drew up plans for a new city on the plain, and he had the authority and wealth of the world at his command. Alexander the Great planned a trade route by sea from Babylon to Egypt. Babylon would become the central headquarters for his world empire. He issued 600,000 rations to his soldiers to rebuild the city. Almost immediately he was struck with a fever, and within days he was dead. The ruins of Babylon stand in mute testimony: "We would have healed Babylon, but she is not healed: forsake her, and let us go every one into his own country: for her judgment reacheth unto heaven, and is lifted up even to the skies" (Jeremiah 51:9).

"Scripture cannot be broken"

One needs only to read through the archeological journals of the last twenty years or so to see a continuing succession of testimonies. As political conditions in the Middle East allow excavations, the weight of evidence will only pile higher. If I wished to doubt, I would get no help from historical, archeological, and textual evidences. As this is written the long wait to see the full texts of the Dead Sea scrolls seems to be ending. Some have said that in those scrolls higher critics will have new proof that the New Testament is dependent on traditions of a dying and resurrected teacher revered at Qumran. But as the scholars dig deeper into the newly released texts, that connection already grows more unlikely.

Critics will continue to make brave assumptions based on the latest source theories, but their evidence turns out to be vague presuppositions, based on the work of some past scholar, who based his work on a skeptic before him. My heart cries for generations of brilliant minds, some of whom have honestly thought they were serving God, whose entire life works have been based upon a delusion. But I feel more sorrow for generations who perish because all they hear from the pulpit is the delusion. That delusion is that somehow one can break open the Bible, push aside the supernatural, and find within some underlying truth. Those who believe such a lie should listen to Jesus when he declares that "the scripture cannot be broken" (John 10:35), and when he prays for his disciples that the Father will "sanctify them through thy truth: thy word is truth" (John 17:17).

The *Westminster Confession* goes on to say something else in the chapter "Of the Holy Scripture" that we will look at more closely in chapter 3. I can read the Bible twenty-four hours a day, and I will only be an exhausted Bible reader. It won't change me and I won't really understand its rule for my life. Sin runs that deep. The *Confession* says: "Our full persuasion and assurance of the infallible truth, and divine authority thereof, is from the inward work of the Holy Spirit, bearing witness by and with the Word in our hearts." This is one reason scholars can spend a lifetime in the Word and never feel the sanctification that Jesus prayed for his people. Only the Holy Spirit can make that truth come alive.

Is there a Source of ultimate truth?

There is but one living and true God, who is infinite in being and perfection. . . . God hath all life, glory, goodness, blessedness, in and of himself; and is alone in and unto himself all-sufficient, not standing in need of any creatures which he hath made. . . . In the unity of the Godhead there be three persons, of one substance, power, and eternity: God the Father, God the Son, and God the Holy Ghost.
[Westminster Confession of Faith, chapter 2]

3

A God Suppressed

In the last chapter I mentioned some wonders of the ancient world. In St. Louis, Missouri, stands a truly spectacular wonder of the modern variety. It is called officially the "Gateway to the West," but most people know it as "the Arch." The world's largest humanly engineered monument, its shining steel frame looks down from a far greater height than the Eiffel Tower, which once held that distinction.

The story of the construction of the Arch is truly one of imagination, daring, and precision. Its foundations lie some sixty feet below the surface of the hill on which it stands overlooking the Mississippi River. Yet the design tolerance for the two bases laid on those foundations was one one-hundred-twenty-eighth of an inch. So critical were the specifications that if the measurements had been off even one one-hundredth of an inch, the two great towers would not have aligned at the top.

I am indebted to a young Puritan scholar and St. Louis minister, David Wynkoff, who not long ago died in a mountain climbing accident, for pointing out a striking analogy between the building of the Arch and the importance of the first two confessional subjects we are considering. Christian faith rests on two pillars: (1) our view of Scripture, and (2) our concept of God.

We can, perhaps, misinterpret some teaching. We can be wrong about our view of baptism or the gifts of the Spirit. We may disagree about how a church should be properly governed, what will happen at the end of history, or any of a number of issues that stir debate among Christians. We should seek to learn the truth about such things, but we can be in error and not go radically astray or lead others to spiritual ruin. But we dare not err or plant our feet in sand regarding the Bible and the person of God. If we do, our entire understanding of Christianity will lack strength or consistency. Our faith will end up looking like the anemic twin arches of a fast-food restaurant instead of a stable, magnificent tower of steel. We will never even know how to live, because ethi-

> *For the wrath of God is revealed from heaven against all ungodliness and unrighteousness of men, who hold the truth in unrighteousness; Because that which is known of God is manifest in them; for God hath shewed it unto them.* [Romans 1:18–19]

cal decisions are meaningless unless founded in the absolute standards of God's revelation and his person.

Isn't it interesting, Wynkoff continued, that over the centuries of Christian history two teachings continually have been twisted one way and then another? Today the two doctrines face bitter attack from within and without Christendom: (1) the trustworthiness of Scripture, and (2) the person of God. At no other points do people seem to be so blind or so relentless to suppress truth.

I was having lunch with a young couple—a man and woman who were articulate, intelligent, sophisticated, urbane, and had delightful personalities. It was a pleasure to chat with them. We got around to the subject of religion, and I shared with them something of the gospel. They let it be clearly known that really "we just couldn't believe those sorts of things."

Actually they were quite involved in the New Age movement. After they rejected the good news of Christ, I shared with them some of the incomparable evidences for the Christian faith and for the resurrection of Jesus Christ. It was fascinating to watch with what facility they were able to invent—sometimes it seemed out of thin air—all sorts of extraneous and absurd objections.

In chapter 2, I presented only some of the evidences for the truth of Scripture. Yet if you have determined in your thinking that the Bible is only a human book that is full of myth and fable, neither those arguments nor any others will be compelling enough to change your mind. At most you now realize that some of your assumptions about the Bible are not as safe as you once thought. Be careful. Once you let in a little light, the darkness never seems quite comfortable again. If I made that young couple a little more queasy about their assumptions, that is fine with me, but uncertainty will not bring salvation. The mind is capable of producing an enormous prolixity of arguments to counter the truth of Christ. The fallen human mind has a stake in unbelief. In the case of this couple at least part of that stake was easy to identify, for they were living together "without benefit of matrimony." After all, the argument goes, what is a marriage certificate but a piece of paper? And if their belief system is correct then they can remain warm and safe in a snug little dwelling place of assumptions they have built around themselves. No real societal pressure stands in their way. In this brave new world of relative truth and morality, how can anyone—even the friendly preacher at their luncheon table—cast stones at their alternative lifestyle of free sexuality?

But this warm, cozy little cabin in the woods of doubt only remains safe so long as the wolf does not enter the door. If there is an absolute right and an absolute wrong that have been established by an absolutely just, holy, perfect, and all-powerful God, then the sanctuary of the warm, fuzzy, fireside feelings of relative truth is no protection. The claws of truth rip away all pretense that we can stand before the God we have spurned.

The darkened room

Am I overstating the dangerous wolf at the door? "The wrath of God is being revealed from heaven against all ungodliness and unrighteousness of men, who hold the truth in unrighteousness," Paul tells us in Romans 1:18. But wait . . . If there is a God, then he doesn't have cause to get too upset with me, does he? I would have been willing to believe if only he'd pulled back the sky or sent me a personal letter. That is Paul's very point. He does not say that human beings haven't had the truth thrust before us. He declares that each person has the truth but suppresses it.

As Paul continues in verses 19–20, "that which may be known of God is manifest in them; for God hath shewed it unto them. For the invisible things of him from the creation of the world are clearly seen, being understood by the things that are made, even his eternal power and Godhead; so that they are without excuse." Psalm 53:1 puts it bluntly: "The fool hath said in his heart, There is no God. Corrupt are they, and have done abominable iniquity: there is none that doeth good." There it is again. We all have a stake in not knowing God, because our ways are vile. It is to our sinful advantage not to know him.

I do not suggest that this decision is conscious. I doubt many people are as forthright as one young college student named Bob who was presented with the claims of Christ.

"I won't believe, because you can't prove what you say is true," came his challenge.

"Well, I'm not so sure that is your real problem. What if I can prove to you beyond any shadow of reasonable doubt that God exists?"

He mulled that over for a second. "I suppose then I would be forced to believe."

"No, not really. No evidence can *force* you to believe anything you have made up your mind to disbelieve. How about it? Are you prepared to really look at the evidence?"

"No, I'm not," Bob said, shaking his head.

Gone was the arrogant challenge of his specious arguments against the existence of God. He was looking at his suppression honestly now. Some years have passed since that conversation. Maybe Bob's moment of self-understanding was a sign that the Holy Spirit was working in his heart. However, the truth-suppressing power of the fallen intellect is indeed capable of enormously potent self-delusion.

How potent? We will look closely at all the effects visited on humankind by the great fall into sin. But before we can understand our society's attempt to sanitize the land of all God-consciousness and we can discern why God's self-revelation goes unheeded, we need to realize something that Romans 1 and the men who wrote the *Westminster Confession* make very clear. Romans 1:28 declares of the human plight that "as they did not like to retain God in their knowledge, God gave them over to a reprobate mind, to do those things which are not convenient [or ought not to be done]." Looking at this and other Scriptures, and just looking around at their violent society, the framers of the *Confession* concluded: "We are utterly indisposed, disabled, and made opposite to all good, and wholly inclined to all evil" (chapter 6). That doesn't mean humanity is as depraved as it could possibly become. It means that the mind of each person who lives without Christ lives in a darkened, shriveled world, blind to what is all around.

Turning on the light of creation

Paul says God doesn't need to pull back the sky to reveal himself. The sky itself reveals him. "The heavens declare the glory of God," cried King David in awe (Psalm 19:1–2), "and the firmament sheweth his handiwork. Day unto day uttereth speech, night unto night sheweth knowledge." This language has stupendous implications for modern sophisticated Westerners who confidently assert that science has disproved God.

Has science disproved God? James Reid's book *God, the Atom and the Universe* states:

Science is preparing a surprise for mankind! At least it will be a surprise for those who are laboring under the misapprehension that science has undermined the Bible. In fact, it may even shock some scientists, who may be startled to find that their newly uncovered fact, or accepted theory, prepares still another link in the chain of evidence that is showing that the facts of the universe support the statements of the Bible, including creation.

As a man of science, Reid endeavored, under the old classic Newtonian physics, to discover support for the Bible. He was unable to do so. But then the old classical physics gave way to the new quantum physics, the atomic theory. A whole new concept of the universe emerged. As Einstein's theory of relativity revealed the inner relationship of mass and energy, Reid suddenly found that the new discoverers of science were establishing the teachings of the Bible. Many years later this process continues, and its consequences are incalculable. It takes a great deal more faith today than in the time of Voltaire to fervently study science and remain secure in materialism—the view that nothing exists but matter—no soul, no spirit, no God.

Astronomy

"The heavens declare the glory of God." No branch of science looks at a larger portion of God's handiwork than do astronomers. Carl Sagan to the contrary, I have read that 90 percent of all astronomers today believe in God. Then a higher percentage of astronomers believe than of butchers, bakers, or candlestick makers.

At the same time as Voltaire and the French Revolution instituted France as the crowning jewel of skepticism, a Frenchman named Pierre-Simon Laplace was establishing the modern marriage of mathematics and astronomy. Laplace said that the proof in favor of an intelligent God as the Author of creation "stood as infinity to unity against any other hypothesis of ultimate causation." No other explanation for both the infinity and unity of the universe seems remotely plausible. It was far more probable, he said, that a set of writing implements thrown promiscuously against parchment produced Homer's *Iliad* than that the cosmos originated by chance.

Of course astronomy has come far since Laplace's work in the late 1700s and early 1800s. So let us listen to one of the leaders of twentieth-century astronomy, Sir James Hopwood Jeans. As he looked out into the cosmos, Jeans said that the more he examined the vast expanses of space and the tremendous complexity of the universe, the more the universe seemed to be one gigantic thought of a pure mathematician.

Those who represent the case for creation call this the *cosmological argument*. It is persuasive, for it applies Psalm 19 to the world of science. "The heavens declare," David said. As Jeans and other astronomers take into account the diversity, complexity, order, beauty, and sheer mathematical precision of infinite space, David's words in Psalm 19:2 seem all the more true: Day after day they pour forth speech; night after night they display knowledge. Quantum physics has demonstrated that when you get down to the subatomic particles there is an irresistible urge of electrons toward symmetry. This same urge is repeated in the very formation of the galaxy and even in the way galaxies move in relation to one another.

Earth science

The findings of astronomy seem so incomprehensibly vast, that perhaps we should move closer to home. The cosmological argument for the existence of God applies here on spaceship earth as well, but let us move to another howl of the wolf lurking outside the cabin in the dark woods of doubt. This is the *teleological argument*. The word *telos* in Greek means the "end." Teleology is that view of philosophy that sees in the universe that things were designed for a purpose—an end. Evolutionists do not like the words *design*, *purpose*, and *teleology*. They believe it is all one gigantic accident, the combination of infinitely long time and chance. With the advances in science over recent decades, it requires a remarkable degree of faith (or suppression, Paul would say) to believe that.

Consider the mass and size of this planet. The gravitational field of objects of certain weight and density allows life to flourish, or even exist. The gravity of Jupiter would give all organic life the dimensions of a pancake. The moon's gravitational field works the tides on earth but is not sufficient to form a life-sustaining atmosphere on its own shores. It is only by taking most of what we need with us that we humans can visit the moon, and the problems of planting a colony there are staggering. Just how much tolerance does the size and mass of a planet allow for life to thrive? One scientist figures that if earth were 10 percent larger or 10 percent smaller, earth would be desolate.

The interplanetary probes have underscored the fact that we are at an unusually precise distance from the sun. We receive just the right amount of heat and light. Our planetary orbit takes us much closer to the sun at some times of the year than at others. If we veered much from this flight path we would become a toasted Venus or a frigid Mars. Temperatures on neither will support life as we can conceive of it. Combine this with the tilt of the axis of the earth. None of the other planets in our system is so tilted at 23 degrees. As the earth slowly turns, all parts of its surface receive the rays of the sun, much like a chicken roasting on a spit. Otherwise a portion would become unbearably hot, and a much greater portion of the top and bottom poles would accumulate masses of ice.

We have already mentioned the moon's pull on the oceans. God provided the moon as a maid service to clean up the oceans and shores of the continents. Without the tides created by the moon there would be too little water movement. Shores and coasts would become one stench pool of garbage.

It would be impossible to live near them. Because of the tides we have continuous waves breaking upon the shores to aerate the oceans. This provides oxygen for plankton. Plankton is the foundation for the world food chain. Without it there would be no chain. Without plankton there would not be enough oxygen to create a living atmosphere.

There is the wonder of our atmosphere, a great envelope of 78 percent nitrogen, 21 percent oxygen, and 1 percent a dozen different trace elements. None of the other planets investigated have anything like this combination, and spectrographic studies of nearby areas of the galaxy show no sign of the necessary elements. In addition, the atmosphere's elements are not chemically combined, which would make them less usable, but they are mechanically mixed by the tidal effects of the moon on the atmosphere. The environmentalists make a point that the atmosphere is something we should steward. But it is not quite as fragile as they usually suggest, or we long ago would have choked in the carbon dioxide we dump into the atmosphere. Where does all this waste go? It is absorbed into the ocean—allowing animal and human life to continue.

Then there is the amazing nitrogen cycle. Nitrogen is extremely inert. If it were not we would all be poisoned as it combined with other elements. But, in fact, it is impossible to get it to combine naturally with other things. Nitrogen is definitely needed for plants, but how does God get the nitrogen out of the air and into the soil? Lightning continually charges the atmosphere somewhere on the planet, daily depositing thousands of tons of nitrogen to nourish the soil and allow plant life to continue.

Much has been said about the depletion of the ozone layer. This certainly is cause for concern, for this is a thin layer of the atmosphere. If compressed, the ozone in this layer would be only a quarter of an inch thick. Without it, however, life would not exist. Eight killer rays fall upon this planet continually from the sun, and without ozone we would be burned, blinded, and broiled. The ultraviolet rays come in two forms. The longer rays are deadly and are screened out by the ozone layer. Shorter ultraviolet rays are necessary for life, and the ozone layer lets them through. Furthermore, the most deadly of these rays are allowed through the ozone layer in just a very tiny amount, enough to kill the green algae. Otherwise algae would fill all the lakes, rivers, and oceans. Just think of it: We live on a tiny crust of earth, comparatively the thickness of an apple peel, bombarded from above by deadly radiation, while just beneath our feet lies an immense core of molten lava. We are suspended between burning from above and burning from below. I would be exceedingly nervous were not I confident that there is a competent Designer who holds me in the balance.

One more natural wonder must be visited before we leave our thoughts on the earth. That wonder is water. Little or no water has been found on our sister planets, though we now have a fairly good idea of their composition. Here water rules the planet. Water, the amazing solvent, dissolves almost everything except those things that are life-sustaining. In its ice form water breaks up rocks and produces soil. As snow it stores itself in the valleys. As rain it nourishes and cleanses. As vapor it moistens the arable land. It forms clouds in just the right amount. At any one moment just about 50 percent of the earth's surface is covered by clouds, filtering sunlight and producing rain. As steam it runs powerful machinery.

Other than bismuth, water is the only liquid that is heavier at 4 degrees above centigrade than it is at freezing. That may not seem such an important quality, but if it were not true, lakes would freeze from the bottom up instead of from the top down. All fish would die and all algae would be destroyed. Without algae there would not be oxygen, and we would perish. The earth continually pours out speech about the person and character of God.

Human physiology

Whitaker Chambers was an atheist and leader in the American Communist Party until he ended his own spiritual wanderings at the cross of Christ. What is interesting is that the turning point that roused Chambers from the cozy fireside in the cabin of unbelief was an ear. He was sitting at the kitchen table feeding his infant son. Like many a new, doting parent he was considering with wonder this miniature person who demanded so much attention. He casually meditated on the shape of the ear, so uniquely formed and perfectly designed to carry out its mission of detecting and channeling sound waves. Yes, designed. . . . There seemed no other word for it. Communism might have a master plan for shaping the world, but its designers lacked the power to shape a baby's ear.

Everywhere we look the body points to God. Our life is based upon the blood that flows in our veins. The amazing red blood cell, created in the bone marrow, immediately gives up its nucleus when it reaches the bloodstream. For any other cell, losing the nucleus means death, like cutting the heart right out of a person. But a red blood cell is formed like a donut with a thin membrane across the hole. Without its nucleus it is able to carry more oxygen for the body because of this membrane and its shape. Were it shaped like other cells our bodies would require nine times as many red blood cells to provide oxygen.

What gives ears and blood cells their shape and provides most of the extraordinarily exact information needed to create a living organism? It took science a long time to break even the most rudimentary secrets of life, the gene. We now have a new kind of applied scientist, the genetic biologist, who has learned how to effect the formation of this chain of amino acids that are part of every cell. In a vastly complex process, which geneticists are only beginning to understand, the genetic code duplicates itself in each cell of the organism, carrying the entire design for a unique individual. These chains must form in very precise order for life to be even remotely possible, yet no one knows why they form at all.

One mathematician with a sense of humor tried to run a computer simulation to calculate the statistical possibility of a genetic code sequence forming by pure chance. The best he could come up with was that the statistical probability is not one chance in 1 million or even in 1 trillion, but in 1 followed by enough zeros to roughly stretch from the earth to the moon. Since the genetic code was broken in the 1960s, being a materialistic evolutionist is about as logically reasonable as being a member of the flat-earth society. We pity the poor soul who believes the earth is flat. We hire the evolutionist to teach our children.

How, for example, could anyone look at a human eye and suppose that it just happened? Evolution operates through the principle that nature provides what an organism needs over the slow process of the survival and reproduction of the more adaptive creatures. But try to imagine what process of natural selection would have adapted a set of nerves that could translate light into electrical impulses that could be translated by a brain. There are no half-way steps between no-eyes and eyes. Nothing less than the fully developed article can do the job. Yet what mindless force could begin the process? For something without eyes the sun would have been warmth. But what conceivable drive could have needed to find a way to turn that energy into sight? And having somehow found the need, what mindlessness evolved the focusing lens, the pupil that opens and closes to control the amount passing through the lens? Where did the clear, gelatinous material come from to conduct light through the eyeball to tiny receptors? And what of the nerve connectors that make the image meaningful to the brain? But even this isn't the whole problem. Having somehow developed the eye, nature wasn't content, but universally created two eyes on a horizontal plane, so that we not only can see but we also have a range finder that determines distance and perceives in three dimensions.

Did you ever wonder why tears continually flow across your eye? To see clearly and comfortably the eye must be continually washed with a secreted brine. The superfluous brine is conveyed to the nose through a perforation in the bone as large as a goose quill. When once the fluid has entered the nose it spreads itself upon the inside of the nostril and is evaporated by the current of warm air that passes over it through respiration. It is easily perceived that the eye must want moisture. But could the need for an eye generate the simultaneous production of the gland that produces the tear and the hole through bone by which it is discharged?

This is the weakness of materialist theories for the origins of life. What we know about the abilities of a creature to adapt to its environment can account for superficial, simple changes. But as complexity rises, so does the evolutionist's need for credulity. To put the matter mildly, the belief that chance evolved sight requires faith presuppositions. Sir Charles Scott Sherrington, an English physiologist who wrote a classic work on the eyes, said, "Behind the intricate mechanism of the human eye lie breathtaking glimpses of a master plan." We have developed some fine cameras and telescopes, but the finest does not even vaguely approach the optical manipulation of light that the eye provides automatically. When the eye got ready to create itself it also had the forethought for its own protection, and built itself beneath the bony ridge of the brow. It even provided a nose on which to hang the glasses that some of us need and its own window shutters, the lids and lashes that bat dust out of the way and spread moisture. Evolution certainly thought of everything, if it thought.

Lastly we mention the incredible brain. Weighing but 3.3 pounds and containing 10 billion to 15 billion nerve ends, each a living unit in itself, it performs incredible feats. Evolutionist Sir Henry Fairfield Osborn said, "To my mind the human brain is the most marvelous and mysterious object in the whole universe." True enough, and creationist researcher Dr. Henry M. Morris holds that mystery up before all of his evolutionist colleagues when he says, "Therefore, men who reject or ignore God do so, not because science or reason requires them to, but purely and simply because they want to!" As Romans 1:28 puts it, "since they did not think it worthwhile to retain the knowledge of God, he gave them over to a depraved mind" (NIV).

Turning on the light

Let us return to my two young friends in the restaurant. Presented with all the evidence in the world, they will not move from the darkened room they have shut themselves into. They will not move by virtue of the facts alone to come to put their trust in any God, let alone the God of the Bible. One thing the Bible makes abundantly clear is that human beings with a stake in their self-centered lives are experts in fooling themselves. We suppress the facts. Materialistic evolutionists aren't the only ones who do it well. Suppose after reading the last two chapters this young man and woman say, "Yes, what you say does seem quite persuasive. It seems difficult to believe in evolution. But our philosophy still works for us. If God is big enough to do all you say, then he certainly isn't concerned about our little lives. And who knows what kind of spiritual life forces may actually be the unseen guides of the universe? Why, there are those who are able to connect into them. We can even merge into that life force and so become one with the God you are telling us about. We have faith."

Their explanation might proceed in any of a number of directions and never stir from the cozy cabin. The occupant need only paint the outside with the colors of a belief system that best fits current needs and desires. Many people are quite willing to accept the Bible on a strictly intellectual basis. Their suppression mechanism simply filters and colors the light so that it no longer carries truth to their heart. After years of study and more years in the study and pulpit, ministers by the thousands continue to deny that God or the Bible has any meaning or gives any hope. I have known a few who came to find true faith and new life in Christ after they were in preaching or teaching ministry. "Why didn't I see it?" they ask. "Such wondrous things were right there all the time. I read about them. I knew about them. But I never took them in." The darkened room looks so gloomy and carries such an odor of death when viewed from the light and life of God's truth.

Who or What is the Source of ultimate truth?

He is the alone foundation of all being, of whom, through whom, and to whom are all things; and hath made most sovereign dominion over them, to do by them, for them, or upon them whatsoever himself pleaseth.
[Westminster Confession of Faith, chapter 2]

4

God Who Grows

C S. Lewis takes us to the heart of Christian experience in his philosophical and logical defenses of the Christian faith, but he slipped some of his most profound insights into the pages of five fantasy stories called *The Chronicles of Narnia*.

The first of these stories, *The Lion, the Witch, and the Wardrobe*, retells in a fresh way the gospel message. Four children are magically transported from our everyday world to a world that seems to be controlled by a wicked witch but is actually ruled by Aslan, a great lion who represents Jesus, the Lion of Judah. As I contemplate the person of God, however, I am reminded of another of the Narnia books, entitled *Prince Caspian*. In this tale the children, Peter, Lucy, Susan, and Edmund, return to Narnia after only a short passing of earth time but many centuries of Narnian history. Lucy is the first one to encounter the lion she has come to love more than life:

> "Aslan, Aslan. Dear Aslan," sobbed Lucy. "At last."
> The great beast rolled over on his side so that Lucy fell, half sitting and half lying between his front paws. He bent forward and just touched her nose with his tongue. His warm breath came all around her. She gazed up into the large wise face.
> "Welcome, child," he said.
> "Aslan," said Lucy, "You're bigger."
> "That is because you are older, little one," answered he.
> "Not because you are?"

"I am not. But every year you grow, you will find me bigger."

How God must enjoy seeing his children grow to see him become bigger. He is no more omnipotent today than when he called the universe into being by the power of his word. He is the Ancient of Days, God Almighty *El Shaddai*, God Most High *El Elyon*, and Sovereign Lord *Adonai Yahweh*. He is the Immortal God, the Invisible God, the Just and Mighty One, the *Alpha* and *Omega*, eternal and ever-present. Once he reached out and pulled me out of the pit

I have heard of thee by the hearing of the ear: but now mine eye seeth thee. Wherefore I abhor myself, and repent in dust and ashes. [Job 42:5–6]

of my sin and I saw him as all-sufficient Savior and Redeemer. But, like Lucy, I have grown older, and now I seem to look higher to gaze into his face. The God I understand and love is still only a micro-version of the reality that is beyond my comprehension. But as I continue to grow, so does my perception of who I am and who he is. That was the experience of Lewis, and of Paul when he wrote in Philippians 3:10–11 of his desire that he might "know him, and the power of his resurrection, and the fellowship of his sufferings, being made conformable unto his death; If by any means I might attain unto the resurrection of the dead." That is the experience of every believer who is growing in his or her chief purpose for living, "to glorify God and to enjoy him forever." I can't imagine a more wasted life than one who has warmed a pew in the church building and has a Bible sitting uselessly on the shelf, but who has never grown older spiritually nor seen God grow.

Through the blast furnace of affliction, Job found his own righteous life in its true perspective in relation to God's size. When his own pretense of righteous living was laid out before him, he said in 42:5–6, that it was like he had only heard of God before. Now that he saw him, all he could do was repent. Isaiah was ushered into the presence of God and he cried out in Isaiah 6:5, "Woe to me! I am ruined!" (NIV).

The straightedge

John Calvin begins his *Institutes of the Christian Religion*, one of the most influential works in the history of Christianity, with this introduction: "Nearly all the wisdom we possess, that is to say, true and sound wisdom, consists of two parts: the knowledge of God and of ourselves." Calvin goes on to observe that it is impossible to truly know oneself without a knowledge of the God in whom we live and move and have our being (Acts 17:28). Our knowledge seems true and logical when we keep our eyes fastened steadfastly on the material things around us. But what happens when we take God into account? Calvin writes:

> Suppose we but once begin to raise our thoughts to God, and to ponder his nature, and how completely perfect are his righteousness, wisdom, and power—the straightedge to which we must be shaped. Then, what masquerading earlier as righteousness was pleasing in us will soon grow filthy in its consummate wickedness. What wonderfully impressed us under the name of wisdom will stink in its very foolishness. What wore the face of power will prove itself the most miserable wickedness. That is, what in us seems perfection itself corresponds ill to the purity of God.

More eloquent pens than mine have failed to communicate what by definition is beyond the scope of language to portray. Even the *Westminster Confession* and catechisms show signs of the struggle these pious, learned men experienced as they contemplated God. They ended up with a compilation of the language Scripture uses, a stringing together of verse after verse after verse after verse. They seem to have been unable to sum up all those attributes and descriptions. Then they came to the writing of the *Shorter Catechism* and the question "What is God?" Now they were stuck. This catechism was to sum up the essentials of faith in a form a child could understand. Long and hard these men discussed all that they knew God to be. It seemed to defy abbreviation. Finally they adjourned for a time of prayer that God might give them special wisdom.

The youngest of the delegates, a Scot named George Gillespie, had not yet seen his thirtieth year. He began to pray: "Oh, God. Thou art a Spirit, infinite, eternal, and unchangeable in thy wisdom, power, holiness, justice, goodness, and truth. . . . "

"Stop the prayer!" shouted a voice from the assembly. "God has answered us." And they wrote down those words, which come down to us as one of the most beautiful and scriptural definitions of the person of God ever written:

God is a Spirit, infinite, eternal, and unchangeable in his wisdom, power, holiness, justice, goodness, and truth.

Most church historians say that story probably is not how it happened, but it does seem true to my experience that, when I try to reason out God, my mind is simply blown away the closer I come. But when I open my spiritual mind in prayer, and apply scriptural precepts with the eyes of faith, I grow older; God grows larger. I can, with Calvin, "begin to raise my thoughts to God, and to ponder his nature, and how completely perfect are his righteousness, wisdom, and power—the straightedge to which I must be shaped."

God is a Spirit

We acknowledge a mystery as soon as we open the first page of Scripture and read that "In the beginning God created the heaven and the earth" (Genesis 1:1). Among the first things Scripture teaches is that God is not from our neighborhood. He is not bound by laws of dimensionality and size and mass as is everything else we know. This is an uncomfortably foreign Being, beyond our control and escape. The *Confession* begins its description: "There is but one only living and true God, who is infinite in being and perfection, a most pure spirit, invisible, without body, parts, or passions, immutable, immense, eternal, incomprehensible. . . . " Where do they get such terms?

> Lo, he goeth by me, and I see him not: he passeth on also, but I perceive him not. [Job 9:11]

> Whither shall I go from thy spirit? or whither shall I flee from thy presence? If I ascend up into heaven, thou art there: if I make my bed in hell, behold, thou art there. [Psalm 139:7–8]

> No man hath seen God at any time; the only begotten Son, which is in the bosom of the Father, he hath declared him. [John 1:18]

> God is a Spirit: and they that worship him must worship him in spirit and in truth. [John 4:24]

> Howbeit the most High dwelleth not in temples made with hands; as saith the prophet, Heaven is my throne, and earth is my footstool: what house will ye build me? saith the Lord: or what is the place of my rest? Hath not my hand made all these things? [Acts 7:48–50]

Theology, the study of God, uses the word *transcendent* to describe such characteristics. God transcends the earth and heavens and my understanding. Yet every time I stand beside a casket of someone I have known I realize that there are spiritual beings besides God, and we human beings are among them. Though the materialistic evolutionist tries to tell me otherwise, there is obviously something going on in my conscious mind besides electrochemical activity. And when a person dies something departs that had been inside the body. There is simply no one at home any longer in the arms and legs and torso and head lying in state. We may gather in the funeral home and observe the craft of the embalmer and remark, "How natural she looks, as if she is there asleep." But this is no sleep. That body lies a ruined house, silent and uninhabited.

For the Christian that relationship of spirit to Spirit is the fantastic hope of our faith:

> For whosoever will save his life shall lose it; but whosoever shall lose his life for my sake and the gospel's, the same shall save it. For what shall it profit a man, if he shall gain the whole world, and lose his own soul? Or what shall a man give in exchange for his soul? [Mark 8:35–37]

> The Spirit itself beareth witness with our spirit, that we are the children of God. [Romans 8:16]

> For if we believe that Jesus died and rose again, even so them also which sleep in Jesus will God bring with him. [1 Thessalonians 4:14]

> Receiving the end of your faith, even the salvation of your souls. [1 Peter 1:9]

The Bible generally speaks of three types of beings in the spiritual sphere: (1) Human beings are spirit as well as flesh. (2) Angels are completely spirit, though they are also finite, even as we. That fact gives me considerable comfort when I think about the spiritual warfare that involves the holy angels, the angels in rebellion against God, and me. Angels are limited, too. (3) Then there is God, the infinite Spirit who is unbound, so that we are never outside his presence.

The *Confession* calls him a "most pure spirit." In the language of the 1640s the writers said that he is "without passions." The meaning of *passions* has changed somewhat over the intervening centuries. They were not saying that God is without emotions, and Scripture has much to say about

God's emotions. In modern language the *Confession* means that God's emotions are never uncontrolled. Given how often my sin gives God cause for uncontrolled anger, I am most thankful that self-control is part of the innate character of his spirit.

In chapter 5 we will consider the Holy Spirit within God's nature as Trinity. I will share then why I am especially grateful for this particular aspect of God's spiritual self.

Infinite, eternal, unchangeable

Considerable nonsense masquerading as theological wisdom has centered in these descriptive terms.

Infinity

God is infinite. He must, then, be unreachable, it is said. He transcends all of the temporal, spatial universe; logically he cannot be imminently in touch with my life. What sanctified baloney. If God's transcendence meant he could not be imminently concerned with the world he would be a very limited God indeed, a Jolly Green Giant too big to help pick the peas. It may not seem reasonable that an infinitely present God would be concerned about this corner of his creation, but it is hardly possible that he would not be *able* to do so as he wills.

"Ah," says the skeptic. "When you speak of God's *will* you have reached the logical impossibility of an infinite God. Your theism has no answer for that old question: 'Can God create a stone so large that he cannot lift it?'" I doubt there are many people serious about talking to lost people who have not heard this trite cliché. The answer is simple. Of course God cannot do so, for if he did he would be acting against who he is as God. To say that God is infinite does not imply that there are no things outside of his ability. The Bible says that God cannot lie, nor go back on his promise (see Numbers 23:19–20; 1 Samuel 15:29); if Jesus had failed in his mission to be the sacrifice for sin, God would have ceased to be an infinite God. That is what God shows Abram in Genesis 15:8–21. Neither can God dwell in the presence of sin, nor anything that is imperfect or unholy. Otherwise Jesus would not have had to die. Could not God simply have invented another way to deal with the sin problem? He could not and have remained true to his infinite holiness. God cannot sin nor tempt others to sin (James 1:13). It was only when Jesus laid aside infinity for a season that he could inhabit an infant's body and could be tempted as the second Adam.

The Children's Catechism, a much more recent writing than the Westminster documents, was prepared as a first step toward understanding God. It is used by several denominations. This catechism sums up the answer to the above objections to God's infinity nicely. The question is, "Can God do anything?" The answer: "Yes, God can do *all his holy will*." God's infinity means he is utterly free: He can do anything that he wants.

Solomon declared the true meaning of infinity when he built a temple, not to box God into a piece of geography, but to demonstrate his boundlessness:

> But will God indeed dwell on the earth? behold, the heaven and heaven of heavens cannot contain thee; how much less this house that I have builded? Yet have thou respect upon the prayer of thy servant, and to his supplication, O LORD my God, to hearken unto the cry and to the prayer, which thy servant prayeth before thee today. [1 Kings 8:27–28; 2 Chronicles 6:18–19]

This is true infinity: to fill all and yet hearken to the prayers offered by small voices in his presence.

Eternality

God is eternal. In his book and television miniseries *Cosmos*, Carl Sagan says, "The cosmos is all there ever was, all there is, and all there ever will be." That is his statement of faith. As we have said, such statements quite ignore the problem of the origin of matter. Some materialists claim that matter and energy are eternal. Certainly no true scientist could miss the problems that theory implies for the laws of physics, but it is the best answer available to solve the problem of the *first cause*. Physicists accept the fact that somewhere there must have been an "uncaused cause," the "unmoved mover," and that first cause cannot have ever been brought into being. Something *must* be eternally existing. There simply is no alternative. For the theist that first Cause and Mover is God. Often the Old Testament saints confessed their praise to a God who is "from everlasting to everlasting" (for example, Nehemiah 9:5). "'I am the Alpha and the Omega . . . which is, and which was, and which is to come, the Almighty" (Revelation 1:8; see also vv. 17–18). The one who makes this last statement is Jesus, the Christ.

Is God, then, totally outside the space-time continuum, so that all times blend into one eternal now? I do not believe so, though God certainly has perfect command and understanding of the future, as well as the past. The Bible uses the metaphorical statement that a thousand years are as a day in the time perspective of God. That would seem to indicate a passage of succeeding moments, though one quite beyond our human perspective. God certainly relates to us in terms of past, present, and future.

Unchangeability

Another word you run across when listening to theological talk is *immutable*. Both words refer to God's utter constancy in being, will, and purpose. One twentieth-century heresy, process theology, claims that God is "in process of becoming." The god behind this statement turns out to be nothing more than a pantheistic being. Certainly the theologians who hold such an idea do not find it in creation or Scripture.

This does not mean the God revealed to us is stagnant. His governance of creation is exceedingly dynamic. Scripture has much to say about what this part of God does and does not mean. The following passages should give us an overview:

The Strength of Israel will not lie nor repent: for he is not a man, that he should repent. [1 Samuel 15:29]

The counsel of the LORD standeth for ever, the thoughts of his heart to all generations. [Psalm 33:11]

But the mercy of the LORD is from everlasting to everlasting upon them that fear him, and his righteousness unto children's children. [Psalm 103:17]

I know that, whatsoever God doeth, it shall be for ever: nothing can be put to it, nor any thing taken from it: and God doeth it, that men should fear before him. [Ecclesiastes 3:14]

For I am the LORD, I change not; therefore ye sons of Jacob are not consumed. [Malachi 3:6]

Heaven and earth shall pass away, but my words shall not pass away. [Matthew 24:35]

Because God wanted to make the unchanging nature of his purpose very clear to the heirs of what was promised, he confirmed it with an oath. God did this so that, by two unchangeable things in which it is impossible for God to lie, we who have fled to take hold of the hope offered to us may be greatly encouraged. [Hebrews 6:17–18 NIV]

Every good gift and every perfect gift is from above, and cometh down from the Father of lights, with whom is no variableness, neither shadow of turning. [James 1:17]

One area of much argument concerns Scriptures that say God repented (or was grieved that he had done something). One place where God "changed his mind" occurs before the flood in Genesis 6:6: "And it repented the LORD that he had made man on the earth, and it grieved him at his heart." Another is God's statement to Nineveh through the prophet Jonah that he would destroy the city and his subsequent decision to spare it (Jonah 3:4, 10).

These two passages tell us something about God's character, but not that he is fickle. In the first instance we see the great decline into evil that humanity had plunged from the fellowship of righteousness God intended. He is shown to be a father whose child has run far into rebellion. The parent is grieved. This Parent was so grieved that his holiness demanded punishment and a new beginning. Yet that punishment also grieved him, so that he made a covenant with the race he had so nearly destroyed (Genesis 8:20–9:17). The clear testimony is not that God would have done things differently if he had had the chance to go back, but that he is touched by both sin and its results. He takes no pleasure in destroying the wicked (Ezekiel 18:23, 32).

The second example says much the same thing, with the difference that the judgment against Nineveh is canceled after the wicked people of the city became frightened enough to repent. Actually it wasn't canceled so much as postponed (see pp. 48–49). God had a lesson to teach Jonah and Israel. As wicked as the Gentiles were, God intended Israel to be a priesthood for the world. He knew he would not destroy Nineveh at this time; what is more, Jonah was pretty sure of it as well. But that did not make Nineveh's condemnation, nor Jonah's responsibility to them, any less real.

Infinite, eternal, unchangeable in wisdom

Infinity, eternality, and unchangeability are three lenses through which we can look at all things we can say about the characteristics or "attributes" of God. They are aggregate in six categories of the *Shorter Catechism*: (1) wisdom; (2) power; (3) holiness; (4) justice; (5) goodness, and (6) truth. These are not six separate pieces of God's being; rather, each of them is descriptive of the whole nature of God. God is all of these things always.

The wisdom of God is infinite. He has been infinitely wise from eternity past to eternity future. Theologians call this God's *omniscience*. That word is interesting, combining the words *omni* for "all" and *science* for "knowledge." All of our search for knowledge—our sciences—attempt to learn what God has known completely and fully. He is the source of the equation for the theory of relativity as well as the theorems of geometry and the concept that $2 + 2 = 4$. Omniscience means that God holds no false beliefs. The range of his knowledge is total, including all true propositions.

Theologians and philosophers worry much about the implications of omniscience. Does it mean that we have no free will because God's copy of the pages of the book of future history is already completely printed? Certainly the Bible speaks of God's knowledge of the future, and it also speaks of Jesus not being fully informed about the future during his time on earth. God chose to limit his own knowledge in that way. We also might deduce that God can know and take into account all possible contingencies of all possible actions. God's understanding would be total, yet each human would be able to do exactly what he or she wanted to do given the choices and limitations God had placed on that point of choice. We have little experience with omniscient beings to know how this works. We will return to this question in chapter 7.

This much we can say with supreme confidence: God's infinitely and eternally wise understandings and decisions have not and will not change.

Infinite, eternal, unchangeable in power

Alongside the infinity, eternality, and unchangeability of omniscience, God is revealed as being all powerful or *omnipotent*. As stated above (see pp. 78–79), God's freedom to act and respond is limited only by his character. He cannot do anything that would make him less than God. But he can do anything he wants and has been able to from eternity past and will be able to do so as the waves of eternity roll on.

In his book *The Concept of God*, Ron Nash mentions one of the more unusual problems that have puzzled philosophers through the years. If God is omnipotent, does that mean he can change the past? Or, to state it another way, if I hear that a plane has crashed, and I realize that my family was flying on this particular plane, is it wrong at that moment to pray that God has saved their lives? The event is over, so he already has or has not done so.

Whether it makes logical sense, I guarantee that this prayer will immediately burst forth from my heart, and bringing any concern to God is certainly not "wrong." Is it useless? Will God hear that prayer and answer it by putting the brakes on time and backing them up to change an event that has happened? Nash quotes Thomas Aquinas to the effect that God cannot cause an absolute contradiction. If I can say that something happened as a true proposition, and the past is changed so that this truth becomes untrue, we have a logical problem of the highest order. Nash prefers to say that God cannot do anything that would reverse cause and effect. That restriction has nothing to do with God's freedom or power.

Infinite, eternal, unchangeable in holiness

The infinite, eternal, and unchangeable holiness of God returns our thoughts to his transcendence or separateness (see p. 76). Surely we know that God is separate from sin. He is also separate and exalted above us and everything else in creation. The Hebrew word used to describe God's holiness carries with it the idea of "heaviness." Remember when young people showed they were impressed by something by saying, "That's heavy, man"? The ancient Hebrews had a similar idea:

> Who is like unto thee, O Lord, among the gods? who is like thee, glorious in holiness, fearful in praises, doing wonders? [Exodus 15:11]

> There is none holy as the Lord: for there is none beside thee: neither is there any rock like our God. [1 Samuel 2:2]

And one cried unto another, and said, Holy, holy, holy, is the LORD of hosts: the whole earth is full of his glory. [Isaiah 6:3]

And the four beasts had each of them six wings about him; and they were full of eyes within: and they rest not day and night, saying, Holy, holy, holy, Lord God Almighty, which was, and is, and is to come. [Revelation 4:8]

From beginning to end, from Genesis to Revelation, nothing is more certain in the Bible than that God is heavy—and beyond our knowing. The Israelites had an object lesson about this holiness in the ark of the covenant, which was given to symbolize God's presence and law. The ark was kept in the Holy of Holies, the innermost part of the tent in which God was worshiped in the wilderness, and an inner room of the temple. The room was shaped as a perfect cube, symbolizing God's perfection, and a great curtain separated this awesome sanctuary from the people. Only the high priest could enter the Holy of Holies, and then only once each year, the Day of Atonement. And on this day the priest offered a sacrifice for his sin and the sin of the people so he would be pure enough to enter. He filled the holy place with a cloud of incense so that he might not look upon the golden cherubim above the ark. And with all this, the early priests wore bells on their clothing and a rope around their waists. They feared God might find the high priest's offering unacceptable and strike him dead. Imagine the other priests listening at the door. Would the bells continue tinkling? Or would they be forced to pull on the rope to remove the dead body of one rejected?

Now remember that day when the lifeless body was that of the holy God himself, who defiled himself by taking on himself our sins. At his death on the cross the curtain that hung before the Holy of Holies to separate humans from God in the temple was ripped from top to bottom. That infinite holiness of God was now shared. The transcendent, "heavy" God has sanctified his people, so we may fellowship in his throne room.

Infinite, eternal, unchangeable in justice

Recently a well-known news figure was interviewed about his religious affiliation. His father, he said, was a very religious man, and he had learned at home to have a deep but private religion, whatever that means. But, he added, "My father did not believe that a good God would send people to hell, and I do not believe there is a hell, either." This man, and presumably his father, have joined the chorus of millions in adoring a God who is infinite in mercy but who is quite willing to let bygones be bygones. This is a gospel of cheap grace, a Christianity needing no Savior, no standard, no cross, no repentance, and no righteousness. By necessity this Christianity rejects both the Bible and Jesus, since both tell us quite plainly that hell exists because God is just: "Behold, all souls are mine; as the soul of the father, so also the soul of the son is mine: the soul that sinneth, it shall die" (Ezekiel 18:4).

Jesus said, "Shall not God avenge his own elect, which cry day and night unto him, though he bear long with them? I tell you that he will avenge them speedily. Nevertheless when the Son of man cometh, shall he find faith on the earth?" (Luke 18:7–8).

A man named Elihu, the wisest of Job's three friends, puts his finger on the questions we need to ask ourselves: "Shall even he that hateth right govern? and wilt thou condemn him that is most just? Is it fit to say to a king, Thou art wicked? and to princes, Ye are ungodly?" (Job 34:17–18). I know that no one hates justice—for the other guy. But it is, in fact, a condemnation of God to say that he offers only forgiveness and will take no action toward those who have rejected him and thumbed their noses at the laws he has made. Is not such a god a weak and despicable ruler? Elihu goes on to say that this is not the sort of God he believes in:

> Is he not the One who says to kings, "You are worthless,"
>   and to nobles, "You are wicked,"
> who shows no partiality to princes
>   and does not favor the rich over the poor,
>   for they are all the work of his hands . . .

God has no need to examine men further
    that they should come before him for judgment.
Without inquiry he shatters the mighty
    and sets up others in their place.
Because he takes note of their deeds,
    he overthrows them in the night and they are crushed.
He punishes them for their wickedness
    where everyone can see them,
because they turned from following him
    and had no regard for any of his ways.
They caused the cry of the poor to come before him,
    so that he heard the cry of the needy. [Job 34:18–19, 23–28 NIV]

A loving god who is not just is not truly loving because he cares nothing for the oppression of the weak by the mighty, and he is not very holy, for he permissively lets people walk all over him. We would call such permissiveness bad parenting or bad governing in our own society, but we demand it of God who is infinite, eternal, and unchangeable. I preach about hell, not because I find the subject pleasant, but because Jesus took my hell on himself, and now no one needs to go there. The good news of the gospel is not that there is no hell, but that its power is broken.

God is so much better than permissive. He is merciful—so merciful that we do have a Savior, a standard, a cross, and a means of repentance and righteousness. "God presented him [Jesus] as a sacrifice of atonement, through faith in his blood. He did this to demonstrate his justice, because in his forbearance he had left the sins committed beforehand unpunished—he did it to demonstrate his justice at the present time, so as to be just and the one who justifies those who have faith in Jesus" (Romans 3:25–26 NIV).

Infinite, eternal, unchangeable in goodness

We praise excellence by calling it "good." Yet Jesus considered "goodness" truly applicable only to God. To ingratiate himself with Jesus, a man called him "good teacher." Jesus immediately challenged this conception of goodness: "There is good but one, that is, God" (Mark 10:18). Jesus *was* the "good teacher" in truth, and the man's big problem was that he did not realize the full truth in what he was saying. God is transcendently excellent in all that he is, the perfect standard for what goodness is. Comparatively, nothing and no one else excels.

God's excellence extends to creation (Genesis 1:31), his love (2 Chronicles 5:13; Psalms 100:5; 106), his blessings (Psalms 31:19; 145), his works (Psalm 52:9), his power to restore (Jeremiah 33:11), his protection of his people (Nahum 1:7), his grace to all (Matthew 5:45; Acts 14:17; James 1:17), his gifts (Matthew 7:11), and his special grace to those who love him (Romans 8:32; 2 Thessalonians 1:11; 2 Peter 1:3).

God is perfectly good in all that he is and does, and the wondrous thing is that he imparts that excellence in the creative expression that uniquely connects all humanity with his creative perfection. Think of some great classic novel by Hugo, a play by Ibsen, a symphony by Beethoven, a poem by Frost, a cantata by Bach, or a dance by Nureyev. Some of our greatest artists and performers and writers and musicians have lived in complete rebellion against God, yet their talents still testify to his excellence. Even the elegance of a pro basketball player soaring toward the goal and the controlled explosion of energy as the Olympic sprinter leaps forward from the blocks offer an out-of-focus photograph of the excellence that is in God perfectly, infinitely, eternally, and unchangeably.

Infinite, eternal, unchangeable in truth

It was one of the saddest questions ever posed, and the most important he would ever ask. He was a judge, and the man on trial before him had said that he was a King, who had come to "testify to the truth."

"What is truth?" asked Pilate.

In a world ruled by deception fostered by the father of lies, truth is a rare commodity. We cynically pride ourselves on not being taken in by the con. We don't know the voice expression with which Pilate asked his question, but I wonder if his tone was not wistful. There was so little truth in his own life, so little truth in those he knew, and he had ceased to look for it. Yet standing before him was not only a man who was telling the truth, but who was the very embodiment of truth. Jesus had told the disciples the answer to this riddle only hours before: "I am the way, the truth, and the life: no man cometh unto the Father, but by me" (John 14:6). All successful searches for truth end in the presence of Jesus Christ.

If God is the Source of all truth, and Jesus is truth, we never know God fully in himself as he is, not even when we arrive in heaven. The full scope of infinity will remain beyond our ken. But we can know God as he is as he reveals himself to us. We can know something of the truth that lies behind the words: "God is a Spirit, infinite, eternal, and unchangeable in his wisdom, power, holiness, justice, goodness, and truth." Here are the sources of truth:

"Howbeit when he, the Spirit of truth, is come, he will guide you into all truth" (John 16:13).

"Sanctify them through thy truth: thy word is truth" (John 17:17).

Who or What is the Source of ultimate truth?

There is but one only living and true God. . . . In the unity of the Godhead there be three persons, of one substance, power, and eternity: God the Father, God the Son, and God the Holy Ghost.
[Westminster Confession of Faith, chapter 2]

5

The Absurd Trinity

The Trinity is a mathematical absurdity. Anyone who has progressed beyond the first grade ought surely to know that one plus one plus one does not equal one." That quote comes from the literature of a certain cult, one of many who have mocked the very idea of a God who is triune. A woman in my church once chided me that I really shouldn't speak of Jesus as God, "because when Jesus was on earth, God was in heaven, don't you know?"

As a matter of fact, I did know that. I also have progressed far enough in my education to know that one plus one plus one does not equal one. Nor do I believe that God is a cherry pie cut into thirds—three pieces, one pie. It has been said that the doctrine of the Trinity is one of the greatest evidences that Christianity is not a humanly devised religion. No one in his or her right mind could have devised such a concept. I think there are better evidences than that, but it does make the point that we need to be clear about what we confess to be true and and what we do not believe. Many errors have arisen in the church in attempts to logically understand God as the Father, Son, and Spirit. This was complicated by trying to explain that Jesus possesses two natures: one divine, one human.

By the year 451 so many problems had appeared that a church council at Chalcedon tried to write a creedal statement that covered all the bases. We might wonder if the Definition of Chalcedon did not overdo things just a little. Part of it reads thus:

We teach with one voice that the Son [of God] and our Lord Jesus Christ is to be confessed as one and the same, that he is perfect in Godhead and perfect in manhood, very God and very man, of a reasonable soul and body consisting, consubstantial with the Father as touching his Godhead, and consubstantial with us as touching his manhood; made in all things like unto us, sin only excepted; begotten of his Father before the worlds according to his Godhead; but in these last days for us men and for our salvation born of the Virgin Mary, the Mother of God according to his manhood. This one and the same Jesus Christ, the only-begotten Son, must be confessed to be in two natures, unconfusedly, immutably, indivisibly,

Hear, O Israel: The LORD our God is one LORD: and thou shalt love the LORD thy God with all thine heart, and with all thy soul, and with all thy might. [Deuteronomy 6:4–5]

inseparably, and that without the distinction of natures being taken away by such union, but rather the peculiar property of each nature being preserved and being united in one Person and subsistence, not separated or divided into two persons, but one and the same Son and only-begotten, God the Word, our Lord Jesus. . . .

I hope what follows will be clearer regarding what we are *not* saying about God, what we *are* saying, and why we *must* say it.

What the Trinity is not

The Trinity is not like anything else

Some say the Trinity is like water, which may be liquid, solid, or gas. This contains some illustrative quality, since all three remain water. Another version of this is that the Trinity is like an egg, which consists of a shell, an egg white, and a yolk. Another is that God is like a person who fulfils different roles at the same time. I am a husband and a father; I am a pastor; I am a citizen and a voter. I am all of these things at the same time and I simply fulfil one role and then another. God is Creator; God is Redeemer; God is Comforter and Guide—isn't this what God is like?

Such analogies break down so quickly that they are more dangerous than they are helpful. One of the first heresies the church faced was Sabellianism or modalistic monarchianism. Its adherents taught that God created the world, then put down that role to assume human form. At the ascension he put down that role or form and became the Holy Spirit. It is like an actor who performs on stage, then runs behind the curtain, changes costumes, and assumes another persona. God is not a thespian, nor is he moving from role to role. Nor is he now vapor, now solid, now liquid, depending on the conditions of the moment. He is Father, Son, and Holy Spirit—fully and at the same time. God does this in perfect unity, while the three natures remain distinct and functionally separate.

You don't understand this? Neither do I. God is not *like* anything else. You will find no corollary in nature. God is. God is who he is. We don't have any choice about what kind of God exists. He comes with the package of life, so to speak. He didn't have to create us, love us, reveal himself to us, die for us—do anything for us. And he doesn't have to fit our mind's ability to conceive of him. The fact that he does do all those things is serendipity, or rather mercy.

Fortunately, God uses illustrations to reveal himself to us. The concepts of Father, Son, and Holy Spirit are his words, and they reveal aspects of tri-unity. Jesus is not a son in the same sense as in a human family. But the picture of sonship tells us much about the relationship of the Father and Son. John Calvin described God's pictures to us as the kind of language we use with an infant. The little one does not understand language yet, so we make sounds for the infant to model in its very first efforts to talk. God describes himself with the metaphors of a Father, an Eagle, a Shepherd, a Rock, a King. These pictures are ideas we can understand. But when Moses asked God his name, the name given was "I AM THAT I AM" (Exodus 3:14). We must hear that bottom-line answer. God can use our categories of knowledge, just as we can use an infant's categories to begin teaching about the world. But the categories only go so far until they grow. At the end, God simply IS, as opposed to every other sort of god, who ISN'T. God IS WHO HE IS, whether we understand or not.

The Trinity is not other

There are three major distortions of the concept of God: *deism*, *pantheism*, and *polytheism*. The woman who advised me not to think of Jesus as God because God is in heaven, is close to the deist frame of reference. The word *deist* means one who believes in a god. But deism is belief in a certain *kind* of being, one who is "other" to our experience. *Deism*, as opposed to *theism*, which is the Christian's view of God, is belief in the existence of a supreme being who is the ultimate source of reality, being, and values but who does not intervene in human affairs and is ultimately unknowable. This defines God as the great clock maker, who assembles the works, winds it up, then sits back and meditates while the clock ticks away on its own.

Deism was popular in the seventeenth and eighteenth centuries because it approached God from a rationalist, Enlightenment perspective. Voltaire and Jean Jacques Rousseau made France a deist nation and paved the way for the atheistic, human-rights-worshiping French Revolution. That bloody time in French history tells us something about deism: The deist god is so out of the picture that he is no God at all in a meaningful sense. It was a short hop from deism to atheism.

A similar progression occurred in German theology, with more long-term results. Immanuel Kant, the father of modern rationalist philosophy and theology, in 1781 wrote a book that rejected all the arguments for the existence of God. He saw that our knowledge of reality is colored by our senses and emotions. So he deduced that we do not know *any* reality beyond what we can learn through our senses. We must reject all metaphysical knowledge. Kant erred, not in his evaluation of the mind, but in his estimation of God's ability to talk baby talk with us. He thought God too big— too "other" than creation. In fact, Kant's god was small. It takes a big God to fill the universe with his presence and remain involved in one speck of planetary dust in a rather ordinary galaxy. The small god remains rather conveniently out of the way, unconcerned with human sin.

German deism immediately attacked the Bible. Scripture's revelation was the point at which their small god collided head-on with the true, infinite, three-in-one God. Two of Kant's contemporaries, Gotthold Ephraim Lessing and Hermann Samuel Reimarus, founded higher criticism of Scripture. They believed the ultimate judge of Scripture was empirical science and said that Scripture's history and truth could be studied to see whether it was true or false. To this add Kant's rejection of human ability to understand the supernatural. Suddenly the idea is born that, if science cannot test God, he cannot be real. That is not quite logical, but that deduction came to be made, alongside the conclusion that we can test Scripture through higher critical theories and find "truth" buried behind the superstitious, unbelievable, unknowable, supernatural parts.

The Trinity is not "the force"

The god of the Enlightenment West is unknowable and transcendently "other," but there also is a tendency to err in the other direction. This concept of god is called *pantheism*. This word comes from the Greek *pan*, meaning "all," and *theos*, meaning "god." It means *all is god*; the universe is god. The immanence of god is emphasized until there is no distinction at all between god and creation. This idea dates at least to the beginning of Hinduism and some forms of Buddhism. A number of Christian mystics have sought to become lost in some great universal pool of God. If deism replaces God with reason, pantheism replaces God with nonreason. God is eternal but impersonal, and reality is a temporary emanation or manifestation—a life force, if you will.

If that language sounds slightly familiar to fans of the *Star Wars* movies, Luke Skywalker's and Darth Vader's universe represents classic pantheism. The good and bad sides of the force are equally "god," and Luke releases his potential as a "Jedi knight" only when he learns to leave behind rational thought and be guided totally by the extrasensory power within him. There is even a pint-sized guru, the mystic Yoda, who leads Luke toward oneness with the "force." Reincarnation in Hindu theology seeks to lose the individual's consciousness, desires, identity, and rationality in the force behind creation. The end comes with absorption into the cosmos. The New Age movement expresses the desire to become one with the infinite. Its forms pervade society—from astrology and horoscopes to transcendental meditation and imaging.

It pervades Christian society as well. Have you heard anyone say, "It doesn't really matter what you believe [rational, substantive faith] as long as you are sincere [emotionally] about it"? That may sound quite open-minded, but the logical end of such thinking may be seen in the following report by a participant in the 1970 World Council of Churches' "Dialogue Between Men of Living Faiths":

> The dialogue . . . introduced most of us to a new spirituality, an interfaith spirituality, which I mostly felt in common prayer: who actually led the prayer or meditation, a Christian, or a Muslim, or a Hindu, or a Buddhist, did not much matter, what actually was said during prayer was not all important, whether a Muslim would say "amen" after a Christian prayer mentioning sonship of Christ, was not the question, what we really became aware of was our common human situation before God and in God.

> We were thus led gradually into a new relation with God, with our own selves, and with others, and this new relation was perhaps to what entire human history was moving.

Pantheistic elements infected Christianity in reaction to Kant's elevation of the rational mind. Three men were crucial to this process. The first was David Hume, who generally agreed with Kant about the mind's inability to comprehend God. Hume, however, saw a continuing nonrational need to believe. In the modern vernacular Hume told us to "Go for it! Don't worry about explaining God. Just pick a faith and make a great leap into the dark, into emotional catharsis."

Hume was a philosopher, but his preference for a nonrational faith bore fruit in the "German idealism" Christianity of Friedrich Schleiermacher. Schleiermacher announced all doctrines and propositional truths of faith to be nonessential "husk" that could be stripped away to expose *inner truth*. He said, in effect, "I agree that however God exists is unknowable. God is too distant to affect human moral reasoning. Who cares? Religion is not really about knowing or doing. It is about feeling, about ecstasy. I can still have a subjective, emotional faith in something out there somewhere that I do not see. So I will leap off this cliff I am standing on, and my 'feeling of absolute dependence' assures me that something out there will catch me." Suddenly theologians were stumbling over themselves to remove the Trinity, the virgin birth, the resurrection, and all supernatural husk. Deism was replaced by idealism, liberalism, modernism, and a host of other isms. The deist other-god had been poured into a bake-it-yourself cake mix of pantheism.

The next major thinker in this train was Karl Barth, a pastor in Switzerland during World War I. Like many who followed liberal Christianity, he was thoroughly disillusioned by the war, for humankind was supposed to be evolving into something better. The horrors of war showed that this was not the trend at all. Barth totally rejected the unaware deist-liberal god, proclaiming an infinite, transcendent, and sovereign God. That sounds good—certainly nothing like the imminent god of pantheism—but with Barth and his followers things are not always what they appear. Bear with me while I sort out a few central teachings of what is variously called Barthianism, neo-orthodoxy, dialectical theology, or crisis theology.

First, Barth taught a creation and a fall of humanity. But this fall did not occur in space and time as we know it. Did it happen in history? That is irrelevant. What matters is that the fall is a principal in all people in all times.

Second, whether or not this fall actually occurred historically, the human being is so totally fallen that he or she can have no point of contact with God. God is totally other and is unknowable. Does that sound familiar? It gets even more complicated, though.

Third, God has overcome this gulf between himself and humanity by incarnating himself in the Word. In some sense the infinite became finite. Barth's view of God is that, in a paradoxical and mystical way, God stopped being infinite and revealed himself to us as Jesus Christ. He was not God and Jesus at the same time. Whether there was a specific time in which God walked on earth and was nailed to the cross and rose again from the dead is, once more, irrelevant.

Fourth, the Bible *contains* God's Word; we can even say that it contains the incarnate Jesus Christ. God's Word has authority. But the Bible is totally a human document. How do we know what is and is not truth? Well, the Holy Spirit incarnates Christ in our heart in the Word. What may be God's Word for you may *not* be God's Word for me. The dialectic push-pull of my emotional response ultimately gives it meaning.

I hope I have given an adequate overview of neo-orthodox teaching. Since truth is relative, its expression varies. Barth worked hard to find an adequate God and leave the pantheistic camp of the liberals. Actually he did neither. The liberals said the fall and the incarnation did not occur in history. Barth said it does not matter to faith. The liberal god was totally absent from the universe and imminent in the emotions. Barth found God unreachable except through a paradox—a putting together of two truths that cannot coexist. Barth saw Jesus Christ as God, but as a God that does not exist in the same time and place as the Father and the Holy Spirit.

The American theologian J. Oliver Buswell once personally confronted Barth on these points:

> I referred to his *Dogmatics in Outline* and asked if his view of the Persons of the Trinity, as there expressed, was not Sabellianism [see our description of Sabellianism or modalism above].
> "Well, you could call it Sabellianism," he frankly replied.
> . . .
> I asked Professor Barth how he explained the prayers of Jesus and His sayings in which He spoke objectively of the Father and of the Spirit. His reply was to the effect that in speaking of the Deity the difference between subject and object completely disappears. I said, "Is that not then mysticism?" to which he replied, "Well, you could call it mysticism."

If I were to poll theological writers and teachers, asking what theologian has most influenced their understanding of God, the Trinity, and Scripture, a majority would name Barth. That is unfortunate. We may admire Barth's courage against Adolf Hitler in Germany and his attempt to stand against the atheist understanding of liberal theology, but the root of Barthianism is mired in the marsh of the unknowable God, a blind leap of faith, and a rationalist view of Scripture.

The Trinity is not three gods

The third major distortion of the idea of God is the concept of polytheism, which says there are many gods. At least polytheism is not one of our problems in Western Christianity and our view of God. Or is it? I would suggest a tendency even in this direction among Christians who see God as something less than all-powerful against Satan. Satan takes the form of God's peer, rather than a limited, controlled, created being. Perhaps you have heard such statements as: "God wants to heal you. He is just waiting for you to unlock his ability by doing this or by praying in this certain way." "I am being besieged by Satan, and I can't get free because I haven't had the right people praying for me." Nobody who says such things would dream of calling Satan an equal of God, but that is an unconscious implication of this small-god thinking.

I am not forgetting that Christians are accused of being polytheists because of the Trinity. Some cults avoid that charge by saying, "Is it not the truth that there is one God, the Father? That Son is just a created being? He is really an exalted man who was created at some point in time, and the Holy Spirit is simply an impersonal force. The Spirit is the active force of God." This actually is an ancient error called *Arianism*. A distinguishing mark of cults is that they deny the Trinity. The defense of the unity of God will never come from philosophy or rational arguments. It is spelled out firmly in Scripture. Without deep roots in the authority of Scripture and a biblical understanding of God as the Bible reveals, the church's protest that Christianity is monotheistic sounds ridiculous.

The Trinity in Scripture

The Old Testament

The Trinity is more fully revealed in the New Testament. In the Old Testament God continually countered the polytheism of other cultures by impressing on the Israelites his *oneness*. But there are shadows of the Trinity in the Old Testament as well.

From the very first verse of the Bible we suspect that something is up, because the plural and singular forms of the Hebrew word for God sometimes appear together. God is plural—and he is singular. Genesis 1:1 says, "In the beginning God created the heaven and the earth." The word used in Hebrew for "god" is *Elohim* (plural), not *El* (singular). It says: "In the beginning God[s] created the heaven and the earth." Genesis 1 then switches to the singular form until verses 26–27: "And God said, Let us make man in *our* image, after *our* likeness. . . . So God created man in his own image, in the image of God created he him; male and female created he them." Genesis 3:22: "And the LORD God said, Behold, the man is become as one of *us*, to know good and evil." Genesis 11:7: "Let *us* go down. . . . "

Higher critical scholars make all sorts of spurious claims about mixed authorship in those early chapters, but that doesn't account for Isaiah 6:8: "Also I heard the voice of the Lord saying, Whom shall *I* send? And who will go for *us*?"

Jesus, of course, doesn't manifest his godhood in the Old Testament, but the prophets had a great deal to say about the coming Messiah, including his deity. Here are just a few of the passages in which the inference that the coming Christ will be God is strong. Psalm 45:6–7 says in reference to the coming King, "Thy throne, O God, is for ever and ever. . . . therefore God, thy God, hath anointed thee with the oil of gladness above thy fellows." Jesus himself and the Book of Hebrews quote Psalm 110:1 as indicating Jesus' deity: "The LORD said unto my Lord, Sit thou at my right hand, until I make thine enemies thy footstool."

Isaiah is explicit. In 7:14 he says, "Therefore the Lord himself shall give you a sign; Behold, a virgin shall conceive, and bear a son, and shall call his name *Immanuel* [Hebrew for 'God with us']." In 9:6–7 Isaiah continues, "For unto us a child is born, unto us a son is given: and the government shall be upon his shoulder: and his name shall be called Wonderful, Counsellor, The mighty God, The everlasting Father, The Prince of Peace. Of the increase of his government and peace there shall be no end." Jeremiah is just as specific, using a name reserved for God in 23:5–6 to refer to Christ: "The days come, saith the LORD, that I will raise up unto David a righteous Branch, and a King shall reign and prosper, and shall execute judgment and justice in the earth. In his days Judah shall be saved, and Israel shall dwell safely: and this is the name whereby he shall be called, THE LORD OUR RIGHTEOUSNESS." There are other texts that state it clearly: The Messiah, King, and Redeemer of God's people is God. Jesus is God.

The Holy Spirit enters Scripture in a full way only after Jesus returned to the Father, but he actively worked in Old Testament times as well. This is true in 2 Samuel 23:2–3: "The Spirit of the LORD spake by me, and his word was in my tongue. The God of Israel said, the Rock of Israel spake to me. . . . " Look also at Numbers 11:17, 25; Psalm 104:30; Isaiah 63:10–11, and Zechariah 4:6.

Some Bible students speculate that the Trinity is referred to in Numbers 6:24–26 when the Lord's blessing is given three times and in Isaiah 6 when the creatures seen in Isaiah's vision of the throne room of God cry out: "Holy, holy, holy is the LORD of hosts."

The New Testament

It is always interesting to hear people say, "You Christians say Jesus is God, when he didn't even claim that title for himself." Bible scholar Walter Elwell, in his *Topical Analysis of the Bible*, notes about 200 passages in the Gospels in which Jesus claimed godhood, claimed the prerequisites of godhood, or taught with an authority only proper to God. Here are some of those texts:

> And Jesus came and spake unto them, saying, All power is given unto me in heaven and in earth. [Matthew 28:18]

> And he [Jesus] said unto her, Thy sins are forgiven. And they that sat at meat with him began to say within themselves, Who is this that forgiveth sins also? [Luke 7:48–49]

> Also I [Jesus] say unto you, Whosoever shall confess me before men, him shall the Son of man also confess before the angels of God. [Luke 12:8]

> Verily, verily, I say unto you, before Abraham was, I am. [John 8:58]

> Why then do you accuse me of blasphemy because I said, I am God's Son? Do not believe me unless I do what my Father does. But if I do it, even though you do not believe me, believe the miracles, that you may know and understand that the Father is in me, and I in the Father. [John 10:36–38 NIV]

Jesus may have been a megalomaniac, a liar, and a blasphemer, but do not accuse him of making fainthearted claims. Nor did he alone make these claims: John 1:1 says, "In the beginning was the Word, and the Word was with God, and the Word was God." John's Gospel refers to Christ, the Word who "was made flesh, and dwelt among us" (John 1:14). The doubting disciple Thomas fell on his knees before the resurrected Christ, saying, "My Lord and my God" (John 20:28). The point of Hebrews 1 is that Jesus Christ is above the angels as God.

We read in the New Testament that the Holy Spirit also is God and that the Holy Spirit is a person with tasks and responsibilities. Here are some of those passages:

> For it is not ye that speak, but the Spirit of your Father which speaketh in you. [Matthew 10:20]

> But when the Comforter is come, whom I will send unto you from the Father, even the Spirit of truth, which proceedeth from the Father, he shall testify of me. [John 15:26]

> But Peter said, Ananias, why hath Satan filled thine heart to lie to the Holy Ghost. . . . Thou hast not lied unto men, but unto God. [Acts 5:3–4]

> Know ye not that ye are the temple of God, and that the Spirit of God dwelleth in you? [1 Corinthians 3:16]

The Holy Ghost also is a witness to us. [Hebrews 10:15]

For Christ also hath once suffered for sins, the just for the unjust, that he might bring us to God, being put to death in the flesh, but quickened by the Spirit. [1 Peter 3:18]

We also can find some passages where all three persons of the Trinity are in view; for example:

And Jesus, when he was baptized, went up straightway out of the water: and, lo, the heavens were opened unto him, and he [the second person] saw the Spirit of God [the third person] descending like a dove, and lighting upon him: and lo a voice from heaven [the first person], saying, This is my beloved Son, in whom I am well pleased. [Matthew 3:16–17]

Go ye, . . . baptizing them in the name of the Father [the first person], and of the Son [the second person], and of the Holy Ghost [the third person]. [Matthew 28:19]

When the Comforter [the third person] is come, whom I [Jesus, the second person] will send unto you from the Father [the first person], even the Spirit of truth, which proceedeth from the Father, he shall testify of me. [John 15:26]

Because ye are sons, God [the first person] hath sent forth the Spirit [the third person] of his Son [the second person] into your hearts, crying, Abba, Father. [Galatians 4:6]

Is it necessary to believe in the Trinity? Certainly if we believe the Bible we must believe this body of evidence. Loraine Boettner has said that, apart from the doctrine of the Trinity, "the Deity of Christ, the incarnation, the personality of the Holy Spirit, regeneration, justification, sanctification, the meaning of the crucifixion, and the resurrection cannot be understood." Jesus said, "This is life eternal, that they might know thee the only true God, and Jesus Christ, whom thou hast sent" (John 17:3). This is eternal life, to know the triune God. Unitarians and Muslims, and others worship someone else, a lone, solitary person who exists alone from all eternity.

What the Trinity is and does

But how can God be three in one? In the Trinity the Father penetrates the Son and the Spirit, and the Son penetrates the Father and the Spirit. Jesus said, "I am in the Father, and the Father in me" (John 14:11). Whatever that exact composition, the fact that God is a Trinity is a fantastic blessing to us, because the three take to themselves different roles. The Father, Son, and Holy Spirit take part in the total relationship the believer has with God in Christ.

First, the Father takes to himself three tasks: (1) creation and governance of all things in creation; (2) election of those who will be saved, and (3) authorship of the plan of redemption. John 3:16 says that God the Father loved the world and sent his only Son.

Second, the Son takes to himself the threefold task of redemption: (1) laying aside his prerogatives as infinite God (but not godhood itself) to assume humanity and live a perfectly holy life; (2) suffering and dying in the place of those who deserved to die, and (3) rising victorious from the dead to ascend to heaven and send the Holy Spirit.

Third, the Holy Spirit (1) draws sinners to God, (2) applies the holiness of Christ to believers and guides us toward true holiness before God in what is called sanctification, and (3) comforts us in sorrow and speaks for us before the Father.

To know God is neither to figure him out rationally nor to rely on mind-submersing emotional catharsis. To strike the balance of faith I recommend that you read the revelation the triune God has given and meditate on what you discover there about the work of these three parts of the perfect oneness of God. All three are available to us in prayer, and it helps me to recognize by addressing each in prayer, remembering what they have done. There are examples of prayer to all three in the New Testament. Worship, praise, and adore each member of the Trinity, separately and specifically.

Hear, O Israel, the Lord our God, the Lord is one. And within that one there is Father, Son, and Holy Spirit—three persons in one God, forever, amen!

Is anyone in control out there?

It pleased God the Father, Son, and Holy Ghost, for the manifestation of the glory of his eternal power, wisdom, and goodness, in the beginning to create or make of nothing the world, and all things therein, whether visible or invisible, in the space of six days, and all very good. After God had made all other creatures, he created man, male and female, with reasonable and immortal souls, endued with knowledge, righteousness, and true holiness, after his own image.
[Westminster Confession of Faith, chapter 4]

6

The God Revolution

Anyone who shares the gospel with men and women in the community, whether using the Coral Ridge "Evangelism Explosion" plan or some other approach, quickly learns something about worldviews. It doesn't take long when discussing spiritual things to discern another person's answers to the quest questions, even if that person would not know how to phrase those answers. How one answers the question heading this chapter, "Is anyone in control out there?" affects every thought more substantive than which shoe to put on first in the morning.

Many years ago a great revolution occurred. Two titanic theories—and only two—exist for explaining the origin of the universe and the meaning of the life inhabiting it, whether on this planet or any other that may turn out to be occupied. When the theory of evolution was introduced it was not that one scientific idea replaced another, nor even merely that one worldview replaced another worldview. A supernatural view with ultimate meaning was pushed aside by an entirely naturalistic set of assumptions. Thomas Huxley announced that there no longer was any room for the supernatural. His equally famous grandson, Sir Julian Huxley, said, "Operationally, God is beginning to resemble, not a Ruler, but the last fading smile of a cosmic Cheshire cat."

A world without its God

I don't think I need to sell any thinking person, whatever he or she believes about God, on the fact that a revolution of monumental significance has altered the mental fabric of much of the world. More Christians have been martyred in the twentieth century for their faith than in all other centuries of the Christian era combined. More people have been killed in wars. In the most medically advanced and best fed

> *Prepare to meet thy God, O Israel. For, lo, he that formeth the mountains, and createth the wind, and declareth unto man what is his thought, that maketh the morning darkness, and treadeth upon the high places of the earth, The LORD, The God of hosts, is his name.*
> [Amos 4:12b–13]

and clothed parts of the world, children are starving to death for food or love in the midst of neglect and abuse. Life in the twentieth century has been as cheap and disposable as in the depths of the cruelest, most degraded societies of the past.

Look at one ongoing example in our own enlightened part of the globe. In 1980, eight years after *Roe* v. *Wade* brought about abortion on demand, a study estimated that 113,000 abortions occurred in the second and third trimesters of pregnancy. By this stage of development few abortionists would seriously argue that the unborn child is a "cellular growth" in the woman's body. At the very latest a developing embryo feels pain and begins responding to his or her environment by the late third month. By the fifth month premature babies are routinely sustained outside the womb in incubators. I find it difficult to imagine that somewhere around 30 million lives have been destroyed through abortion in the United States alone since the fatal Supreme Court decision in January 1973. Those who favor "choice" have all sorts of reasons to justify the majority of those killings occurring in the first trimester. But even if we allowed those arguments to go unchallenged, what about those 113,000, for which only the grossest ignorance of the facts or the grossest disregard for the lives of other human beings could account? Here in one year are 113,000 exhibits of a worldview that says, "Life is meaningful only when it doesn't interfere with my desires." The incidence of post-abortion distress among women of whatever stage of terminated pregnancy shows that not everyone is capable of living so callously.

Disregard for human life also shows itself in the disrespect being shown for one another's bodies. At a recent seminar conducted at a penitentiary by the international Prison Fellowship ministry for inmates approaching release, a volunteer asked a small group of men about the pressures and temptations they expected to face when they returned to the street. The prisoners mentioned several anticipated problems. "What about sexual desires?" the volunteer prompted. One man, a Christian active in the Bible studies, nodded. All the rest shook their heads. No, they responded, this was not something they worried about.

"I've got a girlfriend," one explained. "We're not that close, but we help each other out, and she gives me sex when I want it." The man was not trying to be smug or humorous, nor did he express the least bit of embarrassment at this evident lack of feeling toward his sex partner. Probing further, the leader found that the young man truly did not conceive that such a relationship might not be perfectly moral or healthy for either him or his friend. Two other men were equally unblushing in assuming that life was supposed to be promiscuous. "I use a condom," each explained in turn. The volunteer, a veteran of work in jails and prisons for many years, was hardly surprised that the men planned to have sex outside marriage. He did become thoughtful about the lack of meaning they attached to the most intimate relationship between human beings. "What struck me about these men is the sheer ignorance that there could be any other kind of life. They have committed crimes, but each is intelligent, and the one with the girl-friend is serious, articulate, and from a relatively well-off background. They represent a cross-section of our culture."

In that same culture an organization called, ironically, the North American Man/Boy Love Association (NAMBLA), now openly represents the rights of pedophiles in the United States and Canada, proclaiming that we prudes have inhibited natural, healthy sexual activities between men and the young objects of their desires.

Abortions, "mercy killing," using a woman or child to gratify sexual needs, active homosexuality—these are hardly new tendencies. What is new is that in Western Judeo-Christian culture none of these things were considered acceptable behavior until we convinced ourselves that we are qualitatively no different from a community of over-achieving amoebas. Slowly society has been conditioned, and is continuing to be conditioned, to tolerate, accept, and even value such "modernity." What once was done in hiding is out of the closet. This great divide occurred largely because of the biggest lie to ever come down the pike, a lie that has done and is doing more harm than any other intellectual theory that I know of. I think most people, including most Christians, are abysmally naïve when it comes to understanding how the theory of evolution contributed to all this misery. Evolution devalues humanity. Underneath its scientific facade, the doctrines of the evolutionary worldview demand that the strong survive, the weak must move aside, and that ultimately none of it matters much. Why should not the ends, whether pleasure or peace, justify all means necessary and convenient?

The eyes of the world were on a hot courtroom in Arkansas back in 1925 when Clarence Darrow called to the stand his opponent in the trial of John Scopes, a trial held to see whether evolution might be acceptable in the schools of the country. The great orator William Jennings Bryan was that opponent, and when Bryan had taken the oath and his seat in the box, Darrow asked Bryan if he realized that in his home state of Nebraska there had lived a whole race of men 1 million years ago. Bryan said he didn't realize anything of the sort, and he didn't believe it, either. So Darrow brought in Dr. Henry Fairfield Osborn of the American Museum of Natural History, the most respected paleontologist in America. Yes, Dr. Osborn verified, just three years prior, in 1922, evidence of a whole race of people had been discovered to have lived in Nebraska a million years ago. Bryan was dumbfounded.

The great con?

The discovery was made by a man named Harold Cooke, who christened the find, in scientific terminology, *Hesperopithecus haroldcookii*. Most called it "Western ape-man." Around the world drawings and reconstructions of "Western ape-man" appeared in museums and schools, showing *Hesperopithecus haroldcookii* in all his glory, sitting around the fire with his family, with a club over his shoulder. Everyone knew exactly what he looked like.

What was the great paleontological discovery that introduced us to our ancient ancestors? It was a tooth—not a skull with teeth, not a jawbone and teeth, nor several teeth. It was one tooth. Sometime later, in the same area, they discovered another, identical tooth, this time connected to a jawbone—the jawbone of an extinct pig or peccary. Creation-science researcher Dr. Duane Gish said, "I believe this is a case in which a scientist made a man out of a pig and a pig made a monkey out of a scientist!" Thanks in part to the Scopes trial, the pig made a monkey out of all of us.

The search for human origins has been a comedy of such errors. In 1959 Dr. W. R. Thompson, an entomologist who for years was director of the Commonwealth Institute of

Biological Control in Ottawa, Canada, wrote in the fore-word to the centennial edition of Charles Darwin's *Origin of Species*:

> This situation, where men rally to the defense of a doctrine they are unable to define scientifically, much less demonstrate with scientific rigor, attempting to maintain its credit with the public by the suppression of criticism and the elimination of difficulties, is abnormal and undesirable in science. . . . The success of Darwinism was accompanied by a decline in scientific integrity.

A young man who took a course in anthropology at the University of Florida told me he was very surprised that at the end of the course his professor had the integrity to tell the class that all that they had been told during the whole semester was purely speculation. She did not have one single fact to back it up. Dr. T. N. Tahmisian, a physiologist for the Atomic Energy Commission, said: "Scientists who go about teaching that evolution is a fact of life are great con men, and the story they are telling may be the greatest hoax ever."

I often have given my own opinion of evolution and those who teach it as the irrefutable truth. The purpose of this book is to look at God, not to slam scientists, even those who may deserve it. I do not think evolutionists have set out to perpetrate the greatest hoax in human history. I think they are men and women of faith, who fervently hold a worldview and enthusiastically evangelize for it. They honestly believe they are right and I am wrong, and they read and interpret and teach the facts on the basis of their assumption that evolution is the way it must have happened. For some, including such founders of materialist science as Darwin and Ernst Haeckl, it may be argued that their science sprouted from their intense personal animosity toward Christianity. But they did not, I assume, deliberately set out to mislead. Their rebellious hearts, their prejudice, and their worldview assumptions blinded them, just as Paul said in Romans 1:18–23.

Aldous Huxley, leading atheist and evolutionist and author of *Brave New World*, said this:

> I had motives for not wanting the world to have meaning; consequently assumed that it had none, and was able without any difficulty to find satisfying reasons for this assumption. . . . For myself, as, no doubt, for most of my contemporaries, the philosophy of meaninglessness was essentially an instrument of liberation. The liberation we desired was simultaneously liberation from a certain political and economic system [capitalism] and liberation from a certain system of morality. We objected to the morality because it interfered with our sexual freedom.

Another of the famous Huxleys, Julian, has been equally forthright about the reasons for the immediate acceptance of Darwin's book, *Origin of Species*: "We all jumped at the *Origin* because the idea of God interfered with our sexual mores."

The great revolution?

At this writing the final outcome of the breakup of the Soviet Bloc remains years away. Some new totalitarianism may emerge with promises of economic and social stability to the nations born at the beginning of the 1990s. Nearly three-quarters of a century of economic, social, cultural, and religious repression will not be washed away quickly. Neither will the revolution in worldview unleashed by the events of the last decade be undone. In those early days of openness American Christian booksellers were invited for the first time to show their wares at the Moscow Book Fair. One company brought 50,000 Russian language Bibles to give away. The police stopped them from giving away their Bibles for several hours at the show because such a mob of people rushed the booth that every aisle of the Book Fair turned to gridlock. The police told them to give Bibles away for one hour, stop for two hours, and resume for another hour. The officials were not trying to prevent the distribution. They simply wished to keep the aisles open and to prevent injury. Nearby, Madalyn Murray O'Hair was displaying her wares at the American Atheist Society booth. Someone who was there told me that virtually no one stopped to even see what she had to offer. They knew all too well.

Those of us who have followed life in these countries have heard countless stories of the spiritual revolution that accompanied the political and economic changes. One of the sad elements of this miracle has been that great numbers of Western cultists and radical preachers have flooded into the countries to peddle their own agenda, so many that the government was forced to consider reestablishing restrictions. Even American speakers with something substantive to say alienated listeners by offering great, inspiring messages full of advice without love or understanding of the real spiritual issues the people wanted to hear about.

But there were others, such as one young Michigan layman, who did make a difference. David Marvin was invited, much to his surprise, on a trip to Romania in early 1993. David hurriedly did his best to put together a series of messages, praying that the Lord would show him why he had been given this opportunity. Two things utterly changed his life as soon as he set foot on Romanian soil, causing him to discard those feverishly studied sermons. First, he encountered unimaginable deprivation and poverty. But second, and more important, in the midst of near starvation Christians were the most generous, disciplined, spiritually alive, and joyful he had ever known. In the comparatively well-off home in which he stayed there was not enough money to buy fuel, and the temperature hovered only slightly above freezing. But any extra money after the most basic needs were provided was dropped into a jar on the table so that it would be available to give to those more needy. The $1500 he took with him to distribute was given to a church that had nothing, and the church immediately gave most of the gift to a visiting Russian pastor whose people were worse off—this in a country where hatred for Russians runs deep and predates the Soviet occupation. It didn't take long to learn the reason for this revolutionary Christian discipleship. The Romanian church had been nurtured under the persecution of an atheistic worldview. In such a desert the smallest stream of spiritual water offered soul-quenching nourishment. God was not just there. The Creator of all was seen at work daily among his people.

David tells of his experience: "I learned that I was not sent to Romania to minister to those people. They ministered to me by teaching me what was missing from my own spiritual life and the lives of most American Christians. I could not stand before them to speak without breaking down in tears of shame for the way we have allowed our material gifts to pull our eyes off the Giver."

By the end of his month in Romania, people were crowding to hear the man they called "Dahveed Ahmereeka—the man who cries." We too need to hear what David Marvin said in those meetings: "Some day soon you people of Romania will have a better life, with more money to spend. That will be when you will face your greatest danger. Never become like the people of the West. Reject our lifestyle. Don't lose your hard-won consciousness of God. You are so rich; we are so poor." David now takes that message of shame to his own impoverished countrymen.

It was in a barren wilderness that Moses looked ahead and saw the danger of neglecting the Creator of heaven and earth:

> And it shall be, when the LORD thy God shall have brought thee into the land which he sware unto thy fathers, to Abraham, to Isaac, and to Jacob, to give thee great and goodly cities, which thou buildest not, And houses full of all good things, which thou filledst not, and wells digged, which thou diggedst not, vineyards and olive trees, which thou plantedst not; when thou shalt have eaten and be full; Then beware lest thou forget the LORD, which brought thee forth out of the land of Egypt, from the house of bondage. [Deuteronomy 6:10–12]

Looking back on those years, the writer of Psalm 106:13–15 tells the result of forgetfulness toward God: "They soon forgat his works; they waited not for his counsel: But lusted exceedingly in the wilderness, and tempted God in the desert. And he gave them their request; but sent leanness into their soul."

The wasting disease

How we need a Romanian revolution in worldview! The citizens of the former Soviet states, even those citizens who have not turned to Christ, have experienced the shattering of a society built on the worldview that we are not creatures living in a magnificently created world that was made by an infinitely creative God.

In the late 1950s Dr. Ernest Gordon, dean emeritus of Princeton University Chapel, was invited to address the senior class of an English department in a city high school. He arrived at the office of the assistant headmaster, who guided him to the lecture hall. Twenty years later he was invited to speak at the same school, only it was not the same school at all. The assistant headmaster's office had become the security command post. Corridors and classrooms were monitored by police officers. Dr. Gordon wrote:

> I interpret this scene as evidence of the endtimes of a civilization that had once benefited from the Christian worldview, one that exalted creation and people, and provided the ideals essential for an authentic education. I recognize that civilization does not create Christians. However, the community of faith created and still creates the civility that is evidence of civilization. That demoralized school is the tragic consequence of a society's rejection of the biblical worldview that provided the intellectual dynamic of Western education. What is education but an expression of the prevailing culture?

A newspaper article quoted Harvard scientist Stephen Jay Gould, a leading evolutionist, with this equally disturbing statement: "We're an afterthought, a little accidental twig." I don't know what you do with little accidental twigs that fall on your lawn. I pile them in a heap and throw them in the garbage. That is, I guess, Gould's view of life. We are nothing more than little accidental twigs. The writer of the newspaper article made the aside that "there is nothing quite like a conversation with Stephen Jay Gould to knock a little evolutionary humility into a person." That is more than a little humility. When set alongside the other evidence it seems more the symptom of a wasting disease that is destroying the significance of humanity. The evolutionary worldview immersing our society has declared all-out war with *teleology*—the idea that things exist for a purpose. We already have talked about the Christian's view of the teleology for each human being: to glorify and enjoy God forever. The writers of the *Westminster Confession* described a similar teleology for the creation of all other things, particularly humanity:

> It pleased God the Father, Son, and Holy Ghost, for the manifestation of the glory of his eternal power, wisdom, and goodness, in the beginning to create or make of nothing the world, and all things therein, whether visible or invisible, in the space of six days, and all very good. After God had made all other creatures, he created man, male and female, with reasonable and immortal souls, endued with knowledge, righteousness, and true holiness, after his own image.

God is triune, infinite, eternal, and unchangeable in his wisdom, power, holiness, justice, goodness, and truth. See how all of that fits into the Christian's world-and-life view.

> Have ye not known? have ye not heard? hath it not been told you from the beginning? have ye not understood from the foundations of the earth? It is he that sitteth upon the circle of the earth, and the inhabitants thereof are as grasshoppers; that stretcheth out the heavens as a curtain, and spreadeth them out as a tent to dwell in. . . . Lift up your eyes on high, and behold who hath created these things, that bringeth out

their host by number: he calleth them all by names by the greatness of his might, for that he is strong in power; not one faileth. . . . Hast thou not known? hast thou not heard, that the everlasting God, the LORD, the Creator of the ends of the earth, fainteth not, neither is weary? there is no searching of his understanding. [Isaiah 40:21–22, 26, 28]

The theologians at Westminster and Isaiah agree that the creation and direct revelation of the Bible teach us three magnificent things about the Creator God. First, he is powerful; second, we cannot fathom his wisdom and understanding; and third, he is good. God's is not a strength that must be renewed with rest. His wisdom forgets not where a star has wandered off to. This is not an excellence that begins the job and leaves it half-finished. He still is involved, unwearied and everlasting. What else do we know about God that applies to our culture? Here are just a few things:

This is a Creator who should knock more humility into us than Stephen Jay Gould's ridiculous assessment:

The LORD said unto him, Who hath made man's mouth? or who maketh the dumb, or deaf, or the seeing, or the blind? have not I the LORD? [Exodus 4:11]

You give life to everything, and the multitudes of heaven worship you. [Nehemiah 9:6b NIV]

Thou hast possessed my reins: thou hast covered me in my mother's womb. I will praise thee; for I am fearfully and wonderfully made: marvellous are thy works; and that my soul knoweth right well. [Psalm 139:13–14]

The rich and poor meet together: the LORD is the maker of them all. [Proverbs 22:2]

The heaven is my throne, and the earth is my footstool: . . . but to this man will I look, even to him that is poor and of a contrite spirit, and trembleth at my word. [Isaiah 66:1–2]

This is a Creator whose works are good:

God saw every thing that he had made, and, behold, it was very good. [Genesis 1:31a]

How manifold are thy works! in wisdom hast thou made them all: the earth is full of thy riches. Thou openest thine hand, they are filled with good. [Psalm 104:24, 28b]

For every creature of God is good, and nothing to be refused, if it be received with thanksgiving. [1 Timothy 4:4]

This is a Creator worthy of all my worship and praise:

For great is the LORD, and greatly to be praised: he also is to be feared above all gods. [1 Chronicles 16:25]

Let them praise the name of the LORD, for he commanded, and they were created. He hath also stablished them for ever and ever: he hath made a decree which shall not pass. [Psalm 148:5–6]

But to us there is but one God, the Father, of whom are all things, and we in him; and one Lord Jesus Christ, by whom are all things, and we by him. [1 Corinthians 8:6]

This is a Creator who re-creates in Jesus Christ:

In that day will I make a covenant for them with the beasts of the field, and with the fowls of heaven, and with the creeping things of the ground: and I will break the bow and the sword and the battle out of the earth, and will make them to lie down safely. And I will betroth thee unto me for ever; yea, I will betroth thee unto me in righteousness, and in judgment, and in lovingkindness, and in mercies. [Hosea 2:18–19]

For I reckon that the sufferings of this present time are not worthy to be compared with the glory which shall be revealed in us. For the earnest expectation of the creature waiteth for the manifestation of the sons of God. For the creature was made subject to vanity, not willingly, but by reason of him who hath subjected the same in hope, Because the creature itself also shall be delivered from the bondage of corruption into the glorious liberty of the children of God. [Romans 8:18–21]

God . . . hath in these last days spoken unto us by his Son, whom he hath appointed heir of all things, by whom also he made the worlds; Who being the brightness of his glory, and the express image of his person, and upholding all things by the word of his power, when he had by himself purged our sins, sat down on the right hand of the Majesty on high. [Hebrews 1:1–3]

He that sat upon the throne said, Behold, I make all things new. [Revelation 21:5a]

The re-creation revolution

The revolution that counts grows not from the teaching that a person has evolved. It grows from the re-creation that *revolves* a person's life a 180-degree direction change from that in which he or she has been going. Quite frankly, I fear for the future of the West, a culture whose engine is fueled by the big lie. On the other hand, I am supremely confident in the re-creating power of God the Creator. How ironic, but also how like God, that we must now find our Christian discipleship model in the lives of former Eastern Bloc Christians like those David Marvin met in Romania, those who have lived so long under the thumb of atheism. In the ashes of the most disastrous worldview in history his re-creating power has been fashioning something of quietly spectacular loveliness.

But now we need a similar re-creation revolution in our midst, one that takes us off the sidelines and empowers us with a message of shame that we have been pulled away from God by the evolution revolution. When God first breathed life into humankind he gave us what is called the "cultural mandate." In Genesis 1:28b we have a commission given to us as creatures created in his image in knowledge, righteousness, and true holiness. Our mandate is:

> Be fruitful, and multiply, and replenish the earth, and subdue it: and have dominion over the fish of the sea, and over the fowl of the air, and over every living thing that moveth upon the earth.

Fruitfulness to Adam and Eve meant to have children. Fruitfulness to a church in the late twentieth century means we need to reproduce and multiply spiritually. You who are unbelievers are called by the Creator of heaven and earth to revolve, turning from a worldview of meaninglessness and the big lie, to a worldview of purpose and truth. We are called to do nothing less than to glorify God and to enjoy him forever. We who are already children of God in Christ Jesus are called to go and make disciples. And we also are called to involvement in the declaration of God's glory in the arts, in education, in culture, in business—in every sphere of life.

The Bible's principles apply to the individual, the church, the family, and the school, but too often we have stopped there. God also has principles that apply to the artist, to the writer, to the factory worker, to the senator, to the physician, to the lawyer, to every human being on the planet. The cultural mandate points us at the world in all that we are and says, "Be fruitful. Subdue. Bring every cranny of life under the Word of God as far as you are enabled to do so. Offer all to the glory of God."

Is anyone in control out there?

God, the great Creator of all things, doth uphold, direct, dispose, and govern all creatures, actions, and things, from the greatest even to the least, by his most wise and holy providence, according to his infallible fore-knowledge and the free and immutable counsel of his own will, to the praise of the glory of his wisdom, power, justice, goodness, and mercy. [Westminster Confession of Faith, chapter 5]

7

Plan, Power, and Providence

It is, without doubt, the most popular religious program ever to hit TV. Millions of television sets tune in each week to watch a glamorous high priestess, who always looks somewhat like Vanna White, gracefully push the necessary buttons on a glass altar filled with swirling white objects. All of the people have offered their sacrifices at the local gas station and grocery store. On whom will the gods of fate bestow beneficence? Seven balls—possibly white to symbolize the ethical purity of the religion's rulers, the state lottery commission—dance through a pneumatic tube and display the numbers that will mean a life of total ease and fabulous wealth for some lucky worshiper.

The next day a report appears in the daily newspaper. Some needy soul has been plucked from obscure poverty and is on her way, even as the reporter interviews her, to buy a Maserati. The fate gods have smiled. The fate gods are good. Bow now before the fate gods and buy thirty tickets for this week's $22 million jackpot.

Is playing the lottery worship? Rather, is it idolatry? Yes, I believe it is, and more than a little foolish. I would not like to lay money against such odds. Governments callously play on popular greed. Impoverished people who have trouble putting food on their table voluntarily pay precious dollars with little realistic hope of return. The lottery madness lends a whole new dimension to Jesus' words: "For where your treasure is, there will your heart be also" (Matthew 6:21).

126

There is no Super Lotto god, and I should let everyone in on a secret about these games of "chance": *They are rigged—every one of them.* Winners were chosen untold ages back within the intricate warp and woof of the sovereign plan of God. If the sovereign God who is recognized in the Bible exists, then chance or fate does not exist. The two are mutually exclusive. In *Fiddler on the Roof*, bemused Tevye asks God: "Would it upset some eternal plan if I were a wealthy man?" God's eternal plan for the universe is infinitely larger than whether Tevye becomes financially comfortable, but Tevye's wealth might have ramifications to that plan that he cannot foresee.

> *Remember this, fix it in mind, take it to heart, you rebels. Remember the former things, those of long ago; I am God, and there is no other; I am God, and there is none like me. I make known the end from the beginning, from ancient times, what is still to come. I say: My purpose will stand, and I will do all that I please.* [Isaiah 46:8–10 NIV]

It just could upset some eternal plan if he were a wealthy man. Tevye lacks the wisdom to know.

Sovereignty means God's providential rule over all lives stands within the scope of a divine plan. His divine authority will carry it through. "I trusted in thee, O LORD: I said, Thou art my God. My times are in thy hand" (Psalm 31:14–15a). Scripture teaches that my times are in his hands, and it would be odd if there were any other possibility. The God who weaves amino acids of the genetic code inside the structure of each living cell might be expected to govern how the aggregates of those cells while away their hours.

Fatalism?

The sovereignty of God has never been and never will be a popular subject. Some charge that this doctrine strikes a fatalist's pose: If God commands minutiae, we are simply puppets, dancing out a rehearsed scenario. Others will add that such a view destroys all pretense of human free will. Still others allege that if God exerts such control he must be a monstrous tyrant, allowing the terrors of life to unfold without intervention. Could God be deaf to the cries of people in pain?

Since the beginning of creation, the creature has sought to usurp the place of the Creator. Lucifer, the angel of light, first sought to grasp the divine prerogatives. He and a great multitude of angels with him had to be evicted from heaven. Grasping for God's prerogatives also occasioned the human banishment from Eden; two pretenders to the throne insisted that their own plan was obviously more pleasant and practical than that fixed by their Lord. Yet the plan of God drew one line before them, saying: "Thus far you will go, and no farther. . . . If you eat of that fruit you will die" (see Genesis 2:17).

The skeptic H. G. Wells said that the world is like a great play, produced and directed by God. As the curtain goes up, all is lovely to behold. The characters are fantastically beautiful—a delight to eye and ear. All goes well until the leading man steps on the hem of the leading lady's dress. She trips and falls into a chair, knocking over a lamp that pushes a table into the side wall. This knocks over the back scenery, which brings the entire set crashing down in chaos on the heads of the actors. Meanwhile, God frantically runs to and fro, pulling strings and shouting orders, trying desperately to restore order to the chaos. He is unable to do so. Poor God.

Modern religion prefers such a limited God because this God is not blamable for evil and suffering. "Either God is not good or he is not powerful," runs the popular sentiment. Since most people are unwilling to believe God is not good, they conclude that he is doing the best that he can. He tries and fails. Which horn of the dilemma do you choose?

May I suggest that the God of Scripture hardly fits either description. He is omnipotent and has all power. Therefore his plan will be worked out. He is holy, and therefore his plan is morally right. He is infinite, eternal, and unchangeable in wisdom, power, holiness, justice, goodness, and truth. Therefore his is not the *merely* omnipotent force of fatalism. The biblical picture denies fatalism, because fatalism puts all that happens in the hands of an impersonal force, while Scripture places it in the hands of a Father who is all righteous, wise, and merciful. Fatalism rules out second causes. The stars, fates, gods, or whatever, pull the strings of fate directly. The Bible establishes second causes, declaring that every human being freely does whatever he or she *pleases* at any given moment of time. Unfortunately what pleases the individual outside of Christ is limited to direct disobedience against God. The natural state since the fall has been worthlessness—slavery to sin. "What iniquity have your fathers found in me, that they are gone far from me?" asked Jeremiah. In their freedom these people "have walked after vanity [or worthless idols], and are become vain [worthless]" (Jeremiah 2:5). Romans 1:24 adds that "God also *gave them up* to uncleanness through the lusts of their own hearts." That does not signal the creature's veto power over the plans of the Almighty, but rather a frantic chasing around in circles that accomplishes nothing.

Captain of a ship of fools

How ludicrous and blasphemous to think that the God who by the authority of his word governs creation steps meekly aside as his rebellious creature screams: "I am the master of my fate and the captain of my soul." There is a word for the attempt to master my fate. That word is *futility*. "Has not the LORD Almighty determined that the people's labor is only fuel for the fire, that the nations exhaust themselves for nothing?" asked the prophet Habakkuk (2:13 NIV).

During a flood a reporter was sent out in a boat to find out how the stranded people were faring. Floating down what only days before had been a street, he noticed a woman who was perched on the edge of her roof, staring out into the swirling waters. She said nothing as he climbed up to join her but noticed that she was watching a hat drift with the current.

Or was it? Suddenly the hat turned and started back upstream. The reporter stared in amazement as the hat bobbed back and forth by the house, first with the flow of the water and then against it.

"I just don't understand that at all," he remarked.

"Oh, that's my husband," the woman responded. "He said he was going to mow the lawn come hell or high water."

As futile as mowing grass in a flood is the scramble for life that does not take God into account. "Except the LORD build the house, they labour in vain that build it: except the LORD keep the city, the watchman waketh but in vain" (Psalm 127:1). Most of the world's most graciously appointed mansions hide lives colored by sorrow and meaninglessness. What really is the point of laboring for wealth that requires intricate security systems to protect and may vanish with the next downturn of the stock market? Why go to all the trouble accumulating at all, if there is nothing more lasting than today's work and next weekend's party?

Those wealthy people who have paid large fortunes to have their cadavers cryogenically frozen hope someday to be resurrected to eternal life through the next miracle of technology. Yet immortal existence would become hell itself if life offered no more than sustained breath. It is interesting how many horror novelists write plots fantasizing what it would be like to be cursed with the inability to die. We innately realize that this is a horror, because we were made to glorify and enjoy God—to participate in a sovereign plan that gives eternal worth. The story of the human fall into sin ends on just this sad note. The human residents of Eden are driven into exile into a world of thorns and futile labor. An angel with a flaming sword stands watch over the forbidden entrance to the home from which the man and woman have been evicted (Genesis 3:22–24). But it is not for punishment that this angelic guard watches, but as a mercy. For God declares that the human being must never be allowed to reach for the fruit of the tree of life while in this state of sin. That fruit was made to give eternal life, not ongoing existence entrapped in the futility of sinful flesh.

God's providence is not only logical and true; it is the only view that gives life worth. Psalm 127, which speaks of the futility of building houses and watching cities without God's partnership, contrasts that vain scramble with the blessedness of resting in God's infinitely meaningful purpose: "It is vain for you to rise up early, to sit up late, to eat the bread of sorrows: for so he giveth his beloved sleep" (vs. 2).

Explaining providence

Christian confessions affirm that God's good plan rules his universe through his acts of creation and providence. Creation we have talked about in previous chapters. But just as not all agree on what creation means, there is considerable difference of opinion regarding providence. Its double-minded tentativeness contributes to the church's lack of confidence in an uncertain world. Nothing should give us so hearty a hope on the front lines of a culture war with sensualism, humanism, and materialism as a solid understanding of God's sovereignty over all.

Providence refers to God's omniscient foreknowledge of what will happen; it also depicts God's omnipotent governance of history. One of the most beautiful and pastoral descriptions of God's providence was written into the *Belgic Confession of Faith* by Guido deBres, who later gave his life at the stake, a martyr for the Reformation of the

Netherlands. For deBres the key to God's providence lies in his constancy. He will not walk off and forget his creation, nor his rebellious creatures:

> We believe that the same good God, after He had created all things, did not forsake them or give them up to fortune or chance, but that He rules and governs them according to His holy will, so that nothing happens in this world without His appointment; nevertheless, God neither is the Author of nor can be charged with the sins which are committed. For His power and goodness are so great and incomprehensible that He orders and executes His work in the most excellent and just manner, even then when devils and wicked men act unjustly. And as to what He does surpassing human understanding, we will not curiously inquire into farther than our capacity will admit of; but with the greatest humility and reverence adore the righteous judgments of God, which are hid from us, contenting ourselves that we are pupils of Christ, to learn only those things which He has revealed to us in His word, without transgressing these limits.

Another document of faith, the *Heidelberg Catechism*, stands alongside the *Belgic Confession*. For the question, "What dost thou mean by the providence of God?" the *Catechism* answers:

> The almighty and every where present power of God; whereby, as it were by His hand, He upholds and governs heaven, earth, and all creatures so that herbs and grass, rain and drought, fruitful and barren years, meat and drink, health and sickness, riches and poverty, yea, all things come, not by chance, but by His fatherly hand.

The *Westminster Confession's* statement on divine providence heads this chapter. The *Shorter Catechism* answers "What are God's works of providence?":

> God's works of providence are, his most holy, wise, and powerful preserving and governing all his creatures and all their actions.

In these human explanations lies the exquisite biblical answer to those who would see God sickly or wicked or an impersonal force. Each says that God:

1. *preserves creation.* The sun will not suddenly flame out and send the earth hurtling into a black hole while God has his back turned.
2. *governs all of creation and the natural phenomena.* The stars in our own neighborhood, and those of every other galaxy equally come under God's command, as does the sparrow that falls to the ground (Matthew 10:29).
3. *governs human thoughts and actions.* God so rules in history so that nothing occurs that is not taken into account in God's plan. In fact he foresees and arranges the flow of second causes in history and each individual life according to his infinitely wise will. Yet the evil that occurs among those second causes arises only from the bondage of sin and death upon creation. God uses them for his purposes, but he is not their author.

The logic of a God in control

The preserving governance of God is agreed to by any theist who believes in a Creator as opposed to a mindless, evolutionary, pantheistic force. Belief in the preservation of creation certainly is not much of a stretch for someone who believes in a Being capable of creating the universe in the first place. Could not the designer and manufacturer of a product manage to write and follow the maintenance manual? There are many who disbelieve in a God who is this powerful over creation, but their problem involves disbelieving the more basic assumptions that there exists a Designer and Manufacturer.

Most people with any faith in, and understanding of, the God of the Bible willingly take the second step as well. If God created and maintains, it follows that he established and administers the laws that govern the natural order of that creation.

I should suspect that God, if he desired, could suspend those laws. If it pleased him he could stop or even reverse the motion of the earth relative to the sun (Joshua 10:12–14; Isaiah 38:7–8). And if he could do that he certainly could, without working up a sweat, manipulate the weather to deny rain or send down hail in judgment (Exodus 9:22–26; Joshua 10:11; 1 Kings 17:1; 18:41–45; 2 Chronicles 6:26–27; Revelation 8:7–9). He could manipulate or even create new natural phenomena to turn the day dark (Exodus 10:21–23; Luke 23:44–45) or to cause the light from a distant star to appear on the earth at just the moment and in just the right quadrant of the sky to guide travelers where he wished them to go (Matthew 2:1–2, 9). And if he could do that, I seriously doubt it would be an unreasonable burden for him to calm a storm, walk on water, or control the healing process of the body (for example, Matthew 14:22–27; 15:30–31; Mark 4:35–41). Those who are troubled by such possibilities have a problem somewhat deeper in their concept of God than simply disbelief in what are called "miracles."

It is the governing of thoughts and actions that divides. We should be able to agree that if a God can do such things as already described, he can act with understanding and influence over the affairs of humanity. Certainly he can, for example, exert control over the environmental and genetic and social influences in a life. Surely an omniscient God foresees the individual's future reactions to various situations, particularly if he enjoys total perception of the individual's personality and thought processes. And he would be able to influence, help, guide, or overrule the individual's actions by controlling the flow of experiences and influences that swirl around a life and cause the person to constantly make choices. Certainly in the Christian the indwelling power of the Holy Spirit undeniably influences actions. In such a scenario we might even say that sovereign governance does not truly interfere with the person's "freedom" to choose, so long as the individual is quite free to pick from among available options at each point along the way.

Some Christian traditions zealously guard our freedom as human beings to make choices based on our will. They are afraid that a God who exercises sovereign authority must be a puppet master who sends people to heaven or hell on a whim and is chargeable with all evil that occurs in the world. Others are zealous to protect God's omnipotent control over all people and his mercy in enabling the lost to turn to him in repentance. Our sources for resolving such issues are limited. As deBres wisely wrote,

> And as to what He does surpassing human understanding, we will not curiously inquire into farther than our capacity will admit of; but with the greatest humility and reverence adore the righteous judgments of God, which are hid from us, contenting ourselves that we are pupils of Christ, to learn only those things which He has revealed to us in His word, without transgressing these limits.

We can, however, know *some* things, for the Bible teaches us much about who God is, who we are, and how he acts. We must uphold all that the Bible teaches us. First, free or not, people do make choices freely, based on their will. Yet it is equally clear that God does rule and overrule in the affairs of humanity.

The power and the plan

The Bible does not equivocate about the providential design and authority of the Almighty to control everything from the galaxy to the atom. He governs the angels in heaven, the inhabitants of earth, and the kings and fortunes of nations. He raises them up and casts them down. He brings one to power and removes that power by the stroke of his hand, working through second causes.

The right of lordship

God has the prerogatives to micromanage history, not simply because he has the biggest, most omnipotent club to hold over the heads of people, but because we his creatures belong to him by right. "It is he that hath made us, and not we ourselves; we are his people, and the sheep of his pasture" (Psalm 100:3). "O LORD, I know that the way of man is not in himself: it is not in man that walketh to direct his steps" (Jeremiah 10:23).

There is a current teaching in many churches that declares that one can enjoy the fruits of salvation in the atoning sacrifice of Jesus Christ on the cross without accepting Jesus as personal Lord. That is bunk on three counts. First, Jesus is Lord by right of creatorship and demands submission to his authority whether one accepts or rejects him as Savior. God calls sinful people to acknowledge his lordship but makes it clear the lordship extends to every person—repentant sinner or rebel:

> Look unto me, and be ye saved, all the ends of the earth: for I am God, and there is none else. I have sworn by myself, the word is gone out of my mouth in righteousness, and shall not return, That unto me every knee shall bow, every tongue shall swear. Surely, shall one say, in the LORD I have righteousness and strength: even to him shall men come; and all that are incensed against him shall be ashamed. [Isaiah 45:22–24]

Second, Jesus is Lord by right of his conquest over Satan, the fulfillment of God's sovereign plan. Philippians 2:9–11 (and Romans 14:9–12) says that because Jesus put off his glory as God and humbled himself to death on the cross,

> Wherefore God also hath highly exalted him, and given him a name which is above every name: That at the name of Jesus every knee should bow, of things in heaven, and things in earth, and things under the earth; And that every tongue should confess that Jesus Christ is Lord, to the glory of God the Father.

Third, Jesus possesses lordship most particularly and definitively over the lives of those who have become his personal people through the gift of salvation. The apostle Paul makes this especially plain, as in 1 Corinthians 6:20: "Ye are bought with a price." Paul tells all Christians in Romans 6:20, 22, "When ye were the servants of sin, ye were free from righteousness. But now being made free from sin, and become servants to God, ye have your fruit unto holiness, and the end everlasting life." In Ephesians 2:10 Paul describes the way God has re-created us and redesigned our lives around Jesus Christ so that his lordship might make us a blessing to others: "For we are his workmanship, created in Christ Jesus unto good works, which God hath before ordained that we should walk in them." If we are truly in Christ, Paul adds, his power as Lord works within us (Ephesians 3:20).

Those are the benefits of accepting a plan that includes the lordship of Christ. For those who want the Savior without the Lord, rejecting one means rejecting the other: "Wherefore we receiving a kingdom which cannot be moved, let us have grace, whereby we may serve God acceptably with reverence and godly fear: For our God is a consuming fire" (Hebrews 12:28–29).

The freedom of lordship

God has the prerogatives of authority over every action and thought because that is how he established the universe to function. The difference between us and God is that we are made for his ownership while he has perfect freedom to act in concert with his will. Isaiah 46:10 relates God's ultimate claim that "I will do as I please." He alone makes that statement without fear of contradiction. And the Bible extends that statement over our individual lives and actions.

The LORD killeth, and maketh alive: he bringeth down to the grave, and bringeth up. The LORD maketh poor, and maketh rich: he bringeth low, and lifteth up. He raiseth up the poor out of the dust, and lifteth up the beggar from the dunghill, to set them among princes, and to make them inherit the throne of glory: for the pillars of the earth are the LORD's, and he hath set the world upon them. [1 Samuel 2:6–8]

He shall break in pieces mighty men without number, and set others in their stead. [Job 34:24]

No one from the east or the west or from the desert can exalt a man. But it is God who judges: He brings one down, he exalts another. [Psalm 75:6–7 NIV]

He raiseth up the poor out of the dust, and lifteth the needy out of the dunghill; That he may set him with princes, even with the princes of his people. He maketh the barren woman to keep house, and to be a joyful mother of children. Praise ye the LORD. [Psalm 113:7–9]

A man's heart deviseth his way: but the LORD directeth his steps. [Proverbs 16:9]

There are many devices in a man's heart; nevertheless the counsel of the LORD, that shall stand. [Proverbs 19:21]

This is the purpose that is purposed upon the whole earth: and this is the hand that is stretched out upon all the nations. For the LORD of hosts hath purposed, and who shall disannul it? and his hand is stretched out, and who shall turn it back? [Isaiah 14:26–27]

Freedom under providence

A lack of human freedom may bother others, but I am quite thankful for it, for I am not altogether competent to manage my own affairs. First, God's perfect freedom means I can come to him with my petitions, knowing that he is more than capable of giving whatever I ask, however immense that request may seem to me. Second, in his perfect understanding and care of my life, God knows whether what I ask for is wise or frivolous and even detrimental. So he also is able to say, "No, I have a better plan than you have conceived. I love you too much to give you what you want. But I will provide exactly what you need." Third, sometimes God listens to my petitioning heart and says, "That is something I will give you, but the time is not quite right. Just wait, child; grow up a little more and learn to trust me." And sometimes God listens and says, "Yes. That is something I gladly give. Receive my blessing and follow me on."

Of course this freedom from my own folly means submitting to God's authority when that is precisely the last thing I want. Suppose a doctor breaks the news that I or someone I cherish is facing a painful, debilitating, terminal illness. There is no human hope through medical technology. Now what do I do with God's possible answers to my cry for help? That is when God's freedom will become precious. I can go to him, knowing that he is able to deal with the medical condition immediately and utterly. I can go to him, knowing as well that if he says no to my request for healing it will not be because he is weak or because I lack some magic prayer word formula to make him obey me. It will be because he has a greater plan that I do not see. He has already given me part of the answer to my grief in Romans 8. Paul says that suffering and death continue because of the curse of sin, yet these things can never be out of the Father's control, and they can never separate the sufferer from him. These things will work for good. But if, in my anguish and confusion, I forget or feel unable to accept those realities, and if I become angry with him, God's perfect ability and wisdom will understand what I feel and love and comfort me anyway. And beyond all that I will know that he can give me the grace to bear whatever must be borne.

God's freedom also becomes his great gift when we look at the evil that exists within the world. The Christian is called, as a purchased servant, to stand in the midst of the battle. The purchased servant does not have the options to submit to a world system or to cynically or resignedly stand aside because "That is just the way things are." As God is sovereign, with a plan and power, fatalism can never be the appropriate response. We are empowered by infinite power to do what he has given us to do where he has given us to do it, within the boundaries set by his wisdom, will, and Word. And if we have followed his lead and fall flat on our faces by every human measure of success, we still will have victory in the divine providential perception of things. The battle isn't ours to win but ours to stand.

And if evil vanquishes all apparent hope we should never forget that the providence of God rules beyond our understanding, though Satan throws the forces of hell into the arena. One wicked Egyptian pharaoh thought he was standing firm against the Hebrew God, yet that God said to him: "For this cause have I raised thee up, for to shew in thee my power; and that my name may be declared throughout all the earth. As yet exaltest thou thyself against my people, that thou wilt not let them go?" (Exodus 9:16–17). Proverbs 21:1 tells us that ultimately "the king's heart is in the hand of the LORD, as the rivers of water: he turneth it whithersoever he will."

The power and plan of providence have already won the battle. The kingdom of Jesus is established forever:

> The kings of the earth set themselves, and the rulers take counsel together, against the LORD, and against his anointed, saying, Let us break their bands asunder, and cast away their cords from us.

> He that sitteth in the heavens shall laugh: the LORD shall have them in derision. Then shall he speak unto them in his wrath, and vex them in his sore displeasure. Yet have I set my king upon my holy hill of Zion. [Psalm 2:2–6]

If there is a good God, why . . . ?

Q What was the providence of God toward man in the estate in which he was created?

A. The providence toward man in the estate in which he was created was the placing him in paradise, appointing him to dress it, giving him liberty to eat of the fruit of the earth; putting the creatures under his dominion, and ordaining marriage for his help; affording him communion with himself; instituting the Sabbath; entering into a covenant of life with him, upon condition of personal, perfect and perpetual obedience, of which the tree of life was a pledge; and forbidding them to eat of the tree of the knowledge of good and evil, upon the pain of death.
[Westminster Larger Catechism, question 20]

8

The Sorcerer's Apprentice

"God made man good, and good he remained. We have no sin. Man is incapable of sin. Man cannot depart from holiness."

If Mary Baker Eddy were alive today I doubt she would have written those words. Such a sentiment was popular over 100 years ago in the glow of optimism that humanity was evolving quite nicely. No wonder Mrs. Eddy's Christian Science movement has been on the wane in recent decades, and the old classic liberal Christianity, while still with us in a variety of forms, doesn't make the same old noises as in the late 1800s that "Every day, in every way, I'm getting better and better."

That was before the artillery sounded, and twenty-five allied nations marched off to fight the Central Powers of the Austria-Hungary Empire, the Ottoman Empire, and Bulgaria. Many millions tramped off to the great "war to end all wars," but 10 million never returned; 20 million were wounded at Flanders field, Amiens, and Belleau Wood. When Johnny came marching home, little did he realize that this was only the warm-up for a greater spectacle. This time the arenas were named Dunkirk, Iwo Jima, Normandy, and Hiroshima. Finally the world was "safe for democracy." But we all know that the world has not been safe for anyone. As these words go onto paper, and probably as you read them, children cry from blown-off limbs, civilians crouch in shelters, and young soldiers face one another in any of several "hot spots." This hardly seems the golden age that our liberal great-grandfathers promised, nor the "age of Aquarius" the 1960s radicals saw in the stars.

Those who do not believe in God have mostly turned from optimism to cynicism to nihilism over the last century. The most optimistic form of irreligion with any real influence on the Western scene is an irrational blend of secular humanism and Eastern mysticism that mostly ignores the issue of

> *God blessed them, and God said unto them, Be fruitful, and multiply, and replenish the earth, and subdue it: and have dominion over the fish of the sea, and over the fowl of the air, and over every living thing that moveth upon the earth. . . . And God saw every living thing that he had made, and, behold, it was very good.*
> [Genesis 1:28, 31a]

evil. But cynics of every stripe sneer at Christians with the taunt: "Where is your God in all of this?"

The invisible gardener

At the beginning of this book we set out on a pilgrimage up into the mountains of life for a closer view of God. It has been all too brief a journey, filled with tantalizing glimpses of glory. Human language offers only childish babbling sounds to communicate the Father, Son, and Holy Spirit, one God—"For of him, and through him, and to him, are all things: to whom be glory for ever. Amen" (Romans 11:36).

Now that we stand on a higher plane, however, we have won a new vantage point from which to observe the world. If you can mentally push through the smog, what do you view? Much is beautiful, isn't it? In book one of his meditational studies of Scripture, *Before the Face of God*, R. C. Sproul answers the skeptical philosopher Anthony Flew, who speaks for Western intellectualism. Flew wrote a parable of two explorers who come upon a perfectly cultivated garden in the midst of an impenetrable rain forest. They wait to meet the gardener, but none comes. They string bells around the garden so they can hear if the gardener visits in the darkness, but the bells never sound. One of the explorers concludes that there is no gardener, the other that the gardener is invisible and immaterial.

What practical difference, argues Flew, is there between a God who is infinite, eternal, and invisible and no God at all? The difference, observes Sproul, is the *garden*. As we look down upon creation we see triune fingerprints everywhere. The creative work of the Father, Son, and Holy Spirit interweaves the threads of life as a master composer blends counterpoint harmony, so that the whole is far greater than the sum of its parts. Or, remember that chapter 4 of the *Westminster Confession of Faith* addressed the wonder: "It pleased God the Father, Son, and Holy Ghost, for the manifestation of the glory of his eternal power, wisdom, and goodness, in the beginning to create or make of nothing the world, and all things therein, whether visible or invisible, in the space of six days, and all very good." What is the proof of the Gardener? The bottom line is that there exists a garden. It is there. And it is very good.

Or it *was* very good, Mrs. Eddy notwithstanding.

Covenant of life and death

We Christians become overly sensitive in reacting to the argument that a good God would not allow evil to infect creation. I've heard it called the "fatal flaw" in our faith, and sometimes we sound as if we agree with that assessment and are intent on apologizing for God. Three notions have infected Christians' thinking:

1. Since sin entered the picture, there must have been an inherent weakness in God's plan.

2. The presence of evil obliges God to immediately take away all of its effects if he is all-powerful and all-loving.
3. Ultimate good must aim at the greatest happiness for the greatest number of people.

A flawed design?

Was there a flaw in the design? Consider the lives of the first humans. The *Larger Catechism's* description with which we opened this chapter states that they had:

Nurturing environment

Our first parents were perfectly placed in a garden ideally suited to their needs and purpose (Genesis 1:26–31); theirs was a "paradise."

Significant work

They enjoyed employment for which they were perfectly equipped. They were given what has been called the *cultural mandate*—a mandate that all human culture still shares—to be fruitful through the bearing of and nurturing of children, and to care for the land. Work was no afterthought or punishment. Work fulfilled the joy of accomplishing praise to the Creator. Genesis 1:28 exults in the high calling of humanity.

Sufficient authority

That calling to "dress" the garden includes perfect authority over it (Genesis 1:29–30; 2:19–20). Every seed-bearing plant, every animal, every bird were Adam's for food and enjoyment. When the ancient Jews read that Adam gave names to the animals, they understood something we may not. In ancient culture authority and power in a person were symbolically expressed by the giving of a name. To name something denoted a right of authority over what was named. When God gave new names to certain biblical people he was indicating a new dimension of his involvement in their lives.

Satisfying relationships

Our parents enjoyed perfect fellowship (Genesis 2:18–25). As Adam named the creatures God showed him that these beings would not fulfil his emotional needs. He required continual fellowship with God and with others of his own kind. The fullest expression of interpersonal fellowship was in the mutually completing companionship of man and wife as one flesh.

Refreshing relaxation and praise

Our parents knew seasons of energizing rest and worship (Genesis 2:2–3). Were Adam and Eve ever tired from their labors at the end of the week? Did they need a rhythm of work, rest, and centering on God? The language of Genesis strongly suggests an affirmative answer to both questions.

This is the plan—a life-giving agreement between God and his subjects. What was the weakness of such a *covenant of life*? Its only "weakness" was that God gave to his subjects the choice to love him or to reject him. Adam and Eve were free to trust and love God for who he was, or to selfishly reject him. Those who charge God with allowing evil and suffering to slip from Pandora's box are usually those who demand freedom to live as they please. The Bible identifies that freedom as the key that unlocked and threw open that evil.

Why didn't God intervene?

One of Walt Disney's most noteworthy cartoons is a short segment in his film *Fantasia*. Mickey Mouse is a young, impetuous apprentice to a powerful and wise sorcerer. As the strains of Paul Dukas's delightfully-haunting music carry along the story, the sorcerer leaves his young apprentice in charge of caring for his workshop full of strange potions. He also leaves his book of magic spells within reach. Curious, anxious for a short-cut with his chores, and desiring quick knowledge without waiting for wisdom, Mickey tries out the spells. At first all goes splendidly. The broom comes to life and takes over on its own. The water buckets carry water without the apprentice's muscle-power. Unfortunately the apprentice's commands for stopping do not work nearly as well as those for starting. The animated helpers turn malevolent as action and music whirl out of control.

Just in time the sorcerer walks in, discovers what is going on, and uses his magic to set things to rights. The badly chastened apprentice has learned his lesson, and all live happily ever after.

That is not how it happened in Eden; God does not play the role of rescuing cavalry. Instead, he confronts his miserable little apprentices as they try to squirm out of their mess by casting blame on each other and their serpent co-conspirator (Genesis 3:7–13). Adam finds part of the fault in God for making him a very troublesome wife. All the while the pair is cowering behind leaves to cover their nakedness. The blessings of their covenant of life lie broken at their feet. Instead of sympathy, a stiff lecture, and a pat on the head, God pronounces doom, as he had promised he would if they disobeyed (Genesis 3:14–24). God's judgment included:

Cursed environment

They must leave paradise and face life and death on an unfriendly planet.

Cursed work

Work would be hard and unfulfilling, childbirth's joy mixed with agony. The task of the cultural mandate was not removed, but it would now be won only by sweat and pain.

Cursed authority

Humankind would retain authority, but no longer in smooth partnership. Walls rose to separate people, animals, and plants. The mutually accepted role of headship had been spurned by Adam. The role of mutually blessing partnership, with the husband leading the wife and following God, would now be replaced by a pattern of dissatisfaction with the roles God had given the sexes.

Cursed relationships

This strife between men and women, of course, has an impact on marriage and other interpersonal relationships from Cain and Abel through Democrats and Republicans (though thankfully without too much bloodshed in the latter case). Perhaps most painful is the immense wall between people and their God. From then on, a Mediator and the shedding of blood must stand between human sin and God's holiness. First would come sacrifices of animals, then the system of priests to intercede for the people, then a temple to symbolize both the connection and the great distance between God and humans.

Promised relaxation and praise

Notice that God did not take away the sabbath blessing. As life becomes harder and God more distant, the sabbath takes on new meaning in resting from labor and praising God and hoping for the full renewal under God's promise. That renewal comes in a new covenant to replace the broken covenant of life.

Look what had happened to the holiness of God's fallen image bearer, to the natural righteousness and knowledge of God of unfallen humanity. Remember that God will not—cannot—do what will make him less than infinite, eternal, and unchangeable in wisdom, power, holiness, justice, goodness, and truth. Suddenly the awful situation becomes clear. God would have ceased to be God had he simply waved his sorcerer's wand and cleaned up after his willful creatures. For, in fact, it was the sin of Adam and Eve that they wanted to be apprentices to Godhood. That option was not open to them. And God is no magician. He is God.

But could he not have foreseen what would happen and stopped Eve's grasping hand? God desired something more than coerced, resentful obedience. The prophet Micah expressed what God desired in this way (6:8): "He hath shewed thee, O man, what is good; and what doth the LORD require of thee, but to do justly, and to love mercy, and to walk humbly with thy God?"

As for his foresight, we know from our understanding of his omniscience that he certainly knew and took into account what would happen from the start of creation.

The ultimate good

But were his actions good or right? The question of ultimate good has bothered philosophers for millennia. Our egalitarian culture has made it almost an undeniable axiom of ethics that good is what brings the greatest happiness to the greatest number of people. This is a form of situation ethics, the view that the right response in any situation is the one that shows the most compassion for others. We will look more closely at the fallacy of this ethical standard in part 3.

God's ethical correctness was on trial that day in the garden. Had he acted as the good sorcerer instead of the holy God, humanity would not be better off today. They would have suffered the loss of God's essential being as holy and righteous and just. The garden might have remained theirs, but they would have shared it with the small god of the humanist. That loss of God's godness would have made Satan the victor and Eden a creation without a worthy Creator. It would essentially have differed little from hell. There was another road, full of pain and suffering, but vindicating God's integrity. That was to replace the covenant of life with a *covenant of grace*, when the serpent would strike at the heel of a second Adam, and he would crush the serpent's head (Genesis 3:14–15). Paul explains in Romans 5:12–19:

> Wherefore, as by one man sin entered into the world, and death by sin; and so death passed upon all men, for that all have sinned. . . . Therefore as by the offence of one judgment came upon all men to condemnation; even so by the righteousness of one the free gift came upon all men unto justification of life. For as by one man's disobedience many were made [appointed or declared] sinners, so by the obedience of one shall many be made [appointed or declared] righteous.

The great covenant of grace, and its promise of salvation in Jesus Christ alone, is the highest peak we can reach in our understanding of God, and the subject of part 2. We will not explore that peak just now, but we can stand on its majesty and look down on the world from its point of grandeur.

As we look down at the world we are not so far off as to miss the sight of bloody struggle that is still underway because of sin. We hear the sounds of spiritual warfare. God maintains control of this battle, and the final outcome in Christ no longer remains in doubt. But the battle continues to devastate human society and the natural world. The natural state of humanity was once "to do justly, and to love mercy, and to walk humbly with thy God." With sin in the picture:

> There is none righteous, no, not one: There is none that understandeth, there is none that seeketh after God. They are all gone out of the way, they are together become unprofitable; there is none that doeth good, no, not one. [Romans 3:10–12]

That is a picture of what theologians call *radical depravity*. Unfortunately it is the real state of each unsaved person— what the *Westminster Shorter Catechism* calls a "state of sin and misery." Chapter 6 of the *Westminster Confession* spells it out:

By this sin they [our first parents] fell from their original righteousness and communion with God, and so became dead in sin, and wholly defiled in all the faculties and parts of soul and body.

They being the root of all mankind, the guilt of this sin was imputed, and the same death in sin and corrupted nature conveyed to all their prosperity descending from them by ordinary generation.

From this original corruption, whereby we are utterly indisposed, disabled and made opposite to all good, and wholly inclined to all evil, do proceed all actual transgressions.

At the naked feet of Adam, the covenant breaker, can be laid every act of oppression and suffering yet visited or ready to be visited upon this planet. It was an infinitely vile offense because it impugned the integrity and affronted the majestic prerogatives of an infinitely holy Being. And when we break any command of God are we doing less? As shameful as it makes me feel, I only see two differences between my acts of rebellion and Adam's. First, like Eve, I am not the direct head or administrator of the covenant between God and humanity. Adam was. Second, I know something about evil and its costs. I approach sin with eyes wide open.

In Psalm 51:4 King David asks God for forgiveness after he had committed adultery with another man's wife and then murdered the husband, one of his own trusted lieutenants, in a cover-up. Further, he had betrayed the trust of the nation, yet he says: "Against thee, *thee only*, have I sinned, and done this evil in thy sight." David could not have denied that his evil cost Bathsheba, Uriah, and Israel, but he understood that every crime—regardless of the human cost—ultimately stands committed against God's holiness. God is the ultimate victim, and the penalty for victimizing God is death. Who dares accuse God of being uncaring and unfair when we have seen what sin means in eternal perspective?

The way of the transgressor

Is depravity a reality? In 1648, ironically the year following the completion of the Westminster standards, the world turned a corner in its thinking about good and evil. That year the Treaty of Westphalia ended the Thirty Years War, an unspeakably cruel series of conflicts that devastated Europe as petty regional rulers fought for power and land. These rulers tried to legitimize their greed, however, by trumpeting that they were defending true Christianity against their heretical enemies. In the end there were no real winners, only war weary people who decided to enact a tolerance based upon apathy. They no longer cared who was right and wrong. Surely no faith was worth the price. Religion was to blame. If people minded their own business and quit worrying about right and wrong, everyone would be much happier and peaceful.

This was the hour of decision for the West. The men of faith who wrote the Westminster documents tried to turn their country toward the Bible's view of a desperately bent humanity and an utterly holy and merciful God. Most of the rest of the world turned toward the Enlightenment view that the human mind could reason itself out of depravity.

The Treaty of Westphalia sought to end the slaughter over absolutist beliefs. Our age seeks a new war on the absolutes themselves and those who say that absolutes do exist. Lately the catch-phrase has been "political correctness." As I understand what political correctness means, there is now an intolerance toward those who say that what I want to do might possibly be sinful. There is no truth versus error, no right and wrong, no evil versus good. Actually, the politically correct mentality declares that there is one evil—any narrow prudery that shakes its bony finger in my face and says, "I know you are having fun, so stop it right now!"

Against that attitude a wise man once looked at the facts: Some acts and thoughts are beneficial and helpful; other acts and thoughts are harmful to self and others. Further, some acts and thoughts have been condemned by the Creator of heaven and earth, and anyone who does or thinks them offends God and stands condemned. That wise man wrote: "Good understanding giveth favour: but the way of the transgressors is hard" (Proverbs 13:15). If there is no evil, or if absolutes are identified as the only evil, then there is no transgressor. There is nothing to transgress. Hence, there are no transgressors to have a hard life.

Case in point: The television program *Good Morning America* was filming in Sweden. One particular episode discussed the sexual freedom that exists in Sweden. The film crew interviewed several people who agreed that young people "are going to do it anyway," so rather than force them to have sex in a car parked on lover's lane somewhere, they tell them to "bring the girl home where it's nice and safe; where you can take the proper precautions." Throughout the television program there was never the slightest hint that sexual relations outside marriage are immoral. They lamented the fact that it probably would be years before such "freedom" existed in America, because of the church.

A vice-president of one television network said that what disturbs him is not the immorality that exists in the entertainment media, but the amorality—the total ignoring of any moral standards whatsoever. We have come to joke about the people who appear on talk shows to talk about their involvement in every conceivable sort of immoral activity, without the slightest hint that they are doing anything wrong.

But the evidence suggests that there is a price to pay for amoral attitudes and immoral actions. In South Florida there are now at least twenty-six flagrant sexually-transmittable diseases, not including HIV. In a sermon at Coral Ridge Presbyterian Church I once mentioned that I had observed a young man in the congregation the week before who showed every sign of being in the final stages of the AIDS infection. At that time, just a few years ago, the tragic sight of these men and women who resemble a walking corpse was less common than it has become today. After the service the young man came up to me. He said, "You referred to me in your sermon this morning. I want you to know that last Sunday in the service I found salvation." Praise God. That man today is with his Lord. But salvation and redemption in the blood of Jesus Christ did not take away the consequences of his transgression in the flesh. His way was hard. Murderer Ted Bundy confessed Christ in a moving video with James Dobson just hours before he was strapped into the electric chair. If that confession was genuine, Ted Bundy stands equally forgiven with other redeemed sinners in heaven. But his addiction to pornography led him down a hard road to a hard end. Forgiven by God, he still had to pay the price in his body.

In his mercy God does withhold the physical judgment our sins deserve for a time. I am an example of his forbearance. I was converted when I was almost twenty-four years old. Before that time I lived the life of a promiscuous, unregenerate American heathen. Why did not I become infected with some disease or sink further and further into alcohol abuse or commit a crime deserving a lengthy imprisonment? I would *like* to tell you that there was something in me that made God withhold such judgments. In fact, it had nothing to do with my worthiness and everything to do with grace—God's sheer unmerited forbearance and love. When two people equally abuse themselves or others or God it seems unfair that one dies from his folly at age twenty and the other survives to become an octogenarian. But if God gave us what we deserve he would strike us all down immediately. He is merciful. But don't think you can toy with that mercy. The hard way of the eighty-year-old may be just as arduous a penalty for transgression as that of the man who died in his youth. And both will stand before God condemned for all eternity if they do not have a Savior. That is the way of all transgressors—a hard way indeed.

Groaning, joy, and a Redeemer

Scripture informs us of the consequences of sin and describes its victims. First, creation as a whole was victimized. Second, the breaking of the covenantal relationship so skewed human nature that unsaved people are unable to do anything *except* rebel against God. Third, while not totally gone, the mirror image of God we carry was beaten almost beyond recognition. Fourth, God not only is victimized by every sin; in his love he gave himself to *be* sin, taking on himself the infinite punishment for the infinite crime. God became a victim twice—in the garden and on the cross. That second time was when the mess left by the apprentice sorcerers was set aright and the covenant of grace fulfilled.

The groaning and joy of creation

Proverbs 13:15 not only tells the story of the results of sin today but the result of sin from the beginning. In fact, according to Romans 8:19–23 the way is hard for all creation because of sin. The effects of sin infected the good in which all things originally were created; all things experienced frustration:

> For the earnest expectation of the creature waiteth for the manifestation of the sons of God. For the creature was made subject to vanity, not willingly, but by reason of him who hath subjected the same in hope, Because the creature itself also shall be delivered from the bondage of corruption into the glorious liberty of the children of God. For we know that the whole creation groaneth and travaileth in pain together until now, and not only they, but ourselves also, which have the firstfruits of the Spirit, even we ourselves groan within ourselves, waiting for the adoption, to wit, the redemption of our body.

We did not fall alone. From the beginning the fate of inanimate creation was inextricably bound up with that of its caretakers. And creation's hope is through the redemption that happened on the cross. Someday it will be totally fulfilled when the angel will stand down from his guardhouse at the gate to Eden, and all will be renewed. As John mystically described that moment: "I saw a new heaven and a new earth: for the first heaven and the first earth were passed away" (Revelation 21:1a).

The groaning and joy of the redeemed

John goes on to say that renewed creation will have no "sea" (Revelation 21:1b). In Scripture the sea tends to symbolize that which separates people from people and people from God. Today, like creation, we groan. Some room for argument exists as to whether Paul in Romans 7 is talking about the plight of the unsaved or his continuing frustrations with sin. Whomever he addresses, I also feel frustrated that:

> For that which I do I allow not: for what I would, that do I not; but what I hate, that do I. . . . For I know that in me (that is, in my flesh,) dwelleth no good thing: for to will is present with me; but how to perform that which is good I find not. For the good that I would I do not: but the evil which I would not, that I do. [Romans 7:15–19]

Yet the person in Christ has an answer to this frustration. The depraved Paul shouts: "O wretched man that I am! who shall deliver me from the body of this death?" (Romans 7:24). The redeemed Paul already knows the only answer: "I thank God through Jesus Christ our Lord" (7:25).

The whole message of the Bible is one of *generation*, *degeneration*, and *regeneration*. The human race still bears the image of God, but twisted and perverted. It is like a Cadillac that has rolled off the production line at General Motors, been driven a few miles, and then rolled over a 500-

foot cliff. There is a Cadillac at the bottom, but who will argue that it is the same as it was? The wrecked Cadillac needs to be towed into the garage, have its fenders and doors pounded out, the frame straightened, and the motor repaired. Humanity is a noble wreck, and that alone is the reason for its sin and despair.

The three transforming tasks

For the one who has gone from degeneration to regeneration, however, God's glorious, ever-renewing purpose awaits. Remember what we know of that purpose:

1. Our chief end is to glorify and enjoy God—both now and forever.
2. Our initial instructions, given at the dawn of creation, were to be fruitful, to multiply, to replenish and subdue the earth, and to rule its creatures. All humanity, all cultures, both Christian and non-Christian, own this cultural mandate. Only the Christian, however, can appreciate why we own it.
3. Jesus gave us new marching orders, a Great Commission, at the dawn of new creation. Jesus said:

All power is given unto me in heaven and in earth. Go ye therefore, and teach all nations, baptizing them in the name of the Father, and of the Son, and of the Holy Ghost: Teaching them to observe all things whatsoever I have commanded you: and, lo, I am with you alway, even unto the end of the world. [Matthew 28:18b–20]

How do we participate in those three life-transforming tasks? We must get to know the Father, Son, and Holy Spirit as revealed in Scripture. That can only truly happen as we realize that God's plan for history did include the fall into sin. A kingdom of the redeemed was established from the dawn of time (Matthew 25:34). That kingdom was established in Jesus Christ from the beginning (Ephesians 1:4). Entrance to that kingdom was always, is now, and ever will be based on the sacrifice of Jesus Christ for our sins. That sacrifice was promised at the fall but it had already been planned as the way to God:

> For as much as ye know that ye were not redeemed with corruptible things, as silver and gold, from your vain conversation received by tradition from your fathers; But with the precious blood of Christ, as of a lamb without blemish and without spot: Who verily was foreordained before the foundation of the world, but was manifest in these last times for you, Who by him do believe in God, that raised him up from the dead, and gave him glory; that your faith and hope might be in God. [1 Peter 1:18–21]

It is those who believe Jesus is God, who died and arose in victory from the grave, and who accept his authority as Lord who have escaped the curse of our first parents. It is those depraved but delivered people whose names are "written in the book of life of the Lamb slain from the foundation of the world" (Revelation 13:8).

Redeemed, we still are like that sadly mangled Cadillac that has gone over the cliff. We must be towed to the garage, and the effects of sin must be hammered out and our frame straightened before we can commune with God and glorify and enjoy him. Within the divine body shop we study God's revelation, pray to him, worship him, and follow his commandments, giving thanks for his great glory. And we begin the joy of obeying his Great Commission—making disciples like ourselves, and representing Christ in all the spheres of life, from marriage and parenting to schools and government, music, literature, art, and business.

When our greatest purpose is to offer our minds to knowing God more fully and our lives in testimony to God's lordship over all, then we have truly begun to glorify God and enjoy him forever.

Come with me. Let us walk on together, pilgrims on the adventure of an eternity—transformed and transforming people who know their God.

Part 2

Saved by Grace

Introduction to Part 2

It was first uttered on a night illumined by a singular star.
A whisper issued from a manger.
It had about it the lisp of baby speech, yet the ears of wise
    men tuned to hear across a pain-wracked world.
Behold a promise:
"I am he who makes all things new."

That word was heard again on a night of earnest questions.
Now a Teacher breathed the words.
"Nicodemus, except a man be born again, from above, he
    shall in no wise enter the kingdom of heaven."
"But how . . . "
"I am he who makes all things new."

The words came again, this time with a dolorous tone.
Night fell at noonday without a star.
The Son of God hung outside the wall, as the very triunity
    of God was ripped apart. God become man became sin.
"Tetelestai"—"It is finished."
"Now all things can become new."

The word burst, fire-tongued, on a morning that needed no
    star.
A grave stood gaping.
Death was swallowed; life returned to a shrouded world
    that still listens for a final trumpeted victory salute.
The song will resound:
"I am he who makes all things new."

These words glide gently through the gloom to a twilight
    soul.
Suddenly it's morning.

Though corrupt in flesh, an inner man awakens young and
fresh—everything backwards from what we'd expect.
"Begin again," he calls,
He who makes all things new.

He will make you new. That promise is repeated over and over in Scripture. It is both the promise of God and the experience of history.

The first of our three parts on the transforming doctrines or teachings of Scripture presented a travelogue of the quest toward a higher understanding of ourselves, our world, and the God who is. We ended that part at the brink of a high, dark precipice, where the creature crafted to glorify and enjoy God forever plunged from God's sight. If we can nudge our quest metaphor just a little further, we now stand still and watch God's own quest unfold—the quest of the plan of salvation in Jesus Christ. Only Christ can speak the words with which we begin: "I am he who makes all things new."

For reasons we have already made clear, only one set of truths can unravel the story of this second quest. We can look with confidence only to the Bible, God's sufficient and utterly trustworthy revelation of himself. Again we will also take advantage of one of the most systematic outlines ever written to describe what the Bible teaches. This most helpful outline is called the *Westminster Confession of Faith* and its companion *Larger* and *Shorter* catechisms. Like any creed or confession that Christians have written and used over the years, the Westminster standards are only aids to understanding Scripture. Written in the 1640s, some of the involved sentences in the Westminster standards may seem a lot of trouble to sift through. Yet the trouble is repaid, for the insights of these men of God are the fruits of deep thought, fervent devotion, and earnest prayer. Are there any three things our society needs more than these?

I have three readers in mind in offering this book. First, I warmly desire to share the basics of Christian faith with anyone who does not know the Christ of Scripture and of the cross. For this reason I have made every effort to answer questions that non-Christians have asked me over the years and to be clear about what we believe and why. Second, I hope this book will enable and encourage Christians to share their Lord and Savior with others. Third, in an era in which the Christian church so often speaks with a wavering tongue and a mouth full of mush, may these words call you to deeper, clearer, faith—with love and without compromise. One caveat must be understood: We will approach the transforming themes of salvation. They have utterly changed my life, and they continue to renew my heart at each encounter. Yes, you can reject the Christ of Calvary and go your way, but you will never be the same as if you had never met and heard him speak. You can decide to remain nominally identified with "religion," deciding that wholehearted discipleship and turning from your lifestyle just isn't for you. But you will be forced to make a decision, and it may not be as easy to remain neutral as you think. These themes of Scripture are transformers. One way or the other, you will be changed when you encounter the real Jesus of Nazareth.

Consider, for example, Jacob DeShazer, a crack bomber pilot at the start of World War II. DeShazer joined the elite unit of volunteers who flew with Jimmy Doolittle on that first bombing raid on Tokyo. Only DeShazer was shot down on that historic raid. Captured, and incarcerated in a Japanese prison, he was tortured regularly. As a result DeShazer developed an intense hatred of everything Japanese. He survived with only one thought: to get his hands on the throats of his tormentors.

One day there came into his possession a copy of the New Testament. He opened and heard its mysterious proclamation: "Behold, I make all things new." As he came to understand and believe the gospel, Jacob DeShazer was made new. The hatred drained away, and his heart was filled with love. He returned to Japan as a missionary after the war and wrote his story in a pamphlet distributed around Japan.

Mitsuo Fuchida also was a pilot at the beginning of World War II. In fact, Captain Fuchida led the air assault on Pearl Harbor, giving the final "All squadrons attack!" order that sent 360 planes loaded with death down upon the ships. When the day was over, the planes had killed more American sailors than had died in all of World War I, and Fuchida was the national hero of Japan. Yet in the end came defeat and disillusionment. He dreamed of a world without war, but it seemed impossible. *Peace, brotherhood,* and *love* were meaningless words.

Then one day in a train station Fuchida picked up one of DeShazer's tracts. Here was a man whose heart had been changed by a power Fuchida could not imagine. He read the gospel presentation and right then was transformed by the power of Christ. Fuchida too became a missionary, a preacher to his own people. In the city where both Buddhism and Shintoism had first entered Japan, the commander of the raid on Pearl Harbor spoke to a gathering of 2000 Japanese about the God who can change hearts, no matter who you are.

No matter who

Has your life been transformed? Two kinds of people have trouble accepting the message of transformation. One is the person who feels he or she is "good enough" and in no need of change to be acceptable before God. The other is the person who believes he or she is too bad, that Christ "would never want me." When I think of that second category I recall a man who was about as worthless and derelict a person as I ever heard of. Some decades ago this man was an alcoholic who spent most of his time looking for ways to get a bottle on the streets of Chicago. Whatever little money he could make from the jobs he could keep for a few days was spent on whiskey.

Unfortunately, this man had a wife and daughter. He neglected them, deprived them of food, even beat them during his drunken rampages. One day his precious little blonde daughter became ill. Her mother had hidden a little emergency cash, so there was money to buy medicine. Only the father took this money and went out and bought booze. By the time he sobered up his little girl was dead. He went in to see his daughter laid out dead in her tiny, simple coffin. As he looked down at her through his tears he took off her shoes. He sold them and got drunk again.

This time when he half sobered he figured that he was too bad to exist in the world. Slowly and painfully he began the trek across town to Lake Michigan, intending to throw himself in the lake. On the way he passed a rescue mission where somebody was preaching. A loudspeaker on the street blared out the words of grace about One who could give a new heart, a new character, a new life. As the words flowed over him like fresh water the man was cleansed. His heart was transformed, and he became a new man mightily used by God. Eventually he established one of the most successful missions this country has ever seen. It still is being used to reach and change worthless people.

It is astounding how many are willing to trade the outer trappings of religion for the inner reality that possesses that power. They devour the husk and discard the kernel. As a result, our churches, our lives, our families, and our society are dying from spiritual malnourishment. Many drunks and drug addicts have passed into eternity without a Savior, when the reality was right there, waiting to free and transform them. So have religious people who relied on something other than the reality of a new and changed heart.

Five words that transform lives

In the ministry of Evangelism Explosion we have a simple, effective way to share how Jesus Christ changes lives. As we begin a study of salvation, I want to introduce five words that are easy to remember and stand at the center of all else that will be said here. These words are:

1. Grace
2. Man
3. God
4. Christ
5. Faith

1. Grace

a. Heaven is a free gift
b. It is not earned or deserved

This is the starting point for understanding and sharing the gospel. And what a startling idea it is. Most people think heaven is something you earn by being good. But it is not. Heaven is a gift that is decidedly not earned or deserved: "For by grace are ye saved through faith; and that not of yourselves: it is the gift of God: Not of works, lest any man should boast" (Ephesians 2:8–9).

2. Man

a. Is a sinner
b. Cannot save himself

That seems pretty clear, especially to anyone who has come to understand that each human being stands guilty of breaking God's law. People are sinners and nothing they do could ever make them good enough to earn a place in heaven: "For all have sinned, and come short of the glory of God" (Romans 3:23). The importance of this comes through when you see what Scripture says about God.

3. God

a. God is merciful
b. God is just

God wants us to be with him in heaven. He wants us to have eternal life—to be all that we were created to be eternally. But he also is just. He must judge our sins or he will not be a God worthy of the name. They have to be paid for if his justice is to be satisfied. Though he says, "I have loved thee with an everlasting love" (Jeremiah 31:3b), "Thou art of purer eyes than to behold evil, and canst not look on iniquity" (Habakkuk 1:13a). He does not leave the guilty unpunished (Exodus 34:7).

Here is where Christ comes in.

4. Christ

  a. Who he is: The infinite-eternal God-man
  b. What he did: Died on a cross to purchase a place for us in heaven

God's love is clearly seen in Jesus. He became human, though he is the eternal God. And he died on a cross though he was sinless. He died to pay for our sins. In this he shows God's love and fulfils God's justice. He died so we do not have to. "The Word was made flesh, and dwelt among us" (John 1:14). "He [God] hath made him to be sin for us, who knew no sin; that we might be made the righteousness of God in him" (2 Corinthians 5:21). He became sin so that we might be forgiven.

Now that he has risen from the dead he offers eternal life to anyone who will receive it by faith.

5. Faith

  a. What it is not: intellectual assent or temporal faith
  b. What it is: trusting in Jesus Christ alone

Faith is the key to heaven, but it is not just knowing about Jesus Christ. Nor is it trusting God for such things as safety, health, and wealth, which are temporal and will pass away. Saving faith is trusting in Jesus Christ alone for our salvation. Only as we depend totally on him can we know that God has forgiven us and made us new. "Believe on the Lord Jesus Christ, and thou shalt be saved" (Acts 16:31).

This is the gospel: It is that easy and that impossible. Through such good news Christ transformed Saul of Tarsus on the way to persecute Christians. Through such good news Christ transformed a hateful Jacob DeShazer and a hopeless Mitsuo Fuchida. Through such good news Christ transformed a wretched derelict on his way to die. In our own way each of us who have life in Christ were once wretched derelicts on our way to die.

That is what makes these transforming truths such good news.

How did Jesus Christ make a way to God?

It pleased God, in his eternal purpose, to choose and ordain the Lord Jesus, his only-begotten Son, to be the Mediator between God and man, the Prophet, Priest, and King; the Head and Saviour of his Church, the Heir of all things, and Judge of the world; unto whom he did, from all eternity, give a people to be his seed, and to be by him in time redeemed, called, justified, sanctified, and glorified.
[Westminster Confession of Faith, chapter 8]

9

All Things Are Made New

The Bible addresses itself to all sorts of questions: Questions that are theological and moral. Questions that are ethical and intellectual. Questions that are spiritual and physical. Questions that are existential and eternal.

We sought answers for some of the most basic of these in part 1, finding the only ultimate answer in God. The answers to the "quest questions"—Who am I? What is my purpose in living? Why is the world as it is? Is anyone in control of life?—transform our lives as they unveil the Creator in whom we live and move and have our being. Knowing God lifts human beings from futility to significance.

Yet some of the answers point us to the bad news of humanity's lost condition. It is not enough to know the answers if we cannot use them to transform our ethical, intellectual, spiritual, physical, existential, and eternal selves. The bottom line is this: *Men and women must be made new.* The old analogy of the caterpillar becoming the butterfly has been overused. So have Jesus' words: "Except a man be *born again*, he cannot see the kingdom of God" (John 3:3b). Yet these two pictures vividly tell the story of the gospel, and the reason why that story is so unpopular in our time.

Caterpillars do not live very exciting lives. They never travel far, they must expend much effort to journey what little distance they do move, and when they reach their destination what do they see? More dirt. One day two caterpillars were making their way across a particularly muddy

170

terrain when a butterfly fluttered by. One of the caterpillars stopped to watch as the butterfly dipped and flitted, carried here and there in the wind currents. He turned to his companion in the mud. "You'd never get me up in one of those things!"

What is in a name?

Lots of people feel the same way about being reborn in Christ. Back in the 1970s Watergate scandal conspirator

> *Therefore if any man be in Christ, he is a new creature: old things are passed away; behold, all things are become new. And all things are of God, who hath reconciled us to himself by Jesus Christ.* [2 Corinthians 5:17–18a]

Chuck Colson described his own spiritual journey to Christ in the book entitled *Born Again*. Suddenly everyone in the media and politics was talking about "born-again Christians." A man sitting next to me on a plane at that time asked if these "born-again people" were starting some kind of new religious sect.

"No," I said, "they've been around quite a while. In fact, the only kind of Christian that exists is a born-again Christian, whether he be Presbyterian, Methodist, Roman Catholic, Greek Orthodox, Lutheran, or whatever. Unless a Christian has been born again, that person is not a Christian in anything other than a merely nominal sense of the word."

It is a small wonder those looking at the church from the outside become confused. What a plethora of types of "Christians" and sorts of allegedly Christian behaviors abound! Protestants kill Catholics in Northern Ireland and vice versa. Modernists, Barthians, and inerrantists fight over the sense in which the Bible is God's Word. Colleges that have traditions steeped in faith teach evolution and sponsor homosexual student associations.

At the turn of the century a group of American businessmen and theologians published a series of twelve books called *The Fundamentals* to explain that not all Christians deserve the term. Out of those popular books was born a new category of Christian—*Fundamentalist*. If Muslim fundamentalists blow up airliners and assassinate, what might Christian "fundies," as they are sometimes called, be up to? Some were dissatisfied with the fundamentalist label and founded a new movement to set out the essential differences between true Christianity and the modernist. This movement chose an old Reformation word, *evangelical*, to describe a faith that was Bible-centered, Christ-focused, and evangelism-minded. But before long some began to co-opt the evangelical banner for a wide variety of very bad theological positions. Now we euphemistically call the evangelical churches that have slipped toward heresy "broadly evangelical." They are evangelicals, sort of.

Similar confusion attached to those who have focused on sanctification and the work of the Holy Spirit, while retaining allegiance to the fundamental teachings of Scripture. The names *Pentecostal* or *Holiness* have described such churches, though a variety of teachings, some of them patently unbiblical, have occasionally skewed that focus. *Charismatic renewal* movements have sought to return mainline churches to a purer Christianity from within, but such reformations face the danger of going off in unscriptural tangents. Pentecostal and charismatic fellowships range from the most vibrant centers for worship, discipleship, and witness to anemic, emotion-driven encounter groups with some connection to the "charismatic" gifts of speaking in tongues, prophecy, and healing.

Many other labels have invaded the church of Jesus Christ and hit the secular newsstands. Some labels identify cults whose doctrines have only the most superficial connection to Christianity. Labels grow from legitimate differences of opinion among brothers and sisters who share allegiance to Christ as Savior and Lord and Scripture as the unerring revelation of God to us. Too frequently, however, the labels mask attempts to replace historic faith with something more "relevant" and friendly to the anti-Christian world. My companion on the jetliner had every right to be confused.

Oh, to sweep away the labels. Let the humanists, modernists, and any other "ists" find their own religious names; calling oneself a rocket scientist won't get anyone a step closer to the stars and calling oneself "Christian" or "born again" won't get one a whit closer to God.

A Christian is a life transformed—remade into something new—by God in Jesus Christ.

The life cycle of rebirth

The life cycle stages of a butterfly are egg, larva, pupa, adult. Each signals a basic change in lifestyle and being. But only the metamorphosis from caterpiller to butterfly deserves to be called a rebirth. Likewise, there are passages in the life cycle of a human being, each traumatic and being altering in its own right—womb to infancy; toddlerhood to childhood; adolescence to young adulthood; middle to old ages. Only one metamorphosis is rebirth, however, when a person passes from the living death of the state of sin to the state of eternally living life in a new covenant of grace between human being and God.

The new covenant of grace actually is an ancient agreement. When all things were new, God established another agreement, which sometimes is called a "covenant of life," with Adam, the first human being. Adam was on the spot in this covenant; he was responsible to obey its one command. This was a covenant of life in which Adam and his descendants could live forever, enjoying God and glorifying him, if Adam did not cross the line into disobedient rebellion. When he did cross that line the covenant of life was shattered, but God was ready with another covenant that provided a way back from sin and death (Genesis 3:16–17). This way back was a plan for new birth, newness that could only come through payment of the eternal penalty for sin.

This new covenant could have only a new kind of Mediator, One who was both God and man. From the very moment when he was born of a virgin, until he was laid in a new tomb, Jesus constantly made things new. He took what was old, dying, and dead, and changed them. Now ruling in heaven he continues to make things new, and will until that climactic day when he says, "I make all things new" (Revelation 21:5b). Then he will create a new heavens and a new earth (Revelation 21:1).

Imagine following Jesus around on a day of his earthly ministry, especially during those last months when his work was building to a climax. Had we been there, following a mile or so behind the rabbi from Nazareth, we might have encountered a man and two women who are talking and gesturing excitedly with their friends.

"Sir, I seek the teacher," we interrupt.

"Ah, you want to see Jesus," the man replies with a nod.

"Yes, you must meet him. I have come to love him more than life itself, and he has given me life of more than one kind. My name is Lazarus. A week ago at about this time, I died."

"You mean you became sick enough to die."

"I mean just that I *died*! My body was empty, and it was wrapped with spices and laid in a cave until my flesh would rot away. Then Jesus came by. I was made alive."

Considering this strange story, we proceed down the road until we come to the tax booth of Zacchaeus. We have heard about this agent of Rome who is particularly hated because of the unfair fees he charges. But now the fee is quite reasonable, lower than that of any other tax collector.

"Oh, pay what you can afford," he says with a laugh. "I *was* a cheat and a thief, if the truth be known. But then

Jesus passed by. When everyone else hated me, he singled me out from the crowd to love, and now my life is new."

We meet a lame man who runs and jumps. We encounter one who had been a stinking leper, but who now hurries from person to person to show that his skin is fresh and pure, like that of a baby. A once-blind beggar embraces us with the exciting news that Jesus of Nazareth has come by and heard his cry for mercy. He marvels for the first time at the colors of the surrounding hills and sky.

Children and adults, young and old. The Master has left a wake of change. All things and all people are changed, one way or the other, when they encounter Jesus. Some are hardened to hate him; others are forever softened by renewed body, mind, and spirit.

To understand the dynamics of rebirth we must understand two people. First we must meet Jesus, the One in whom a person can become reborn. Second, we must get to know the changed person who has met Jesus along the way.

One who changes things

When an informed Old Testament believer took a dove or a lamb to the temple at Jerusalem the worshiper understood that this sacrificed animal's death would not take away sin. In those times when Scripture was taught, prophets and priests clearly explained that sacrifices were a shadow—a token of love and obedience by the worshiper, and a token of the true removal of sins that would occur when *Messiah* came.

Messiah. The very word told something about this future person, for the word means "the anointed one." The messiah would be miraculously empowered by God, anointed and ordained for the great task. There was much Old Testament people did not know about this coming Savior, but those who studied the prophets could have explained that the anointed one would be a Prophet, a Priest, and a King:

A Prophet

A prophet is one who speaks for God among the people. Old Testament prophets were directly inspired by God and spoke out from a direct communication. Much of the writing of the Old Testament, such books as Isaiah, Jeremiah, Hosea, Amos, and Malachi, record these inspired prophetic communications. Prophets were middle-men, mediating God's Word to his people. The Anointed One would be the once-and-forever Prophet:

> The LORD thy God will raise up unto thee a Prophet from the midst of thee, of thy brethren, like unto me; unto him ye shall hearken. . . . I will raise them up a Prophet from among their brethren, like unto thee, and will put my words in his mouth; and he shall speak unto them all that I shall command him." [Deuteronomy 18:15, 18–19; see Matthew 21:11; Luke 24:19; John 4:19; Acts 3:22; Acts 7:37]

> The spirit of the Lord GOD is upon me; because the LORD hath anointed me to preach good tidings unto the meek; he hath sent me to bind up the broken-hearted, to proclaim liberty to the captives, and the opening of the prison to them that are bound. [Isaiah 61:1; see Matthew 11:5; Mark 1:14; Luke 4:14–21; Luke 8:1]

The *Westminster Shorter Catechism* describes Christ's prophetic work this way: "Christ executeth the office of a prophet in revealing to us, by his word and Spirit, the will of God for our salvation."

A Priest

Protestants tend not to talk of priests. We do not have such mediators—but that is not true at all. We have a priest. The point where we differ is that we believe no *other* priest is needed. For our Priest also is the King. Genesis 14 introduces a king who was a priest, a mysterious character named Melchizedek. Abraham encountered him at Salem, the mountaintop Canaanite village where, centuries later, the city of Jerusalem would stand. We know only two things about Melchizedek. First, he ruled the peoples who had settled this land. Second, he represented the people in worship before God.

A priest became a vitally important person centuries later when the nation of Israel received God's laws. The primary function of priests was to slaughter the animals brought by the people as sacrifices for sin. Priests burned those sacrifices on the altar as offerings to God. They also prayed for the people and participated in celebrations of worship. Once each year, on the Day of Atonement, the high priest entered the Holy of Holies, the room set apart to symbolize God's holiness, containing the ark of the covenant that symbolized his presence. For one moment each year this mediator offered full intercession for the people, asking that God's wrath for their disobedience might be turned away. But the nation awaited the coming of an ultimate priest who would be the final mediator of the law and the one who would offer the final cleansing sacrifice for sin:

> The LORD hath sworn, and will not repent, Thou art a priest for ever, after the order of Melchizedek. [Psalm 110:4; see Hebrews 5:5–10; 6:19–20; 7:15–25]

> Therefore will I divide him a portion with the great, and he shall divide the spoil with the strong; because he hath poured out his soul unto death: and he was numbered with the transgressors; and he bare the sin of many, and made intercession for the transgressors. [Isaiah 53:12; see Hebrews 7:26–28; 9:11–14, 24]

> Behold the man whose name is The BRANCH; and he shall grow up out of his place, and he shall build the temple of the LORD: Even he shall build the temple of the LORD; and he shall bear the glory, and shall sit and rule upon his throne; and he shall be a priest upon his throne: and the counsel of peace shall be between them both. [Zechariah 6:12b–13; see Hebrews 9:24; 1 John 2:1]

The *Westminster Shorter Catechism* describes Christ's priestly work in the offering up of himself as a sacrifice to satisfy divine justice, his reconciling people to God, and his continual intercession before God for us.

A King

Even without the example of Melchizedek, Old Testament people knew that the Messiah would end the need for a king or any other ruler. His heritage would be of the royal family of David, and his dynasty would never end. Some things only a few Old Testament prophets understood. Surely Isaiah had the clearest picture of it. The new kingdom would be no earthly empire, but rather a spiritual realm. It, therefore, could cross national and ethnic boundaries. It was a rule of the heart. Also, the reign of the King himself, and not just a king's family, would be eternal.

Did Jesus fulfil all of this prophecy? After all, the line of kings was established through the father, and we say that Jesus was the Son of God, not of Joseph. The early readers of Matthew's and Luke's genealogies were not bothered by this in the least. There was no distinction between sons by blood and sons by adoption in that culture. The declaration of sonship was the deciding factor, not genetic relatedness. Joseph readily adopted Jesus into the Davidic family. This custom prepared the people, not only for Jesus' unique sonship, but for ours in him—adoption as the children of a heavenly Father. The following are just a few of the prophecies that the Anointed One would be the final Mediator of the kingdom and family of God:

> Yet have I set my king upon my holy hill of Zion. [Psalm 2:6]

> The days come, saith the LORD, that I will raise unto David a righteous Branch, and a King shall reign and prosper, and shall execute judgment and justice in the earth. In his days Judah shall be saved, and Israel shall dwell safely: and this

is his name whereby he shall be called, THE LORD OUR RIGHTEOUSNESS. [Jeremiah 23:5; see John 1:49; 18:33–37]

David my servant shall be king over them; and they all shall have one shepherd: they shall also walk in my judgments, and observe my statutes, and do them. And they shall dwell in the land that I have given unto Jacob my servant, wherein your fathers have dwelt; and they shall dwell therein, even they, and their children, and their children's children for ever: and my servant David shall be their prince for ever. [Ezekiel 37:24; see Matthew 2:5–6; Luke 1:32–33]

The *Shorter Catechism* says that "Christ executeth the office of a king, in subduing us to himself, in ruling and defending us, and in restraining and conquering all his and our enemies."

The Head and Savior of his church

Other religions have had messiahs of a sort. Confucius was a great teacher, Mohammed a self-styled prophet who became much like a king to the nomadic peoples of his time. But as a Prophet, a Priest, and a King, Jesus uniquely came to save a people for God. His was a "search and rescue mission." Moreover, he did not found an empire but an international refuge, gathering from among every people those he had rescued. This is something the likes of which the world has never seen except in the church, a society of worshipers without ethnic, nationalistic, class, cultural, or racial barriers, whose charter was signed in blood and whose bylaws were founded on love for others before self. The church hasn't always lived like that, but the church truly headed by Jesus Christ is supposed to be that kind of nation.

This unique relationship often allowed those early prophets to see their coming anointed one as mediator of a new kind of nation:

Also the sons of the stranger, that join themselves to the LORD, to serve him, and to love the name of the LORD, to be his servants, every one that keepeth the sabbath from polluting it, and taketh hold of my covenant; Even them will I bring to my holy mountain, and make them joyful in my house of prayer: their burnt offerings and their sacrifices shall be acceptable upon mine altar; for mine house shall be called an house of prayer for all people. [Isaiah 56:6–7; see Romans 10:12–13]

And it shall come to pass, that whosoever shall call on the name of the LORD shall be delivered: for in mount Zion and in Jerusalem shall be deliverance, as the LORD hath said, and in the remnant whom the LORD shall call. [Joel 2:32; see John 4:21–24]

For he hath looked down from the height of his sanctuary; from heaven did the LORD behold the earth . . . to declare the name of the LORD in Zion, and his praise in Jerusalem; When the people are gathered together, and the kingdoms, to serve the LORD. [Psalm 102:19, 21–22; see Acts 15:12–18]

In chapter 25 of the *Westminster Confession*, the headship of Christ over the church is described: "The visible Church, which is also catholic or universal under the gospel (not confined to one nation as before under the law) consists of all those, throughout the world, that profess the true religion. . . . Unto this catholic visible Church Christ hath given the ministry, oracles, and ordinances of God, for the gathering and perfecting of the saints, in this life, to the end of the world; and doth by his own presence and Spirit, according to his promise, make them effectual thereunto."

Heir to and Judge of the world

The irony of describing Christ as Heir is that he is the Creator, and all things have been his from the beginning. Still, in the plan of grace Christ gave up what was his by right and assumed the subordinate role of servant. Even those looking forward to the coming of their Anointed One, however, knew that the role of servant would fall away in the day of accounting, revealing a Messiah who was also Judge.

Christ, then, is the Mediator of justice. He truly defines what justice is, and the day of his coming is a day of uncovering truth and dispensing judgment:

> He shall not judge after the sight of his eyes, neither reprove after the hearing of his ears: But with righteousness shall he judge the poor, and reprove with equity for the meek of the earth: and he shall smite the earth with the rod of his mouth, and with the breath of his lips shall he slay the wicked. And righteousness shall be the girdle of his loins, and faithfulness the girdle of his reins. [Isaiah 11:3b–5]

> Behold, the LORD hath proclaimed unto the end of the world, Say ye to the daughter of Zion, Behold, thy salvation cometh; behold his reward is with him, and his work before him. [Isaiah 62:11; see Luke 2:11; John 4:42; 1 John 4:14]

Chapter 33 of the *Confession* points to the final day of justice, administered by Jesus, the anointed Judge: "God hath appointed a day wherein he will judge the world in righteousness by Jesus Christ, to whom all power and judgment is given by the Father."

These and many other prophecies tell the ways that Jesus Christ mediates the covenant of grace and the plan of God. The most important of these to remember are the first three. Jesus Christ is Mediator of the covenant of grace as a Prophet, as a Priest, and as a King. All other ways can be thought of as fitting under one of those headings, but all are important to our understanding of the Messiah and the changes he brings.

The question for all time

If that is the shape of the Christ who makes people new, what is the shape of a new person? We can see the difference when the pupa cocoon of a caterpillar discloses its changed inhabitant. Reborn people are not quite so obvious. What is new about the newborn child of God? A man named Nicodemus was a teacher of the law, yet he did not understand the answer to that question. As told in John 3, he sought Jesus out at night, whether secretly out of fear to be associated with this new teacher or because he wanted uninterrupted time in which to be taught. But Jesus immediately understood Nicodemus's lack of awareness and answered the question that Nicodemus and every other person in history had feared to ask:

"No one can see the kingdom of God unless he is born again."

Jesus laid it on the line. He was saying something much like this:

"Nicodemus, here is the teaching you are missing, and it is not optional. If you are not made new, you are outside the kingdom of God; you are blind to spiritual reality; you cannot understand spiritual truths, and you shall never enter the kingdom of God."

What imperious words, yet they stand eternally true. Unfortunately, the ways people try to become new show no more understanding than did Nicodemus.

"What do you mean, Lord? Do I have to go back into the womb again?"

"No, Nicodemus. You must be born from above. Only the Holy Spirit makes you new."

Had we been standing there, listening in, we might have jumped in at this point.

"What do you mean, Lord? Will not my good works suffice?"

"If you had any piety (and you have none) it would not make you new. Only perfect righteousness is good enough. Come to me and believe."

"What do you mean, Lord? Surely my baptism and church membership punch my ticket?"

"I alone am the way, the truth, and the life. No other ticket exists. Come to me and believe."

"What do you mean, Lord? Surely if I follow the 'golden rule' and live by the Ten Commandments you won't turn me away?"

"If you come before me on that basis you will not see God. Only trusting in me makes all things new."

"You must be born again." What a sweeping condemnation of all that we are, all that we have, and all that we have done. We need an entirely new life, a new heart, a new soul. True religion begins on the inside. But again the Nicodemus in us asks: "How does one know?" In response, Jesus took Nicodemus back to one of the first stories he had probably learned as a child (Numbers 21). During their years of wandering in the wilderness the children of Israel had rebelled against God (as usual), and in judgment he had sent venomous snakes through the camp. Only Moses had the antidote: God instructed Moses to make an image of a snake wrapped around a staff. Those who looked on that cross-like form did not die from the venom. Now Jesus reminds Nicodemus of how those snake-bitten Israelites had passed from death to rebirth:

> As Moses lifted up the serpent in the wilderness, even so must the Son of man be lifted up: that whosoever believeth in him should not perish, but have eternal life. . . . And this is the condemnation, that light is come into the world, and men loved darkness rather than light, because their deeds were evil. For every one that doeth evil hateth the light, neither cometh to the light, lest his deeds should be reproved. But he that doeth truth cometh to the light, that his deeds may be made manifest, that they are wrought in God. [John 3:14–15, 19–21]

We are so familiar with John 3:16 that we may overlook its main point. God so loved that he gave his only Son in Jesus that whosoever looks on the cross in the same way those sinful, dying Israelites looked on that other cross will live. That is the way to become new. The Israelites were in the darkness of rebellion. They were dying from God's judgment for that rebellion. They had to:

1. *Realize* their true condition. Realization meant confession that the serpents were sent from God, who had afflicted them for good cause.

2. *Believe* the promise.
3. *Obey*. Literally lift venom-clouded eyes from the darkness to the light of that gleaming cross.

Paul says that the secret to becoming a new creation is to be "in Christ. . . . old things are passed away; behold, all things are become new" (2 Corinthians 5:17). Paul tells us the same thing Jesus told Nicodemus. To be reborn three crucial things are necessary.

1. The sinner must *realize* that he is a sinner, dead to God and bound for damnation through the venomous serpent's bite of rebellion against the God of the universe.
2. The sinner must *believe* the gospel: that God sent his one and only Son, who became sin and paid the penalty, crucifying the serpent of sin in his own body on the cross; that Jesus arose victorious over death and the grave on the third day.
3. *Obey*. The sinner must look on that cross as his own, accepting Jesus as Savior and Lord, stepping from darkness into the light so that everyone can see what has happened in the sinner's life.

Are you a creature made new? If so, has your life stepped into the light so that the world can see that most dazzling of miracles—not the caterpillar turned gossamer butterfly but the rebel turned reconciled child of God?

How can someone come to Christ?

All those whom God hath predestined unto life, and those only, he is pleased, in his appointed and accepted time, effectually to call, by his Word and Spirit, out of that state of sin and death, in which they are by nature, to grace and salvation by Jesus Christ; enlightening their minds, spiritually and savingly, to understand the things of God; taking away their heart of stone, and giving unto them a heart of flesh; renewing their wills, and by his almighty power determining them to that which is good, and effectually drawing them to Jesus Christ; yet so as they come most freely, being made willing by his grace. [Westminster Confession of Faith, chapter 10]

10

The Hound of Heaven

Francis Thompson's vivid metaphorical poem, "The Hound of Heaven," portrays a great chase. A fugitive seeks to escape a relentless hunter. The pursuer is always coming, never hurrying yet never breaking off nor slowing. He does not see but he knows, for he hears the footsteps and the voice—the voice reminding him that flight is futile.

> I fled Him down the nights and down the days;
>   I fled Him, down the arches of the years;
> I fled Him, down the labyrinthine ways
>   Of my own mind; and in the midst of tears
> I hid from Him, and under running laughter,
>   Up vistaed hopes, I sped;
>   And shot, precipitated,
> Adown Titanic glooms of chasmed fears,
>   From those strong Feet that followed, followed after.
>   But with unhurrying chase,
>   And unperturbèd pace,
> Deliberate speed, majestic instancy,
>   They beat—and a Voice beat
>   More instant than the Feet—
> "All things betray thee, who betrayest Me."

Here and there he runs, always coming eventually to a dead end. Finally cornered, the vanquished waits, seeing at last the approaching conqueror:

> Naked I wait Thy love's uplifted stroke!
> My harness piece by piece Thou hast hewn from me,

And smitten me to my knee;
I am defenceless utterly.
I slept, methinks, and woke. . . .
I stand amid the dust o' the mounded years—
My mangled youth lies dead beneath the heap.
My days have crackled and gone up in smoke,
Have puffed and burst as sun-starts on a stream.

> *Lo, every one that thirsteth, come ye to the waters, and he that hath no money; come ye, buy, and eat; yea, come, buy wine and milk without money and without price. . . . Incline your ear, and come unto me: hear, and your soul shall live.*
> [Isaiah 55:1, 3a]

Part 1 proclaimed that God is sovereign Ruler of the universe. He does not work helter-skelter, nor does he ad-lib as he goes along day by day. Rather, he laid the architectural plans for all his work before he created the world. He sovereignly controls and ordains that which shall come to pass, managing the greatest star and the least atom.

Yet this governance leaves a certain natural liberty to people. Adam and Eve were created and given a covenant of life by God. They stood with a choice before them: They could submit to God and his wonderful plan for their lives, glorifying God, administering his creation, and enjoying his fellowship forever. Or they could cross the line into disobedience by breaking the one negative command God had given, expressing rebellion that desired to usurp God's prerogatives and authority. The choice was ultimately between life and death. The freedom of all the human race rested on the shoulders of its first member.

"I fled him"

The choice, of course, was made, plunging humanity with all creation into a chaotic bondage and condemnation. Knowing all things, the Creator had already planned for the consequences of this rebellion. The covenant of life lay in pieces, but he raised a greater covenant in its place, a promise of grace that rested in a new Adam, one provided personally by God. By this grace a call goes out to all God's enemies. A life of blind hopelessness—a starvation of the soul—afflicts those who have not trusted in Christ for redemption. A life of futility and an eternity of hell await.

Yet the voice of God calls: "Come to the waters, all who are thirsty. You who have no money, come and eat! All of you, Hear me and live." Some seem to hear only a faint echo off distant mountains; some hear the footsteps distinctly but successfully evade the persistence of the call, until its sound finally fades to silence. And for some, the hound of heaven persists, on and on and on and on—never hurried but never stopping, until the restless soul is invaded by love.

"All things betrayest thee"

We should not say more than does the Bible about God's call to the soul, but we also must say as much, so we can better understand salvation in Jesus Christ. Scripture tells us of two calls:

The external call

There is an external call to every human being on planet earth. God's plaintive invitation reaches out in love to all humanity. It is that free invitation of the gospel that we share universally (see, for example, Matthew 28:19–20 and John 3:16). Accompanying this invitation is the command to repent and turn from sin to Christ or face destruction (for example, 2 Chronicles 30:8; Jeremiah 4:4; Nahum 1:2–3; Romans 2:5–8).

The internal call

There is an internal call that the heart hears and answers. God's call through the Holy Spirit enlivens the dead hearts of those he has chosen from all eternity to save. Scripture refers to these as the *elect*. Those from every tongue, kindred, nation, and tribe who hear this call answer, because they know God sent his Son to die and to procure eternal life for them.

> *Moreover whom he did predestinate, them he also called: and whom he called, them he also justified: and whom he justified, them he also glorified.* [Romans 8:30]

This question of how God calls is answered through the doctrine of predestination, a subject that divides Christians, who interpret the passages on predestination with some variation. If you trust in Christ as the Son of God, born of the virgin, crucified on the cross in your place, resurrected and seated at the right hand of God the Father, your Savior and Lord, then I will not withhold fellowship from you as a brother or sister in Christ because we disagree about what the Bible teaches regarding election and predestination. I hope you feel the same toward me. At the same time, I am writing about tenets that transform faith and churches as we better understand and apply them. I place God's predestinating love and his "hound of heaven" call among the transforming articles of faith.

The Bible speaks of a call that is effectual and a call that does not lead to new birth. When I say in the name of Jesus Christ, "Ho, every one that thirsteth, come ye to the waters, and he that hath no money; come ye, buy, and eat; yea, come, buy wine and milk without money and without price. . . . Incline your ear, and come unto me: hear, and your soul shall live," I address non-Christians who do not feel the slightest spiritual thirst. Their soul-throats are parched and dry, but they do not see their need. Their emotions are hardened and their ears blinded because that is the natural state of each fallen man and woman. Therefore, something more than an external invitation must happen. There must be an inward work of the Spirit of God, effectually drawing the individual and opening his or her eyes to see the real situation. Only then is the person able to be willing to choose Christ freely.

That the *outward* call of the gospel is of limited effect may be seen in Matthew 22:14: "For many are called, but few are chosen." That "few" still contains a multitude no one can number. That the *inward* call of the Spirit is effective can be seen in John 6:37: "All that the Father giveth me shall come to me; and him that cometh to me I will in no wise cast out" and Romans 8:30: "Moreover whom he did predestinate, them he also called: and whom he called, them he also justified; and whom he justified: them he also glorified."

Those God called came, even though they did not deserve to hear that call because of any good in themselves. Those God did not call did not come, but they did not deserve to hear it either:

Reprobate silver shall men call them, because the LORD hath rejected them. [Jeremiah 6:30]

What then? Israel hath not obtained that which he seeketh for; but the election hath obtained it, and the rest were blinded (According as it is written, God hath given them the spirit of slumber, eyes that they should not see, and ears that they should not hear:) unto this day. [Romans 11:7–8]

For this cause God shall send them strong delusion, that they should believe a lie: That they all might be damned who believed not the truth, but had pleasure in unrighteousness. [2 Thessalonians 2:11–12]

"Thy love's uplifted stroke"

But what of the inward call, the one God works in the heart through the Holy Spirit? The *Westminster Confession of Faith* says at least six things about it:

First, grace irresistibly draws a person in God's time, not ours. A delightful Southern preacher named Kennedy Smartt has dedicated his life to evangelism and has introduced perhaps thousands to the Savior, but he has felt a particular burden for one of his friends. Unless that prayer has been answered before you read this, Kennedy still prays each day for his lost friend, anticipating God's saving work in this man's life.

This prayer for his friend has only been part of his daily routine for a little over sixty years.

Acts 2:39 suggests that we should look for God to work in us and our children and even those who are far off, perhaps both in geographical distance and in their distance from God. It is a bittersweet moment when a sinner who comes to the Lord wishes to share that moment with a believing mother who has gone to the Lord. The mother never saw her prayers answered. Yet they were answered.

Second, grace irresistibly draws as the Holy Spirit applies the content of God's Word. "So then faith cometh by hearing, and hearing by the word of God" (Romans 10:17). I remain skeptical of great, emotional conversion experiences that arise from a vision or emotional event, having little or no discernible connection with the reading or teaching of the content of Scripture. Experiences that are real come because the Holy Spirit uses what the individual knows of Scripture (2 Thessalonians 2:13). But I fear that many come not to Christ but to psychological catharsis.

Third, grace irresistibly draws the person away from a life and worldview. Early in Billy Graham's crusade ministry he achieved a great deal of publicity when the mobster Mickey Cohen came forward and confessed Christ. But Graham quickly saw that Cohen was making no noticeable move to distance himself from his criminal empire. Billy made an appointment to see Cohen and confronted him with Scripture's demand for holiness. The mobster was surprised. If Christians could continue in their life's occupations, why should he have to change his? He, like the rich young ruler confronted by Jesus, turned away. This does not mean the newly saved person has left behind all sin, but it does mean the time to begin turning has arrived. The old ways should become uncomfortably foreign and undesirable, for "it is God which worketh in you both to will and to do of his good pleasure" (Philippians 2:13).

Fourth, grace irresistibly draws the mind to desire to know and love God. The enlightened mind of which the *Confession* speaks has no room for a vacuum. As the new believer turns from the old ways and ideas, his heart hungers to replace those things with truth and wholeness, "that by his power he may fulfil every good purpose of yours and every act prompted by your faith" (2 Thessalonians 1:11b NIV). The most beautiful sign that a miracle has occurred is not that a person stops swearing or using drugs or gossiping or flying into a rage at the least provocation. The beautiful thing is when swearing *is replaced* by words of kindness, when using drugs or sex to escape is replaced by an energetic aliveness to God and healthy relationships with others, when rage and bitterness are replaced by patience and emotional maturity. Such healing takes time, and often help from counselors and loved ones. That it can happen is a miracle.

Fifth, grace irresistibly renews the heart. "Create in me a clean heart, O God; and renew a right spirit within me," pleaded a repentant David in Psalm 51:10. Paul saw such a change in the Thessalonian believers: "Knowing, brethren beloved, your election of God. For our gospel came not unto you in word only, but also in power, and in the Holy Ghost, and in much assurance" (1 Thessalonians 1:4–5a). This heart renewal is the preeminent miracle of salvation, for it begins the restoration of what was lost in the fall. The writers of the *Confession* saw this as (1) taking away the heart of stone and replacing it with a heart of flesh, (2) renewing the will so that it desires to *serve* God and not to *be* God, and (3) focusing the mind on a new set of ideals—those that are "good." This is where irresistible grace tears out my old principle for living and installs a new principle. At this point Jesus becomes not just Savior, but also Lord.

Sixth, grace irresistibly draws the saved sinner ever closer to fellowship with Jesus Christ. In 2 Corinthians 5:11–21 Paul describes this drawing to Jesus Christ as reconciliation. Paul speaks of Christ's love constraining him, compelling him into the world as a witness, for Paul's wants have died in the One who died for him. Once he had a fleshly view of Christ and the world, but now "If any man be in Christ, he is a new creature: old things are passed away; behold all things are become new. And all things are of God, who hath reconciled us to himself by Jesus Christ, and hath given to us the ministry of reconciliation" (vv. 17–18). God has reconciled Paul irresistibly and irrevocably to himself. That could happen because Paul is identified in Christ crucified. That fellowship in the cross now impels Paul back out into the world as Christ's ambassador, imploring others: "Be ye reconciled to God" (v. 20).

"I am defenseless utterly"

What an incredible story this is: Jesus Christ, the Hound of heaven, tracked my fleeing soul down the immense halls of the years. The Holy Spirit called me irresistibly into the banqueting hall of the Father to partake of an eternal repast set with my name on it before the world began. And he has set me apart to be his ambassador to call the world to share in this meal of life in Christ. He has given me a share in searching out those others he intends to call to his great feast. There are two immense implications to the Bible's teachings about predestination and election. First,

I am utterly ennobled and empowered by what has been done on my behalf. Second, I am utterly cast down and my egocentric spirit broken by how little all of this has had to do with me. The Christian who truly considers his or her salvation must be nearly pulled apart by the conflicting themes of glory and worthlessness.

> For whom he did foreknow [set his love upon], he also did predestinate to be conformed to the image of his Son, that he might be the firstborn among many brethren. Moreover whom he did predestinate, them he also called: and whom he called, them he also justified: and whom he justified, them he also glorified. [Romans 8:29–30]

> I will say to them which were not my people, Thou art my people; and they shall say, Thou art my God. [Hosea 2:23b; see Romans 9:25]

Paul presents a progression of events that have taken place in the name of each elect person. God *foreknew* them. There are two meanings this Greek word translated "foreknew" could take, but it can have only one meaning in Romans 8:29. The meaning this word does *not* have is that God knew what was going to happen ahead of time, saw who was going to choose him, and elected them. "Foreknew" here means that God set his intimate affection on the people he predestined, called, justified, and glorified.

One reason I believe this is verse 28. Paul says that all things work together for good—but *only for those who love God*. That makes sense, but Paul isn't finished yet. He says these people who love God are those who have been called according to his purpose. So which comes first, our love or God's call? It would seem most definite that those who love are those who were called. Now add in verse 29, as Paul explains further what he means in verse 28. Who loves? Those who are called. Who are called? Those on whom God has set his affection. Does it really make sense that we love *because* we were called, and we were called *because* God saw that we would love?

Another reason is that through all of Romans 7 and 8 Paul is speaking of the powerlessness of the individual over the law of sin and death. The human being is part of a frustrated creation. Suffering and degradation is the lot of all things, until God sets them to rights. Paul has particularly said in 8:5–8 that the mind of the sinful human being is set on death. The natural human being is hostile to God. The human mind "is not subject to the law of God, neither indeed can be. So then they that are in the flesh cannot please God." So where does this love arise in the human mind?

Third, Paul seems to anticipate our natural inclination not to want to accept this, for the primary purpose of Romans 9 addresses this very matter. The bottom line answer is 9:16: "So then it is not of him that willeth, nor of him that runneth, but of God that sheweth mercy." As the old hymn put it:

> I sought the Lord, and afterward I knew
> He moved my soul to seek Him, seeking me;
> It was not I that found, O Saviour true,
> No, I was found of Thee.

Fourth, only a view that God chose those he had set his intimate love upon conforms with the rest of Scripture, for the Bible says that faith is a gift (John 6:44, 65; 1 Corinthians 4:7; Ephesians 2:8; Philippians 1:29). The idea of this divine affection is found in Genesis 18:19 and Jeremiah 1:5. In fact, it pervades Scripture.

Many—a majority of Christians, in fact—do not agree with this position. There are two schools of thought, or two theological systems within Protestantism, which attempt to answer the question of how we come to choose God. The system I believe Scripture teaches is called *Calvinism*, after the Reformer John Calvin. Actually he took the concepts (aside from his reading of Scripture) in earlier Christian thinkers, especially Augustine. Most Christians take the other view and are called *Arminians*, after the theologian

Jacob Arminius, though he was also teaching the thoughts of others before him.

Why do some accept and some reject the gospel? The Calvinist believes the difference is to be found in *God*, while the Arminian finds the difference in the *person*. The Arminian believes that God certainly provides the way of salvation, but each person makes the final determination about the fate of his or her eternal soul. The old saying is: "God votes for us; Satan votes against us, and we cast the deciding vote." This is an interesting little ditty, which would sum up salvation handily if it were true. The Bible-believing Arminian believes that salvation is a gift—unearned, unmerited, undeserved. But at the same time he or she wants to keep the human free will autonomous to choose God. And if both of those statements are true, and the Bible's picture of the human fall also is true, then not a single person will choose God, and no one will be saved. "What good is a 'whosoever will' in a world where everybody won't?" asked Charles Spurgeon.

Spurgeon is making the crucial point: The Calvinist is not saying that a person is not free to do what he or she *wants* to do. Every person is always free to do what he or she *wants*. The person is not free—does not have the power because of sin—to do what he or she *ought*. The person who ought to love God with heart, strength, mind, and soul is shackled by sin, and only the power of God, working through the Spirit in the inner call to the heart, can hold down the rebellious prisoner and break off the shackles that have made all the *wants* the *ought nots*.

"Those strong Feet that followed"

This may seem a minor shading in the big picture of salvation, hardly one of the life-transforming concepts promised. Also, many Arminian brothers and sisters have been far more humble servants of the Father and more aggressive ambassadors for Christ in the last century than many Calvinists. The story is told that nineteenth-century revivalist Charles Finney was accosted by a woman who said, "Mr. Finney, I don't like the way you do evangelism." Finney is said to have replied dryly, "Madam, I like the way I do evangelism a lot better than the way you don't do it." Finney's theology was superficial and appealed to an emotional response in a manner that has haunted American evangelism ever since. Yet many, many people truly came to know the Lord through his ministry because he gave himself wholeheartedly to the gospel.

However, the effectual call of God cuts to the heart of where we stand in relation to ourselves, to God, and to the unbelieving world. There are reasons God has gone to great lengths through Scripture to make it known to us.

In relation to ourselves

It seems a great danger that Christians who believe in the autonomy of the human will should set themselves on a higher moral plane from the non-Christian. The Arminian system says God offers eternal life to everyone, and some will believe and accept it and others will not, only because of some personal openness or closed-heartedness to Christ within the heart. "I have heard the gospel; I believe and accept Christ, therefore, I have eternal life," thinks the Christian. "You, neighbor, have heard the same gospel but because of your sinful and hard heart you've turned your back and rejected it. Therefore, you are not saved and I am. You are a different sort than I. In fact, I am more spiritual, more religious, more softhearted, less in love with sin and the world. Therefore I will cling tenaciously to something in which I can boast. If I cannot boast of my good works, I shall at least boast of my faith."

A person who has come to believe in the effectual call of God on his or her life cannot make such a statement and be consistent. In the presence of the non-Christian the believer must think: "I am truly no different than you. I could never have freed myself from my sins, just as you cannot. Eternal life is only mine because of the strong Feet that followed as I fled the Hound of heaven. I was in bondage, and only the Son of God could set me free (John 8:36). I was an unclean thing and nothing clean could have come from me (Job 14:4)." Lazarus, whom Jesus raised from the dead, would have sounded pretty silly if he had shouted into the tomb where a deceased friend lay buried and said, "I was obviously a lot more alive than you are, Eleazer. I hopped out of my grave, and I wasn't even stinking."

A spiritual Lazarus who understands fully that the only thing that makes his call from the tomb different was the authority of the caller, is transformed in self-awareness. A proper understanding of the call of God to our carcasses should squelch our feelings of self-sufficiency and lay us in awed, worshipful silence. "But he that glorieth, let him glory in the Lord" (2 Corinthians 10:17). This is a transforming glorying in Christ.

In relation to God

If God offers to all the choice and it is up to each person to accept, the implication is that God is desperately scrambling around the earth to coax all he can into the kingdom. Again, there is a grave danger, perhaps unconsciously, for the Arminian to hear God saying, "It is my will that everybody in the world should be saved. But, alas, in the end I must say, 'Not my will but yours be done. For you, O man, are the sovereign lord of this world, not I.'"

Through just such a view of dependent God and autonomous humanity did the pollution of humanism pollute the church, poisoning its pure waters. This is especially true in the popular theology that came into the church through such evangelists as Finney, who held just such a view of God and people. Finney wrote a book, which is still widely read and lauded today, called *Revivals of Religion*. It was the premise of this book that the salvation of people is not a supernatural work. Finney believed that revivals and other works of evangelism simply use the means God has afforded us to convince others. Finney was trained as an attorney, and he saw the witness for Christ as arguing the case for Christ as in a courtroom. How persuasively the Christian presents the evidence and uses good psychology to work on the emotions and break down that autonomous will are the fundamental factors of revival. Finney specifically rejected the effectual call of Christ and made the Holy Spirit subservient to the wit and cunning of the witness who pleads Christ's case.

Yet Ephesians 1:9 and other Scriptures state unequivocally that God is absolutely sovereign over all things, including the spirit, will, and heart. Romans 9:19 says that none resist his will. Do we have a God who is desperately trying to save everybody and is, for the most part, failing? Or do we have a God who has set his purpose and fixed his intimate delight upon a remnant for himself, those chosen from the foundation of the earth and unfailingly brought in his time into glory? God could be equally just and merciful if he never saved anyone. Spurgeon said that the amazing thing is not that everybody is not saved, but that anybody is saved. God issues the call to all humanity, commanding, "I have no pleasure in the death of the wicked; but that the wicked turn from his way and live: turn ye, turn ye from your evil ways; for why will ye die, O house of Israel?" (Ezekiel 33:11b). God loves to see rebellious sinners turn to him, and he orders them to do so. But the depth of sin is such that they will not, so he has ordained to call some. Those he called he also justified. Those he justified he also glorified. This is a transforming view of God.

In relation to the unbelieving world

A transforming understanding of God's effectual call frees the Christian to be a witness before the watching world. The Christian becomes God's ambassador, not God's lawyer, offering a testimony of reconciliation while leaving the rest to God. Witnessing becomes an outgrowth of love for God and for others, without the burden of having to argue someone into the kingdom, for the witness knows it is impossible to argue someone into the kingdom. There are rational proofs that God is real and has revealed himself in acts of creation and providence. There are proofs that the Bible is God's Word. The Christian should know and share these proofs for the sheer joy of giving an answer for the hope he or she has. The news is too good to keep silent, and God has invited us to be used as his witnesses throughout the world. The Christian is called to knock down the walls that separate the rationalistic human mind from God. There is a plan of salvation we are responsible to present as well as we can at each opportunity. God will judge harshly the believer who shrugs off the call to witness with the words: "Well, I'm a Calvinist, and I know the Lord will do fine in calling his people without my help."

There is a danger in Calvinism of entertaining such thoughts, but one who does so has missed the point. God chooses to work out his plan through his people when they make themselves available, and if the person with "correct theology" stands disobedient God will raise up a Finney, whose heart of hearts is stayed on the joy of seeing a lost sinner come to know abundant life.

Oh, may he use each of us, his children, to be the strong feet that follow the Hound of heaven. Once he followed us; now we follow at his side. The transformed and still transforming is used as a tool of the Transformer.

What do we do about guilt?

Those whom God effectually calleth he also freely justifieth; not by infusing righteousness into them, but by pardoning their sins, and by accounting and accepting their persons as righteous: not for any thing wrought in them, or done by them, but for Christ's sake alone; not by imputing faith itself, the act of believing, or any other evangelical obedience to them, as their righteousness; but by imputing the obedience and satisfaction of Christ unto them, they receiving and resting on him and his righteousness by faith; which faith they have not of themselves, it is the gift of God.
[Westminster Confession of Faith, chapter 11]

11

Forgiveness to the Uttermost

About a dozen of London's most illustrious citizens of a century ago received a singular correspondence. The envelope was quite plain, with no return address. Yet the story is told that each blanched after they tore the envelope open and read its unsigned communication. The succinct note read:

All is discovered! Flee at once!

Not one who received it thought the letter had been delivered by mistake. Each knew precisely what it meant. Some quickly found reasons to go on seaside vacations far from London as quickly as possible. And yet they were safe, for the letters were sent as a practical joke by Sir Arthur Conan Doyle, author of the Sherlock Holmes stories. Dr. Karl Menninger of the Menninger Psychiatric Clinic relates a similar story:

On a sunny September day in 1972 a plainly-dressed, stern-faced man stood on a street corner in the busy "Loop" area of downtown Chicago. The man stood there stiffly, watching each pedestrian who passed. Then he fixed a cold eye on one, raised his hand, and pointed as the passer-by came abreast.

"Guilty!" said the man with the piercing glare.

This eerie pantomime occurred several times, Dr. Menninger said, and the effect on the people was electric. The people stopped, transfixed, to stare at their accuser for a moment. They would look down, look back at him, glance at one another, and then hurry on down the street. One of the men so arraigned was overheard saying in bewilderment: "How did he know?"

The just shall live by faith

We come to holy ground, the great central theme of redemption. The doctrine of justification broke the shackles

> *Who shall lay any thing to the charge of God's elect? It is God that justifieth. Who is he that condemneth? It is Christ that died, yea rather, that is risen again, who is even at the right hand of God, who also maketh intercession for us.* [Romans 8:33–34]

from the soul of Martin Luther and became the very heartbeat of the Protestant Reformation. "This is the foremost pillar of religion," said John Calvin. "It is the pivotal point around which all else turns," said Geerhardus Vos. "This is the article of the creed by which the church either stands or falls," added Herman Bavinck.

The doctrine of justification *is* the gospel of our Lord Jesus Christ. Without at least a rudimentary understanding of the basic principle involved in this doctrine, no person will see heaven. That principle, as stated in the *Westminster Shorter Catechism* (question 33) is this:

Justification is an act of God's free grace wherein he pardoneth all our sins, and accepteth us as righteous in his sight, only for the righteousness of Christ imputed to us, and received by faith alone.

This is the total answer for the great dilemma facing humankind: If God is truly holy and people are truly unholy, is there any hope for anyone to become acceptable to God?

The answer: "Yes, there is, but we have nothing to do with it."

Justification is an act of God—It could not be an act of a human being, because we humans are by nature offenders of God's justice. Justice had to be satisfied *for* the offended one. Only a holy and omnipotent God on his judgment throne can declare someone just.

Justification is an act of free grace—Only one reason exists as to why any person should be declared just by God—Jesus of Nazareth. No one else has earned justification; to the contrary all have earned condemnation.

Justification is an act of pardoning all sin—Pardon does not mean the criminal is declared "not guilty." It means he or she is declared "not *liable*" for the penalty fitting the crime. As we saw in looking at the character of God, each sin is an eternal affront to God's character and deserves eternal separation from God. If one crime against God remains unpardoned there is no hope of reconciliation.

Justification is an act of acceptance as righteous—But to stand before an almighty, holy God requires more than a blank slate. The person must become holy, must have a positive righteousness. Justification means that the positive righteousness of Jesus Christ's life and sacrificial death is applied to the sinner's account. The person is allowed to stand under a righteousness that is not his or her own by personal character or action. Both the absence of guilt and positive righteousness enable God's acceptance to be just.

Justification is an act received by faith—God takes something else from the sinner in lieu of positive holiness and righteousness. Belief and trust in Christ, acceptance of Christ's sacrifice, and submission to Christ as Lord are accepted as righteous perfection in God's declaration that an individual is justified.

All of this may seem to be old news, but think what it first meant to Abraham (Genesis 15:6), the writer of Psalm 130:3–4, Isaiah (53:11), Paul (Romans 3:21–5:21), and saints such as Martin Luther. Habakkuk 2:4 makes the classic statement that the righteous will live, not by righteousness, but by faith.

Guilty!

From Job (9:2b) came the cry, "How should man be just with God?" The twentieth century has been an incongruous age. Dr. Menninger's book, *Whatever Became of Sin?* was dedicated to confronting the denial by modern people that any such thing as sin objectively exists. We are in a phase of denial. Yet Chicago street corners are not the only places where guilt clings to people as if attracted by a charge of static electricity. A psychologist in California reported, after a study of people in mental institutions, that those who are not there because of organic brain dysfunction are there because of guilt. Almost without exception, guilt is responsible.

Or should we say a *"sense* of guilt" or "guilt *feelings*"? There has been great debate, especially in the twenty years since Menninger's book was published, about whether to blame objective guilt or subjective feelings of shame for the obvious psychological and spiritual trauma professionals see. Actually this debate has been in progress since Sigmund Freud theorized that neurosis is the product of harsh socialization during childhood. Freud did not believe in an absolute standard of conduct, and so he did not believe in such a thing as actual, existential guilt. But some other psychologists who do approach their study from a more or less biblical reference have come to conclude that Menninger's appeal to call sin what it is may tell only part of the story, and Freud's view that we become sick because we make mountains out of moral molehills is not altogether wrong. Christians need to be quite careful. To be transformed and transforming people of God we must deal realistically and biblically with sin and guilt—and the prescription for both. From Scripture and experience with my own guilt and the guilt of others, I would suggest that we can helpfully think of four kinds of guilt and shame:

1. *A dirtiness clings to fallen human beings.* This is actual, not just psychological, guilt. It also may be called *ultimate guilt.* In the tribunal of God, each person stands ultimately guilty. Romans 1:18–32 speaks of the picture of God that lies in the heart of every human being, a sense of what holiness and righteousness is. While humans subvert true righteousness, trading it for their own pitiful version, each has a natural awareness that they are basically unsound in life. This feeling of not being what one was made to be is the dis-ease that accompanies the disease of depravity. Even Christians whose sins have been taken away, can feel this dis-ease. We see the effects of this guilt in the remaining sin in our lives.

2. *Unhealthy guilt attaches to legalistically measuring self-worth by doing or being the "right thing" in our own strength.* This actually is not far from the kind of neurotic guilt that Freud saw rising from Victorian society, in which works righteousness was understood better than grace. S. Bruce Narramore believes many conservative Christians who know their salvation is a gift of God still feel a badness and the desire to be punished. Narramore believes the Christian who feels such guilt would likely describe it as: "A painful, negative emotion that somehow comes from God and is a consequence of our misbehavior, in order to motivate us to improved behavior and to serve as a form of mental punishment for our sins." Such false guilt often is a painful legacy of being brought up in an abusive home or a family where legalism, rather than true faith, measures acceptability. For others it is a desire for self-atonement and an insidious sin in itself.

3. *Akin to these false guilt feelings is a childish pouting that lashes out irrationally at God or others through self-punishment.* Rather than maturely admitting that an action was sinful, stupid, rebellious against God, and has led to some unfortunate penalty, some people retreat into self-destructive attitudes or

actions. This kind of childish guilt feeling can be complex; the person feeling it doesn't understand the rebelliousness of these inner motivations. Professional help may be needed. A philandering husband turns to alcohol after his wife leaves. An abused child grows up to become a drug user or anorexic. A businessman whose investment collapses commits suicide. The guilt may be true or false. Its origin may not be anyone's "fault" in particular. The person becomes his or her own judge, jury, and executioner in anger at "the unfairness of it all."

4. *There is, finally, objective guilt.* A person disobeyed and feels guilty and ashamed as a result. It is good, healthy guilt, that makes the non-Christian understand the need for a Savior and can help a Christian grow. However, it certainly is frustrating and painful. Paul describes its pangs in Romans 7:7–24: "O wretched man that I am!" he shouts out in verse 24. "Who shall deliver me from the body of this death?"

The answer to all four kinds of guilt feelings is found in Romans 7:25–8:2:

I thank God through Jesus Christ our Lord. . . . There is therefore now no condemnation to them which are in Christ Jesus, who walk not after the flesh, but after the Spirit. For the law of the Spirit of life in Christ Jesus hath made me free from the law of sin and death.

The fruit of guilt

The sense of guilt that pervades our society has debilitating and disastrous effects upon human life. I am not thinking of the actual results of sin and death upon our bodies and planet, but the fruits of sin and guilt upon our spirit—the oppression that true and false guilt allow.

Anxiety

Guilt creates a sense of anxious fear. A sense of angst hangs over the heads of many people, who look over their shoulder when they walk down the street. They feel some goddess of vengeance following. Psychologists and philosophers have struggled to define this plague of the soul. Paul Tillich, for example, called it "the existential awareness of nonbeing." One of the clearest clinical descriptions, however, is one of the oldest. The Book of Job offers great insights into anxiety, depression, and guilt:

The wicked man travaileth with pain all his days, and the number of years is hidden to the oppressor. A dreadful sound is in his ears: in prosperity the destroyer shall come upon him. He believeth not that he shall return out of darkness, and he is waited for of the sword. He wandereth abroad for bread, saying, Where is it? he knoweth that the day of darkness is ready at his hand. Trouble and anguish shall make him afraid; they shall prevail against him, as a king ready to the battle. For he stretcheth out his hand against God, and strengtheneth himself against the Almighty. He runneth upon him, even on his neck, upon the thick bosses of his bucklers [shield]. [Job 15:20–26]

Yea, the light of the wicked shall be put out, and the spark of his fire shall not shine. The light shall be dark in his tabernacle, and his candle shall be put out with him. The steps of his strength shall be straitened, and his own counsel shall cast him down. For he is cast into a net by his own feet, and he walketh upon a snare. The gin shall take him by the heel, and the robber shall prevail against him. The snare is laid for him in the ground, and a trap for him in the way. Terrors shall make him afraid on every side, and shall drive him to his feet. His strength shall be hungerbitten, and destruction shall be ready at his side. It shall devour the strength of his skin: even the firstborn of death shall devour his strength. His confidence shall be rooted out of his tabernacle, and it shall bring him to the king of terrors. [Job 18:5–14]

Depression

Guilt also produces depression. In the comic strip "Li'l Abner," there was a pathetic little character who was always accompanied by his own private cloud. His little cloud was always raining. That is a good picture of the kind of depression and unhappiness that guilt creates in the human life. Guilt always rains on our parade.

The late O. Hobart Mowrer was a Christian who pioneered in trying to relate biblical faith and the findings of psychology. He saw both depression and schizophrenia as profoundly guilt related. More recently researchers have looked for some organic factors as well; still Mowrer's description has a ring of truth when he calls it "self-inflicted suffering," which would make it part of the third sort of guilt listed above (pp. 206–207). Mowrer said that depression "looks very much like an act of 'serving time,' comparable to what happens in such other places of penance as penitentiaries where legally convicted offenders are sent."

King Saul is the classic picture of a depressive personality whose psychological illnesses were assuredly the result of personal sin. David, Saul's successor, gives a good description of the feelings inside in Psalm 38:

> There is no soundness in my flesh because of thine anger; neither is there any rest in my bones because of my sin. For mine iniquities are gone over mine head: as an heavy burden they are too heavy for me. My wounds stink and are corrupt because of my foolishness. I am troubled; I am bowed down greatly; I go mourning all the day long. . . . My heart panteth, my strength faileth me: as for the light of mine eyes, it also is gone from me. My lovers and my friends stand aloof from my sore; and my kinsmen stand afar off. [Psalm 38:3–6, 10–11]

An inflamed conscience

Dr. John R. W. Stott, who was chaplain to the Queen of England, tells of a speaker who was addressing a Pakistani university audience concerning the Christian faith. At the conclusion of his speech, 121 people asked for private counseling. As Muslims, they did not want to know about the Trinity or the incarnation or resurrection; they wanted to know how their soiled consciences could be cleansed. Dr. Stott took a survey of his own congregation, asking: "At the time of your conversion, what was your understanding of sin and guilt?" Their responses included:

"I felt unclean."

"I felt dirty."

"I felt worthless."

"I felt like a dirty rat."

"I felt I was no good."

"I felt vile."

Is it any wonder that when guilt makes life seem unbearable, people slip into neuroses, manic-depressive states, or even schizophrenia?

A bad image

Guilt also creates a bad self-image, something we hear a great deal about today. There are many books on the subject that will never solve the problem because they don't deal with the problem of sin. As long as a person is mired down in sin and its consequent guilt, he or she is always going to feel like a louse. In fact, *louse* is a fairly accurate description. When Christians refuse to deal with sin, Satan uses that rebellion to steal away what is theirs in Christ. He simply reminds them of their louseness.

As the philosophizing opossum Pogo of the old comic strip said, "We has met the enemy and he is us!" We are our own worst enemy. Satan and his demonic horde are only created beings who cannot be omnipresent and cannot wreak all the emotional havoc with which they are blamed. Our own conscience arraigns us before the bar of justice, crying, "You are guilty! Guilty! Guilty!"

Imagine the state of the disciple Peter's emotional health after he had bragged that he would follow his Lord to the death and then denied and disowned him in cowardice.

What kind of self-image problems did the risen Lord see when he looked into Peter's heart by the seashore and gently asked, "Simon, do you really love me?" (see John 21:15). Jesus, the great Physician, knew that our understanding of who we are is tied up in our affections and allegiances. Jesus alone could understand the confusion Peter felt about himself as his allegiance to Jesus had been stripped away by guilt. It would not have helped Peter for Jesus to have said: "Peter, just don't worry about it anymore." The guilt was too awesome, too real. Instead, Peter was forced to again swear his love and belongingness, once for each time of denial. This was not what Dietrich Bonhoeffer called "cheap grace" but grace that Peter now could know had been purchased with blood.

Physical illness

Time and again physicians have reported that many, even most, of their patients have more emotional than physical distress. That is not to say the illnesses are imaginary. But it is to say there is a *psychosomatic* element to them. *Psychosomatic* means that something amiss in the mind has caused something to go amiss in the body. Emotional stress has been studied in its relationship to everything from ulcers and colitis to arthritis and cancer. Even when there are underlying organic causes, the feelings of guilt may trigger them to erupt. David, perhaps after his egregious sin with Bathsheba, said, "When I kept silence, my bones waxed old through my roaring all the day long . . . my moisture is turned into the drought of summer" (Psalm 32:3–4).

Guilt and guiltiness

What truly is guilt? If you had been asked that question at the beginning of this chapter would you have responded as Narramore says the average Christian would—that guilt is "a painful, negative emotion that somehow comes from God and is a consequence of our misbehavior, in order to motivate us to improved behavior and to serve as a form of mental punishment for our sins"? Perhaps you still think of guilt as a bad feeling you get when you have done something you know to be wrong. If so, you are wrong. That is not guilt, nor what the Bible means by guilt, nor even what the law means by guilt. There is a great difference between *guilt* and *guilt feelings*. If you ask a person who is in a trauma center burn ward what "burn" is, the person may describe the searing pain experienced in his or her mind. But that pain is not why the burn patients are being treated. Their flesh has been damaged, probably several layers deep. The burn is different from the feeling of pain it inflicts in the mind.

According to the Bible, *true guilt is liability to punishment*. Suppose you have been arraigned before a court of law, charged with murder. The trial takes weeks, and the jury is out for days, and they finally reassemble.

The judge takes his place behind the bench and asks: "Ladies and gentlemen of the jury, have you reached a verdict?"

"We have, your honor," responds the foreman.

"The defendant will please rise. Ladies and gentlemen of the jury, what is your verdict?"

"We find the defendant guilty as charged."

Now there would be a catch of the breath, a closing of the throat, an increase of the pulse, an additional flow of adrenaline, perspiration, clammy hands, dizziness, a sense of nausea, and fainting. All of those would be *feelings of guilt and fear of impending punishment*. But the *liability to punishment* is the real source.

How to remove guilt and its feelings is the premier question of psychiatry and psychology. You often will hear or read that some psychiatrist now has come up with a great new insight into emotional distress. Don't believe it! According to the *Saturday Review of Literature*, there are 230 differing psychological philosophies being practiced in the United States, many of which completely contradict one another. We are fortunate that some psychology now is practiced from a Christian perspective, but not all "biblical" psychological and psychiatric models are worthy of the name; they so easily become tainted by humanistic presuppositions. Also, psychology in itself can only confront and treat guilt feelings—not the guilt itself.

Unfortunately, many psychologists simply try to deaden sensitivity—to rationalize and explain. They try to take away the pain of the burn, without healing the spiritual skin tissue that has been destroyed and is threatening to destroy the soul. One psychologist, a Dr. Gershenfeld, says that we should use words like *confused* or *mixed-up priorities*, rather than *guilt*. Should we not, as one pastoral counseling theorist suggests, deemphasize the concepts of sin and guilt, speaking, rather of a "distortion" or "inadequacy in human nature," a "sickness" that has infected the covenant relationship? By emphasizing the "judgment-justice-justification" model, he suggests, the church has been stuck in legalism when it should be offering the healing available through God's unconditional grace. There is some truth to all of these metaphors, but they fail if they suggest that sin is sickness only, and therefore not truly the person's fault. It is not legalism when Scripture says that "all have sinned, and come short of the glory of God" (Romans 3:23), and it is the individual's "fault." "There is none righteous, no, not one" (Romans 3:10). That doesn't leave out grace; rather, correct understanding of sin is a prelude to correctly understanding what grace is:

> But now the righteousness of God without the law is manifested, being witnessed by the law and the prophets; Even the righteousness of God which is by faith of Jesus Christ unto all and upon all them that believe: for there is no difference: For all have sinned, and come short of the glory of God; Being justified freely by his grace through the redemption that is in Christ Jesus. [Romans 3:21–24]

There it is, the introduction of unmerited, unearned love, directed toward those who both *feel* guilty and *are* guilty. The apostle John says if we do not acknowledge our guilt—if we claim to be innocent—"we deceive ourselves, and the truth is not in us" (1 John 1:8b). That is not neurosis. It is honest self-reflection of a kind that helps us out of our neurotic attempts to deal with sin on our own. John goes on with one of the most comforting promises in all of Scripture: "If we confess our sins, he is faithful and just to forgive us our sins, and to cleanse us from all unrighteousness" (1 John 1:9). If this is a "judgment-justice-justification" model, then I will take it over a "sickness" model any day. God has judged sin to be sin and worthy of condemnation; Christ has satisfied the just liability for punishment that is guilt; I am justified freely by grace.

A troubled young man came to see me. Years before he had broken the law and had been placed on probation. That probation was almost up, but now he had committed a relatively minor infraction, but one that called him to court before someone who well-deserved his reputation as the "hanging judge." The young offender could be sentenced to several years in prison and he was petrified. But he told me he did not want me to help him get out of it; he simply wanted me to give him something to take with him. I could do better than that. I could give him *Someone* who would go with him. He received Jesus into his life.

Jesus Christ is the perfection of justice. He is the absolutely holy and just One. His eyes are too pure to look upon iniquity. Before him if we offend in one point we are guilty of all (James 2:10–11). He will say to many, "Depart from me, ye cursed, into everlasting fire, prepared for the devil and his angels" (Matthew 25:41b). Jesus, however, is in a far different sense the "hanging judge." He is the Judge who was hanged on the tree. Jesus is the Judge who came down from behind the bench, took off his robes of glory, and went to the cross in our place.

The final answer for guilt

In Romans 8:33–34 Paul asks the most important questions one oppressed by guilt will ever hear:

> *Question:* Who will bring any charge against those whom God has chosen?

Answer: It is God.

Question: Who is he that condemns?

Answer: No one for the Christian. The Judge who is Jesus Christ, who intercedes for me.

Question: Paul, is this God the same God who also justifies?

Answer: It is the very same.

Question: Paul, is this the hanging judge—the one who died and was raised to life? Is this the same judge who is at the right hand of God and is interceding for us?

Answer: Yes, that is the One.

All this happens through a process called justification. God in Jesus Christ freely justifies; he pronounces, accepts, and treats as just one who is no longer liable for punishment. The *Westminster Confession* makes an important distinction at this point. The law has been disobeyed, and God does not justify by simply waving his hand and saying, "All is well. I will forget about the broken law and infuse you with righteousness." God would not be just if he did that. The skeptic who joked that God would forgive him, "because that is God's business" will be sadly disappointed. Rather, said the Westminster divines, God "accepts sinners as righteous" who have come under the blood of Christ. Charles Wesley described it as having an interest in Christ's blood:

> And can it be that I should gain
> An interest in the Savior's blood?
> Died He for me, who caused His pain?
> For me, who Him to death pursued?
> Amazing love! How can it be
> That Thou, my God, shouldst die for me?

The *Confession* says that when I stand before the Judge, he looks at me and sees nothing but Christ's obedience and the satisfaction of the law's demands. "For the wages of sin is death; but the gift of God is eternal life through Jesus Christ our Lord" (Romans 6:23; see also Ephesians 1:7). All the sinner adds is faith, believing "on him that raised up

Jesus our Lord from the dead" (Romans 4:24). "If thou shalt confess with thy mouth the Lord Jesus, and shalt believe in thine heart that God raised him from the dead, thou shalt be saved" (Romans 10:9). No, Paul says, we do not really even add the faith. God gives us the faith to place in Christ—something we would never do on our own (Ephesians 2:8–9; Philippians 1:29). Wesley's hymn continues:

> No condemnation now I dread,
> Jesus, and all in Him, is mine!
> Alive in Him, my living Head,
> And clothed in righteousness divine,
> Bold I approach the eternal throne,
> And claim the crown, through Christ my own.
> Amazing love! How can it be
> That Thou, my God, shouldst die for me?

This is forgiveness to the uttermost. Condemnation is replaced with a crown.

What justification is not

We have said a great deal about what justification does in freeing us from the penalty for sin. We should also say what it is not and what it will not do.

Justification does not change our hearts, souls, or lives one whit. It has to do with what God declares about our guilt, and what he sees when he looks at us in Christ. The declaration that we are righteous is entirely external to us. Indeed, God does internally change us, but that is *regeneration* and *sanctification*. The implication of this is that the problem with sin and guilt in our lives will not go away once we trust in Christ and are reborn. You are no better after you are justified than before. You are not one bit holier. We can not separate justification from sanctification.

Yet its significance in changing us is fantastic in two senses.

First, no one who understands justification will ever again try to cling to good works for salvation. John Gerstner has described the plight of the proud man in this way:

Christ has done everything necessary for his salvation. Nothing now stands between the sinner and God but the sinner's "good works." Nothing can keep him from Christ but his delusion that he does not need him—that he has good works of his own that can satisfy God. If men will only be convinced that they have no righteousness that is not as filthy rags; if men will see that there is none that doeth good, no, not one; if men will see that all are shut up under sin—then there will be nothing to prevent their everlasting salvation. All they need is need. All they must have is nothing. All that is required is acknowledged guilt. But, alas, sinners cannot part with their "virtues." They have none that are not imaginary, but they are real to them. So grace becomes unreal. The real grace of God they spurn in order to hold on to the illusory virtues of their own. Their eyes fixed on a mirage, they will not drink real water. They die of thirst in the midst of an ocean of Grace.

Right now you are clinging to something in your hope that you are acceptable to yourself and to God. There will be one day, said Jesus, a great wedding feast (Matthew 22:10–13). All who come will have on beautiful white garments—the righteousness of Christ. But one man comes into the wedding feast in Jesus' parable who does not have on a wedding garment. Likely he supposes himself to be dressed in his Sunday best, dressed in morality, money given to charity, commandment keeping, Golden-rule living, and general "niceness." Unfortunately, the guest doesn't truly see his clothing very well. To the king he is filthy, foul-smelling, and louse-infested. "Friend," the king asked, "how camest thou in hither not having a wedding garment?" Jesus said the man was speechless. He had no defense. "Then said the king to the servants, Bind him hand and foot, and take him away, and cast him into outer darkness; there shall be weeping and gnashing of teeth."

Second, justification should transform the sinner's self-image. The great malady of our age is conquered. We have been forgiven. This is fact, not surmise. Someone from an Evangelism Explosion calling team asks: "Suppose that you were to die tonight and stand before God and he were to say to you, 'Why should I let you into my heaven?' What would you say?" What a feeling it is to know that you could answer: "I am declared just, only in the blood of Jesus Christ, my Savior and Lord."

With that out of the way, I have peace with God and access to God and hope of glory (Romans 5:1–2). Peace, access, and hope are the great needs of the age of guilt, the great antidotes to depression and feelings of guilt. If we cling to Christ we have peace, access, and hope.

Therefore, the dirtiness that clings to us as ultimate guilt also is ultimately powerless. As fallen human beings we will die, and death will take us into the glory of God's presence. Original sin's guilt is taken care of on the cross. Cling to Christ, and the depression that comes from the human condition loses its power to oppress.

Therefore, the guilt of trying to do the right thing and failing is absolutely powerless to oppress. If salvation is a gift of God and not of works, the filthiness of a person's own good works truly is irrelevant. What I do, I do to the glory of God, and he will accept it as praise on that basis. Cling to Christ and the need for self-punishment loses its power to oppress.

Therefore, the childish desire to lash out at oneself, God, or others can be replaced by mature dealing with mistakes. An adult way has been made for the Christian to be forgiven of sin. Emotional bondage loses its power to oppress.

Therefore, objective guilt is gone, so far as God is concerned. Yes, the person will do wrong and be liable to chastisement by God and civil/criminal/social penalties imposed by society. However, what penalties I must pay in the flesh for sin are God's disciplining hand to help me be more like Christ (Hebrews 12:4–13). Unpleasant though they be, at least I know they will be used to strengthen and further sanctify me. I am forgiven to the uttermost and guilt has no oppressive power over me.

What does it mean that Christians are adopted?

All those that are justified God vouchsafeth, in and for his only Son Jesus Christ, to make partakers of the grace of adoption; by which they are taken into the number, and enjoy the liberties and privileges of the children of God; have his name put upon them; receive the Spirit of adoption; have access to the throne of grace with boldness; are enabled to cry, Abba, Father; are pitied, protected, provided for, and chastened by him as by a father; yet never cast off, but sealed to the day of redemption, and inherit the promises as heirs of everlasting salvation. [Westminster Confession of Faith, chapter 12]

12

Abba, Daddy

They had studied for years. They had planned, designed, tinkered, built, attempted, and failed. Then on a December morning on the sand dunes of Kitty Hawk, North Carolina, Orville and Wilbur Wright broke the shackles of gravity and lifted humanity upward in the first powered flight. They knew the significance of their victory and immediately sent a telegram to their sister Katherine. She ran right down to the newspaper office and showed it to the editor.

"We have actually flown 120 feet. Will be home for Christmas," the telegram said. In his hands that editor held the scoop of the year, the story of the decade, perhaps the most significant news of the new century. The editor read it carefully and smiled.

"Well, well! How nice. The boys will be home for Christmas," he said.

He had planned and designed before the first star burst into flame to light the darkness. Then, when the world was in the grips of sin and distress, at just the right moment, the triune God undertook a flight far greater than that of Orville and Wilbur's. Christ flew through the galaxies, from the mansions of glory, into the filth of a cave used as a stable. Millions have heard of that flight and said, in the midst of their slavery to fear, "Well, well. Jesus was born at Bethlehem. That's sweet."

Others have looked at the same event and become more frightened of it. "Well, well. Now don't talk about such things. We want to stress the brotherhood of all people instead of one set of narrow religious interests."

As a result of both answers, our society is wracked by what Romans 8:15 calls a spirit of fear, when a Spirit of sonship with God would break the shackles of fear and lift humanity. That sounds like the greatest news of this or any other century, for verses 16 and 17 continue: "The Spirit itself

> *For ye have not received the spirit of bondage again to fear; but ye have received the Spirit of adoption, whereby we cry, Abba, Father. The Spirit itself beareth witness with our spirit, that we are the children of God: And if children, then heirs; heirs of God, and joint-heirs with Christ.* [Romans 8:15–17a]

beareth witness with our spirit, that we are the children of God: And if children, then heirs; heirs of God, and joint-heirs with Christ; if so be that we suffer with him, that we may be also glorified together." In Christ the believer has been *adopted* by God.

That implies wonderful things. Already we see one wonder. We need no longer be slaves to fear. We shall see that it also denies universalism, the great error of our time.

Fitting adoption into the big picture

We have seen two great covenants or promises that were given by God, the covenant of life, and the covenant of grace. The Bible speaks of being adopted as children of God within the covenant of grace. Adoption returns to us something that was lost after the covenant of life was broken.

God had created the world and made Adam in a perfect, sinless state when he gave him the covenant of life. While this covenant was operating we see the wonderful picture of fellowship between creature and Creator (Genesis 1:27–2:25). While any analogy falls short, the closeness depicted by Scripture resembles the intimacy of a parent-young child relationship—the relationship of a parent and child when both are functioning in their proper roles and intimate communication and love flow back and forth easily. The child feels most comfortable when in touch with the parent. There is no desire to break away or rebel.

The promise of the covenant of life was based on a probationary command. Adam had one command he was to keep to show his obedience and devotion to his God. If he kept it he would earn for himself and all his children eternal blessedness, bliss, and peace. He would, through this command, be enabled to fulfil the purpose for which people were created: to glorify God and enjoy him forever. However, he chose to rebel, plunging the human race into sin and fear, death and misery.

Why should God care to set in place his second covenant—the covenant of grace? God certainly could have let men and women go their own way, or wiped them out and started over. Instead, he offered another way to eternal life, a way that took into account the true condition of the fallen, who "glorified him not as God, neither were thankful; but became vain in their imaginations, and their foolish heart was darkened" (Romans 1:21). Left alone, the human heart opposes God. No human heart understands or appreciates the things of the Spirit (Romans 3:11).

Therefore, God determined to select a great mass of men and women out of every nation and language. These were individually chosen before even one of them was born, in fact before the fall into sin itself had occurred (Ephesians 1:4–6; Revelation 5:9). Into the hearts of each of these dead individuals he sends his Spirit, irresistibly, unfailingly drawing them to him. The Spirit makes their hearts and minds new, brings their souls, dead with sin, to life in Christ

(Ephesians 2:1–10). They come most willingly, made willing by his grace.

Still, none of this would have been possible if the guilt-price of sin had not been paid. To purchase salvation for all who come to him, so that he might remain the just Judge, God gave his unique Son, a part of himself, to pay for their transgressions. At just the right time in each life, God sent his Holy Spirit to effectually call them through their individual experiences and background. In some great outpourings of grace in history, hundreds, even thousands have laid their lives at the cross in a brief time. This still was no mass production operation of the Spirit. In each heart the Spirit worked through that mind and those life experiences to individually relate the gospel to them in their situation and cultural background. By understanding through the Bible and renewal through the Spirit a dead mind leaps to life, a soul is reborn, a will is made malleable. After hearing God's voice and knock at the door, each sinner says in his or her own experience, "Come in, my Beloved." After receiving trusting faith from God as a gift, the individual is justified (declared to be righteous) on the basis of that faith God has given.

At every point salvation is from God. If you want the theological term for all of these steps God has taken the sinner through toward himself, it is called the *ordo salutis*—"the way of salvation." While these steps may take some time, or they may seem to happen over an instant, the *ordo salutis* is a logical progression for us to use in understanding the process. However, the steps of this path are not yet completed, though even some of the great Christian thinkers stopped at this point, neglecting entirely what happens in *adoption.* Scripture has some things to say about it, though, and the writers of the *Westminster Confession* were careful to give it its due place in how we understand what God does for us. We are predestined or chosen by God so that we may be adopted as children of God, brothers and sisters of Christ. This is the ultimate blessing of the Christian life.

Child of God, or of Satan?

Adoption is also the point at which we confront a serious error—*universalism*. The universalist says that somehow, somewhere, sometime, every one of God's creatures will ultimately arrive in paradise. Universalism has been strongly preached from many pulpits by those who are so caught up in the idea that God is love that they abhor the thought that anyone could be eternally punished in hell. Yet the Bible plainly teaches that those who reject Christ will be forever separated from God. Jesus Christ himself made it plain:

> Enter ye in at the strait [narrow] gate: for wide is the gate, and broad is the way, that leadeth to destruction, and many there be which go in thereat: Because strait is the gate, and narrow is the way, which leadeth unto life, and few there be that find it. [Matthew 7:13–14]

> When the Son of man shall come in his glory, and all the holy angels with him, then shall he sit upon the throne of his glory: And before him shall be gathered all nations: and he shall separate them one from another, as a shepherd divideth his sheep from the goats: And he shall set the sheep on his right hand, but the goats on the left. . . . And these shall go away into everlasting punishment: but the righteousness into life eternal. [Matthew 25:31–33, 46]

> And if thine eye offend thee, pluck it out: it is better for thee to enter into the kingdom of God with one eye, than having two eyes to be cast into hell fire: Where their worm dieth not, and the fire is not quenched. [Mark 9:47–48]

> He that believeth on the Son hath everlasting life: and he that believeth not the Son shall not see life; but the wrath of God abideth on him. [John 3:36]

Universalism impinges upon the doctrine of adoption when universalists speak of the "fatherhood of God and the brotherhood of man." It sounds very loving and spiritual to sing, with the once popular chorus, "With God as our Father, brothers all are we. Let me walk with my brother, in perfect harmony." Many believe that sentiment to be from the Bible, but the idea that God is Father of all and that all are brothers and sisters is utterly foreign to the Scriptures. This false unity is true to the ideals of humanism, not Christianity. Jesus looked at the religious people of his day, who thought themselves children of Abraham, and said, "Ye are of your father the devil, and the lusts of your father ye will do" (John 8:44a). Paul takes an equally pessimistic view of those outside the kingdom of God: "And you hath he quickened, who were dead in trespasses and sins; Wherein in time past ye walked according to the course of this world, according to the prince of the power of the air, the spirit that now worketh in the children of disobedience" (Ephesians 2:1–2).

The state of the one who has not accepted Christ is hardly one of brotherhood with those who have. The disobedient child of the devil is under God's anger; his or her only connection with the kingdom of God is enmity. True connection with God comes only as we are transformed from the kingdom of darkness into the kingdom of God's dear Son: "But as many as received him, to them gave he power to become the sons of God, even to them that believe on his name" (John 1:12).

Childhood and citizenship

Can anyone *become* something he or she *already is*? Of course not. Romans 9:8 makes it clear that it is not the natural children who are God's children, but it is the children of the promise who are regarded as Abraham's (Romans 9:8). Abraham's offspring? It was Abraham who was declared righteous (justified) by his faith. He looked forward to the coming of a Savior for his sins. Now we can look back on the cross (rather than forward as did Abraham), but we are declared righteous in the same way he was, and through justification become the true children of Abraham. The justified ones, as children of Abraham, are children of God. This is not a promise to children of the flesh but children of the Spirit. In fact, in a spiritual sense the children of the Spirit are to stand apart:

> Wherefore come out from among them, and be ye separate, saith the Lord, and touch not the unclean thing; and I will receive you, And will be a Father unto you, and ye shall be my sons and daughters, saith the Lord Almighty. [2 Corinthians 6:17–18]

The deception of the devil may be that all people are the children of God, that God is Father of all, but this is not the teaching of Scripture.

To be perfectly accurate we should notice three meanings for the term *sons/children of God* in Scripture. First, when God made Adam he was the son of God. That special status was obliterated in the fall into sin. Second, those in Christ are *adopted* children of God by receiving him as Savior and believing on him (John 1:12). Third, in its most restrictive and unique sense, the term applies to Jesus Christ, the eternal second person of the Trinity, who has forever been the Son of God (p. 104).

Adam was both son and subject. He was a member of the divine kingdom and of the divine household. God, to him, was Sovereign and Lord; he also was Father and Friend. If Adam had obeyed, we would all have an eternal citizenship in the kingdom of God and eternal sonship in the house of God. But Adam sinned against the magisterial favor of the King and against the paternal regard of the Father. In one act he sinned in both ways. As a result he became an outlawed citizen and a disinherited son. Therefore, all his children are born out of relationship with the righteous Judge and the benevolent Father. The human condition was described succinctly by Robert Webb, who said concerning Adam and all his natural children:

> There was, there could be, there ought to have been, but one denouement to such a situation—a child with a heart so per-

verted ought to have been excluded. God dismissed him. Today he has neither the right nor spirit of a child. He is legally disowned because he is morally bad. He is ungoverned, because he is ungovernable. He has thrown off his Father's authority, because he has cast away his Father's disposition. Moral gravitation has naturally and logically carried him into that fellowship where the outraged sensibilities of his Father have justly consigned him. Parental discipline has dealt with him according to the demands and desires of his own degenerate nature. He has been permitted to have his wilful way; and the misery of his course will be the just retribution of his heady and impertinent career. He is a child of Satan; therefore a "child of wrath."

This dreadful condition needs a twofold remedy. As proscribed citizen and disinherited child, each person must be restored to legal citizenship and be recovered into the bosom and household of the Father. This double remedy is clearly stated in Scripture. On one hand, the problem of citizenship is dealt with by justification. In justification the transgressed law of God is fulfilled by Christ and the penalty paid by him. The sinner is clothed in the righteousness of Christ and restored to the kingdom of God. Sonship is taken care of in adoption. The saved sinner is adopted into the family of God and restored to his household.

Obviously adoption is closely related to justification and to the overall process of being born again (regenerated). Not only must the child be restored to a filial disposition; the child must also be given a filial nature, the nature of a child. The spiteful attitude of natural humanity says to the parents: "I hate you; I never want to lay eyes on you again. I couldn't care less what you have done for me." The regenerated person has a new heart and nature and acts like a child, in keeping with the new rights and privileges of son and daughterhood.

The errors of universalism

Let us compare that with the theology of the fatherhood of God/brotherhood of man. This is a new religion of paternalism. It is interesting that universalism should rise in the twentieth century, at a time the Western European and North American governments have been exercising a more paternalistic attitude toward citizens. People have come to believe they have a right to be taken care of. In keeping with that, God must be the Father of everyone.

Universalism fails to realize God's absolute perfection. It would be unfair for him to leave out anyone. He did not create people because he was lonely; he existed in perfect fellowship with himself. God created humans for his own glory.

Universalism fails to understand the difference between divine government and divine discipline; between the rule of a Sovereign and the rule of a Father. A sovereign-state ruler exercises justice and punishes the rebellious. A father operates out of love, chastening instead of punishing. There is a great difference between chastening and punishing. Punishment is retrospective—it looks back to the broken law and is not done to make the criminal better. A law-breaker is punished because the law has been violated. Chastisement is prospective—it looks forward to future behavior. It is given to correct a fault, to make the child better. An electric chair makes no one better. It may make society better since one of the reasons for justice is the protection of society; but the reason for chastening is to make a better child.

Universalism denies the need for an atonement. It reduces the Bible to the story of the prodigal son, where the father embraces the son without payment for sins. But that is the nature of fatherly discipline. All the father requires is repentance and evidence of a desire to do better. So people who suppose this to be the way of salvation believe that if a person merely wants to do better in the future, all will be well. This is to suppose a murderer who has been given a life sentence rattles the bars and says to the warden: "Warden, I've had a change of heart. You will be delighted to know that I'm sorry about the whole thing. I've decided I shouldn't have killed all those people. Please tell the jailer to open the cage and let me out because I'll never do that again."

The universalist fails to understand that only identification with Jesus Christ can make a sinner both a member of God's kingdom and of his family. Jesus was the suffering Servant who remained subject to the King—obedient to God in all his ways. Jesus paid the penalty as the Servant; thus God restores him to legal citizenship in the kingdom. Jesus is also the very Son of God because it takes the Son by filial obedience to restore the sinful, disobedient son to a filial relation. So Christ the suffering Son provides for us both justification's restoration to the kingdom and adoption's reclamation into the family.

Gifts from the Father

The *Westminster Confession of Faith* notes that we should think of adoption as growing from justification. "All those that are justified God vouchsafeth, in and for his only Son Jesus Christ, to make partakers of the grace of adoption." To vouchsafe means to condescend to give. Adam's and Eve's original rights and privileges were based upon a wonderful act of condescension that was possible because they stood as righteous in God's sight. God can vouchsafe nothing for those he cannot look on because of their sin. This was the Westminster writers' way of saying that adoption presents the proof that the guilt of sin has been removed. Restoration has occurred, so reclamation is possible. Our God can bend down to pick us up and hold us again in his arms. What is vouchsafed for those who are taken into the number and enjoy the liberties and privileges of the adopted?

God gives them his name. I have always felt a special admiration for those who are willing to become foster parents. Foster parents, as the state usually defines them, are parents who temporarily take over parenthood for children who cannot remain with their natural parents. Some sort of intervention is required to get the child's own family functioning again. It is not the nurturing environment that child needs for the moment. The child goes to live with the foster parents for weeks, even months; yet when the child returns to its birth parents the foster relationship is broken. The foster mother and father must say good-bye and put away the special affections they may have enjoyed for this child. The foster parent can not give the child a new name. There can be no permanent relationship signified by the change in name. In biblical times a change in God's relationship with a person often accompanied a new name. *Abram* and *Sarai* became *Abraham* and *Sarah*; *Jacob* became *Israel*. In the New Testament *Simon* the fisherman became *Peter* the "rock."

God gives them his Spirit. Every child has something of the nature of his father and mother within him. There is a genetic connection. Our hair may be the same color, our build the same type, and some natural affinities and abilities may be similar. Also, by virtue of being together through those formative years of childhood, children who have had a strong bond with their parents often seem to have a sort of kinship in spirit. This may return in adulthood even if there has been a tumultuous breaking away time when the parents and the child see almost nothing the same way at all.

But with God this spiritual connection is an actual Spirit connection. It is like the genetic link between blood relatives in that the Spirit of God takes up residence in the Christian's inner being. Holiness becomes part of who we are as new creatures. Those that become the children of God have a new desire for holiness, and even wisdom, which is one of the attributes of God. God gives to every child of his a certain divine wisdom, a wisdom of things eternal, which the world, regardless of its knowledge or education, knows nothing about. We receive the divine nature.

Singer Amy Grant expressed what this ought to mean for the Christian in a song entitled "Father's Eyes." The theme of the song is that we may have many traces of our family in our lives, but the Christian should most desire to see one's self and other people through the eyes of God's perspective.

The Holy Spirit is just as much a part of who God is as the Father and Son. This Spirit of adoption gives us gifts and direction from God and intercedes with God on our behalf.

Therefore we have access to the throne of grace with boldness. One lasting impression of John F. Kennedy's presidency was that of his toddler son's constant access to his father. Heads of state might be gathered in the oval office, yet on the rug in the center of the room little John was absorbed in his toys, knowing that daddy's lap was available if he wanted it. As the child of the King of the universe, we may push our toy trucks and other trappings of earthly preoccupation around on the floor, knowing we are in the presence of *Abba* and his lap is not too big to climb upon. And while a parent may not always understand what needs are expressed by those sniffling, incoherent cries of anguish, the Holy Spirit is our Translator, explaining what we want and what we really need.

God allows us Abba *intimacy.* Within our relationship we are pitied, protected, provided for, and chastened by him as by a father; yet never cast off. How sad a commentary on the godlessness of society that we have to be a little cautious in describing God as a Father. For many people, a father is the last thing they want God to be if that makes God what their own father was. We have come to the point where a minority of children know a stable father-child relationship. Father tends to be abusive or weak or absent. So God as father seems an ogreish, self-centered, or irrelevant image.

God has made us heirs. All that the Father has will one day be ours. "All things are yours," said the apostle Paul—the things in this world and the things to come. I am the heir of God, included in the will—only a living inheritance from a living Father. The New Testament of our Lord and Savior Jesus Christ is the will of God. And all who will receive Jesus Christ have their names in the Lamb's Book of Life and are heirs of God.

God gives us access to his home. Jesus has gone to prepare, in his Father's house, a place for each Christian. We are brought into the family of God, given his name, and made heirs by an act of God's grace. We also have the promise that we have his Spirit within us. He pities us as a Father, provides for all our needs, watches over us, defends us from our enemies, and one day will take us to our mansion in glory—the mansion he has prepared for us. How wonderful it is that because of the Spirit of adoption we can look up into the face of God, whom many fear, and say, "*Abba*, Father" (Romans 8:15b).

Love without measure

I once pointed out to a Jehovah's Witness that the New World translation is not correct when it includes in the New Testament the word *Jehovah* as the name of God, since it does not appear once in the New Testament Greek text. *Theos*, the generic Greek word for god is used often, but never the word *Yahweh* or, as the King James Version expresses it, *Jehovah*. "Why would God not use his Name in the New Testament?" the person asked. I cannot answer for God, but I have an idea as to the reason. When my little girl, Jennifer, was about five years old she passed through a phase when she began to call her mother and father by our first names—Anne and Jim. She heard others use these words and didn't see why she couldn't use them too. After a few weeks of this I sat her on my knee and said, "Jennifer, darling, there are thousands of people in this world who can call me Jim, but there is no other person on this earth who can call me 'daddy' except you, and to you, Jennifer, my name is Daddy." So also God revealed his name in the Old Testament as *Yahweh*—Jehovah, the Ever-Living One. But in the New Testament, when we are given the Spirit of adoption and brought into that intimate relationship as sons and daughters of God, we can look up into the face of our Father and say, "*Abba*," a diminutive of the Aramaic word for "father" that means, essentially, "daddy."

You may feel bruised and battered by life. You may feel all alone and cast down. If you are a parent you know something of the love of a parent for a child, the love that reaches out after a child even in its waywardness, a love that reaches out to a child in pain, a love that reaches after a child who has deserted the family, a love that never lets go. All of that tender compassion of a human parent's love is but the faintest shadow of the infinite love of God, which knows no measure—a love that could never let us go. When we become children of God we enter into that parental love of God. Have you came to the place when you can say, "I'm a child of the King. I can go to God as *Abba*"? If so then you know how transforming love can be. If not, then you can experience it—not the sickly passed-around love of the universalist's god, but the God who sets his love on those who are justified in Christ.

What is a sanctified life?

They who are effectually called and regenerated, having a new heart and a new spirit created in them, are further sanctified, really and personally, through the virtue of Christ's death and resurrection, by his Word and Spirit dwelling in them; the dominion of the whole body of sin is destroyed, and the several lusts thereof are more and more weakened and mortified, and they more and more quickened and strengthened, in all saving graces, to the practice of true holiness, without which no man shall see the Lord.
[Westminster Confession of Faith, chapter 13]

13

The Glint of Gold

When I was a seminary student I heard a story, told by a preacher from Canada, that I shall never forget:

One day a young woman in the church came to him for counsel. She had a terrible situation at home. She lived with a man who was an ogre. She got along fine with her husband, but her father-in-law had come to live with them. He was mean and bitter. He had a vile mouth and a blasphemous tongue, and it cut loose on her every time she did anything that displeased him in the slightest.

Now this woman had some spirit herself and was not about to be used as anyone's doormat. So when he gave it to her she gave it right back. Only later she always felt bad about it. Her anger hadn't accomplished anything, and these continual altercations were hard on everyone. She wondered what she should do.

The pastor was new to the ministry, and this problem sounded like it was beyond his meager store of wisdom. But he did have one idea.

"What is a food your father-in-law loves to eat?" the pastor asked.

The woman was taken aback by the question. She thought, "I knew I shouldn't have come to such a young man for advice. What does he know about anything?" But after a moment she answered that her father-in-law loved fudge.

238

"Next time he gets angry with you, make him some fudge," said the pastor.

She left, despairing of preachers not yet dry behind the ears. A few days later the next explosion occurred. She was going about her business in the kitchen. It was a wintry day, and this ugly man was sitting with his feet propped up on the potbelly stove. He had gout in one foot, and the heat helped. There he sat, his feet up and his hands folded around an opulent belly, when she accidentally splashed

> *Sanctify them through thy truth: thy word is truth. As thou hast sent me into the world, even so have I also sent them into the world.* [John 17:17–18]

hot water on his hurting foot. He explained the full depth of his feelings in the most colorful language. Her blood pressure rose until red reached the tip of her ears. She was ready to blow him off his seat when she remembered the preacher's insane advice. She stopped, counted to ten, turned around, and started to make fudge.

Meanwhile the bear settled back into his den, folded his hands, and went back to sleep. He slept while she mixed the ingredients, made the fudge, and cooled it. She cut some pieces, put them on a plate, and stuck the plate under her father-in-law's nose. One eye opened, then the other. He looked down at the plate of fudge, but he didn't move for a long time. He sat there thinking about his hurtful words and the fudge, his blasphemies and the fudge. A large tear slid down his cheek and dampened one of the pieces. He slowly slid out of the chair onto his knees, put his arms around her waist, and said, "Daughter, I want you to forgive a mean and ornery old man."

That day she had the joy of leading her father-in-law to the Lord.

Fudge grace

Wouldn't it be great if all interpersonal problems could be solved with a plate of fudge? Perhaps more could than we might imagine. The secret ingredient wasn't in the fudge, however. Something more intangible and mysterious was going on in two hearts. In the father-in-law's soul the Spirit of God drew the old man and made him willing. This transformation used the Word of God that had been placed in his mind in the past and the words his daughter-in-law used to share the gospel. This was God's grace.

The Spirit also used "fudge grace." Through the plate of an undeserved gift of grace the old man saw his own sin in stark contrast. Words of bitterness that had long been a habitual way of life were seen in all of their true ugliness against the backdrop of an act of sacrifice. He wasn't simply told about Jesus' sacrifice; he would have scoffed at such words from a daughter-in-law who traded insult for insult. Rather, he saw a demonstration of Jesus' sacrifice mirrored in a life.

It is like a prospector who fills a pan with riverbed rock and dirt. Most of what he pans is worthless sludge and splashes over the side of the pan. But occasionally the sunlight hits something small but sparklingly different in the pan. That sparkle makes the prospector's heart beat faster, for this is what his back-breaking labor and nights sleeping in the cold have been about. This is the glint of gold.

The Holy Spirit was also at work in the woman. Remember her reaction to the pastor. His advice only applied Scripture. Had she read those verses for herself she might never have connected them with the man whose feet were warming on her stove. Yet now the Holy Spirit took Scripture, mediated in the willing mind of the pastor, and gently applied it like sandpaper. The Spirit molded, smoothed, and shaped her mind. Fudge was not the natural reaction to abuse, but it was God's way. A growing child of God put off anger and became a vessel of love. That is the fudge grace called sanctification that God promises to every believer, the transforming power to be holy like our Lord.

The doctrine behind the life

The exceedingly important doctrine of sanctification reaches us right where we are. It has to do with life as we are living it now. Sanctification seems such a simple matter—merely living the Christian life. But not one church member in ten has the foggiest notion of what the biblical doctrine of sanctification really is. This is partly why there is so little true sanctification in the church. Sanctification is a doctrine as well as a life.

Sanctification is closely related to justification—so closely that the two often are confused. Though they can never be separated, they must be distinguished. One way to make the distinction is to place the definitions side by side as they were set out by the writers of the *Westminster Shorter Catechism,* questions 33 and 35:

What is justification?

Justification is an act of God's free grace, wherein he pardoneth all our sins, and accepteth us as righteous in his sight, only for the righteousness of Christ imputed to us, and received by faith alone.

What is sanctification?

Sanctification is the work of God's free grace, whereby we are renewed in the whole man after the image of God, and are enabled more and more to die unto sin and live unto righteousness.

Act and process

The first difference is that justification is an act; sanctification is a process. Justification takes place once for all and is complete and perfect. Sanctification is imperfect. It is a long process that lasts from the moment Christian life begins until the moment earthly life ends.

Courtroom and hospital

Second, justification is entirely external, while sanctification works in us. Jesus satisfied the penalty for our sins. We had nothing to do with his sacrifice on the cross. Justification is the act of God as Judge declaring us righteous in his sight through the death of Christ. We had nothing to do with that declaration. We are entered into the book of the kingdom of God. We did not write our names down. Nothing happens in justification inside us at all.

Sanctification takes the metaphor from the courtroom to the hospital. A trauma victim enters on a cart and is immediately wheeled to surgery. The condition is stabilized, but other treatments and therapy may take time. Sanctification begins with the work of a Surgeon within our persons. We are made holy before God when we are justified and clothed with Christ's righteousness. But then comes a lifelong patient-Physician relationship. We are actively involved in becoming what God has declared us to be. This process is intimately connected with our thoughts and actions. To change the image slightly, we are saints under construction—a hard-hat work site.

Guilt and corruption

The third difference involves God's purposes in the act of justification and the work of sanctification. They deal with two very different aspects of sin. If you do not distinguish these aspects you will have difficulty understanding Christian theology.

The first aspect of sin is its guilt, what we have described as liability (see pp. 212–14). The lawbreaker in the civil realm is liable to punishment. This is guilt. Anyone who sins against the law of God is liable to punishment. But justification reverses this liability. The righteousness of Christ has been imputed to the sinner. God tolerates no unrighteousness. If you have been made acceptable your account stands spotless so far as God is concerned. You are clothed with the garment of grace. In your flesh you may pay the penalty for sins committed. In God's sight no penalty is due.

The second aspect of sin is its corrupting power. In this aspect lies the filth with which sin stains our personalities, minds, and actions. Sanctification is the operation of doing away with the corruption. This is not done by imputing Christ's righteousness to us. It is accomplished by infusing Christ's holiness into us.

Anyone who has bitten into a rotten or wormy apple has experienced the nauseating reality of corruption. After a few days a corrupt apple need not be tasted for its problem to be identified. A glance reveals the brown, wrinkling decay, a touch the squishy unwholesomeness. Keep it around a little longer and a strange odor pervades its surroundings. Rottenness no longer needs to be tasted, seen, or touched. Likewise, humankind stinks to high heaven. Not a flattering thought. From the top of our heads to the soles of our feet there is nothing but corruption within. In the English language *holiness* relates to the word *whole*—as in wholeness, soundness, oneness. We know how to make a good apple rotten, but only God can make a rotten apple sound. A corrupting human apple can become whole again by connection to the Tree, the Source of soundness. Jesus used a slightly different picture to make the same point, that wholeness (and holiness) occurs only through connection:

I am the true vine, and my Father is the husbandman . . . Abide in me, and I in you. As the branch cannot bear fruit of itself, except it abide in the vine; no more can ye, except ye abide in me. I am the vine, ye are the branches: He that abideth in me, and I in him, the same bringeth forth much fruit: for without me ye can do nothing. If a man abide not in me, he is cast forth as a branch, and is withered; and men gather them, and cast them into the fire, and they are burned. [John 15:1, 4–6]

Take an apple off of the tree, leave it around long enough, and rottenness results. If we are severed from the Vine we will become corrupt. Holiness is an attribute of God alone, and holiness in anyone or anything in this world exists only in relation to God. The holiness of God flows into it in some way.

The call to connection

The justified Christian has been removed from liability. But establishing the vital vine-branch connection is only the beginning. While God accepts the new believer, the connection is weak because of the ongoing effects of the sin-nature: "Thou art of purer eyes than to behold evil, and canst not look on iniquity" (Habakkuk 1:13). God is intolerant of *all* sin, in the unbeliever and the believer. If you have never truly experienced intimacy with God, and I believe few Christians enjoy that experience, it likely is because much of your life remains contrary to the holiness of God. Your rebellion remains an abomination. The vine-branch connection remains weak. True holiness needs to replace remaining unholiness that God hates. Sanctification is the answer.

But the need for sanctification may raise a few questions:

1. Why, if the penalty for sin has been taken care of, must I be so concerned with holiness?
2. On the other hand, when Jesus talks about remaining connected to him in John 15 he warns about branches being cut off and thrown into the fire. Can I lose my salvation if the process of sanctification doesn't "take"?
3. But sanctification is a work of God. So isn't it really out of my hands?

Why be concerned?

Our Father is God of the universe, holy and perfect, omniscient and omnipotent. I should be careful about making him angry if I am his child. He is a loving Father, but he is no wimp. And he has made a world in which sin has consequences, some of them drastic. Ananias and Sapphira were early church members who thought they could keep God as a convenient fire escape (Acts 5:1–11). We are not told whether this man and wife had come to a saving knowledge of God. Perhaps they had. Yet God required their lives when they thought they could lie to him with impunity. The lesson was not lost on the rest of the Christian community. The church was strengthened by their deaths, for "great fear came upon all the church, and upon as many as heard these things" (Acts 5:11). Sanctification begins with a healthy sense of awe for the God in whose presence we serve.

God hasn't struck anyone dead in your church lately? That may have been what the Corinthian Christians thought as well, but I believe Paul described physical sickness and death that had befallen abusers of the worship sacrament of the Lord's Supper: "For he that eateth and drinketh unworthily, eateth and drinketh damnation to himself, not discerning the Lord's body. For this cause many are weak and sickly among you, and many sleep" (1 Corinthians 11:29–30). Certainly the God who struck down Ananias and Sapphira hasn't changed his opinion of sin in his body, and he is one who should be regarded "acceptably with reverence and godly fear: For our God is a consuming fire" (Hebrews 12:28–29).

A more positive reason to be holy is that the transforming life should hunger for fellowship connection with the Beloved. If we were created to glorify God and enjoy him forever, the path of maturing holiness is the only way to achieve our most transforming purpose. Jesus came so that we may have life to the full (John 10:10). Why should we let anything keep us from enjoying all that life can be in Jesus?

Another reason for concern may seem obvious, but many overlook it: If we love God we should be willing and anxious to obey him. "If ye love me, keep my commandments," Jesus said in John 14:15, 23. Holiness is commanded.

Can I lose my salvation?

A child of God, bought with the blood of Christ, will not lose the salvation Jesus purchased. Not ever. Not under any circumstances. Theologians call this promise the doctrine of *eternal security* or the *perseverance of the saints.* According to Psalm 37:23–24, "The steps of a good man are ordered by the LORD: and he delighteth in his way. Though he fall, he shall not be utterly cast down: for the LORD upholdeth him with his hand."

This must have been a particularly important promise to John, for his Gospel quoted several of Jesus' statements regarding this assurance of life:

> Verily, verily, I say unto you, He that heareth my word, and believeth on him that sent me, hath everlasting life, and shall not come into condemnation; but is passed from death unto life. [5:24]

> All that the Father giveth me shall come to me; and him that cometh to me I will in no wise cast out. And this is the Father's will which hath sent me, that of all which he hath given me I should lose nothing, but should raise it up again at the last day. And this is the will of him that sent me that every one which seeth the Son, and believeth on him, may have everlasting life: and I will raise him up at the last day. [6:37, 39–40]

> My sheep hear my voice, and I know them, and they follow me: And I give unto them eternal life; and they shall never perish, neither shall any man pluck them out of my hand. My Father, which gave them me, is greater than all; and no

man is able to pluck them out of my Father's hand. I and my Father are one. [10:27–30]

My salvation is as certain as the promise of God and the oneness of the Father and the Son (see also Romans 8:29, 38–39).

But as clear as this promise stands, those who teach that one can lose salvation have a point: The one who claims Christ, yet shows no turning from sin or growth in Christian maturity and righteousness that naturally accompanies sanctification, has no ground for assurance of salvation. Such people have not *lost* salvation; they have not had it to lose. Jesus told a parable of a sower who scattered seed throughout his field (Matthew 13). One of the soils where seed landed was mostly rocks. At first the seed showed every appearance of sprouting but there was nothing for it to take root in, so the plant quickly withered in time of trouble (Luke 8:13).

Likewise seed fell among weeds. Again, it showed some signs of germination, but the weeds never moved over to allow room for a plant. This, Jesus said, represented the souls in which God's Word is choked out by worldly care. How many people seem to come to Christ (perhaps again and again), but their approach seems all emotion, with no change of direction or mind? They are not in love with Christ, nor do they make him Lord of their life. They wish an emotional high, a feel-good glow. Be cautious of such cathartic experiences. They are easy for Satan to mimic, and they often have little or nothing to do with the content of God's Word. At the first descent into the valley of life cares the person falls away. Others believe all of the right things, but their faith is so filled with shallow pride that love for God finds no place to take root. Such people may be filled with self-righteousness and very Bible literate, but they are bound for hell and never notice their plight.

In its chapter on the assurance of grace and salvation (18) the *Westminster Confession* speaks of times when assurance is lost:

When one who has confessed Christ does not persevere in faith and commitment

When one falls into a sin that wounds the conscience and grieves God's Spirit

During times of severe temptation

When one perceives that God has withdrawn—usually because we have withdrawn ourselves emotionally from God's presence or are in depression

There are indeed times when we need to look at our lives honestly and confess: I don't feel connected to God. Am I living in rebellion or forsaking his gifts of Scripture, prayer, and worship? If so, maybe I have not truly accepted him as Lord and need to approach God in repentance and submission.

We must be clear about the difference between believing intellectually or emotionally, but without submission. That is not faith. Evil spirits fell down before Jesus with the confession, "Thou art the Son of God" (Mark 3:11), but Jesus did not say, "Bless you, demon. You have finally seen the light." He told the devils to shut up, for he would accept no such belief or confession. The neighbors of the Gadarene demoniacs believed Jesus had power. But they wanted none of it (Matthew 8:33–34). The people of Nazareth heard Jesus and were amazed at his wisdom and miracles, yet he condemned their faithlessness (Matthew 13:56–58). Many in Jerusalem saw his miracles and "believed in his name," records John 2:23, "But Jesus did not commit himself unto them, because he knew all men, And needed not that any should testify of man: for he knew what was in man" (2:24–25). Paul (Ephesians 2:8–10) and James (James 2:18–26) distinguish intellectual assent, which we share with demons (James 2:19), from saving faith that flows into sanctification. Works of obedience, righteousness, growth, and repentance do not save, but they are prerequisite to assurance of true redemption in Christ.

What do I have to do in sanctification?

Sanctification is a work of God in me, yet Christians are continually called to obedience as part of the working out of salvation. This sounds confusing, but it isn't so difficult to understand. Any large construction project is the work of more than one contractor, and God is pleased to sub-contract part of this mammoth undertaking to the Christian. Or think of it as a partnership in which God provides the strength and will with which I keep my end of the contract. It is a good thing we have such assistance, for the goals of sanctification are perfection, identification with God, conformity to Christ, and a life of good works.

Through the process of sanctification the Christian joins in the work of God and others. As already stated, the Christian's perfection is an accomplished work of the Father, who sees us as perfect in Christ (1 Thessalonians 5:23). It also is a work of the Son. Jesus offered complete sanctification to the Father, fulfilling all righteousness (Matthew 3:15). The author of Hebrews says that Christ's obedience through suffering was a perfection that enabled him to be the perfect High Priest who offered himself as a perfect Sacrifice to be the Source of our salvation (Colossians 1:22; Hebrews 5:9–10). Jesus said in his prayer to the Father on the night before he was crucified: "For their sakes I sanctify myself, that they also might be sanctified through the truth" (John 17:19). And sanctification continues through God the Holy Spirit. "To the end he may stablish your hearts unblameable in holiness before God, even our Father, at the coming of our Lord Jesus Christ with all his saints" (1 Thessalonians 3:13).

The completion of sanctification in the individual extends beyond God to the work of the church, which prays for and enfolds the developing saint. Each member of the body strengthens the others and is strengthened in the Word by the others: "We are glad, when we are weak, and ye are strong: and this also we wish, even your perfection"

(2 Corinthians 13:9; see also Colossians 1:28; 2 Timothy 3:16).

Perfection in sanctification holiness is aided, too, by circumstances—especially those we might prefer not to have. But as we work through them with growing dependence on God, we are working through our construction in holiness: "My brethren, count it all joy when ye fall into divers temptations; Knowing this, that the trying of our faith worketh patience. But let patience have her perfect work, that ye may be perfect and entire, wanting nothing" (James 1:2–4). In this we are actively involved: "Do all things without murmurings and disputings: That ye may be blameless and harmless, the sons of God, without rebuke, in the midst of a crooked and perverse nation, among whom ye shine as lights in the world" (Philippians 2:14–15; see also 2 Peter 3:14; 1 John 4:12).

In sanctification's growing holiness the believer identifies with the perfection of God. Identification with the Father is what Jesus calls for when he says, "Be ye therefore perfect, even as your Father which is in heaven is perfect" (Matthew 5:48). Though God makes us holy, the Christian is commanded to take off the old attitudes and desires and to put on a new self, "which after God is created in righteousness and true holiness" (Ephesians 4:24). God is working behind the scenes on such a reconstruction job, but he wants us to pound in some nails. Ephesians 5:1–2a tells us to "Be ye therefore followers of God as dear children: And walk in love, as Christ also hath loved us." Adds Paul elsewhere in Ephesians, God has chosen us "that we should be holy and without blame before him in love" (Ephesians 1:4b). Children imitate the father they love, and shouldn't we be merciful, just as our Father is merciful (Luke 6:36)? Shouldn't we be kind one to another, tenderhearted, forgiving one another, even as God for Christ's sake forgave us (Ephesians 4:32)? Following in Father's footsteps here is working alongside of him for my sanctification. My work so fits into God's that I cannot say where my effort fades into his.

Conformity to Christ means that sanctification makes us think and act more like him. Again, we know that this conformity isn't anything we do (see pp. 242–44). In a real sense every Christian is conformed to Christ the moment Christ's Holy Spirit dwells within. The Christian has the mind of Christ (1 Corinthians 2:16) and increasingly reflects Christ's glory (2 Corinthians 3:18). But look at who all is at work in Ephesians 4:11–13, conforming us to Christ:

> And he gave some, apostles; and some, prophets; and some, evangelists; and some, pastors and teachers; For the perfecting of the saints, for the work of the ministry, for the edifying of the body of Christ: Till we all come in the unity of the faith, and of the knowledge of the Son of God, unto a perfect man, unto the measure of the stature of the fulness of Christ.

Our lives, as we become sanctified, should be reflected in works in keeping with who we are. What we do certainly reflects on the One we name as our master: "No man can serve two masters: for either he will hate the one, and love the other; or else he will hold to the one, and despise the other. Ye cannot serve God and mammon" (Matthew 6:24). "Let your light so shine before men, that they may see your good works, and glorify your Father which is in heaven" (Matthew 5:16). Peter tells us to be sanctified before the watching world: "Having your conversation honest among the Gentiles: that, whereas they speak against you as evildoers, they may by your good works, which they shall behold, glorify God in the day of visitation" (1 Peter 2:12). James is caustic on this point:

> What doth it profit, my brethren, though a man say he hath faith, and have not works? can faith save him? If a brother or sister be naked, and destitute of daily food, And one of you say unto them, Depart in peace, be ye warmed and filled; notwithstanding ye give them not those things which are needful to the body; what doth it profit? Even so faith, if it hath not works, is dead, being alone. [2:14–17]

Even here we do not work alone. Paul says to be filled with the fruit of righteousness "which are by Jesus Christ, unto the glory and praise of God" (Philippians 1:11b). Ephesians 2:10 fits the partnership together: "For we are his workmanship, created in Christ Jesus unto good works, which God hath before ordained that we should walk in them."

Knowing the holiness of God

Having been justified, we are removed from our liability to punishment. Clothed with the garments of Christ, we stand judicially pure before God. In that context we are commanded to put sanctification into operation, to become pure on the inside so as not to dishonor those garments of grace. This is the matter to which sanctification addresses itself: "For I am the LORD your God: ye shall therefore sanctify yourselves, and ye shall be holy; for I am holy" (Leviticus 11:44a). Without holiness no one shall see God (Hebrews 12:14).

We are to perfect holiness in the fear of the Lord. If there is any one thing the church needs today it is a view of the holiness and majesty of God and a consequent view of his demand upon us. John calls us to look honestly on the worldliness that continues to corrupt our lives.

> If any man love the world, the love of the Father is not in him. For all that is in the world, the lust of the flesh, and the lust of the eyes, and the pride of life, is not of the Father, but of the world. And the world passeth away, and the lust thereof: but he that doeth the will of God abideth forever. [1 John 2:15b–17]

What is your particular form of corruption? Does it steal into your heart as a craving of the flesh? God calls us to holiness in body, mind, and spirit. Replace rottenness with that which is sound and holy. How many minds today are virtually pornographic? How about the body, which God commands to be presented as a living sacrifice, holy and acceptable and unconformed to the pattern of the world (Romans 12:1–2)? Is it holy or contaminated by vile deeds and habits? Is your spirit holy? What about the lust of the eyes (covetousness)? The Bible says covetousness is corruption in his sight (Matthew 5:28). What about boasting pride in what you have or do? Vain ambition, pride in appearance, pride in knowledge, pride in ability? These are forms of vile rottenness, out of conformity to Christ who says, "Take my yoke upon you, and learn of me; for I am meek and lowly in heart: and ye shall find rest unto your souls" (Matthew 11:29).

We are called to use the means of sanctification—the Word of God, prayer, obedience to God's commands, the sacraments, and worship together with a family of believers. The Holy Spirit takes our use of these means and makes them the method by which he sanctifies us. If you would know God's holiness, then use the means he has given you to know it.

1. Spend time in prayer.
2. Seriously, systematically meditate upon the Word of God.
3. Walk in a more determined obedience. Many a Christian is determined to walk in *most* of the ways of God's commandments, yet gets nowhere because of the unexplored areas that seem too much trouble. Repentance requires determination after total new obedience.

Would you know the holiness of God? Then you will have to know him who is holy, for apart from him, the thrice-holy God, nothing inhabits this sin-tainted world but death and corruption. Draw near to him. Show the glint of gold—the fruitful holiness of sanctification.

What is saving faith?

The grace of faith, whereby the elect are enabled to believe to the saving of their souls, is the work of the Spirit of Christ in their hearts, and is ordinarily wrought by the ministry of the Word; by which also, and by the administration of the sacraments and prayer it is increased and strengthened.
[Westminster Confession of Faith, chapter 14]

14

Three-Dimensional Faith

It was a dark night on the Mississippi highway from Jackson to Vicksburg. The sky was overcast, but at least the heavy rains of the last few days had stopped. The truck driver relaxed in the cab of his truck and watched the broken line of the road disappear monotonously beneath his cab, thankful that at least now the roads were dry and much safer.

Suddenly the twin taillights on the car in front of him melted into the road and disappeared! He sat bolt upright in his cab. That was inexplicable. It could not happen, and yet it just had. That thought went through his mind in a fraction of a second. In the next fraction of a second he saw the gaping black hole where a bridge had stood over the river.

He slammed on the brakes. The wheels stopped instantly, but there was no longer any road beneath them. His truck sailed silently and eerily into the black void. Breaking glass, he extricated himself and managed to swim to shore. He scrambled up the embankment, all the while hearing one car after another zoom smoothly into the gap, and disappear, followed by shrieks and a booming splash.

Finally he reached the road and frantically waved his hands at oncoming cars. They were no doubt surprised by this dripping scarecrow, but at least three passed him by before he was able to stop a driver from speeding over the edge. Sixteen people died that night. Each had faith in a bridge that the swollen river had torn away—a bridge that was out.

Many suppose that by the bridge of good works—morality, piety, church membership, good character, and religiosity— they can somehow make their way across that dark river safely into paradise. That bridge is out. The abyss is real, and it is eternal. I cannot imagine how frightening it must be to feel yourself, at the end of life, silently slipping over the edge into eternity without heeding God's call—without being justified, adopted, and sanctified.

> *For by grace are ye saved through faith; and that not of yourselves: it is the gift of God: Not of works, lest any man should boast.* [Ephesians 2:8–9]

We have seen what is required of God for salvation to become a reality. In chapters 14 and 15 we will see two things that are required of us: saving faith and repentance. Actually we have already looked at the first of these. Faith is step five in the outline of a plan of salvation that was presented in the introduction to part 2. Here is the bridge that crosses the river safely:

5. Faith
   a. What it is not: intellectual assent or temporal faith
   b. What it is: trusting in Jesus Christ alone

Saving, sanctifying faith is a work of God in our lives, but a mysterious work of God in which we play an active part. Growing in that faith is the transforming enterprise of sanctification, as we grow in seeking to glorify God and to enjoy him forever. It is the one most important ingredient in a life lived for God—a life worth living, and a life that stretches beyond the shadows of earth.

Unraveling the mystery

The *Westminster Confession of Faith* defines saving faith as "the work of the Spirit of Christ" that enables the elect to believe. Once again, the belief in view is no intellectual assent, nor is it emotion, though the Holy Spirit works both in the mind and the emotions to produce it. Saving faith is a reordering of mind, emotions, and will around a central proposition that we are absolutely certain is true. The *Confession's* chapter on saving faith carefully describes what this means in daily life terms:

> By this faith a Christian believeth to be true whatsoever is revealed in the Word, for the authority of God himself speaking therein; and acteth differently upon that which each particular passage thereof containeth; yielding obedience to the commands, trembling at the threatenings, and embracing the promises of God for this life and that which is to come. But the principle acts of saving faith are accepting, receiving, and resting upon Christ alone for justification, sanctification, and eternal life, by virtue of the covenant of grace.

Notice that the Christian does not work to *find* this faith. He or she *has* it. But *by this faith* Christianity becomes a living force in the individual and in the individual's world. *Faith* is the ultimate action word of Christianity. Grammatically it may be a noun, but in our sanctification faith acts as the empowering verb.

A mind in submission to truth

By this faith the Christian *believes to be true whatsoever is revealed in the world*. This does not mean the rational mind jumps over a mystical precipice. Quite the opposite. The rational mind is confident in the truth of the Scriptures because the authority of God is known to stand behind them. When a proposition comes along that seems to refute some truth in God's Word, saving faith is grounded in a firm base of authority and so is not blown away with the first cannonade volley. Rather the intellect, in submission to the Scriptures, kicks into a higher gear to investigate, knowing that all is not as it appears:

1. Is this new fact as factual as it appears, or is someone blowing smoke to make it look like unshakeable truth?
2. What is the logic of these facts? Have they been arranged in such a way as to bias the results? (This is a particularly important question in thinking through claims made in the sciences where researchers unintentionally color their findings according to what they "know" to be true. Recall part 1's example of the prehuman tooth that actually came from the mouth of a pig.)
3. Similarly, what are the presuppositions of those who have come up with this new "truth"? Do they have a hidden agenda?
4. What, precisely, does Scripture say about this subject? Have I been reading more into the text than is actually there, or misinterpreting something as literal that was written as figurative?

Many dates have been set for the Lord's return and the end of the world, using a creative reading of Scriptures. When the key date passed, some fell away from faith, when they should have fallen away from their naïve Bible teachers. Saving faith disciplines the mind under God's authority, correctly interpreting Scripture and carefully evaluating teachings in the light of solid personal study. We should heed Paul's advice to Timothy to be "a workman that needeth not to be ashamed, rightly dividing the word of truth" (2 Timothy 2:15).

When thoughtful, disciplined submission to the Word is practiced, faith is strengthened, rather than destroyed, by attacks on the authenticity of the Word. The Christian builds a healthy skepticism about human experts and the latest "revelation from God" received by some supposed evangelist.

One rather humorous case in point occurred recently in a gathering of New Testament scholars who decided that they were going to settle once and for all what Jesus did and did not say among his words quoted in the Gospels. The media evidently found this symposium particularly significant, for most newspapers and magazines disseminated the experts' astute findings to an extent unusual for an academic convocation. I don't know how many people really took these proceedings seriously, but the scholars took themselves seriously. That made their report all the more amusing. They divided all the quoted sayings of Christ into two categories: (1) his teachings on social justice and (2) everything else he is reported to have said, such as his uncomfortable moral commands or statements that he was God and the only way to salvation. Can you guess which statements were found to be genuine? At the feet of these scholars we learn for certain that Jesus wasn't God, but at least he was politically correct. Many attacks on Christianity are not quite so ridiculous, but most can be seen for what they are under critical examination with the mind of faith, the mind submitted to Scripture.

A life in submission to truth

By faith a Christian is prepared to change his thinking and his actions on the basis of what Scripture says. This faith also is based upon the certain knowledge that the very authority of God stands behind what is taught in his Word. Saving faith is ready to act upon what Scripture says. According to the *Confession*, the man or woman of faith reads Scripture diligently and attends to the preaching of the Word. The mind works critically in this regard. Using the example of setting a date for the return of Christ, suppose you are listening to a preacher who has discovered a hidden message in the number of letters contained in the King James text of Daniel 12. With some additional help from Matthew 24 and the number of words printed in red in his copy of Revelation, this teacher proclaims that the tribulation will strike next year, probably in February, and that you are called upon to sell all of your belongings and come gather to await the return of the Lord seven years hence.

A life in submission to the authority of God would not rush right home from hearing this dire message and hold a garage sale, selling even the garage. The mind disciplined by saving faith would have to be satisfied first about what Scripture really says and so asks more questions:

1. Does this interpretation of Scripture go along with clear passages through the rest of the Bible (for example, about not knowing the day or the hour at which the Master will come)?

2. Is this interpretation based upon clearly revealed teachings of what the text actually says? If this interpretation differs from what the church historically has taught in this regard, are there solid grounds for believing this particular Bible scholar has found something that has been missed by most others (which is seldom the case)?

3. Is the teacher basing all that is said on the authority of God or upon his or her own "new light"? If the teacher claims some new revelation of truth, the answer is obvious—that claim must be rejected on the basis of Hebrews 1:1. All revelation is now from Christ, and Christ has revealed himself in Scripture. There are new applications as the Holy Spirit relates the never-changing words of God to the changing context of our lives, but no new precepts.

You have the practice of reading your horoscope column each morning and ordering your life according to what an astrologer sees in the stars. Then you come to Christ, are regenerated, and begin to seek to follow God's will through faith. At first, as a new believer with a lot of old ways of living, you may not make a connection between reading the horoscope column and trusting the God who rules the heavens and the earth. You might even decide that God put the stars where they are, so that is why they influence our lives. Then one day a neighbor takes you aside and lovingly points out that the Bible has strong words to say against astrology and that the Christian is to leave behind those elements of the world and conform to a new pattern of faith. A choice must be made: Will you submit to God's revealed authority and repent of what he condemns?

The person with saving faith may have problems getting rid of the old habits, but he or she has no question about who has the authority and must be obeyed.

What if the application to life is not so clear-cut? A teacher says you must live one way because that is what the Bible says. You read those passages yourself, and you aren't so certain that this is a correct interpretation. Or another teacher contends that the text says something entirely different. Such questions must be answered carefully, with much prayer for discernment and the help of others more mature in faith. When a text is unclear and seems open to more than one view, there is a more certain text elsewhere that covers at least the principle behind the question. God sometimes makes us dig for the truth, but he never leaves important truth unavailable. However the search for truth proceeds, if the heart is intent on obeying what Scripture actually says, faith will be nurtured toward maturity (James 1:2–5). The key principles of saving faith involve where the individual looks for ultimate authority and whether the individual is willing to submit to that authority.

Mind and life in submission to Christ

Submission to the authority of Scripture obviously has much to do with God's working of saving faith in the believer's life. However, the *Confession* goes on to relate that this is a subordinate part of the story. "But the principle acts of saving faith are accepting, receiving, and resting upon Christ alone for justification, sanctification, and eternal life, by virtue of the covenant of grace." Faith is at its most active when pointed at Christ as Lord of the covenant of grace. We *do* faith through three dimensions:

1. accepting
2. receiving
3. resting

Those may not sound like very active words, but in God's economy they act within the mystery of the dual source of faith—God and the believer. Saving faith has its source in us as we live accepting, receiving, resting lives of submission to Christ and his truth. And the source of saving faith is in God. It is his Holy Spirit that accepts, receives, and rests through us. But where does our part leave off and God's begin? When does intellectual assent to the truth, which does not save, become righteousness-dispensing grace that does?

Living faith in three dimensions

Accept, receive, and *rest* are three separate, repetitive actions of the sanctifying Christian life. They begin in a once-for-all act. The lost, hopeless unbeliever is confronted with the claims of Christ and sees in them the only hope for peace with God. Christ extends the good news, asking, "Will you accept me into your life as Savior and Lord?" The Holy Spirit enables the words of this message to sink into the consciousness and a life of rebellion to be turned to faith that this message is true and available. The response: "Yes! Yes, I believe, that Jesus is the Christ, God become human of a virgin, who died to take the penalty for my sins and conquered death so that I may never die. Yes, I cast myself on you."

In that moment of *accepting*, the Holy Spirit already is working another sort of faith in the one who is being reborn. The truth and lordship of Christ have been accepted mentally and emotionally; now the cleansing, justifying, adopting work of Christ is *received* and the faith worked in the person by the Holy Spirit is accounted by the Father as righteousness in the sacrifice of Christ. At the same time a third dimension of spirituality is born into the soul: a new worldview or organizing principle that revolutionizes the reborn life. The person's life foundation had been built upon external morality and selfishness, but now the basis for making choices and relating to self, others, and God *rests* upon submissive, obedient, saving faith:

1. The reborn Christian *accepts* the gospel as a personal reality.
2. The reborn Christian *receives* Christ's righteousness before God.
3. The reborn Christian *rests* his or her life on a new foundation.

All three are God's works and our acceptance of Christ in faith comes through the Holy Spirit. It is "not of works, lest any man should boast" (Ephesians 2:9). The founder of Gordon College and a missions leader of the nineteenth century, A. J. Gordon, once was riding on a train when he presented the gospel to the man seated next to him. He had explained that it is through faith in Christ that we are redeemed, when the man broke in, "Sir, I heartily disagree with you. I do not believe for one instant that God is going to admit a man to heaven merely on the basis of some little scrap of theological paper which you call faith. But, rather, I believe that God will make a searching inquiry into one's character and morals and his good works." As he said this the conductor came by, and they offered him their tickets.

"Did you notice," asked Gordon a moment later, "how that conductor eyed our tickets very carefully and paid virtually no attention to our persons or our character?"

Even the dimension of receiving, which would seem utterly passive, has an active element. I have known people who refuse to take the action of receiving righteousness. They may, in fact, be saved children of God, but they seemingly have never mentally received as theirs the assurance of forgiveness promised by Scripture. For whatever reason in the past or present, such people live as if unforgiven and fret that the joy and victory that other believers experience have not come. There is no victory of faith, for the sin of self-unforgiveness affronts the God who has forgiven. Failure to receive God's promises is a self-induced birth defect in faith that nurses a grudge and denies that God can keep those promises. It might be that faith has never been born, but possibly it means the person rebelliously gets perverse, childish satisfaction in self-punishment.

Faith is recumbency

Three-dimensional faith does not just work at the moment of salvation. The process works over and over, every day of the born-again life. Living, saving faith is not *just* the bridge over the river we will someday cross. If that is all it is in one's thinking, saving faith is not yet part of the life. Nor is saving faith a toll booth we pass to get to God's super highway. Saving faith is both the bridge at the end of earthly life and the highway beneath the wheels. Through that faith the Christian "believes to be true whatsoever is revealed in the Word" for today, whether faith that God can help overcome some illness, face the challenge of service, or deal with a problem with sin. Through three-dimensional faith God enables his child to

1. *accept* what the Bible says as a personal reality,
2. *receive* the promises that pertain to God's presence and direction in that kind of situation, and
3. move out with assurance that *rests* on the foundation of Christ.

The Puritans of the seventeenth and eighteenth centuries used an interesting term to describe this faith. Saving faith, said the Puritans, is *recumbency*. Missionary John Paton grasped the meaning of that word when he began to translate the Gospel of John for the natives of the New Hebrides. He discovered that their language seemed to contain no word for *faith*. Yet the gospel would hardly make sense without it. After weeks of mulling over this linguistic puzzle, he returned to his home after a long journey with his guide. His native friend sat in a chair on the porch, put his feet up on a stool, heaved a great sigh of relief, and said something Paton could not understand. After some explanation Paton finally understood that the single word his native guide used meant, "I have rested all of my weight here."

That was it! That was what the Puritans had meant by *recumbency* or recumbent faith. Saving faith rests all the weight upon the Lord.

Charles Spurgeon had a similar illustration for recumbent faith. A limpet is a small mollusk with a cone-shaped shell that lives by the seashore. It does one thing outstandingly: It has a foot by which it clings tenaciously to a rock or the underneath side of a ship. Spurgeon said that if you sneak up quietly on a limpet and hit it with a stick it will fall off the rock. But then try to hit another limpet nearby. It has been warned. You can hit it until you break your stick, but you will not knock it from the rock. It will hold on as if it knows its very life depends on clinging to the rock. "Faith," said Spurgeon, "is clinging to Jesus Christ." In the midst of the tumultuous seas of this world it is clinging to Christ as if salvation itself depends on him. Faith is the key to heaven, but it is not just knowing about Jesus Christ. Nor is it trusting God for such things as safety, health, and wealth, which are temporal and will pass away. Saving faith is clinging to Jesus Christ alone for salvation. Only as we depend totally on him can we know that God has forgiven us and made us new. "Believe on the Lord Jesus Christ, and thou shalt be saved" (Acts 16:31).

This is faith that behaves differently and thinks differently because it is focused on Jesus Christ and his work to bring the Christian through justification, sanctification, and eternal life into a covenant relationship with God. The Christian's presuppositions about the world differ from those of others because of the working of scriptural truth into the mind—the foundation. Saving faith cannot help but make substantive changes in all that a person is. That is the distinction James makes between faith and works (James 1:22–27; 2:14–25). There is a kind of faith that is intellect or all emotion—all bells and whistles, flash and mirrors—but no substance. That is the sort the Bible calls "dead." To understand the dimensions of alive faith we begin with Ephesians 2:8–9. By God's grace we are saved *through faith*. Here is the first clue to the mystery.

Faith is the conduit

Through faith means "by" or "by means of faith." Yet we can speak of *through* in another sense as well, for faith acts as a conduit. Through it courses the grace of God. In the Holy Land I remember visiting a massive Roman aqueduct along the eastern shore of the Mediterranean. It stretched as far as the eye could see. This aqueduct was perhaps fifteen or twenty feet high and massive, supported by thousands of arches. The centuries have not been kind to this wonder, and for many centuries it has lain unused. There were great gaps in the aqueduct, and it no longer carried water to the Roman capital. That is what our faith is like. It is the aqueduct that brings to us the water of grace. The water of grace is the important thing, but grace moves through an intact aqueduct of faith.

An elderly woman was known to have led a serene, victorious life. People were curious to know the secret through which she had been so blessed and had blessed others. One person looked her up and asked, "Are you the woman with the great faith?" She responded, "No, but I am a woman with a great God." She had learned that it is not the conduit that helps us; it is the water that flows through it. In the great cities of the Roman world aqueducts channeled water to fountains where the people drew water in pots for their families. The Romans enjoyed giving things an aesthetic appeal, and they developed fantastically carved stone and bronze statuary to decorate their fountains. The life of faith is attractive. God crafted the faith of this woman into something lovely to behold, something whose very beauty pointed others to Christ. The important thing of the aqueducts and fountains, however, was the water, and the importance of faith is the grace it carries. That is what the writers of the *Westminster Confession* realized when they said of saving faith, the conduit of grace:

> This faith is different in degrees, weak or strong; may be often and many ways assailed and weakened, but gets the victory; growing up in many to the attainment of a full assurance through Christ, who is both the author and finisher of our faith.

Nurturing three-dimensional faith

Time, conquerors, and the elements ravaged those strong Roman conduits. Throughout the New Testament Christians are being urged to keep in good repair and strengthen their faith, so that it can quench the flaming arrows of Satan in the day of battle (Ephesians 6:16). The *Confession*, then, gives some good advice to those who feel weak and uncertain. This advice begins in the observation that saving faith usually comes into an unbeliever as the Holy Spirit applies Scripture. God normally chooses to bring saving faith through the ministry of the Word. It may come as a preacher applies a Bible passage, or as a seeker remembers some long-ago Sunday school lesson or opens the Bible to seek answers. It may come through the witness of a believer who shares the good news. The point is that the Holy Spirit applies the content of Scripture in the context of the sinner's experience.

If that is how one comes to have saving faith, faith for living also is strengthened through the same combination of Scripture and experience: "the ministry of the Word, the administration of the sacraments, and prayer." One comes to experience a recumbent faith as one experiences God. The longer and more fully the conduit has been carrying water, the more natural comes the trust of God as Friend. The friend of God is blessed whose delight is in the law of the Lord, attached to the conduit of grace, "and he shall be like a tree planted by the rivers of water, that bringeth forth his fruit in his season; his leaf also shall not wither; and whatsoever he doeth shall prosper" (Psalm 1:3).

Scripture sets before us a model for what living, three-dimensional faith should look like. If the life of faith can be seen as an Olympic event Abraham is scored as the record holder. A close look at that record-shattering event, however, tells us a lot about how faith is nurtured. Abraham's life shows the attainable faith that fails more often than it succeeds, but in the end still stands. Abraham's faith faltered more often than it conquered, and it matured over many years.

God's call on Abram in Ur of the Chaldees was unexpected and possibly unwanted. Ur was the foremost city of the world, and Abram was a well-connected Ur urbanite whose family had likely bowed for generations to the moon god, the chief deity of the Chaldeans. God called on Abram to leave behind the settled lands of Ur and Haran and make a career move at age seventy-five—to become a wandering patriarch. He was to leave behind all but his own immediate family and strike out alone. He was to leave behind allegiance to old relationships and former gods to follow the God who would make of him a nation, at best a long-term project. Abram accepted the call and immediately obeyed all of God's direction in faith, right? Not quite.

Abram took along much of his family, including Lot, whose lifestyle and godliness were anything but exemplary.

At the first sign of famine, Abram left the land to which God had sent him for the safety of Egypt. While in Egypt he passed off his wife Sarai as his sister in an act of cowardice. He only returned to where he was supposed to be when he was deported. When God wasn't quick enough to give him a son he tried to help God out, first by offering his servant to be his heir and then fathering a child by a servant girl. When God told him that the promise would not come through this son Ishmael, but through a son yet to be born, he argued to try to place the blessing on Ishmael instead. And to show that he was, indeed, a slow learner he then became afraid of another king and tried to pass off his wife as his sister once again.

Throughout these years the Bible also records how Abram, whose name became *Abraham*, called upon God and slowly learned more about God's covenant promise with him and God's great provision for him. Ever so slowly his faith was taking three-dimensional form. But the final test of that mature faith came perhaps fifty years after Abram received that first call of God. His son Isaac was born when he was 100 years old, and he saw that child of promise grow into adulthood.

Only then did God give Abraham his final challenge, one that thrills and horrifies us in Genesis 22: "Take now thy son, thine only son Isaac, whom thou lovest, and get thee into the land of Moriah; and offer him there for a burnt offering upon one of the mountains which I will tell thee of" (v. 2). It sounds a monstrous thing for God to suggest, but oddly we are not told that Abraham presented any of his usual arguments. He simply got up, cut the wood, gathered Isaac and his servants, and set out.

When Mount Moriah was visible in the distance, Abraham and Isaac left their servants with a singular confidence about what was to come: "Abide ye here with the ass; and I and the lad will go yonder and worship, *and come again to you*" (v. 5). Isaac turns to his father, remarking that they have not brought the lamb of sacrifice. His father answers, "My son, God will provide himself a lamb for a burnt offering" (v. 8). Yet God does not provide until the altar is built, the wood is placed, Isaac is bound and placed on the altar, and the knife is raised to strike. Only in that last second did an angel intervene with the ram that was to replace the son.

Living faith took the chance that God was faithful, based on the faithfulness God had shown in the past, based on the Word of God, based on long conversations and even arguments with God in prayer, based on past personal failures through which God had been faithful.

Not yet ready to sacrifice a son on the altar for God? Through faith we realize that in Jesus that will not be necessary. For we know what Abraham could only dimly see, that Mount Moriah would, many hundreds of years later, be the site of a city called Jerusalem, where God would place his Son, his only Son Jesus, whom he loved, on the altar for us.

Only he did not stay his hand. Such love is strong enough that we can take recumbency in it. And when we realize that through growing faith, then we are ready for our own walk up Moriah.

What does it mean to repent?

Repentance unto life is an evangelical grace. . . . By it a sinner, out of the sight and sense, not only of the danger, but also of the filthiness and odiousness of his sins, as contrary to the holy nature and righteous law of God, and upon the apprehension of his mercy in Christ to such as are penitent, so grieves for and hates his sins as to turn from them all unto God, purposing and endeavoring to walk with him in all the ways of his commandments.
[Westminster Confession of Faith, chapter 15]

15

The Gift of a Broken Heart

Repentance and faith are inseparable in Scripture. There can be no genuine repentance without faith. There is no genuine faith without repentance. The two are heads and tails of one coin.

On the day the church was born, the day of Pentecost, pilgrims from all over the Jewish world were visiting Jerusalem. A multitude of them gathered to see the strange happenings outside one house that was perhaps not far from the temple. A group of men shouted to them in all of their own languages. The city was packed with people for the holy day, and dozens, then hundreds, then thousands strained to hear the story of Jesus of Nazareth. They heard that this teacher and healer was the very Son of God, the long-expected Messiah, that he had been killed by the religious leaders, and that God had raised him from death. Many had heard of this man, whose words and touch brought healing to the body and to the soul. Now they learned that he could make all things new. Thousands as one came to believe Peter's words that day. They knew that if all of this was true, then a response surely was demanded.

"Brothers, what shall we do?" they asked.

Peter did not launch into an explanation of justification by faith by the blood of Jesus Christ. Obviously, the Holy Spirit already was working faith into thousands of hearts. And with faith came understanding that it was their sins that had nailed God to a cross. The Bible says this thought pierced them emotionally as they had pierced the Christ physically. They were cut, wounded, and probed to the heart.

"What shall we do?"
"What is required of us?"
"What response is appropriate to such news?"

Peter told them to take the step that would seal their new allegiance to Christ—repent.

> *When they heard this, they were pricked in their heart, and said unto Peter and to the rest of the apostles, Men and brethren, what shall we do? Then Peter said unto them, Repent, and be baptized every one of you in the name of Jesus Christ for the remission of sins.* [Acts 2:37–38a]

Faith and repentance

Repentance will not save. Yet you cannot be saved without it. Merely repenting of sin does not guarantee an entrance into heaven, any more than being sorry for committing murder guarantees that the prescribed penalty will not be exacted. Even repentance with true contrition, confession, and a promise not to do it again will not impress a judge and jury at a murder trial. It won't work with God either. A person also must give Jesus Christ a proper place as Lord of life.

Some people have a false faith that is merely intellectual assent. Counterfeit faith contains no tempered steel to cut to the heart. It accepts the facts, opines that they are interesting and even significant in a historical sort of way, and then turns to other matters. There is no crisis of understanding that this news demands personal attention, commitment, and an amended lifestyle. Some people have false repentance, deciding that what Christ requires is for them to try harder to keep the rules.

Counterfeit repentance decides that one can do enough to approach God. Counterfeit repentance of another sort endeavors to do better but trusts only in its own works.

True repentance in faith, by contrast, changes a person's perspective of God and the world, so that all things center in Jesus Christ. Through true repenting, faith changes God's perspective of the person, in that God no longer sees a rebel sinner, but rather a child whose sins are covered in the righteousness of Christ. True repentance changes a person by instilling God's perspective of the world and of life. Nothing so transforms a person's wants and wishes and loves as to see things from God's perspective. The *Westminster Confession* lists transforming elements that come with this new view of things:

1. The sinner sees and senses the danger of rebelling against God.
2. The sinner sees and senses how dirty and disgusting his or her sins appear to God.
3. The sinner sees and senses how holy and pure God is and what righteousness before God truly means in the light of Christ and the Word.
4. The sinner sees and senses that forgiving mercy has become available in Christ to the penitent.
5. The sinner grieves for and hates sins and turns from them all.
6. The sinner purposes and endeavors to walk with God in all the ways of his commandments.

The human soul is made up of mind, heart, and will, so all three are involved in these aspects of repentance. The person intellectually grasps that sin, because of its heinousness, will be punished, and that there is a divine remedy for sin. The sinner must come to know the way of salvation as it has been divinely appointed by God. Only through Christ, his grace, and death on the cross can eternal hope be found.

Legal strivings

Some of the deepest thinking on what it means to repent comes from an eighteenth-century pastor named Jonathan Edwards. The First Great Awakening in the 1730s turned a large portion of the population of New England back to God from a life of superficial faith and works righteousness. Edwards was one of the keenest tools of God in that revival. He is called by some the greatest theologian ever born on this continent. Observing how repentance and faith and how mind, heart, and will worked together in those he had seen turn to God, Edwards described a "legal striving" that first occurred when "the corruption of the heart first discovered itself." He observed how awakened understanding of God's holiness and personal sinfulness emotionally afflicted the soul:

> As they are gradually more and more convinced of the corruption and wickedness of their hearts, they seem to themselves to grow worse and worse, harder and blinder, and more desperately wicked, instead of growing better. They are ready to be discouraged by it, and oftentimes never think themselves so *far off* from good as when they are *nearest*. . . . When awakenings first begin, their consciences are commonly most exercised about their *outward* vicious course, or other acts of sin; but *afterwards* are more burdened with a sense of heart-sins, the dreadful corruption of their nature, their enmity against God, the pride of their hearts, their unbelief, their rejection of Christ, the Stubbornness and obstinacy of their wills; and the like. In many, God makes much use of their own experience, in the course of their awakenings and endeavors after saving good, to convince them of their own vile emptiness and universal depravity. [*A Narrative of Surprising Conversions*, section 2, italics in original]

Can such a discouraging view help the sinner find God and be part of faith and repentance? Edwards said that the deeper the sinner is drawn to probe the inner person and the more aware he or she understands this utter depravity, the greater the conviction of "absolute dependence on his sovereign power and grace." This feeling of absolute dependence transforms the heart of the sinner coming to God and the Christian who should be closer to God. It knocks out all the human props. The heart is broken as the mind understands the necessity of a Mediator. It hurts to contemplate personal wickedness and guilt, insufficiency and pollution, vile emptiness and lawlessness. But to the extent that I do understand those things I depend on God in faith, and my will is turned to wanting those things that benefit me and please God. Heart affections converge on God.

When Paul tells us in Ephesians 6:10–17 to put on the full armor of God so that we can stand against Satan, he starts with the belt of truth that is to be buckled around the waist. People in Paul's day knew that affections could take away appetite and give a flutter to the stomach, and so the seat of the emotions often was placed in the intestines, the belly and bowels. What could a greeting card company have done with that? There is no area of our being so prone to delusion as the emotions, so Paul tells us to clamp a solid belt of truth around them. No one comes to God or grows as a Christian without searching into the inner person, the dark corners that are often subconscious dwellings for dirty little creatures we didn't even know existed within us. To probe the self and repent of heart sins is a wrenching experience, but one King David knew was unavoidable if he were to find peace from the sin in his own life:

> Behold, I was shapen in iniquity and in sin did my mother conceive me. Behold thou desireth truth in the inward parts: and in the hidden part thou shalt make me to know wisdom. . . . Create in me a clean heart, O God; and renew a right spirit within me. . . . The sacrifices of God are a bro-

ken spirit: a broken and a contrite heart, O God, thou wilt not despise. [Psalm 51:5–6, 10, 17]

These legal strivings of the heart break the spirit as they show the cost of sin. In Old Testament times repentance for sin involved a demonstration of sin's offensiveness. The repentant worshiper purchased to sacrifice the best animal available—unblemished. Repentance came with cost. It involved cost for the one who brought the sacrifice and rather more cost for the animal whose throat was cut. A great many of those who came with their sacrifices to the altar were going through the motions of religious tradition, but those who got the point God was making saw that their sins inflicted hideous cost. That thought must have broken their heart as they contemplated the implications of the chasm between humanity and God. In Psalm 51 David saw that price, saying that a broken heart is the true sacrifice God wants. In Romans 12:1 Paul applies this brokenness to all of the life of faith. He urges us, "by the mercies of God, that ye present your bodies a living sacrifice, holy, acceptable unto God, which is your reasonable service." The broken and contrite believer continually brings the self and lays it on the altar in repentance and submission. A broken, contrite spirit is pliable, able to be bent and smoothed into the shape God desires, not the shape of the world pattern (Romans 12:2). Faith and repentance, resting in God and being broken to absolute dependence: This is the proper act of worship.

The lost doctrine of repentance

R. B. Kuiper wrote that people have lost sight of two things, and as a result, the church of the Lamb slain for sins no longer preaches that sinners must repent. First, they have lost the meaning of sin. It is seen as a trifle, a peccadillo, something that can be excused as part of being human. Even those set apart to lead seem to have forgotten that their nature is fallen, debased, depraved, and nothing like

God first made it. They do not see that sin inevitably brings death. Second, people have lost the real vision of the holiness of God. They do not lift their eyes, so they never undergo the awakening described by Jonathan Edwards. They never abhor themselves and repent in dust and ashes.

Scripture stresses the importance of repentance. Both Old and New Testaments call upon people to repent. Noah was a preacher of righteousness, calling the doomed people around him to leave their wicked ways and turn to God. All the prophets called for a leaving of sin and a radical turning away to God. Ezekiel 18 proclaims one of the best explanations of how and why to repent:

> The soul that sinneth, it shall die. . . . But if the wicked will turn from all his sins that he hath committed, and keep all my statutes, and do that which is lawful and right, he shall surely live, he shall not die. Repent, and turn yourselves from all your transgressions; so iniquity shall not be your ruin. Cast away from you all your transgressions, whereby ye have transgressed; and make you a new heart and a new spirit: for why will ye die, O house of Israel? For I have no pleasure in the death of him that dieth, saith the Lord GOD: wherefore turn yourselves, and live ye. [vv. 20a, 21, 30b–32]

John the Baptist took up this refrain as a new day dawned over the world: "But when he saw many of the Pharisees and Sadducees come to his baptism, he said unto them, O generation of vipers, who hath warned you to flee from the wrath to come? Bring forth therefore fruits meet for repentance" (Matthew 3:7–8).

After Jesus reached his thirtieth year and began his ministry, Matthew records: "From that time Jesus began to preach, and to say, Repent: for the kingdom of heaven is at hand" (4:17). The burden of his heart and ministry for a world of sinners was that they should repent. One of his most beautiful parables concerned an errant, prodigal child who came to repentance (Luke 15:11–32). In nearby text he described the joy in heaven over a sinner who repents

(v. 7). In Luke 13 disciples ask Jesus why "bad things happen to good people," to use the contemporary expression. They gave the example of an incident in which Galileans who came to the temple to worship were killed in a confrontation with Roman soldiers. What had these people done wrong to bring such judgment upon themselves in the very act of worship? "Suppose ye that these Galilaeans were sinners above all the Galilaeans, because they suffered such things? I tell you, Nay: but, except ye repent, ye shall all likewise perish" (vv. 2b–3).

Christians are to be about the proclamation of repentance. After Jesus' resurrection he told his disciples that repentance and forgiveness of sins was to be preached in the name of Jesus in all the world, for "ye are witnesses of these things" (Luke 24:47–48). The call to repentance was to be integral to gospel proclamation. At the end of Scripture this word still is on the lips of Jesus. Eight times in the Revelation of John he commands that his church should repent. In all, fifty-three times the New Testament commands men and women to repent.

One can't help but be struck by the theme of repentance when reading accounts of the awakenings in Edwards's Massachusetts, Asahel Nettleton's frontier West of the early 1800s, the Welsh revival in the early 1900s, or Korea's of the 1960s. There was an intensity of realized sin and absolute dependence on Jesus as Mediator. It was the seriousness with which Martin Luther appraised his own sin that gave justification by grace its revolutionizing power in the 1500s. Many church historians have tried to psychologize such workings in the heart, calling them products of an unhealthy society and self-image. But isn't it interesting that where deep repentance has oppressed, deep faith has flourished? Those who saw how much God had forgiven felt a debt of love.

Debtors to mercy

Indebtedness surely changes people. In Romans 1:14 this feeling of owed love empowers the apostle Paul: "I am debtor both to the Greeks, and to the Barbarians; both to the wise and to the unwise." What an enigmatic text. How could Paul have been a debtor to the Greeks and to the non-Greeks? What had they done for him? Let us look at some of the things they did for him:

> Five times he was beaten with thirty-nine lashes.
> Three times he was beaten with rods.
> Once he was stoned and left for dead.
> He was shipwrecked.
> He was in danger from Jews, in danger from Gentiles, in danger from robbers, without food, sleep, clothing.
> He carried around the burdens of hundreds of Christians around the known world (2 Corinthians 11:23–33).

Nevertheless, Paul felt a debt, a master motive that impelled a forceful life: Jesus Christ had given him everything. He could only give obedient love and faithfulness in return. Paul had life everlasting, forgiveness for the "chief of sinners," pardon, reconciliation, adoption into the family, sonship with the most high God, and an inheritance with the saints forever. "For to me to live is Christ," summarized his outlook (Philippians 1:21a). Paul owed an incalculable debt. But when he approached Christ on bended knee with overflowing heart to try to repay this debt, he ever found the Savior with outstretched hand and pointed finger, saying, "Go ye into all the world." This incalculable, inestimable debt was transferred by Christ toward those who needed Paul's ministry. He owed to them all that he owed to Christ. They held the promissory note.

The indebtedness that grows from repentance pertains to every believer. It attaches to all who receive forgiveness. Each Christian comes to the Lord and says, "I know you don't need anything, let alone anything I have to give. But, God, what I do have is yours, and I will regard the debt I owe to you as owed to whomever you wish me to serve in your name." Everyone who has received the gospel has received it as a steward, responsible to the God who gave it and to all others for whom it is intended. The obligation is universal in the church. It descends upon each of us.

Thanks for nothing

I talked to a man who said he had given up the church and Christianity because it seemed to him that the idea was that he was supposed to be under some debt of gratitude to God. He did not like that idea. He did not feel grateful at all, so he quit going to church. It soon was obvious why he felt that way. Unlike Paul, he had not received salvation; he had not received an inheritance with the saints; he had not become a new creature in Jesus Christ; he had not been given all things. So far as he knew, he had received nothing at all. He was precisely that grateful.

One cannot share what is not possessed. For many the attitude of Paul is absolutely alien. They cannot understand him at all. For Paul it was equally unthinkable that he had been given much and would do nothing in return. "I am obligated," he said to the world. And with that he set forth to cut a swath across the continent with the glorious gospel of Christ. And the cause of Christ has advanced around the globe to the extent that repentant people felt that way:

"I am debtor," cried William Carey as he sailed for India with the gospel.

"I am debtor," cried David Livingstone as he plunged into the interior of Africa, going where Europeans had never before been seen.

"I am debtor," cried Hudson Taylor as he approached the hundreds of millions in China.

"I am debtor," cried Lord Shaftsbury as he gave himself to the poor, helpless, homeless, ragged urchins of the slums of London.

"I am debtor," cried Florence Nightingale as she followed the trail of battlefield blood to bind the wounded and care for the dying.

"I am debtor," cried Kagawa as he took the gospel to the slums of Tokyo.

We are morally bound to pay the debts of forgiveness. Unfortunately, what most of us must now repent of is how little we have regarded what God has done for us. If you do not feel that he has, that is your problem.

Your first love

If you do know Christ you may be like many who began their walk of faith aflame with love for God. But somewhere along the line the flame has dwindled from lack of fuel. You have not continued to put on the belt of truth of Ephesians 6, digging out those dark corners and filling their emptiness with affection for God.

Jesus came by way of letter to the great city of Ephesus, which was renowned for its idolatry, in particular its licentious worship of the goddess Diana. Ruins have been uncovered from vast brothels that flourished in the city. But Jesus did not condemn those things with laser-like words. He took aim instead at the Christian community and said, "I have somewhat against thee, because thou hast left thy first love. Remember therefore from whence thou art fallen, and repent, and do the first works; or else I will come unto thee quickly, and will remove thy candlestick out of his place, except thou repent" (Revelation 2:4–5).

Surely these words cut to the hearts of the Ephesian Christians. This was meant to be radical surgery. Today he comes to us with eyes of flame to illumine the deep, dark corners we have failed to sweep out ourselves. He pronounces his judgment: "You have left your first love!"

For all the blessings we have received, few feel Paul's obligation; most have never lifted a finger to labor for Christ. Some think coming to church, sitting in a pew and listening half-attentively to a sermon is labor. The lips strain to mumble a prayer. The mind struggles to pay attention rather than think of the ball game that will be on television in the afternoon. This is the life that needs to be transformed through the religious affections that grow out of awakened feelings of obligation to God. The life of the Christian needs to be rebroken and reshaped.

There was much for the Ephesians to rejoice in. They had labored tirelessly and borne persecution in the midst of an ungodly city. They had had no truck with wickedness. They had rebuked those who taught impure doctrine. Were we members of that church we probably would be feeling smug about our high level of spirituality. Yet Christ does not rebuke the village atheists, the debauched revelers, and the frauds outside the community of faith. The Ephesians' problem lay in a lack of heart affection, the fruit of thankful, contrite repentance. No matter how a married couple works to keep the house tidy, the dishes washed, and the beds made, if their hearts lack love for one another that marriage is in trouble. In Revelation 2 Jesus Christ the bridegroom draws the bride to the side and says, "What has happened to your love for me? There is something amiss with our relationship because your ardor for me has cooled."

Take a moment to put on the belt of truth right now and evaluate your heart response of affection. If you are a Christian there was a day—you remember it well—when God lifted the veil from your mind and the scales from your eyes and you looked upon the cross. The twins of faith and repentance overwhelmed you as, for the first time, you understood for whom the Savior died. How your heart melted by the fire of that redeeming love. You embraced Christ with tears of gratitude. You were made new, and all things around you seemed new. Your heart nearly burst with song, and you delighted to go to him in prayer. It was pure joy to meditate on new truths in Scripture. Times spent with God's people in worship were sacred. It was so disappointing that there were no more times your small group could meet for prayer and fellowship. Why did so few seem to come back for Sunday night worship when the praise songs and sharing times were so edifying? You loved Christ with a love like that of Samuel Rutherford. One of the authors of the *Westminster Confession*, this Puritan's love for Christ was intense. Rutherford said that, though a river drawn from hell separated Christ from him, he gladly would have plunged in and waded across, so that he might be with his Beloved. This is a first love.

But something happened to your first love. It became harder to get up on Sunday morning. The preacher was invariably boring and talked far too long. The day that was holy became a day of chores or personal or family fun. You can't wait to get out to desecrate the Sabbath, to give it over to things of the world. The glitter and allure of worldliness once seemed to be of little interest as you basked in Christ's sun. Now it seems strangely bright again, and you cannot seem to see heaven as clearly. The pleasures of the body have become more important than the prosperity of the soul.

Remember the height

There is a two-part remedy for the sickness of having left your first love: (1) remember and (2) repent. Repentance again holds the key to renewal. Scripture often calls us to remember the eager times gone by. For the Ephesians it wasn't that long. This was the A.D. 90s, and many older members of the church could remember the glory years when Paul taught daily and the people grew in numbers and spiritual life.

Do you remember the joyous discovery that life could be different than it had been, that hatred and bitterness and strife did not have to rule, that the past did not have to enslave? Remember that freedom?

Do you remember the intimate quiet times alone with him, perhaps by the beach or under a sharply scented pine tree? Remember the serendipity of being shown a new idea by the Holy Spirit?

Do you remember . . . ?

If we find ourselves far from God, he has not moved. Remember the height from which we have fallen? Notice that Jesus does not tell the Ephesians that they have slipped or declined in their love but that they have fallen. It is a drastic, serious thing. But we are not far from where we were in the proximity of repentance. Charles Spurgeon said:

> Men come to Christ for the first time, of a sudden, in a moment. We receive it in an instant, like a gift from a king, the gift of eternal life. We are born anew in a moment as a child is born into this world. It is of a sudden that we repent and are converted the first time. And so it is, as I have noted throughout all the years of my ministry, that when people return unto God, they come back with a leap, in a moment; of a sudden they repent and return to him.

You can no more return to Christ slowly than you could come to Christ slowly. You just remember, repent, and return, doing what you did in the beginning.

As a faithful Physician, Christ not only prescribes the remedy but observes the consequences for failing to take it. For a church this was serious—"I will come to you and remove your lampstand from its place." You will cease to be a functioning part of the body of Christ, disqualified as a true church. A great many religious organizations get together to "play church" but have no reality. They are just going through the motions and will likely never repent because they have few or no saved members. They are a ghost ship cast adrift.

In freezing temperatures a person suffering from exposure and hypothermia may suffer at first, but then the pain lessens and a certain feeling of warmth spreads through the body. It would be fine to simply sit in the snow and go to sleep. There will be time to get inside later. Only later never comes. It is so with the church. We will either repent and do the first works or we will rebel against the Spirit of God and find ourselves slipping deeper into a fatal slumber from which we shall never rise. Individuals cannot lose their salvation if in Christ. Churches have no such assurance, and I fear that a great many have already slid into oblivion without missing a single Sunday service.

Brokenness before God—the buckling on of the belt of truth—means ultimate victory. Weakness in God's army assures strength: "To him who overcomes, I will give the right to eat from the tree of life, which is in the paradise of God." We started in a garden, and life is pointed toward another garden, one in which our first place of fellowship with God will be re-created. Meanwhile we are in the spiritual battlefield, where we need absolute dependence on God—the dependence that only repentance grows.

What assurances does the Christian have in death?

Death, being the wages of sin, why are not the righteous delivered from death, seeing all their sins are forgiven in Christ?
The righteous shall be delivered from death itself at the last day, and even in death are delivered from the sting and curse of it; so that, although they die, yet it is out of God's love, to free them perfectly from sin and misery, and to make them capable of further communion with Christ, in glory, which they then enter upon. [Westminster Larger Catechism, question 85]

16

The Stinger Is Gone

Evangelism Explosion witnessing teams have asked millions of people a question that I now ask: Have you come to a place in your spiritual life where you know for certain that if you were to die today you would go to heaven?

You may think you don't have to face that issue today, but you really don't know whether you will see another sunset. Unless Christ returns soon, there will be a day on which you will die. At this point, earthly life is not open-ended. Your situation is terminal, and you will either face that final day of change with confidence or with dread and fear.

This book is about transformed living through Jesus Christ, who makes all things new. No one lives a transformed life until he or she settles the matter of death. I believe one reason for the fear that so infests our churches arises from a weakness in faithfulness to the Word of God regarding the future hope of the believer.

I see three reasons for fearing death:

1. You have no adequate answer to the question of where you will spend eternity. You are in rebellion against God, and you have no ground for hope that he will accept you.
2. You have accepted Christ as Lord and Savior but believe that, at any moment, you may sin and fall from grace. Perhaps you have been taught that even one

unconfessed sin will send you to hell or to some neth-
erworld of purgatory. Perhaps you believe that you will
be prepared for eternity only through doing the right
things in the right way and having the right prayers
said over your dying form.

3. Something clouds your eyes. Maybe it is worldliness, for
you have neglected your love of the Lord. At the very
least you would feel uncomfortable standing in God's
presence when you have sought to be with him so rarely.
Or perhaps you feel depressed and confused as you now
approach death through age or illness. You should be

> *I am the resurrection, and the life: he that believeth in me, though*
> *he were dead, yet shall he live: And whosoever liveth and*
> *believeth in me shall never die. Believest thou this?*
> [John 11:25–26]

happy about going to be with the Lord, but pain, fear
of the process of dying, and the prospect of being cut off
from those you love have stolen away any joy.

If you are in any of those categories, life is just waiting
to be transformed. Death is an enemy with a poisonous
sting, but the stinger has been pulled for the Christian. You
can know how to answer the question of where you will
spend eternity. You can be transformed by that knowledge.

Living with dying

To put into perspective our fears and hopes regarding death,
we need to be certain we understand that three periods of

life are involved. First, there is a time of preparing to die and of dealing with death. How a person lives tells a lot about how prepared he or she is to die. But feelings grow more intense when someone we love, whose fellowship and presence are important, is taken. Feelings intensify when a physician gives us the news that some illness or physical condition has erupted to herald the end of earthly life. That news is a shock for which few are immediately ready. Feelings intensify when we begin to experience the draining of vitality or mental coherency and bouts of searing, unbearable pain.

Second, there is the moment of death itself. It is a dramatic point of passage, about which those who have undergone clinical death and been revived can perhaps tell us a little. The closest analogy that the dying human has personally experienced previous to this moment is birth. Not many remember that day in their lives, and few infants seem thrilled to be going through it. One anticipating heaven may be forgiven a little queasiness about that instant when the body shuts down and an unknown reality opens.

Third, there is the new reality itself, what theologians refer to as the "intermediate state" between death and the resurrection and the "final state" after the resurrection and last judgment.

The Bible shares some very human reactions to death, and a surprising divine reaction. Jesus, who in John 11 said, "I am the resurrection, and the life" moments later watched the sorrow of the grieving friends and family of Lazarus and the look of the enclosed tomb—and cried. Jesus was about to raise Lazarus's body from the grave. He knew that this episode would have a joyous ending for these standing around the final resting place. Yet he still cried. Jesus' tears say something significant: Death doesn't just hurt us. It also hurts God. Death and hell were never intended to be our best. They have become our best through the cross of Jesus, but they still hurt God because they are the grievous fruit of human corruption in sin.

Death, then, is not in itself a joyful occasion. The Old Testament in particular records a human perspective of death as separation and ending. This sorrow is not condemned by Scripture. Rather these bittersweet passages reflect that people were made to give glory to and enjoy God forever within bodies. Sin has affected this ideal in life and in death:

There the wicked cease from troubling; and there the weary be at rest. There the prisoners rest together; they hear not the voice of the oppressor. The small and great are there; and the servant is free from his master. . . . One dieth in his full strength, being wholly at ease and quiet. His breasts are full of milk, and his bones are moistened with marrow. And another dieth in the bitterness of his soul, and never eateth with pleasure. They shall lie down alike in the dust, and the worms shall cover them. [Job 3:17–19; 21:23–26]

Be not thou afraid when one is made rich, when the glory of his house is increased; For when he dieth he shall carry nothing away: his glory shall not descend after him. [Psalm 49:16–17]

There is no man that hath power over the spirit to retain the spirit; neither hath he power in the day of death. [Ecclesiastes 8:8a]

For the grave cannot praise thee, death can not celebrate thee: they that go down into the pit cannot hope for thy truth. [Isaiah 38:18]

But one morning the sting was taken out of death. On that morning the grave became a less fearful place. A little boy with a serious allergy to bee venom was riding in the car with his father. It was a warm day and the windows were rolled down. Suddenly the two of them heard an angry buzz from the back seat. The air currents had pulled a bumblebee into the car, and he was angry, just looking for someone to sting. Knowing that a bee sting could bring on a fatal allergic reaction, the boy started screaming as the bee came over the seat, closer and closer. Then suddenly the bee just disappeared.

"It's all right, son," said the father. "That bee can't sting you now." It was true, for the father had reached out and caught the bee in his hand and thrown him out the window. All that was left was the stinger in the father's palm. Paul said:

O death, where is thy sting? O grave, where is thy victory? The sting of death is sin; and the strength of sin is the law. But thanks be to God, which giveth us the victory through our Lord Jesus Christ. [1 Corinthians 15:55–57]

As a result the New Testament looks not at the lonely grave but at the victorious sunrise. Death continues what the Christian has in life—the opportunity to glorify God and to enjoy him forever:

But ye are come unto mount Sion, and unto the city of the living God, the heavenly Jerusalem, and to an innumerable company of angels, To the general assembly and church of the firstborn, which are written in heaven, and to God the Judge of all, and to the spirits of just men made perfect, And to Jesus the mediator of the new covenant, and to the blood of sprinkling, that speaketh better things than that of Abel. [Hebrews 12:22–24]

Death is a time of freedom from the bonds of sin:

For we know that if our earthly house of this tabernacle were dissolved, we have a building of God, an house not made with hands, eternal in the heavens. For in this we groan, earnestly desiring to be clothed upon with our house which is from heaven: If so be that being clothed we shall not be found naked. For we that are in this tabernacle do groan, being burdened: not for that we would be unclothed, but clothed upon, that mortality might be swallowed up of life. Now he that hath wrought us for the selfsame thing is God, who also hath given unto us the earnest of the Spirit. [2 Corinthians 5:1–5]

Death is a time of intimacy with our Lord:

And he [the thief hanging next to Jesus on the cross] said unto Jesus, Lord, remember me when thou comest into thy kingdom. And Jesus said unto him, Verily I say unto thee, Today shalt thou be with me in paradise. [Luke 23:42–43]

Therefore we are always confident, knowing that, whilst we are at home in the body, we are absent from the Lord: (For we walk by faith, not by sight:) We are confident, I say, and willing rather to be absent from the body, and to be present with the Lord. [2 Corinthians 5:6–8]

For to me to live is Christ, and to die is gain. But if I live in the flesh, this is the fruit of my labour: yet what I shall choose I wot not. For I am in a strait betwixt two, having a desire to depart, and to be with Christ; which is far better: Nevertheless to abide in the flesh is more needful for you. [Philippians 1:21–24]

Death is a time of peace:

And I heard a voice from heaven saying unto me, Write, Blessed are the dead which die in the Lord from henceforth: Yea, saith the Spirit, that they may rest from their labours; and their works do follow them. [Revelation 14:13]

Getting ready for the last day of life

It is no longer necessary to fear death. Yet, given the sinfulness of human beings and the holiness of God, one who has not repented of sin and rested in Jesus Christ for salvation has every right to be afraid to die. It would be irrational not to be afraid to stand before the God of the Bible without a covering of righteousness.

The way modern men and women have chosen to deal with that fear is through denial. Take for example these new trends in mortuary science:

The body is no longer a corpse. It is "the departed," "the loved one," or "Mr. Smith. "

Mr. Smith is no longer "laid out" for viewing. He is in the "slumber room."

Lipstick and rouge have been making departed ones look "so natural, just like he's sleeping" for a long time. But at some funeral parlors Mr. Smith may be stretched out on a couch with a book or his favorite pipe, waiting to greet visitors.

Death, like religion and politics, is not polite conversation. Was it ever? Well, yes. One group of Christians who spoke about death quite a lot were the Puritans. That may seem to go along with history's portrait of them as morbid killjoys. The Puritans actually were among the most joyous and fun-loving of peoples. They were nothing like the romanticized portrayal on Thanksgiving cards or the superpious fuddy-duddy image that goes with the epithet *puritanical*. But the journals, letters, books, and sermons they left mention death far more often than would make modern Americans comfortable. One reason the Puritans in the American colonies had much to say about death was that frontier life was hard and often brief. But also, Puritan writers speak of contemplating their own death each day to keep things in perspective, to grow in wisdom and self-understanding. Thinking of their death was a reality check on evaluating the important things. It helped the Puritans fasten their thoughts securely on the "sweetness of the Savior." That gave life and death full meaning. They put to practical action the words of Psalm 90:12: "So teach us to number our days, that we may apply our hearts unto wisdom."

If you want to judge what gives life meaning, I direct your attention to a number of testimonies—the last words of those who had contemplated the sweetness of the Savior and those who had not. Some had answered that question of where they would go if they died today, and some had not given it a thought.

W. C. Fields was quite ill in the hospital, and a friend was astonished upon entering the hospital room to find this irreligious man thumbing through the pages of a Bible. The friend remarked, "Is that really you, reading the Bible?"

Fields replied, "I'm just looking for a loophole."

Even for Fields, such flippancy rings hollow as he wandered from a godless life toward a godless eternity. The loophole he sought was there in those pages he was holding: He could become a man made new through the blood of Jesus Christ. One man who found that loophole was Hermann Lange, a young German preacher who stood among the Christians who spoke out against Adolf Hitler's repression of the gospel. Like many others Lange was arrested, interrogated, tried as a criminal, and condemned to die before a firing squad. On the last day of his life he wrote a farewell letter to his parents:

> When this letter comes to your hands, I shall no longer be among the living. The thing that has occupied our thoughts constantly for many months, never leaving them free, is now about to happen. If you ask me what state I am in, I can only answer: I am, first, in a joyous mood, and second, filled with great anticipation. As regards the first feeling, today means the end of all suffering and all earthly sorrow for me—and "God will wipe away every tear" from my eyes. What consolation, what marvelous strength emanates from faith in Christ, who has preceded us in death. In him, I have put my faith, and precisely today I have faith in him more firmly than ever. . . . Look where you will [in Scripture] . . . rejoice, once more I say to you, rejoice. And as to the second feeling [of anticipation] this day brings the greatest hour of my life! Everything that till now I have done, struggled for, and accomplished has at bottom been directed to this one goal, whose barrier I shall penetrate today. "Eye hath not seen, nor ear heard, neither have entered into the heart of man, the things which God hath prepared for them that love him" (1 Corinthians 2:9). . . . Should I not then be filled with anticipation? What is it all going to be like? . . . I return to the home of my Father. . . . Until we meet again above in the presence of the Father of Light,
>
> Your joyful Hermann.

Juxtapose the last words of unbelievers and the last words of believers, and it can hardly be imagined that they are speaking of the same event. Lange approached death with such anticipation and joy. Was it feigned? The result of psychological stress from imprisonment? Or had he come to grips with the question of his eternal destiny and as a result faced death with confidence? Contrast the following deathbed statements:

"I am going into eternity, and it is sweet for me to think of eternity," said David Brainerd, missionary.

"I am abandoned by God and man! I shall go to Hell!" cried Voltaire.

"Doctor, I am dying, but I am not afraid to die. 'Tis well," said George Washington.

"It is hell to be left alone," said Thomas Paine.

"I die in the faith of Jesus Christ, and in the firm hope of a better life," said Michelangelo.

"How were the circus receipts today at Madison Square Garden?" asked P. T. Barnum, who had judged himself in his famous line: "There's a sucker born every minute."

"Earth is receding, and heaven is opening, and this is my coronation day," said evangelist Dwight L. Moody.

Many such last lines have breathed remorse, horror, fear, grief, pained acceptance, hope, contentment, and joy. Few approach the end of life without two strong emotions, one that looks back on what has been and one that looks forward on what will come next. Except for a Barnum who is counting his receipts to the last, death has a way of changing one's perspective. In my collection of dying words I even have one from the militant atheist Robert Ingersoll, who spent his adult life trying to convince the world that God did not exist. "If there be a God, may he have mercy on my soul," cried this suddenly uncertain atheist.

If you have not come to the point where you know for certain that you are called, justified, adopted, and sanctified, I direct your attention to the day of your death. It may come when you least expect, and when you are unprepared to take up unfinished business with the Creator of heaven and earth.

But it need not be like that. Death left its stinger in Jesus. It can no longer destroy those who have taken refuge under his scarred hands.

Held safely

There are Christians who yet live in the oppressive fear that they may face God without Christ. We have already said that it is not possible to fall from God's grace before the end (see p. 246). Can a person who has been regenerated ever become unregenerated? Can a person who has received eternal life at the hand of an unchanging God go to hell forever or to a place somewhere between heaven and hell as the Roman Catholic Church has described purgatory? There is neither truth nor victory in such theology. It needlessly steals away the transforming hope that is by right the Christian's.

Let us look at the various answers to this question.

The Roman Catholic Church historically says that yes, a person can fall away. One can no longer speak of a mono-lithic Catholic theology, for the church of Rome stands divided over many of its historical doctrines. A modernism that looks only to this life for the coming of the kingdom of God and regards hope in heaven to be a distraction from the fight for social justice has pulled the church from one side. A new openness to study the Scriptures has pulled many Catholics in the evangelical direction. A charismatic renewal movement pulls in yet a third way. Historically and still dom-inant in Roman theology, however, is a belief that salvation belongs not to the individual Christian but to the institu-tional church as a community of believers. The church is the tap that dispenses God's grace. Individual faith pleases God only if accompanied by righteous living in connection with the sacraments and love. At the very least, the Roman Church teaches, a time of purging will prepare one for heaven. But no consistent Roman Catholic is ever even certain to qualify for purgatory. No consistent Catholic says, "I know I am eter-nally in the hand of God."

Lutheran doctrine likewise makes perseverance uncertain, teaching that a truly converted Christian can come to lose or reject faith, and as a result lose grace as well, forfeiting justification by treason. No consistent Lutheran says, "I know I am eternally in the hand of God."

Neither does that group of churches whose theology is known as *Arminianism* teach that Christians are safe. Since their view of salvation is born of a high view of the individual will, many say emphatically that a person may be saved and then lost. Many ride a roller coaster of emotion, now high and secure, now backslidden and unsure. A person may be saved and lost literally hundreds of times, and at the grieving loved ones must wonder, "In which state was his or her soul at the moment of death?" That will determine whether the person is in heaven or hell.

Calvinists can consistently say that no person who has been truly saved can ever be lost. I have listed biblical reasons for their statement (see pp. 246–48). Romans 11:29 (NIV) summarizes the trust that "God's gifts and his call are irrevocable." Salvation is as certain as the promise of God. Security has limits. Jesus warns in Matthew 10:22; 24:13, and Mark 13:13 that "But he that shall endure unto the end, the same shall be saved." It doesn't mean that any confessor of Jesus lives for the world, the flesh, and the devil and then goes to heaven. There is no question about the fact that those who do not persevere to the end will not be saved. But the one who has turned away from sin to live for God need never fear disqualification from sin or failure. Christ intends that those who come to him share the confidence of the Christian who was asked, "Are you not afraid that you will slip through his fingers!"

That Christian replied, "I *am* one of his fingers."

The rescuer

Then there are those in that third category, Christians whose knees knock and whose feet shake. They are like the preacher who had just seen the Holy Spirit work in a revival service until he felt giddy with rejoicing in God's love and mercy as he returned to his hotel room for the night. He hardly noticed the storm clouds boiling in overhead, and when he dropped to his knees he prayed, "Oh, that right now might be the moment of your final return!"

Just then a bolt of lightning split the sky just outside his window, and the accompanying thunder crack just about sent him through the ceiling. "Wait! Not *quite* yet!" he shouted above the din.

My own emotions remain quite mixed as I contemplate the Lord I serve reviewing the most intimate details of my weak discipleship. I am sure I shall feel quite naked and unprepared. Yet I also know that this will be a judgment of love. Contemplating death, the Christian, like the Puritans, should use that expectation to judge life now, so as not to fear words of rebuke later. "I must work the works of him that sent me, while it is day," said Jesus, "the night cometh when no man can work" (John 9:4).

The mind contemplating death can certainly think of much unfinished business. What can a pastor say to a dying young cancer victim with a toddler at her knee who will not be there to care for the hurts or know the joys of seeing this young one reach adulthood. When a child dies or a newlywed buries her young husband, doubts cloud the mind. Where is God's love and plan in this? And I must say, "It is there, just beyond sight." For I don't know the plan, but I know the Planner. He wept at the grave of Lazarus, feeling the suffering that sin's legacy on humanity was causing. He hurts when his children hurt, and he will work it all for good in a way we may least expect.

The mind contemplating death may also be distracted by a fear that the final struggle with pain or the loss of mental function that comes with some diseases may be more than bearable. A time may come when pain or sorrow steals away the feeling of victory. The believer may slip and fall flat as upon the deck of a rolling ship. That is when the *Westminster Confession's* promise of perseverance becomes so precious. A dramatic film was made on the life of Jan Hus, the

Bohemian preacher who read the works of John Wycliffe and was transformed in his faith. In 1414 he was called to defend his teachings at the Council of Constance. Though promised safe conduct to present his case, he was arrested upon his arrival at the council, summarily tried for heresy, and sentenced to burn. One scene of the film shows the reformer writing by the light of a candle in his cell. He puts down his quill and studies the flame, then puts his hand above it. The pain makes him draw back quickly. Will he be able to stand when he can no longer draw away from the heat?

I don't know whether the real Hus went through the moment of doubt this film portrayed. I do know that as he was chained to the stake Hus looked upward to heaven and said, "Father, into thy hands I commit my spirit."

When Jesus said those same words on the cross he had become sin for all of us, and had experienced the most terrible experience the Son of God could possibly know, the wrath of a just God punishing sin. The Father turned his back on the Son, yet at the moment of death the Son knew that the Father was the One into whose hands he could commit his spirit. For he had already breathed the shout of victory: "It is finished!" Sin's atonement was accomplished. The stinger of death was still releasing its venom, but it was pulled from the bee, never again to strike out at the people of God. So when Hus reached his moment of crisis, he knew there was One on whom he could cast himself, with all his natural human feelings of pain and terror.

Deliverance assured

The question from the *Westminster Larger Catechism* heading this chapter addresses a natural human response: If our sins have been taken away, why do we still have to go through death at all? Why not just be translated from one shore to the other, as an Enoch or an Elijah? The answer gives two responses. First, a day is coming when that will indeed happen. Second, meanwhile, the death of a Christian has been transformed from something dreadful to a beautiful response of God's love. It has become a door to freedom from the state of sin and misery that still plagues the world. It has become a door open to communion with Christ in glory, which the Christian may freely enter and partake. "Precious in the sight of the LORD is the death of his saints" (Psalm 116:15).

If you fear the accompanying pain and affliction of the last enemy or the moment of passage into something unknown, you have a God on which you can cast that burden—a God who has blazed the trail before you. He has defeated the enemy and removed the stinger.

If you fear death because you have no answer for the question of where you would spend eternity if you died today, then you do not have the transforming salvation this book has explained. You may have gone to some altar rail forty years ago. You may be a deacon, an elder, a minister, a teacher, but if your heart holds the dread of uncertainty, you need to give your life to the Christ who has taken the fear out of death for the child of God.

Why does the Christian not fear death? Most simply, it is because the Christian will never die. Someday, when my friends and family gather around for the obsequies, I want you to know that I will be more alive then than I am at this moment. Our bodies may be laid out, but we shall be very much alive, and the bonds will be broken forever.

Part 3

Purposed for Good Works

Introduction to Part 3

I remember a time when I thought that if ever I really let God get hold of my life he would, no doubt, make me miserable. I was not a new believer at the time. Actually I was in seminary studying to be a minister.

I had heard a preacher say, "If you really believe God, you surrender yourself to his hands. Just step out in faith and he will lead you. If God wants you to be a missionary he will lead you. If he does not he will close the door. Do you believe that?"

"Yes," I said in my heart, "I believe that."

"Then sign up!" he continued.

"Yes," I said in my heart, "I should sign up."

He was talking about signing up to go to the Belgian Congo. To this day I do not know why I went to the mission board to sign up to go to the Belgian Congo. I did not want to go to the Belgian Congo. I did not feel called to go to the Belgian Congo. But I was going to do what this fellow said. I then learned that in the middle of the Belgian Congo was the world's largest leper colony. I had had a lifelong phobia about leprosy, and I was convinced that if ever I came within 100 miles of the disease I would be stricken. Now I was probably going to be plopped right down into the middle of a leper colony. Soon I would be one little quivering lump, sans toes, sans feet, sans hands, sans all the rest of me.

This was ridiculous. Why was I working myself into such a state? Now I think I understand myself and my enemy a little better. Satan had been telling me that God was mean, and now he was really going to fix me because he had me right in the palm of his hand to do whatever he wanted.

God's good, transforming will

You can imagine what the Lord did with my uncalled "call" to the Belgian Congo. He tossed me out on my ear and slammed that door hard. God said, "I need you in the Congo like I need a hole in the head. With your neuroses you wouldn't last six months." Instead he plopped me down in Fort Lauderdale, Florida, which he knew I could handle a lot better. I learned a great truth about the will of God for my life—God is good, and what he wants is good for me.

This is the third part in a trilogy about the life-transforming doctrines of Christian faith. Part 1 looked at what we believe about God as Father, Son, and Holy Spirit—a quest up the life-transforming mountain of the understanding of the Creator and the creature. Part 2 answered basic questions about salvation—why Christ had to die to save us, how God's grace works in our lives to save us, and how God continues to change us through sanctification. We finished with a look at assurances the believer has for an eternal life to come. We now look more closely at the Christian life itself. If all the Bible teaches about God and the gospel is true, what should I do? The answer starts again in God and the Holy Spirit's residence within the heart. It involves all that we think, say, and do—our worldview, ethics, worship, citizenship, relationships. It involves where we think history is heading, so we will make some observations about how Christians should live as they await the culmination of history in Christ's return and judgment.

As in parts 1 and 2, our guidebook for this tour of transforming Bible precepts will be the *Westminster Confession of Faith* and the *Westminster Larger* and *Shorter* catechisms. I chose to follow these statements, not because they are inspired, but because they closely reflect what the Bible teaches and are clear, uncompromising statements of faith and life. These documents were written in the midst of national spiritual crisis, the English Civil War of the 1640s. I believe they offer keen insights for our own day of spiritual and cultural crisis. Ours is an era of malnourished church members who have been spoonfed tapioca and cheesecake religion until their spiritual stomachs are bloated and their hearts are clogged with the cholesterol of meaningless "I wanna be me" self-fulfillment.

One preacher commented that the church began its life conquering Roman idolatry and seems to be losing the battle to survive "egolatry." Paul told Timothy,

> This know also, that in the last days perilous times shall come. For men shall be lovers of their own selves, covetous, boasters, proud, blasphemers, disobedient to parents, unthankful, unholy, without natural affection, truce-breakers, false accusers, incontinent, fierce, despisers of those that are good, traitors, heady, highminded, lovers of pleasure more than lovers of God; having a form of godliness, but denying the power thereof: from such turn away. [2 Timothy 3:1–5]

That sounds like such a shopping list of the ills of our day that one wonders how "last" these days are. I don't know. I do think it noteworthy that Paul told Timothy not to have anything to do with such people, so they must have been around even in the first century!

The world-infected church of the last days has been around a long time. But now it has reached a state where a minority of preachers and teachers faithfully impart life-transforming scriptural doctrines. The drift away from biblical truth in the Western European and North American churches began long ago, and generations have been born, lived, and gone into eternity without even a rudimentary understanding of the life-transforming teachings. If everything in these books is old news, wonderful! Rejoice as you meditate on their meaning with me. If this is new news, that also is wonderful. I delight to share these truths with someone hearing them for the first time.

Thy will be done

Each of these three parts has a theme idea that helps organize, at least in my mind, the topics covered. Part 1 searched out the path of quest toward knowing God. Part 2 looked at the Christ of our salvation who "makes all things new." Now we turn to the words of Jesus as he prayed in a garden, facing the worst trial any human being ever faced. His prayer: *"Not my will, but thine, be done"* (Matthew 26:39; Mark 14:36; Luke 22:42).

To live a victorious life we must believe that God is good and that his will for our lives is excellent. We know well his will for humanity: to repent and believe. The Lord God advises post-modern twenty-first century Western culture as he advised the prophet Jeremiah's generation—that we stand at the crossroads and must consider carefully the road to take:

> Stand at the crossroads and look;
>   ask for the ancient paths,
> ask where the good way is, and walk in it,
>   and you will find rest for your souls. [Jeremiah 6:16 NIV]

We are to "glorify God and enjoy him forever." The prophet Micah observed what that means in the day-to-day nitty-gritty of life:

> Wherewith shall I come before the LORD, and bow myself before the high God? shall I come before him with burnt offerings, with calves of a year old? Will the LORD be pleased with thousands of rams, or with ten thousands of rivers of oil? shall I give my firstborn for my transgression, the fruit of my body for the sin of my soul? He hath shewed thee, O man, what is good; and what doth the LORD require of thee, but to do justly, and to love mercy, and to walk humbly with thy God? [Micah 6:6–8]

But God also has a unique and excellent will for each of his children, for those who have come to Christ to be Savior and Lord. Christians will only come to believe that

God's will for us is excellent, however, to the extent that we place our hands, our lives, in the hands of God—the hands that are pierced for us. Those words of Jesus, "Not my will but thine be done," make us want to start back in horror and terror. Surely there is a Congo leper colony hiding within. But God has not called *us* to be the savior of the world. That job is taken. Rather, we are called simply to follow the God who loves us with an everlasting love.

We must also believe that God is wise. Our parents did what they thought best for us, and often they fouled it all up. How many parents have tried to make football players out of poets or physicians out of football players? As a parent I know that a superabundance of ignorance resides within us. But think about what we learned about the wisdom and omniscience of God. Now think about how foolish our way, plans, and desires can be. Honestly, who do we really want calling the shots? If we could comprehend the wisdom of God and the goodness of God, we would say, "Into those hands let me cast my life." God's plan for every sphere of life is vastly better than any that our paltry minds can devise.

Meaning for a meaningless world

> Vanity of vanities, saith the Preacher, vanity of vanities; all is vanity. [Ecclesiastes 1:2]

Ecclesiastes is an odd book of Scripture, for in it King Solomon (the wise Teacher) discusses at length the meaning of life lived in the will of the human individual. Only occasionally, slipping in around the edge, does he refer to God's will for life. Then at the end of the book he throws open the door and proclaims that only God's will offers any meaning at all for the inhabitant on planet earth.

Solomon tells us that he had sampled life from all sides, and he also perhaps met some of the same types of people I have encountered in thirty-five years of ministry. Solomon finds that each kind of person has one of only two centers of consciousness and desire.

One type of person is worldly-wise or "street smart." This person has it all together, or seems to. Solomon was one of these himself, a Renaissance man who studied and pondered and became wise in the ways of life, self-sufficient and knowledgeable in many disciplines. As the wizard of the land of Oz gave to the scarecrow, Solomon had a doctorate in thinkology. But what he learned with his wisdom was that "what is twisted cannot be straightened; what is lacking cannot be counted" (1:15 NIV). Looking for satisfaction only in knowledge, the worldly philosopher said, "My will be done." But all he learned was how bad off he was. It was a "chasing after the wind" without eternal meaning. In modern philosophical terms Solomon relates that looking to self for wisdom leads only to nihilism.

The second kind of person Solomon introduces has a life focused on self-fulfillment. This is the child of our age, who believes we only go around once in life, so we must grab all the fun we can. We work hard to get ahead, so we deserve the best. Sensual desires rule. "My will be done." The person centered in self-fulfillment strongly believes in being what secular humanist psychology calls "self-actualized." If this person makes any sort of profession for God at all it is a religion built upon emotion and "what the church can do for me and mine." This person, if awareness of sin enters into the picture at all, considers that at least 51 percent of goodness will be enough to satisfy God, who is loving and wouldn't really send anyone to hell anyway. Yet hell is where this person is bound, and all the grasping selfishness of this lifestyle will not buy happiness or contentment in the meantime. This is of all lives the most wasted.

Akin to the one interested only in self-fulfilled desires is the third person—one who desires to collect as much wealth as possible. Work becomes an obsession and the wealth in a stock portfolio the barometer of success. Through money, "My will be done." But Solomon warns us that

He that loveth silver shall not be satisfied with silver; nor
he that loveth abundance with increase: this is also vanity.
When goods increase, they are increased that eat them: and
what good is there to the owners thereof, saving the behold-
ing of them with their eyes? [5:10–11]

A fourth kind of person seems far different, yet perhaps
not so different. This person centers life in altruism. This person lives a harried and outwardly fulfilling career of serving
others. At the root is a strong sense of works righteousness
that may hide feelings of guilt and worthlessness and inadequacy. Certainly such a life is good enough and worthwhile.
But alas, for all the sweat, blood, and tears expended in the
name of human betterment, this person seems unsatisfied
and embittered by it all, sarcastically saying there is "one
upright man among a thousand, but not one upright woman
among them all" (7:28 NIV). The righteous get what the wicked
deserve, and the wicked what the upright deserve, so that
there is no justice anywhere (8:14). Amazingly enough, students of human behavior say that the altruist rarely comes
to the land of contentment. Self-sacrifice will not bring grace.
Grace, rather than justice, is what this person is working so
hard to find. In his or her heart the focus still is on self and
desires. "My will be done." This is a life of work and worry
but not of worth.

There are other kinds of people we might name; Solomon
mentions a few others in passing, all of whom are assigned
the same fate—meaninglessness, arising from the cry, "My
will be done!"

Finally, in Ecclesiastes 12 the teacher drops the other
shoe. Yes, there is meaning in life, but only for the one who
says, "*Thy* will be done." Don't wait to find meaning in life,
Solomon counsels us:

Remember now thy Creator in the days of thy youth, while
the evil days come not, nor the years draw nigh, when thou
shalt say, I have no pleasure in them. [12:1]

The Hebrew word for "remember" is an interesting one; it means "to act decisively for." To act decisively for God, Solomon goes on to say, is the only way to find eternal significance:

> Let us hear the conclusion of the whole matter: Fear God, and keep his commandments: for this is the whole duty of man. [12:13]

What is the chief purpose of humanity but to glorify God and to enjoy him forever? Only in Jesus Christ is that possible, for only Jesus Christ moves the center of consciousness from self to God's will—a good and perfect will.

What makes an ethical standard "Christian"?

What is the moral law?

The moral law is the declaration of the will of God to mankind, directing and binding every one to personal, perfect, and perpetual conformity and obedience thereunto, in the frame and disposition of the whole man, soul and body, and in the performance of all those duties of holiness and righteousness which he oweth to God and man: promising life upon the fulfilling, and threatening death upon the breach of it.
[Westminster Larger Catechism, question 93]

17

The Cut-Flower Generation

When you know what God has done in Christ, you will know what you ought to do," said the eminent Scottish Christian leader James Stewart.

If this is true, then Christians should, above all others, know what they ought to do. Christians alone have experienced firsthand what God has done in Christ.

That experience of coming to Christ—of being justified, adopted, and sanctified by the grace of God—is the foundation for a life-transforming way of living. It is an ethic that fulfils our primary reason for existing—*to glorify God and enjoy him forever*. By now most readers are familiar with the question and answer from the *Westminster Shorter Catechism*: "What is the chief end of man? Man's chief end is to glorify God and enjoy him forever." We have looked at the God we are called to glorify and enjoy and at God's plan of salvation in Jesus Christ. Because Christ stepped into our shoes and took on himself our sin, we can have a relationship with the God we are called to glorify and enjoy.

So now the Christian man and woman stand in the presence of God. The Christian can call the Father *Abba*—Daddy! The Christian knows that the penalty for breaking the law of God no longer hangs over his or her head like a sentence of death. Such love from God deserves a fitting response from the one who is called to glorify and enjoy.

316

So how do we live for God today? Three resources stand at our disposal, and this book is about those great gifts God has provided to the one who is called to glorify and enjoy:

1. *We have newness.* We just aren't the same fallen creatures who were lost in rebellion against God; who were not able to fulfil God's purpose. We no longer are under

> *The heart is deceitful above all things, and desperately wicked: who can know it? I the LORD search the heart, I try the reins, even to give every man according to his ways, and according to the fruit of his doings.* [Jeremiah 17:9–10]

the curse of the lawbreaker. We are a new creation, a re-creation. We still sin, but we have new options.
2. *We have an ethical system that works.* No way of living ever devised by the human mind can fulfil God's purpose for humanity. That wasn't why these ethical systems came into being, so they simply cannot meet the need. Ours was designed by the Designer of all things. He revealed it to us in the Bible. It is compatible with how we are made.
3. *We have God's presence within us.* The Holy Spirit now pervades the Christian's being. God the Holy Spirit lives in the heart of every Christian, revealing God and empowering us to glorify and enjoy him.

A lifestyle of newness

The *Westminster Confession*, in its statement on the law of God (chapter 19) is helpful for understanding what it means to have a lifestyle of newness. First, God gave to Adam a promise or covenant of life. This covenant had two provisions. If Adam obeyed God's one rule, he and his children would live in close relation with God forever. If Adam disobeyed, broken relationship and death would result. Second, after Adam disobeyed, God unveiled a new covenant of grace and a more detailed set of laws so men and women would know how to live. These covenantal laws find their most basic expression in the ten commandments— ten principles explaining our duty toward God (the first four commandments) and our duty toward one another (commandments five through ten). Other laws were given to the nation of Israel as God's covenant people, to guide their worship and actions. All of these laws provided principles for understanding God and his will, they restrained the evil in fallen humanity, and they pointed toward the final answer for sin, Jesus Christ.

Third, God's law still stands as a set of principles, which are summarized in the law of love, what Jesus said are the greatest commandments: "Thou shalt love the Lord thy God with all thy heart, and with all thy soul, and with all thy mind. . . . Thou shalt love thy neighbor as thyself" (Matthew 22:37–39; see Deuteronomy 6:5 and Leviticus 19:18). Explains Galatians 5:6: "For in Jesus Christ neither circumcision availeth any thing, nor uncircumcision [the keeping of the law of the Jews or the Gentiles]; but faith which worketh by love."

So the law of God is useless, right? Hardly, according to the *Westminster Confession*:

> Although true believers be not under the law as a covenant of works, to be thereby justified or condemned; yet is it of great use to them, as well as to others; in that, as a rule of life, informing them of the will of God and their duty, it directs and binds them to walk accordingly.

The law informs Christians of the will of God and "binds them to walk accordingly," not out of fear but out of faith, expressing itself through love. It shows how far the believer's actual behavior is from God's ideal and so restrains the evil that remains in the heart of any human being. Its threats show us how God feels about sin; its promises show how he desires obedience. It encourages a closer walk with God.

Fourth, such purposes are God's grace to us. Once the law promised only death; but now it helps us live our new life.

The *ought* and the *is*

Without fear of contradiction I will relate that the Christian ethical system is the only system that really works, if by "working" we mean a system that brings justice and peace to a world in the throes of pain, discontent, dissatisfaction, and meaninglessness. First, it has a source of power in the Holy Spirit that is not found in any other ethic. Second, it works through love, rather than fear. Third, it is built upon the revealed will of God, the Master Architect of life and the Giver of its meaning.

"Ours is a cut-flower civilization," said Elton Trueblood. He explained that a cut-flower civilization has much beauty—its technological advances are stirring; its quality of life is unequaled for the availability of luxury and ease; its thought is capable of great literature and magnificent art. But this momentary beauty hides the fact that the society is terminal. Civilization is cut off from the source of its life and is inevitably decaying. Surely no one in the know can miss seeing the wilt of the petals and the droop and drop of the leaves. Our state is one of advanced degeneration.

This moral crisis is unlike any the world has ever before known, remarks Will Herberg, graduate professor of philosophy and culture at Drew University in an article, "What is the Moral Crisis of Our Time?" Herberg describes this crisis as fundamentally different from the crises of war or riots or crime. "The trouble seems to come, not from the breaking of moral laws, but from something far more serious—the rejection of the conception that there is any moral law at all." We live in what is, to a great extent today, an amoral society.

What is ethics anyway? First of all, note that ethics does not declare what *is*. It declares what *ought to be*. It enunciates norms or standards of conduct. It condemns, condones, or commends. It makes *value judgments;* therein lies the rub.

Everyone has some sort of value system, an ethical framework on which the person builds and lives. So deep within us that we hardly know they are there lie presumptions and assumptions about what we "know" to be true and good. These assumptions color virtually everything we see and hear. Now those perceptions seem to be colored by the assumption that no action is always, under every circumstance, right or wrong. No course of action is morally superior to all others. This assumption lies at the heart of the moral revolution of our time.

Rules for the game

Secular ethics is speculative. It must speculate or rationalize what courses of action are right for human beings to follow because no master plan set of rules is recognized. One of the most influential secular ethical systems has drastically influenced the late twentieth-century church. This system is called situational ethics. The situation ethics movement is no longer a major force, but its ideas remain entrenched. Joseph Fletcher coined the term *situational ethics* and based it upon the philosophy that there can be no absolute set of rights and wrongs. What is important is to show love to other people. Whatever is the most loving response in a particular situation is right. H. Richard Niebuhr applied this to Christian conduct in a church that no longer believed in absolutes or a divinely revealed Scripture. Niebuhr said that morality should be built upon love for God. But how does one know how to love God in a given situation, for the Bible is no longer to be believed. We must speculate. T. Ralph

Morton, a proponent of this "new morality," admitted it makes "Christ-centered" decision-making more complex:

> Even to speak of "exceptions" is to presuppose that there are "rules" laid down somewhere, and it is here that the Protestant Christian, seeking to come to a Christian decision, is at his greatest loss; there simply are no commonly accepted rules in Protestantism for making ethical decisions.

How then does a Christian know what behavior is Christ-centered? What the Bible said Christ himself did is irrelevant, because that was another time and set of situations, and it is not real history anyway. Rather, we know what to do when we see what God is doing in a situation and act accordingly. Niebuhr said the decisive ethical question to ask is, "What is happening?" and then find the fitting response.

What a remarkable admission. God has no definite pattern of behavior, no goal, no law. We are simply winging it. Nothing is revealed. We have joined the team in the middle of the game, and no one can tell us what game we are playing or its rules. We must go out on the field, imagine what is the loving thing to do, and just make up the rules as we go along, according to what seems right. It is all subjective and open to the interpretation of the moment. The prophet Jeremiah sneered at the individual's ability to come up with an ethic without help:

> The heart is deceitful above all things, and desperately wicked: who can know it? I the LORD search the heart, I try the reins, even to give every man according to his ways, and according to the fruit of his doings. [Jeremiah 17:9–10]

Absolutely no absolutes

Without any light to guide their speculations, secular ethicists disagree wildly among themselves. There is only one point on which these systems agree: There is absolutely no absolute standard of morality for all people everywhere.

Many times I have heard critics of the Christian principles of conduct remonstrate that some element of the biblical ethical system seems unwarranted, confining, or oppressive. One thing that might do all these complainers some good is to take a very close look at secular ethics and see the infinite gulf that separates the best efforts of the secularist from Christian ethics.

It only takes a quick survey of ethical systems devised by the ethical speculators to see that all have elements of truth, with a large admixture of error. Satan rarely uses the total lie as his tool. He blends truth and falsehood—a little bait on the hook.

Consequences

Who lived an ethically superior life? Florence Nightingale? Al Capone? Nero? The apostle Paul? Without an absolute standard there is no possible way to prove that any of these people is superior ethically to any other. That applies to mass murderers and despots. Is it better to save life or to take life? Can a massacre be ethically good or bad? There are large numbers of people who might take either side of such questions, at least under some circumstances. Ethical systems have advocated genocide, infanticide, abortion, and mercy killing. What good, then, is any ethical system at all?

Usually no good at all. To qualify as an ethical system a philosophy must attach itself to one of the three parts that are involved in any human deed:

1. the *motive* that lies behind the act;
2. the *act* itself;
3. the *results* or consequences of the act.

Most ethical systems focus on the third aspect—the end to which a deed is directed, or its consequence. These systems of ethics are *teleological*, from the Greek word *telos*, meaning "end." Teleological ethics establish right or wrong by seeing if the end justifies the means. How do you know whether the end is worthwhile? That all depends on your perspective. If no God has revealed himself, the most powerful person has the most important perspective and sets the ethical agenda.

So what kinds of teleological ethical systems have been devised? One of the oldest and most common is *egoism*, from the Greek word *ego*, meaning "I." Egoism is straightforward: What is ultimately good (called the *summum bonum*) is whatever is ultimately good for me. I decide how to act by determining which course of action will do me the most good or the least harm. If that seems selfish, remember that no one has ever demonstrated that genocide or torture is wrong. A little old-fashioned selfishness should not bother us. To say selfishness is "wrong" is to lean on Christian standards, with absolutes of right or wrong. Such value judgments are quaintly irrelevant or even harmful for social evolution.

In her book *The Virtue of Selfishness*, Ayn Rand argues that the only ethical system worth following is egoism, or "enlightened selfishness." As an atheist, Rand believes that most of the world's problems are caused by muddle-headed altruists who are trying to do something for somebody else. How much better if everybody would just take care of "number-one." A selfish society would want to make the streets safe, would want to deal with social problems that might erupt into class warfare, would want to progress in technology to make life easier and more enjoyable, would want good marriages and family relationships, since those make life more bearable, and would want world peace. This does seem a sensible program, even from purely selfish motivations. If we condemn egoism out-of-hand are we saying it is right for an individual to seek his or her own ultimate harm? One definition of insanity is that the person lacks concern for his or her own well-being. Why wouldn't enlightened selfishness make the world a utopia? Or perhaps we should ask why egoism has not led to such fine things, since that is the philosophy under which most of our own society operates. There must be a flaw somewhere.

A second teleological system of ethics was originated in the 1800s by Jeremy Bentham and popularized by the famed philosopher and essayist John Stuart Mill. *Utilitarianism* adopts the principle of utility—an act is only as good as its benefit for larger society. Here the focus is not on the individual but on humankind. This sounds much better than egoism as a way of life, especially when we hear the utilitarian maxim: *"The greatest good for the greatest number."* That seems a fine way to live, and many governments operate on this principle. Utilitarianism is the value system of evolution. The greatest good for the greatest number is the good that advances the species. If someone is sick, has bad genes, or is deformed, the greatest good for the greatest number is for the person to die. Such is the mindset behind genetic testing—the goal to make humanity better and better. Eugenics, a system of trying to weed out the racially or culturally inferior stock, grew out of this ethical system early in the 1900s. Planned Parenthood was founded on eugenic principles. The most famous experiment in utilitarian eugenics was in Germany in the 1930s and 1940s. If 90 million blond, Nordic, blue-eyed Aryans are developing a super-race, and a few million miserable Jews are fouling up the gene pool, then what could be more virtuous than to exterminate them? If the greatest good for all future people of the world is the destruction of every European Jew, East European gypsy, mentally or physically impaired person, and subversive Christian, then this destruction is the *summum bonum*. Utilitarianism also is the basic ethical system underlying communism. The end is the good, and the end is the communist society. Is murder right or wrong? That depends on whether it advances the communist state. So 15 million Ukrainians, 40 million Chinese, and 20 or 30 million Russians are killed. What is that compared to the infinite bliss of a future paradisiacal world?

The apostle Paul headed off utilitarian religion when he foresaw this response to the gospel of grace in Jesus Christ: "God's grace is a wonderful thing. I want more and more of it. And I get more grace when God forgives my sin. Therefore, it is good to sin, since that unleashes grace." Imagining such a response nearly gave the apostle apoplexy:

> What then? shall we sin, because we are not under the law, but under grace? God forbid. Know ye not, that to whom ye yield yourselves servants to obey, his servants ye are to whom ye obey; whether of sin unto death, or of obedience unto righteousness? [Romans 6:15–16]

This sounds like total rejection of teleological thinking. But another teleological ethic outwardly looks very like the sort of ethic Paul himself describes, the system of *altruism*. Altruism says that the only thing I must consider is my neighbor's well-being—the individual with whom I happen to be dealing. I will decide not to follow my own desires. In fact, I will go out of my way to reject my own interests if my actions will help another human being. How gracious this sounds, but on what basis am I to deny myself? This may cover a great act of philanthropy or the self-sacrifice of throwing one's body on a hand grenade to save one's buddies, but it breaks down in daily reality, which is, after all, where most ethical decisions are made.

Altruistic ideals must have an object more definite than "humanity" to be a basis for life. Why should I consider the well-being of my brother rather than my own? In an evolutionary worldview there is absolutely no reason at all, for neither my brother nor sister nor I have eternal value. The only value is in momentary well-being. I may get a good feeling inside when I give of my substance to make another's lot more bearable. But even this satisfaction must be tinged with bittersweet. For if I sacrifice so that someone is fed today, the person is nothing more than an animal who will have other needs tomorrow and next week and on and on until death. My act of kindness does no more than to stave off the inevitable, so why bother? It is, as Solomon saw, a chasing after the wind. King Louis XIV of France put his finger on the flaw with altruism in his line: "After me, the deluge!" In other words, why should I care about the human race? I'll have my fun, and then let the rains come.

Pragmatism presents another ethical option. The maxim of the pragmatist is: "You can't fight success!" Whatever works is right. By this concept many govern their lives, yet how does one build a life on this pattern? How does one know, when making a decision, whether one course of action is going to work, and another is not? The pragmatist, therefore, must build an ethical system upon experience and statistical probability. Something has worked, so likely it will work now. But if it has worked nine times out of ten and we are the tenth, the statistics may spell disaster. Also, how well do we know all the consequences of past actions? Perhaps a decision has not worked as well as we think. The pragmatic way provides no certain guide for humanity because ends do not justify the means.

Motives

If the result is not the proper test for an ethical system, then what about the motive? A number of philosophers have said, correctly, that we cannot rationally compute what the results of an act will be. The important thing is just to act, for by acting in any way we attest that we are alive and acting upon our environment—we prove that we exist. So this philosophy came to be called *existentialism*. While teleological ethics is subjective without admitting it, existentialism brags about its subjective decision-making. Its maxim is the bumper-sticker proverb: "If it feels good, do it." Its theme song is: "There's no tomorrow. Tonight's the night for love."

For obvious reasons this became a popular ethical response, and at least it is more honest than teleological ethics. The existentialist sees no absolute pattern for ethics, admits it, and glories in it. But its result is the same: If I can equally display my existence by helping a little old lady across the street and by kicking her brains in, the ethical system is not very helpful.

We already introduced the variation of altruism in situational ethics, which also deals with motives. We have no ultimate standards, no laws from God but that we love one another. Look at the situation and form an ethical decision that seems the most loving, all things considered. The same act might be virtuous or evil, depending on the motive. The loving act might be to rob a bank, to kill someone, or to give away your shoes. All sorts of examples were concocted by these moralists, frequently in the area of human sexuality: Here is this poor woman who is unmarried and psychologically fouled up. What she really needs is a man. Now, if you sir, being a happily married man, really *love*, then you'll just do this young lady the self-sacrificing thing and have sexual relations with her. This will, no doubt, open up her personality and do her a great deal of good.

But how do you know that this girl might not end up far more unhappy and messed up than before because of your "loving" act? What about the guilt she may end up feeling? What of the sexually-transmitted disease she may pass on to you? What about the child that may be conceived? If you are going to fully compute the consequences you need to take into account what will happen in the life of the child and in society as a result of the birth. What if you conceive the next Joseph Stalin? How much good or love have you actually given?

Deeds

Some argue cogently that we cannot base ethical guidelines on the motive or the results of an action. That leaves us with the deed itself. This is a difficult path to take, without looking at motives or results. One popular approach is *statistical ethics*, determining morality by counting noses.

How many believe it is right to kill people from Iowa? How many do not believe killing Iowans is a good idea? Only in a day of mass polling and demographic studies could such an ethic be possible. What is the proper sexual conduct for American families? Read *The Kinsey Report*! It tells what everybody's doing. Is abortion right or wrong? Consult the latest survey barometer of the standard. What is pornography? Most laws regarding pornography are established on the basis of statistical ethics: "prevailing community standards."

A rather obvious problem is that statistical ethics can only measure what *is*, never what *ought to be*. Kids have been using the statistical argument for years—for millennia, probably ("But Dad, everybody's doing it!"). Few parents, certainly few intelligent parents, buy the statistical argument. You can never extract an *ought* from an *is*. Any decision can be justified through statistical data. All one must do is pick the public to sample. But what if we used a larger sample—the whole human race? But what if the entire human race is morally skewed? A universal sample could not be trusted, given the moral standards for the world.

The late Dr. Gordon Clark studied all possible ethical systems and stated unequivocally that no consistent ethical standard can be developed by the secular world. "It is their secularism," Clark said. "They are cut off from God." It is the cut-flower syndrome. The only health in secular ethics is that which has slipped in from Christianity. A cut-flower generation, without absolutes, is a sickly and degenerating way of life.

Connecting with the Source

Now that we have shot down most of the ethical systems around us, why do we think the Christian ethic meets the challenge? Why is our way superior?

First, the Christian ethic includes absolutes. It is wrong to murder someone in cold blood—always and under every circumstance. And we know the reason behind the absolute: Every human being is an image-bearer of God. Each life is in God's hand, and to take life is to take what belongs to God alone. We are not left in the dark about any of this. The rules are spelled out. We know how the game is played. In the case of murder, some of those instructions and warnings include Genesis 9:5–6; Exodus 20:13; Leviticus 24:17; Numbers 35:16–31; Proverbs 28:17; Revelation 21:8; 22:15. Further, Scripture deals with nations as well as individuals in assessing behavior (regarding the sanctity of life see, for example, Psalm 106:38; Isaiah 59:3–7; Jeremiah 7:9–10; Nahum 3:1; Matthew 23:35).

Second, Christian ethics have helpful parameters, which also are revealed to us. Is it murder to kill someone in war? What culpability does a person have if he kills to protect his or her own property or life? Are circumstances to be taken into account? What about accidental death? Is it murder when the state executes someone? Is an unborn child regarded as a person in relation to the laws regarding murder? Scripture covers each of these situations.

Third, Christian ethics alone of all ethical systems considers the thoughts as well as the actions of an individual (Ezekiel 35:5–6; Matthew 5:22; James 4:1–2; 1 John 2:9–11; 3:15).

Fourth, Christian ethics takes into account the larger motives behind the thoughts. In sanctity of life issues, for example, the motives God looks at include neglect or unconcern for others (Ezekiel 16:49; Matthew 25:31–46); passing judgment (Matthew 7:1–5; Romans 2:1–3; 14:2–4; James 4:12); feeling scorn (Proverbs 19:29; Isaiah 29:29; Jude 18), and slander (Matthew 15:19–20; Romans 1:30; Colossians 3:8; James 4:11).

Fifth, only Christian ethics of all ethical systems offers a twofold perfect standard by which to judge all thoughts, motives, and actions: *Love the Lord your God with all you are. Love your neighbor as yourself* (see Matthew 22:37–39).

Sixth, only Christian ethics offers redemption that transcends all actions and their penalties. If we murder we may have to suffer for our actions, but no mass murderer is beyond the reach of God's forgiveness.

Seventh, only Christian ethics has the indwelling power of the Holy Spirit in our hearts to work obedience and purity and holiness within us. Take away all other differences, and this alone gives ultimate freedom and joy to ethics. All other ethical systems are cut off from the Source. The Holy Spirit keeps us from being cut-flower people.

If we are going to live a successful Christian life, if we are going to be able to follow Jesus Christ and live according to the Christian ethic, it can only be done by the power of the Spirit of God. We say when we come to Jesus Christ that we will, by the power of his Holy Spirit endeavor to live lives as becomes the followers of Jesus Christ. But then we get into trouble because we forget. We endeavor to live lives that will glorify Jesus by our own strength and determination and will. This can never be. It is only the Spirit of God that gives us the power to live the Christian life. Ephesians 5:18 tells us: "Be not drunk with wine, wherein is excess; but, be filled with the Spirit." The Greek word for "be filled" means "to be continually getting filled" with the Spirit. The Holy Spirit comes to us through Jesus Christ. It is through Christ that we are enabled to have the Holy Spirit. God has given the Holy Spirit without measure to his Son. When we receive his Son we receive the Holy Spirit. But we are leaky vessels and need continually to be refilled with the power of God. This sets us apart from the cut-flower generation.

The *Westminster Confession* says that the Spirit of God subdues and enables our will, helping us freely and cheerfully to do the will of God that is revealed in the law. God's promise is not to give us a once-upon-a-time filling that leaves us struggling with our connectedness to God. It is not that the Holy Spirit leaves and we have to struggle to get more of him. He is fully inside every child of God, asking for more of us. God's promise for our life and living ethically is that, if we are thirsty for him, his Spirit will descend upon us abundantly:

I will pour water upon him that is thirsty, and floods upon the dry ground: I will pour my spirit upon thy seed, and my blessing upon thine offspring. [Isaiah 44:3]

God will give the Holy Spirit to those determined to obey him. It is only a lie of Satan that we can have just a little bit of fun through just a little bit of disobedience. At his right hand is joy forevermore, not at a distance from him, but just alongside. Why should we live as cut-flower people when connection is ours to enjoy, both now and forever?

What makes an ethical standard "Christian"?

Although true believers be not under the law as a covenant of works, to be thereby justified or condemned; yet is it of great use to them, as well as to others; in that, as a rule of life, informing them of the will of God and their duty, it directs and binds them to walk accordingly.
[Westminster Confession of Faith, chapter 19]

18

Good Advice and Good News

Scorching desert. Impenetrable clouds. Smoke as of a furnace. Leaping flames. Trembling mountain.

This was no movie set with special effects crew at work. Charlton Heston was not standing by in bearded makeup. It was one of the most significant moments in all history. The Creator of the universe had descended to give his creatures a reflection of his nature, a revelation of his will. He was establishing a set-apart way of life. In all other things God spoke through Moses or one of his prophets; now he came directly to the people. Their hearts melted, and they fell prostrate before thundering authority:

> I am the LORD thy God, which have brought thee out of the land of Egypt, out of the house of bondage. Thou shalt have no other gods before me.

> Thou shalt not make unto thee any graven image, or any likeness of any thing that is in heaven above, or that is in the earth beneath, or that is in the water under the earth: Thou shalt not bow down thyself to them, nor serve them. . . . Thou shalt not take the name of the LORD thy God in vain [misuse it]; for the LORD will not hold him guiltless that taketh his name in vain.

> Remember the sabbath day, to keep it holy. . . .

> Honor thy father and thy mother. . . .

Thou shalt not kill.

Thou shalt not commit adultery.

Thou shalt not steal.

Thou shalt not bear false witness against thy neighbor.

Thou shalt not covet. . . .[Exodus 20:2–17]

The people drew back in terror and cried to Moses: "Speak thou with us, and we will hear: but let not God speak with us, lest we die" (20:19). Thus we received "ten words," ten commands of the moral law of God, from the voice of God.

Down through history individuals and nations have dashed themselves against that law, trying to break it. The fragments of their remains may be found in cemeteries, asylums, prisons, and skid rows. His law does not break; anyone who tries to break his law is broken.

Columnist Cal Thomas quoted a moralist who had addressed the National Press Club in Washington, D.C., with an ominous message about the state of America. This man warned: "At no time in my life has our culture been so estranged from spiritual values. . . . Our problems lie beyond the reach of politics alone." He went on to blame materialism and "a numbers-oriented culture based on what we can grasp and count. We have lost touch with the best of humanity—the inner life."

The speaker was Norman Lear—television producer and founder of People for the American Way. Lear has hardly distinguished himself as a friend of spiritual values. His philosophy has been part of the problem, instead of the solution. Lear and I do not agree on what needs to be done, yet we can agree on the diagnosis. Said Thomas of Lear's speech:

Virtue, morals, respect for law and other people are not concepts that are caught like a strain of flu. They are not acquired by human nature. In fact, they must be taught, even imposed. . . . News reports suggest the beginning of what may be a spiritual revival in Russia. It appears many Russians are recovering what they once had but lost. It also appears too many Americans have abandoned what we once had but gave away—not to a dictator but to decadence. These two nations are like huge ships passing in the night, headed in opposite directions.

What Lear calls losing touch with the inner life, the Bible calls *lawlessness*. In 2 Thessalonians 2 Paul writes that the days before Christ returns will be an era of rebellion and lawlessness. Paul says of his own day that the power of lawlessness was already at work (2:7). Ours is an age where people have kicked off the traces and thrown off the restraints. On every side the moral law of God is abandoned. Within the church itself false teachers tell those who follow Jesus Christ: "You, too, may ignore the law of God. It does not apply to the believer, so live as you like."

Getting to know the law

It is good in these days of lawlessness to recognize that God's law still does apply—even to Christians. It applies *especially* to Christians.

"Oh, but we live under *grace* today!"

Yes, we do, so we must understand how the Bible keeps two great forces in tension—law and gospel. The law is important, for the unbeliever stands under its condemnation. But it helps the believer. As the *Westminster Confession of Faith* explains, Christians stand outside the *guilt* of the law; we are neither justified nor condemned by the thunder from the mountain. Yet, the Westminster framers remind us that the law still is a *rule for living*, especially for God's people. It is his good advice and far more: The law delineates principles of God's will for human behavior. To obey is nothing more than to act as an obedient child. Therefore, the law *directs* and, in a different sense than for the one outside of Christ, it *binds* the child of God.

Lots of laws are spread through the Old Testament. Are we to keep them all? We need to understand that God gave different types of laws for different purposes. Not all have the same importance today, but all have some meaning. Some people say Christians are under none of the laws and are called *antinomians* (*anti*, "against"; *nomos*, "law"). Another group teaches the opposite— that all laws (except sacrificial or temple laws) apply totally to all people and governments. These people are called *theonomists* and stir up serious arguments among those who want to take Scripture seriously but who do not want to apply Scriptures in ways God does not intend.

I suggest that we look to the laws for principles. What God hated he still hates; what he treated with approbation is still good. There are some judgment calls, some places requiring prayer, humility, and sanctified common sense. What follows attempts a simple overview of laws and what they mean today.

Foundation for a nation

When God brought the people of Israel out of Egypt his laws shaped a whining mob of ex-slaves into a nation—a uniquely set-apart people. This government was not to be ruled by King Moses or President Joshua. Leaders were God's intermediaries and the people's servants (a novel thought for politicians). Israel was not initially a monarchy or a democracy, but a *theocracy*—government by God. Therefore, although the laws were, in general, like other laws archeologists have discovered in ancient inscriptions, they also were distinctly different. *Civil*, *social*, *criminal*, *family*, and *ceremonial* laws in the Old Testament made this people radically God's. Jesus, in fact, made the meaning of the laws richer still, even as he took their penalties on himself. "Think not that I am come to destroy the law, or the prophets," he said in Matthew 5:17. "I am not come to destroy, but to fulfil."

So what do they mean if they are not *abolished* but *fulfilled* in Jesus' life and death? Jesus answered that all the commandments of God are summed up in two rules: (1) *Love God.* (2) *Love your neighbor.* Do such rules apply? Is not the church a people ruled by love? Said the Old Testament:

> Ye shall be unto me a kingdom of priests, and an holy nation. [Exodus 19:6a]

Wrote Peter to the church:

> But ye are a chosen generation, a royal priesthood, an holy nation, a peculiar people. [1 Peter 2:9a]

Adds John in Revelation 1:5b–6, we are to live in praise to Jesus—

> Unto him that loved us, and washed us from our sins in his own blood, and hath made us kings and priests unto God and his Father; to him be glory and dominion for ever and ever.

At Sinai the thunder from the mountain called for obedience to the God who had brought the people out of Egypt, out of the land of bondage. From the edge of the throne room in glory John calls us in Revelation 1 to obey the God who loves us and freed us out of sin, out of the land of bondage by his blood. The laws are organized as rules for civil interaction, criminal law, family life, social obligations, and religious life and worship.

Civil laws

Civil laws handle the private interaction and disputes between citizens, in which the state steps in as an arbiter. If a farmer borrows someone's ox and it dies, how should the disputing parties resolve the matter? If you borrow someone's Mazda and it dies. . . ? The Old Testament offers basic principles of fairness and wisdom, good advice for a society that runs to the law courts at every turn. And for Christians the principle of fair play is tempered by the command to love. If I can show love to my neighbor in a dispute, even if it means worrying less about my own rights, God's love constrains my actions. Many non-Christians have been won to the Lord by seeing open-handed mercy when they expected tight-fisted self-interest. *The principle of God's civil law is that loving mercy extends the open hand to others.*

Criminal laws

Ancient Israel had a special covenant connection with God; therefore, we cannot apply their criminal laws in all aspects to our own government. Some laws seem harsh: Sabbath breaking, for example, was punishable by death, as was blasphemy. Man and woman offenders could be stoned to death for adultery. But in a theocracy, in which God was covenantally connected to the nation, any act that fundamentally violated the purity of the covenant relationship threatened national security. In the end Israel was destroyed because the people did not take seriously their obligation to remain undefiled.

And impurity is criminal in God's sight. We who are Christians also live in covenantal connection with God. Should we institute the death penalty for sinners in the church? This is hardly the prescription of the New Testament. Our personal relationship is founded in the blood of Christ and so is unbreakable. But not all who have their names on the church roll are God's people. We should love them and witness to them, but there are occasions for harsh sanctions, even excommunication from the church. Criminal immorality brings dishonor. I strongly believe that God punishes or has withdrawn from congregations—even denominations—who have not held themselves pure. Exercising church discipline must be done carefully, but the congregation that allows a practicing adulterer or a practicing malicious gossip to tear down the holiness of the body is in danger of a corporate death penalty (1 Corinthians 5:9–13; Revelation 2:5; 3:2–3, 16).

We also live under a civil government in which criminal acts given in God's law are rightly punished. As citizens we should promote an Old Testament principle that is often misunderstood. People say, "The Old Testament law was cruel, for it commanded us to take 'an eye for an eye and a tooth for a tooth.' How wonderful that Jesus canceled that law." Did he really? Here is what Jesus taught:

> Ye have heard that it hath been said, An eye for an eye, and a tooth for a tooth: But I say unto you, that ye resist not evil: but whosoever shall smite thee on thy right cheek, turn to him the other also. And whosoever shall compel thee to go a mile, go with him twain. Give to him that asketh thee, and from him that would borrow of thee, turn not thou away. [Matthew 5:38–39, 41–42]

Notice that Jesus does not say, "It is written." Rather, he remarks, "You have heard that it was said." Jesus is not dispatching Old Testament law into oblivion but correcting an invalid interpretation—that God allows private revenge. Quite the opposite is true. God's people are to prefer personal injustice against themselves to taking vengeance. Their attitude is to go beyond what people expect in forgiving. The criminal laws of the land do not come into the discussion at all, and Jesus never says that they no longer apply. Their principle is justice itself—Let the punishment fit the crime. Don't take barbaric delight in torturing the law-breaker. And don't give preferential treatment to one evildoer over someone else who commits the same crime. God's criminal code took into account circumstances but never social standing. Judges were not to give preference in sentencing. Higher social status was not reason for easier punishment. Nor was punishment mitigated because of a difficult childhood or social disadvantage. "Let the punishment fit the crime," God demanded:

So shalt thou put the evil away from among you. And those which remain shall hear, and fear, and shall henceforth commit no more any such evil among you. And thine eye shall not pity; but life shall go for life, eye for eye, tooth for tooth, hand for hand, foot for foot. [Deuteronomy 19:19b–21]

During its rare times of obedience Israel did inflict the death penalty and the lash, but their stress was on restitution of two, three, or four times the amount of damage, depending on the circumstances of the crime. Dehumanizing penal servitude was unknown. The principles of God's department of criminal justice were:

1. Purge the evil, by death or banishment if such extreme punishment is appropriate.
2. Make justice certain and painful enough that the law might be feared.
3. Use restitution and reconciliation of the offender when possible.
4. Fit the punishment to the crime.

We are not commanded to return our nation to Israel's theocracy, but we would do well to examine the principles of God's criminal law that apply to the household of faith and to society.

Family laws

In the ancient world most societies had similar family laws. Children were the property of parents, who held power of life and death. A wife was the property of the husband. She could own nothing. The husband was under a clan patriarch who had final say over the family circle. Israel was never more set apart than in its ideal for the family. Respect, obedience, and honor were demanded of children. Parents could not kill or treat their children cruelly. Marriage and divorce laws protected the woman to an extent unknown in other cultures. Women even could own property.

Some of these family laws sound strange in our culture, for they were tailored to the situations of that time. Still, the principles of the law apply today:

1. Husband, wife, and children owe mutual respect and honor.
2. A chain of loving, serving authority, with perfect equality, flows from God through husband to wife to children.
3. The family unit must be protected by the community in time of disaster.

Social laws

Some might say that we can still benefit from the principles of the civil, criminal, and family laws of the Old Testament, but they certainly lacked our cradle-to-grave social care. Yet look at the record: Our various plans for "warring on poverty" have come a long way in cataloging all the ways that will *not* end poverty. The more social programs at our disposal, the more degrading poverty seems to become. Actually, ancient Israel did not do so well in this arena either. Greed and personal interests interfered with love, then as now. But the Old Testament's humanitarian instructions covered a vast number of situations. Here are some general principles:

1. Each person is responsible for helping those in need.
2. Financial and social status never affect an individual's worth.
3. The worshiping community provides the safety net.

The principle that each person helps his or her neighbor does not mean a handout, but a hand up. For example, loans must be repaid, but at no interest. If that sounds impractical, I would point out that the average interest rate for the ancient Near East was 25 percent and up! Charging no interest was radical thinking in that time, too. Is it better for government to dole out money? The money runs out, but need keeps coming as dependency dehumanizes generations of recipients. Where Christians have taken Old Testament mandates seriously, those in poverty have purchased homes through creatively built and remodeled housing and no-interest loans. They have learned to budget, parent, work, and keep surroundings clean, to pay for what they receive or "glean" through food cooperatives and work programs. It is interesting how often government praises the creative innovations of biblical social programs. But government seldom copies their basic point—the respectful helping hand that pulls those in poverty out of its degradation.

A last resort for a poor person who had fallen upon hard times in Israel was to sell himself into slavery. The law, however, forbade a Hebrew master from looking down on one who had become a servant, for God's law reminded that they had all been slaves in Egypt. The slave was to be provided for, treated with respect, and freed after no longer than seven years, with as much of a stake as the master could afford to break the cycle of poverty.

A return to slavery today is not the application; the principle is that love and respect offer a powerful force for change. A prison guard in Missouri was devastated to learn that his child had a life threatening illness requiring expensive treatment. As word got around about the family's plight one of the inmates figured there had to be some way to help. But how? Inmates could not have cash, and what little money they earned or their families sent to their accounts would do little. Undaunted, the inmate talked to believers who were part of the prison chapter of Jaycees. A plan evolved. A Jaycees photographer was allowed to take pictures to sell on family visiting days. Officers at the front desk handled the cash transactions. Hundreds of dollars accumulated toward the guard's medical bills. Other inmates became involved. For some it may have been the first time they had sought to help another without seeking something in return. Respecting love broke down barriers with creative love and the open hand. It testified that we all were once slaves in the land of bondage.

The worshiping community should provide for the helpless. God established no Department of Health and Human Services. Help flowed to the family from the worshiping community, not the government, when the breadwinner died, crops failed, or some other crisis knocked them off of their feet. Church and family partnership before God still provides the best safety net. How sad that we have turned over to government what is not a proper governmental task. We reap the results in high taxes, corruption, inefficiency, and programs that hurt more than help.

Religious laws

Ceremonial issues involved in the worship of God don't concern us today, do they? Let us look at the principles and see. God took a detailed interest in worship. Not just any form of worship would do. If an interesting form of ceremony was noticed among pagan idolaters, there was a simple rule to follow for using it to worship the true God: Don't!

We no longer go to a temple or have priests sacrifice animals to appease God's anger at our sins. But we still are part of that system. The Book of Hebrews tells us that the temple at Jerusalem has been superseded by the real temple of God's presence. A priest still intercedes for us—the Messiah Jesus. One sacrifice on the cross has replaced all the bulls and sheep and doves. They were a shadow of the real thing. When Christ, the substance, came, the shadows faded. No longer do we keep the Passover or the Day of Atonement, for Christ our Passover has accomplished it all (1 Corinthians 5:7).

Old Testament patterns do speak to us. First, God wants us to come before him in humility, repentance, praise, and thanksgiving. The form of worship must mirror the reality; worship must be in Spirit and in truth (John 4:24). Second, we are not to make up new ways to worship, though we have lots of room for creativity with those he has given. God's Word outlines worship. Third, time must be set aside for God. Though Sunday as the day of resurrection has replaced the Saturday Sabbath, the Sabbath principle still works. It is good for us (see pp. 374–75). Those who must work on Sunday miss an important blessing and will be easily distracted from God if they do not find alternative times to come to him in worship and serving with a community of believers. Keeping a sabbath of service and worship can be difficult, but it seldom is impossible. Talk to your pastor about alternative ways to set aside time if your work schedule is a problem.

Law and gospel

Yes, we should study the Old Testament laws with joy, thankful that their precepts are good, even as their applications may have changed in the power of the gospel. All of the Bible basically contains two elements: law and gospel. We have looked at the fact that the gospel proclaims "good news." The Bible is not just "good advice"; neither is its basic message found in laws. The laws voiced from the mountain anticipated a night when angel voices burst the sky: "We bring you glad tidings of good news." The good news is that those who have not followed the good advice from the mountain can have God's mercy. Only after trusting in Christ for the good news of God's grace—only after being redeemed from the penalty for lawbreaking—do we find that the commandments of God show a lifestyle that pleases God and that works.

But like everything else in the spiritual sphere, we confuse good advice with good news. Suppose you live in rural America of a century ago. One day you go to the city. To your amazement you discover that horses are not being used to pull carts. Instead, people have rigged their buggies so the horses push the carts. Confusion reigns. People sit in their buggies, staring eyeball to eyeball at their horses, pleading with them to "Giddyap! Push! Push!"

Somehow it doesn't work nearly as well. You can only shake your head at the incredible stupidity of these city folks.

But look around at a society that once had a Christian superstructure and churches where the gospel was declared. Everyone from Norman Lear on down looks for a moral structure without the gospel. Although they may not admit it, they want some version of God's good advice because deep inside they know that some things are right and some are wrong. Yet, in their godless versions of God's good advice they refuse to recognize absolutes. They have hooked up the buggy backwards and substituted the horse with a blind laboratory rat. At this writing Russia has enormous problems to overcome after three-quarters of a century under communism. But Thomas is right in his column: Millions of the Russian people are "rushing toward God like a repentant sinner," while the West runs toward self-salvation. New laws go on the books each year, but no good news.

Every other religion in the world, except atheism and paganism, speaks from law. The law says: "Keep me in order to have merit before God. Do this. Do that. Don't do something else." Christianity sets the horse before the cart. Christ says, "I am the Lord, your God, who can bring you out of the land of death through my blood, out of the house of bondage to sin. I change your heart and give you salvation and my Spirit. *Therefore*, keep my commands. Having first been brought to God, we do these things. The difference between Christianity and the other religions of the world is the difference between *in order to* and *therefore*.

"The world has many religions," said George Owen. "It has but one gospel." When people say, "All religions are the same," they are saying that Christianity, like the others, is all *do* and *don't do*. It is an *in order to* sort of faith. In other world religions men and women must reach up and somehow find God. The word *religion* means "bind oneself to." Only in Christianity is God reaching down to men and women. Only the real God does what is necessary for us to be reconciled to him. The basic message of Christianity is not *do* but *done*. "It is finished!" were Christ's words on the cross (John 19:30). It is complete! It is enough! The gospel is not a challenge to do; it is an offer to receive.

What the law does

What, then, does the law do for those who are outside of Christ? First, it reveals their sin. Second, it reveals how bad our sin truly is. Third, it actually makes people more rebellious and sinful. Fourth, it shows how hopeless the situation is.

The law reveals sin

Without understanding sin, no one would understand the need for Christ. "I had not known sin, but by the law," explains Paul. "I had not known lust, except the law had said, Thou shalt not covet." (Romans 7:7; see also Romans 2:15). Many do not realize that lusting in the heart is adultery in the sight of God, or that anger in the heart is murder in the sight of God. When the law reveals these things, we see our guilt.

The law reveals the awfulness of sin

The law shows us how guilty guilt is. People want to live in the grays. They don't want to be "evil," really. They want just to sample the edges of evil, to push the boundaries a bit. God's ethics knows no middle ground. There are no "white" lies. Lies are black and abominable to a God who is total truth. His eyes are too pure to look upon shades of sin. All sin means corruption, and he cannot but punish it.

The law aggravates the motions of sin

You are driving down the street at fifty miles an hour. The radio plays a song you like, and all is well with the world. Suddenly you pass a sign that declares: "Speed limit 25." The law has come and declares that you are not in conformity. Now there is struggle. Will you continue to sail along at fifty or reduce your speed? You don't want to reduce your speed. You are in a hurry. You are late for an appointment. You feel rebellious that fences are set around choices. Law makes sin into struggle.

John Bunyan in *The Pilgrim's Progress* explains this nicely. The hero of his story, "Pilgrim," is taken into a large, beautifully appointed parlor. However, it has not been dusted or swept in many a year. Cobwebs are thick. His companion, "Interpreter," calls in a maiden with a broom and bids her to sweep. The dust she stirs up chokes Christian until he asks its meaning. Interpreter replies, "This is the work of the law in the heart. The dust is the sin that is accumulated there for years, and then the law comes and stirs it up."

Romans 5:20 says that "law entered, that the offence might abound." It stirs up sin that we choke on it. In the story, Interpreter calls in another maiden and bids her sprinkle the room with water. Once the dust settles it is easily cleansed. These, he explains, are the sweet influences of the dew of the gospel, which takes away and makes easily removable the sin in our hearts.

The law shows human hopelessness

How well must one keep the law to be accepted? By now you should immediately hear the answer: "Perfectly." A number of years ago my wife and I had dinner at the home of one of our church families. Seated across from me was the hostess's mother, a woman of about seventy. She said to me, "Oh, Reverend Kennedy, I am so happy to be able to ask you something I've always wanted to ask a minister. How good does a person have to be to be good enough to get into heaven?"

"Oh, that is an easy question to answer."

Her face broke into a huge smile. "Do you mean you *know*? You'll never know how relieved I am. I have been worrying about that for years."

"You'll never need to worry about the answer to that question again. Jesus said it very clearly: 'Be perfect, as your heavenly Father is perfect'" [see Matthew 5:48].

She looked like a cartoon character that had been hit by a skillet! She sat silently for a long time, then said, "I think I'm going to worry about that more than ever."

"I did not go into the ministry to make people worry, but to deliver them from their worries," I assured her. Then I shared the gospel of Jesus Christ: Though none of us lives up to God's standard, Jesus came to do what we have been unable to do. The law shows how much we need Christ.

For as many as are of the works of the law are under the curse: for it is written, Cursed is every one that continueth not in all things which are written in the book of the law to do them. But that no man is justified by the law in the sight of God, it is evident: for, The just shall live by faith. And the law is not of faith: but, The man that doeth them shall live in them. Christ hath redeemed us from the curse of the law, being made a curse for us: for it is written, Cursed is every one that hangeth on a tree: That the blessing of Abraham might come on the Gentiles through Jesus Christ; that we might receive the promise of the Spirit through faith. [Galatians 3:10–14]

The great difference

What then is the difference between law and gospel?

The law binds the unbeliever; the gospel of grace frees the believer to obey God's will.

The law is condemnation; the gospel of grace is mercy and justification.

The law convicts; the gospel of grace relieves.

The law produces rebellion; the gospel of grace produces submission.

The law depresses us with inability; the gospel of grace delivers us in power.

The law produces pride in those who suppose they can make the passing grade; the gospel of grace produces thankfulness in those who know they cannot, those who have been accepted anyway.

The law says, "Do in order to"; the gospel of grace says, "Done."

The law says, "Go and work"; the gospel of grace says, "Come to Christ for rest."

We are not saved by the law; we are not saved by the gospel plus the law; we are not saved by faith plus works. We are saved by faith alone, forgiven, and empowered to keep the law in its purest form of love.

How is life made free in Christ?

The liberty which Christ hath purchased for believers under the gospel consists in their freedom from the guilt of sin, the condemning wrath of God, the curse of the moral law; and in their being delivered from this present evil world, bondage to Satan, and dominion of sin, from the evil of afflictions, the sting of death, the victory of the grave, and everlasting damnation.

[Westminster Confession of Faith, chapter 20]

19

"Give Me Liberty!"

We in the West face a subtle adversary in humanism, the philosophy that humankind is the measure of all things, and that spiritual values are irrelevant, or dangerous. The subtlety and seriousness of the enemy was forced into my consciousness as I spoke with someone and happened to mention Patrick Henry.

"Who?" she asked.

It turned out this was not a momentary memory lapse. This young woman, as best she could recall, had honestly never heard of the Christian statesman and orator who, perhaps more than any other, ignited the sparks that caused the independence of this nation to come to pass. Then I remembered reading that some history texts have expunged the name of Henry and the speech for which he is most famous, his call to "Give me liberty or give me death!" Henry's thundering sentiment, I understand, is not deemed appropriate to teach. It is thought inconsistent with the ideal of peaceful coexistence and acceptance of others. Back in the anti-war protest days this feeling was summed up in that heart-fluttering cry from the college campus: "Better red than dead!"

Henry was hardly a menace to world order. In fact, he was elected governor of Virginia six times. Yet on the day he made the statement he was only a spectator in the Virginia House of Burgesses. He listened with growing frustration, as the delegates considered why the colonies should not go too far in offending mother England. When he could stomach no more of it he rose to his feet, at first speaking softly, then building up a crescendo of passion:

They tell us, sir, that we are weak—unable to cope with so formidable an adversary. But when shall we be stronger? Will it be the next week, or the next year? Will it be when we are totally disarmed, and when a British guard shall be stationed in every house? Shall we gather strength by irres-

Now the Lord is that Spirit: and where the Spirit of the Lord is, there is liberty. [2 Corinthians 3:17]

olution and inaction? Shall we acquire the means of effectual resistance by lying supinely on our backs, and, hugging the delusive phantom of hope, until our enemies shall have bound us hand and foot?

As he continued his words became thunderbolts falling on the seats around him. People moved forward in their seats and strained their necks to see who was talking. He concluded:

There is a just God who presides over the destinies of nations, and who will raise up friends to fight our battles for us. The battle, sir, is not to the strong alone; it is to the vigilant, the active, the brave. Besides, sir, we have no election. If we were base enough to desire it, it is now too late to retire from the contest. There is no retreat but in submission and slavery. Our chains are forged. Their clanking may be heard on the plains of Boston. The war is inevitable, and let it come! I repeat it, sir: Let it come!

> It is in vain, sir, to extenuate the matter. Gentlemen may cry peace, peace—but there is no peace. The war is actually begun! The next gale that sweeps from the north will bring to our ears the clash of resounding arms! Our brethren are already in the field! Why stand we idle here? What is it that gentlemen wish? What would they have? Is life so dear, or peace so sweet, as to be purchased at the price of chains and slavery?
>
> Forbid it, Almighty God! I know not what course others may take, but as for me, give me liberty or give me death!

As he finished, such astonishment fell upon the legislators that most could think of only one course of action. They took steps that would lead inexorably toward revolution and American independence.

The meaning of liberty

When Christians speak of liberty they often narrow the focus to questions of how freely we may behave and still be considered saved. People want to know what they can get by with. Some of this discussion has been practical and important in dealing with matters that are not specifically addressed in the Bible. An example is whether Christians should participate in the secular trappings of Christmas and Easter, decorating trees, giving presents, and hiding colored eggs. Other examples involve what kinds of songs may be sung in worship or whether Christians have liberty of conscience about whether to run for public office, drink alcoholic beverages, dance, play cards, go to movies, own a television, smoke, participate on a jury, carry a gun in the military, work in a store that sells *Playboy,* or a large variety of other matters. Each issue involves its own underlying biblical principles, even if the activity itself is not specifically mentioned in Scripture.

But a larger question of liberty must be answered before we counsel or condemn. If we seem to regulate behavior without laying the groundwork of understanding what Christian liberty means, we surely will come off as the self-righteous prigs many in the secular world believe Christians to be.

Any biblical discussion of Christian liberty proceeds from the attitude of a Patrick Henry, an attitude of controlled, disciplined defiance in the face of force. A few of his listeners must have thought Patrick was making a lot of fuss. "Aw, come on! We don't have it so bad. The English tax our tea, and their laws are rather arbitrary, but after all, we are just a weak little colony. Why rock the boat?"

"NO!" was the rejoinder. "A greater principle is involved than taxes, and some principles are more important than life itself. Giving them up voluntarily is not an option." Henry was not concerned that life would be more carefree if Americans didn't have to pay taxes for tea. The control of the national destiny of America was the issue. Here was a non-negotiable.

Now listen to another voice that began to speak softly but soon was roaring with indignant passion:

> I marvel that ye are so soon removed [literally, becoming a turncoat] from him that called you into the grace of Christ unto another gospel: Which is not another; but there be some that trouble you, and would pervert the gospel of Christ. But though we, or an angel from heaven, preach any other gospel unto you than that which we have preached unto you, let him be accursed. As we said before, so say I now again, if any man preach any other gospel unto you than that ye have received, let him be accursed. [Galatians 1:6–9]

Surely some people in the Galatian church were surprised by the hot words. "Cool down, Paul. Aren't you getting exercised over very little? What can it hurt if we set a few stipulations on people coming into the church? We still look to God for our salvation. We only want to add something. People will be saved by grace, *and....*"

"NO!" came the rejoinder. "A greater principle is involved—the very freedom for which the Son of God died, the freedom of grace over sin and death. That freedom is no option. If anyone tries to throw away the atonement of Christ, let him be damned!"

That was the attitude with which the framers of the *Westminster Confession of Faith* gathered in the midst of the English Civil War to set forth principles they believed were worth dying for. These men knew that, should their king be victorious over the forces of Parliament in this bloody war, all of their lives might well be forfeit.

When they came to their own statement, "Of Christian Liberty, and Liberty of Conscience," they wrote carefully and sought balance. "God alone is Lord of the conscience," they declared, "and hath left it free from the doctrines and commandments of men which are in any thing contrary to his Word, or beside it in matters of faith or worship." All people did not have to believe as they did. However, no human government or doctrine or church had the right to bind the destiny of God's people to a philosophy that violated God's Word. Liberties purchased by the blood of Christ were non-negotiable:

> Christ purchased freedom from the guilt of sin.
> Christ purchased freedom from the condemning wrath of God.
> Christ purchased freedom from the curse of the law.
> Christ purchased freedom from bondage to an evil world system.
> Christ purchased freedom from bondage to Satan.
> Christ purchased freedom from the dominion of sin.
> Christ purchased freedom from the afflictions brought on the body by sin.
> Christ purchased freedom from the power of death, the grave, and everlasting damnation.

The *Confession* makes a connection that American Christians seem to have forgotten, though it has been proven by world history. The moral ethic of civil liberty and the Christian reality of spiritual liberty interlocked. Where Christianity has become a vital force in society, freedom and liberty have expanded. Does this equate loving America with loving God? Some have mistakenly made that connection and created an idolatrous civil religion. However, the principles that built stable, freedom-living democracies in the Christian West have grown out of the hearts of those who love God. Christians who understood biblical freedom in Christ were salty enough that they influenced the creation of an American Constitution. Even those who hated Christianity among the framers of the Constitution were profoundly aware that its ethical principles worked. They knew that where men's and women's hearts were truly different in the liberty of Christianity, their behavior was more caring and serving. Where the Spirit of the Lord was, there was liberty.

That first became obvious one day in an ancient synagogue in Nazareth when a young local man who was making a name for himself as a rabbi stood and unrolled the scroll of the prophet Isaiah (61:1–2a). He read:

> The spirit of the Lord GOD is upon me; because the LORD hath anointed me to preach good tidings unto the meek; he hath sent me to bind up the broken-hearted, to proclaim liberty to the captives, and the opening of the prison to them that are bound; to proclaim the acceptable year of the LORD.

Jesus announced in that moment that he came to proclaim deliverance—to set the captives free. We know that the great work of Christ is the work of redemption, to "buy back out of bondage," to restore from slavery. "Stand fast therefore in the liberty wherewith Christ hath made us free" Paul said (Galatians 5:1). Jesus said, "If the Son therefore shall make you free, ye shall be free indeed" (John 8:36). Right away two implications of the freedoms listed in the *Westminster Confession* become obvious: First, this list in no way invites us to "get by" with loose living. We are freed from the bondage of sin to live in Christ's presence. Our conscience is unchained from the guilt of a lifetime in sin without Christ. We are unchained from rebellion against God. Paul advises us that, since we were called to be free, "use not liberty for an occasion to the flesh, but by love serve one another" (Galatians 5:13). This is an invitation to self-discipline. Second, this freedom is that of a freed slave, so it certainly doesn't make Christians better than anyone else. Among Christians "there is neither Jew nor Greek, there is neither bond nor free, there is neither male nor female: for ye are all one in Christ Jesus" (Galatians 3:28). Among other unbelievers we are called to continue the task of proclaiming liberty to the captives. Now, imagine what that attitude does to the life of a nation founded upon Christian principles. To the extent those principles are known and believed, exactly to that extent government establishes true freedom and justice for all. Where humanistic principles are believed and proclaimed there is no reason not to cheat and enslave, for there is no absolute standard for justice (see pp. 320–28).

The loss of liberty

The American Declaration of Independence and Constitution were written, we are told, to secure, among other things, the blessings of liberty to ourselves and our children. Throughout the long history of this world, those times and places where people have enjoyed true liberty have been few. The vast majority of people have never enjoyed the blessings of liberty. These blessings, so rare, are easily taken for granted. Liberty cannot be seen, tasted, or smelled. Those who have it come to prize it not at all. In the late 1980s and early 1990s, a group of nations began to feel the new birth of freedom after decades under a totalitarian rule. Yet we saw how fragile, indeed, that freedom could be in the civil wars and political unrest that followed. George Orwell was a journalist who saw firsthand the influences of Nazism and communism. Then, to his horror, he saw his own England being subverted by a strong communist movement during World War II. His warning to England was the bitter allegorical story *Animal Farm*— a description of what was at risk. He was asked one time about his vision of the future. "The future," he said, "is a picture of a boot stomping on the face of a man forever." Without faith in the Christ who proclaimed liberty to the captives, Orwell could see no hope for liberty. And without the Christ who proclaims liberty, Orwell is correct.

Abraham Lincoln, who was a Christian, understood better the danger and the hope: "Our fathers brought forth upon this continent a new nation, conceived in liberty. . . . Now we are engaged in a great civil war, testing whether that nation, or any nation so conceived and so dedicated, can long endure."

I am afraid modern blessings of liberty are threatened in some of the same ways the government of Charles II threatened the freedoms of English citizens in the era before the Westminster Assembly. Not all Bill of Rights liberties are made sacred by Scripture, and the writers of the *Confession* said Christian liberty is not a pretense to "oppose any lawful power, or the lawful exercise of it, whether it be civil or ecclesiastical." Yet there is a place to stand with Patrick Henry in defiance of societies or governments or the powers of demons. No legitimate power on earth or in heaven or hell can impinge upon that liberty that, "being delivered out of the hands of our enemies, we might serve the Lord without fear, in holiness and righteousness before him, all the days of our life." Does this statement from the *Confession* chapter 20 repeat a familiar strain?

"What is our chief purpose for existing?" asked the Westminster writers.

"To glorify God and enjoy him forever," came their answer.

Who has given us the freedom to fulfil God's ultimate purpose for us?

God in Christ has died and risen so that we might freely glorify and enjoy him.

Who dare trade that freedom for fake self-righteousness on one side or unholy living that makes light of Christ's death on the other? Even if angels teach such things, let them be damned.

"Is life so dear, or peace so sweet, as to be purchased at the price of chains and slavery? Forbid it, Almighty God! I know not what course others may take, but as for me, give me liberty or give me death!"

I am afraid that our blessings of liberty are under great threat for want of men and women whose love extends to sacrifice. Spiritual liberty, and even liberty to live as a disciplined citizen, come out of hearts that know liberty in Jesus Christ, for where the Spirit of the Lord is, there is liberty. Martin Luther used to refer to himself as *Martin Elutheras. Elutheras* is the Greek word for "free." In Christ he was *Martin the Free.* Does the name *Elutheras* belong to you as well? Have you been set free by Jesus Christ? If Christ has set you free, the Spirit of God dwells in your heart and there is a burning flame for Christian liberty. I am confident that all of the oppressors and all of the tyrants in all of the world will not be able to finally stamp out that flame. We need men and women with that burning passion for Christ and for the freedom that he alone can give—a freedom from sin and a freedom from tyranny and oppression.

For want of such men and women the Christian witness in America has withdrawn over the last century. The church stopped moving forward to proclaim liberty in every sphere of life. A defective view of Christianity, called *pietism*, produced this retreat. Pietism emphasized a very personal and private spirituality. Personal spirituality is good. But pietism excludes the world. Instead of effecting positive change, pietists confine spirituality to their own lives. The very first mandate God gave us in the Garden of Eden is ignored, to subdue the earth and have dominion over it (Genesis 1:28). God called his creatures to involvement in the business of the world. That mandate was never rescinded by the fall into sin, though it became a great challenge in a world degraded by sin and shame.

As pietism pushed the faithful into their holy corner, ominous movements crept in and various spheres were turned over to the unbelievers. The movements slowly became crowding weeds in the garden of liberty, imperiling religious freedoms in the arts, the media, science, law, politics, the social sciences, and education. The authority and genius behind these movements is satanic. Their intent is to take away, where possible, the authority and ability to glorify God and enjoy him in the very spheres of life most important to subduing and ruling creation today.

Our adversaries have willingly persevered and watched for each step back. Paul Blanshard, one of the best known humanist educators in America, wrote an article in *Humanist* magazine looking back over the last seventy-five years. He noted with satisfaction that those years were "full of rebellion against religious superstition." In fact, he also says that after sixteen years in school Johnny may not be able to read, but at least we have rid his mind of the religious superstition that he brought to school from home. Blanshard goes on to say that he doubts that any span in human history has carried the world farther along to honest doubt. Robert C. Hawley, an architect of values clarification education, wrote in his book *Human Values in the Classroom* that the battle for humanistic values is not yet won:

> Still, we must make a beginning. And we can see already signs of hope in such things as the increasing interest in the open classroom, individualized instruction, integrated-day-type classrooms, schools-without-walls, alternative schools, etc. But these beginnings have still left the lives of millions and millions of children unchanged. We must persist, we must step up our efforts, we must persevere: The time is growing short, the time to teach the human values is now, the time to teach survival is at hand.

Anyone who has followed the course of education since 1973 when this book was published knows that some of the great steps Dr. Hawley foresaw have been tried and have failed and been dropped by educators. But those ideas were not the real agenda. They only were signs of moving in the right direction. The goal was to "teach human values," to replace the old educational measures of excellence and absolutes with a moral philosophy of relativism and human-centered religion. And the fruits of those advances have devastated a generation. John J. Dunphy wrote, also in *Humanist*,

> I am convinced that the battle for human kind's future must be waged and won in the public school classroom by teachers who correctly perceive their role as proselytizers of a new faith. . . . They will be ministers of another sort, utilizing a classroom instead of a pulpit to convey humanist values in whatever subject they teach. The classroom must and will become an arena of conflict between the old and the new—the rotting corpse of Christianity . . . and the new faith of humanism.

These visionaries have pushed on toward their goal— what they saw as a better world. Their vision is stronger and clearer than that of many Christians. Such atheistic leaders believed in the importance of fighting for their mission persistently and patiently. True, its end has already achieved the destruction of important aspects of liberty, but the humanists seek what they see as a greater ideal— an ideal they view as non-negotiable. Their ideal has advanced for want of more Patrick Henrys in the church. We left the field, and our more dedicated opponents were waiting. The same has happened in every sphere of life, even the church.

One of the most disastrous consequences has involved the law, as judges reinterpreted the First Amendment to push Christians aside. The founding fathers of America believed something diametrically opposed to what is taught now about the First Amendment. Does the First Amendment teach the separation of church and state? Ask almost any person on the street today and that person will say that, of course, it does. Everybody knows that. Separation has become the overwhelming assumption and a legal doctrine is justified by this interpretation. Yet any objective study of the Bill of Rights and the background of the First Amendment shows that this is not so. The founding fathers of this country resolved the issue of church and state in a marvelously balanced fashion. The First Amendment states:

> Congress shall make no law respecting an establishment of religion or forbidding the free exercise thereof.

What does that say about what the church can and cannot do? What does that say about what the citizen should or should not do? It says nothing about such things. It says nothing about the church whatever. The rule does not protect the state from the church; it protects the church from the state.

Where, then, did we get this idea of a "wall of separation between church and state"? It comes from a letter Thomas Jefferson angrily wrote in 1802 to Baptists and Congregationalists in Danbury, Connecticut, because they had attacked him when he ran for President. They had called him an infidel, an atheist, and a few other uncomplimentary things. In his letter he told them, in effect, to shut up and stay in their place. He said there should be "a wall of separation between church and state." Jefferson certainly was welcome to his opinion, and certainly he was not the only one who has felt that way. That is not, however, what went into the Constitution, and it is my opinion that Jefferson himself would not have wanted to put it there once he got over his snit with the Baptists. Not all the framers of the Constitution were Christians. Not all were deists either, as some historians seem to believe. Whatever their religion, however, they valued a stable government and found the most tested and successful values for that stability in the Bible. What they did not appreciate was the custom of government supporting one religion with tax dollars or passing laws mandating presence in Sunday services.

The criminality of Christ

Our religious liberties as Americans depend on understanding the difference between protecting religion from the state and protecting the state from religion. The First Amendment is a one-way street. All of the Bill of Rights—the first ten amendments to the Constitution—was written to restrain the federal government from interfering with the liberties of the people. Their very reason for the passage of the Bill of Rights amendments to the Constitution was that those at the constitutional convention were afraid of a centralized government and refused to accept one unless the rights of the people were further defined and protected.

And their very first right priority guaranteed freedom of religion and expression, both of which are regularly denied to Christians. The wall of separation doctrine that made a private letter into public constitutional law is emphatically a two-way street. It prohibits and restrains both state and church. But even that two-way protection has been denied by some major church-state decisions of the last thirty years. Courts have tended to restrict the church and allow as little interaction from the church side as possible. That is exactly 180 degrees from what those at the constitutional convention—I suspect even Jefferson—would have wanted.

Several years ago the state of California moved to tackle one of its great criminal activities—home Bible studies. The newspaper account of this action said that the Bible studies were shut down despite the fact that the people said they would not sing songs and would disperse their cars. They were told that if one person outside the family was involved in studying the Bible it was an unlawful church activity. How far is this from the long-standing persecution of unofficial house churches in China? Actually it is even more restrictive, for these Bible studies were not even acting as churches, as do the illegal Chinese bodies.

California also made headlines some years back with a survey that went out to the churches asking such questions as: "Have you in the past year made any statements concerning such political matters as abortion? homosexual rights? ERA?" More than eighty churches declined to answer such statements, and their churches were immediately thrown onto the tax rolls. Buildings were confiscated.

Such an outcry went up that the intolerable tyranny was stopped, but this is the kind of action and reaction taking place. The government most recently has moved to apply antiracketeering charges against abortion protesters. We may soon see a test case in which an organized church that speaks out against the murder of unborn children will be charged with being an organized crime ring.

Another ominous tendency is seen in the legal revolution going on in the West. Ask the person on the street the question: "Can you legislate morality?" The answer will come back: "Of course you can't, and you shouldn't try." If you can't legislate morality, what can you legislate? Immorality? The fact is that you cannot legislate anything but morality. We have laws against stealing because it is immoral to steal; rape because it is immoral to rape. The issue is whose morality is being legislated. Recent attempts to legislate home schools out of existence—even when the home schooled children do exceptionally well in achievement tests—operate from the premise that the only moral way to educate children is in schools. Society has an obligation to protect children from the immoral educational standards imposed by the home schooling parents. Refusing to hire an active homosexual has been declared immoral in the halls of legislatures and courts. Increasingly Western conceptions of immorality are quite clearly those actions or beliefs that do not conform to the humanist agenda. Look closely at any law or court decision that seems wrong-headed or controverted in its reasoning. Someplace under the surface something is being declared moral and something else immoral. Usually it isn't too hard to figure whose morality is being legislated.

The American legislative system was founded upon the Judeo-Christian ethic of the founding fathers. Jefferson wrote the charter for the University of Virginia that the proofs for God as the sovereign Lord and Creator and Ruler of this world and of the moral requirements and obligations that flow from that, must be taught to all students. Is this the same wall-of-separation Jefferson? One would almost think he approved of a theistic ethic at the very foundation of education's contributions to society and government. Perhaps he didn't mind religion's place in moral leadership; he simply disliked Baptist preachers who got personal about it.

Significant changes have appeared in the moral fabric of legislative and judicial theory. One worldview system seeks to push away another. Once the substitution is complete society may be very alien in its approach to human rights and freedoms than anything known to date. Think of the changes that have appeared in the last half century in the areas of infanticide, euthanasia, homosexuality, marriage and divorce, pornography, gambling, suicide. . . . This is not to say that the founding fathers were moral giants or that our grandparents of fifty years ago did not see fundamental flaws in the character of their society and government. All governments, from the national to the local levels, have blind spots, and ours have been serious. Liberty and equality for all has been more of an ideal than a reality. But it was an ideal even when it wasn't practiced or applied justly. A moral ethic operated, even when people didn't cooperate with it. James Madison, the primary author of the U.S. Constitution, said that we cannot govern without God and the Ten Commandments. The Supreme Court Building in Washington, D.C., has those Ten Commandments inscribed on its wall. Yet the Ten Commandments cannot be put up on the walls of a school in Kentucky. Why? The Supreme Court says doing so violates the Constitution that Madison wrote.

The call to non-negotiables

The wise and godly Bible teacher John Murray said that it is impossible to segregate ethics from the transcendent holiness, righteousness, and truth of God taught in Scripture. We may draw from this a linked chain of truths:

Only when the church holds a high view of a holy God and his self-revealing, inerrant Word to be non-negotiable does it have the moral ability to understand Christian liberty and its limits.

Only when an individual Christian submits himself or herself to a holy God through believing in Jesus Christ and repenting of sins, is Christian liberty in its fullest sense possible.

Only when the individual Christian becomes mature in sanctification will some questions about Christian liberty fall into place. Meanwhile, be careful not to offend God or a weaker brother or sister by pushing to the limits of ethical propriety. Yet imposing ethical restrictions on oneself or others without strong biblical warrant also offends God and fellow Christians (see, for example, Romans 14 and 1 Corinthians 8).

Only when individual Christians join Christ in proclaiming liberty and living in it will they become salt and light in local and national public life.

Only when secular governments honor and listen to the Judeo-Christian faith of Scripture will liberty become important enough to be a non-negotiable once again.

How is life made rich in Christ?

As it is of the law of nature, that, in general, a due proportion of time be set aside for the worship of God; so in his Word, by a positive, moral, and perpetual commandment, binding all men in all ages, he hath particularly appointed one day in seven for a Sabbath, to be kept holy unto him; which, from the beginning of the world to the resurrection of Christ, was the last day of the week; and, from the resurrection of Christ, was changed into the first day of the week, which in Scripture is called the Lord's day, and is to be continued to the end of the world, as the Christian Sabbath.

[Westminster Confession of Faith, chapter 21]

20

A Day Saved for Eternity

In the last chapter I considered that God has given us the liberty to fulfil our chief reason for existing—to glorify and enjoy him forever. We looked at some of the ways our enemy seeks to rob us of that liberty in Christ and how seriously the apostle Paul viewed any attempt to steal away what Christ has given to us. He angrily called down God's damnation upon human or angel who would subvert what belongs to the believer by heritage.

I wonder, though, should Paul walk around our nation on a typical Sunday, if he might not first vent his anger upon those who do not bother using what they possess. Do most Christians really want to enjoy God's company and fellowship? Do they wish to truly enjoy him through eternity? Do not our Sundays tell a different story? In the mid-1980s one of the last large cities to keep at least a token set of restrictions on Sabbath-day commerce was St. Louis County in Missouri. Time and society had eroded away most of the laws' enforcement, but some groups were miffed that government might still abide by the archaic custom of "blue laws." Particularly harmful was the fact that package liquor stores and most bars and restaurants were not allowed to serve alcohol on Sundays. A referendum was put on the ballot, and it received a lot of publicity. Some Christians campaigned fervently under the banner of the S.O.S. (Save Our Sunday) organization. They waged an heroic battle, but few were surprised that the election resoundingly voted to strip the legal codes of their Sunday provisions. Evidently not many who would have identified themselves as Christians cared to set aside a special day for worship and rest. Why should they? Some of them had stopped even attending church, and though many did go, at least occasionally, the day had become nothing truly special. It was a time for enjoying time off work to sleep in, golf, watch

> *Remember the Sabbath Day, to keep it holy. Six days shalt thou labor and do all thy work, but the seventh day is the sabbath to the LORD thy God.* [Exodus 20:8–10]

sports programs, or be with the family. Monday would do as well. Is Sunday anything special to God? Didn't the Sabbath used to be on Saturday anyway?

Remember the Sabbath

When Adam walked out of Eden he took with him two institutions that have immeasurably blessed the human race—the institution of the home, and one even older, the Sabbath. The Sabbath was the first institution God gave. Its benefit can hardly be overestimated. An old maxim states: "As goes the Sabbath, so goes the nation." We might do well to ponder that thought in the light of what happened in St. Louis, which was one of the last holdouts of a set-aside Sabbath. We live in a time when the Sabbath has come under great attack from several different points of view. There are those who declare that Christ abolished it, so it no longer is in effect. That view badly distorts what

Christ said, that he is Lord of the Sabbath (Matthew 12:8; see Matthew 12:1–13). Jesus abolished some teachings that were circulating in his day about the Sabbath. It is right, above all else, to do acts of love and mercy on that day. It is not designed to be a burden but a blessing. One may certainly take care of what needs to be done. But abolish the Sabbath? If he is Lord of it, he surely plans to keep it around. The Scriptures at no point teach that Christ annulled, abrogated, or abolished any of the Ten Commandments. On the contrary, the Scriptures plainly teach that the Commandments remain in effect and have been strengthened by Christ, who declared that we are to keep them in thought, word, and deed if we love him (see pp. 337–38).

It is interesting that when Jesus describes the end of the world, his second coming, and the destruction of Jerusalem in A.D. 70 (Matthew 24), he tells his followers to pray that their flight from the great calamity befalling the nation will not be in the winter nor on the Sabbath (v. 20). Bible scholars divide over whether Jesus refers here to an event at the end of the world, or to the destruction of Jerusalem forty years later. If it was the latter he meant the time when the New Testament was mostly written and the New Testament church well established. He certainly intended that the Sabbath would continue.

But did he intend that Sabbath would be on Sunday, the first day of the week, rather than Saturday, the seventh? Seventh-Day Adventists and some other groups maintain that the Sabbath was changed by Constantine around A.D. 325 when he, the first Christian emperor of Rome, made the first day of the week into the legal Sabbath. Anyone who supposes that Constantine changed the Sabbath day makes an error, for the Christian record is that from the beginning the church recognized that the symbol of God's rest on the seventh day was fulfilled when Christ arose on the first. And Sunday represents in the fullest sense the rest of all Christ's people from the burden of their sin. Let us take a brief look at the record of the Sabbath:

1. Jesus rose from the dead on the first day of the week; he appeared to the women and to the disciples on their way to Emmaus on that day of resurrection.
2. On the following first day of the week he appeared to Thomas and the other disciples.
3. The Holy Spirit was poured out on the church on the day of Pentecost, the first day of the week, and so the church was founded on this day, and Acts reports that Christians assembled on the first day of the week. The word used in Acts is the word from which we get "synagogue"; they "synagogued" together on the first day of the week. Collection for the poor was made on the first day as well.
4. It was on the first day, "the Lord's Day," that John was in the Spirit and saw Christ, high and lifted up and mighty (Revelation 1:10).
5. In A.D. 120, less than twenty-five years after John died, Barnabas, one of the early church fathers, wrote: "They kept the eighth day with joyfulness, the day in which Jesus rose from the dead." In A.D. 150 Justin Martyr recorded: "Sunday is the day on which we all hold our communion assembly because Jesus Christ, our Savior, on the same day arose from the dead."
6. In A.D. 194 Clement of Alexandria declared of the Christian: "He, in fulfillment of the precept according to the Gospel keeps the Lord's Day."
7. In about 200 Tertullian, another church father, added, "We solemnize the day after Saturday in contradiction to those who call that day their Sabbath [namely, the Jews]."

Beyond all this, do you suppose Constantine, who legalized the day to keep the support of the Christians who had helped him come to power, would have alienated those Christians by changing the day of their worship?

No, Sunday is the proper day for Christians to keep, though those who meet to honor and worship the Lord in Spirit and in truth, will hardly be turned away from his throne because they missed their appointment. Still, the keeping of Sunday is the keeping of the biblical "Lord's Day," the day for remembering that God created the world and rested therein, for Sabbath comes from the Hebrew *Shabbot*, meaning "rest." We further remember the Son's resurrection and the Holy Spirit's outpouring, and we look forward to the Christian's ultimate fulfillment of the Sabbath: "There remaineth therefore a rest to the people of God. For he that is entered into his rest, he also hath ceased from his own works, as God did from his" (Hebrews 4:9–10).

God's cycle of blessing

Yes, I think Sunday is a special day on God's weekly calendar, but the Sabbath principles transcend a day of the week, for they reflect an attitude of focused heart and desire for God's company. God offers his presence lavishly. God's presence is not the problem. The problem is me. I am a fickle lover of my God. I ask for his nearness and begin to offer my adoration, and then I am distracted by some more immediate desire. I will get back to God as soon as there is time, and I know he will understand. No, I need the Sabbath desperately: It demands that my attention be pulled from other distractions and set upon my Lover and Savior and Lord. Were it not for the discipline of Sunday, I would have a great deal more difficulty glorifying God and enjoying him any day of the week.

Certainly I also would be poorer without one time to worship alongside those of my fellow lovers in Christ. For as hard as it is to get together one day each week, imagine what it would be like to have no one time when our assembly was called. I am convinced that keeping one day in seven expresses God's best desire for the well-being of the believing—and even the unbelieving—world.

Sunday blesses those who have never set their foot inside a place of worship. The very distinction that one family sleeps in and lounges in robes for brunch, while their neighbors get up early to shepherd the kids through breakfast and corral them in the car, remains a vital witness before the watching world. Assuming that the busy Sunday morning family walks their witness all week, and assuming they go to worship out of love rather than self-righteous religiosity, their children may complain, but they will remember. And the neighbors may politely joke about it, but they also will be impressed, respectful, and maybe a bit envious. Why? Because holding that one day of the week as special flows into the rest of the week. And walking a higher plane from Monday through Saturday makes Sunday a greater joy. Life becomes a revolving cycle of devotion for God, fueled by a day each week set aside for absorbing eternal values. This is no magic formula that makes all family problems disappear and all frustrations cease. Yet I know of few suicides, divorces, and irretrievably broken relationships with children among families that set aside Sunday as a day saved for eternity. Certainly crises happen in a world of imperfect, sinful people, but not often and almost never without hope of repair. It is one of Scripture's most precious promises:

> If thou turn away thy foot from the sabbath, from doing thy pleasure on my holy day; and call the sabbath a delight, the holy of the LORD, honourable; and shalt honour him, not doing thine own ways, nor finding thine own pleasure, nor speaking thine own words: Then shalt thou delight thyself in the LORD; and I will cause thee to ride upon the high places of the earth, and feed thee with the heritage of Jacob thy father: for the mouth of the LORD hath spoken it. [Isaiah 58:13–14]

The Sabbath principles

So what are the principles that empower the Sabbath? Chapter 20 of the *Westminster Confession of Faith* suggests several that deal specifically with worship and the Sabbath day. Here are some of them:

1. *Worship belongs to God.* It is his to demand by right, and he has revealed the pattern for the worship he desires us to follow.

2. *The pattern of acceptable worship directs itself to God,* to the exclusion of all else. Its focus sees only the lifting of the heart to fellowship with Father, Son, and Holy Spirit.

3. *True worship has a Mediator in Jesus the Christ* (see pp. 174–75). Other faiths may have an emotionally pleasing worshipful experience, but the only genuine worship occurs in the presence of the crucified and risen Lord.

4. *True worship revolves around communicating fellowship between people and their God* in prayer, the reading of Scriptures, sound preaching, listening with understanding and faith, singing with thanksgiving in the heart, and receiving God's sacraments as seals of his grace.

5. *Worship does not belong solely to a place or time.* Fellowship can take place anywhere and at any time, alone, in a family, or a congregation, under a roof or without one. We need not stand in a cathedral, nor face a Mecca.

6. *Yet God set aside a tithe of time each week* when he is to particularly have our attention, and that day is most appropriately Sunday.

7. *The Sabbath is a holy cessation, a set-apart stopping,* for which we should prepare our hearts during the rest of the week.

Standing apart in joy

Humankind has wandered long and far seeking these principles. The heart is unfilled without the blessed fellowship of God, without knowing once more the restoration of the communion Adam and Eve knew before the fall. One of the most incredible thoughts the mind can contemplate is that the majestic God who guides galaxies in their courses through the heavens desires to walk with us as well. I would that this thought could sink into my mind adequately. How thrilled you would be to receive an invitation to the White House because the President wants to meet you. What if the Queen of England communicated with you that she desires the presence of your person and the fellowship of your company? Yet, what is that to fellowship with the Creator of the universe?

Why do multitudes of church members never know anything vaguely approaching the joy of this fellowship? Charles Spurgeon offered a parable in illustration:

Suppose that a great plague comes upon the city of London. The population is decimated, and every heart is filled with terror at the sight of death on every side. Now in the city dwells a man of noble lineage with his son, who is a wonderful physician. They determine to give themselves to reclaiming the sick. The son unbars the great front gate to their estate and makes his way into the dismal streets where piles of the dead and dying lie about. Finding those who still live, he picks them up in his arms and brings them back to his father's house, where gradually he uses his marvelous skill to restore them to wholeness. The father smiles benignly upon his son, in whom he has such great delight and who is exposing himself to grievous dangers by returning again and again to the city to bring back another victim.

Let us suppose that you are one of those lying in the street, contorted with pain. The virulent disease is making its way through your body. He picks you up tenderly in his arms and carries you back to the house. There he bends over you to begin his ministrations. You will never know anything of the fellowship of God unless you have experienced that healing balm that restores your life. Only in the house of this noble man and his healing son can you enter into an understanding of this great enterprise that is being accomplished. You allow him to touch your body, and you feel the health restored to your limbs. You begin to find that life once more pulses throughout your frame; you know restoration to health and soundness.

But even then you will not be able fully to enter into that fellowship. First, you must come to some sort of understanding of what is really happening around you. You must see that there is nothing in London, nothing indeed in all the world, that begins to compare in significance to the tremendous work going on in these rooms before your eyes. Day by day, as you watch the work of this great father and son, you become more impressed. You realize that this is the only hope of this town, and you enter sympathetically and understandingly into what they are doing. Yet you must go further to enter into fellowship. You must come to the place where you say timidly, "Sir, is it possible that such a one as I could have some small part in this great work that you are doing?"

You are given the task of carrying basins and bringing towels. You begin to understand more fully what is involved and to have a part in the fellowship and communion that goes on between these two, for it has become part of your life as well. Still, you are not ready to fully understand and enter into that fellowship until you come to that day when you say, "Sir, I want not only to have some small part, but I see that this is the only thing in life which is really worthwhile. I want to give my whole self over to it. I yield myself, body and soul. I want to go out and join your son in bringing in the ill. I want to expose myself to the dangers and even the taunts of those who do not understand. I will give even my life for this cause."

At that point you begin to enter in and understand the deep mystery of the fellowship of the father and his son.

One day in that great house you meet a young man who announces that he, too, is one of those who has been brought in and healed and restored and has been adopted into the family. You find out a little about him. He is dressed in a sporting way. He has a tennis racket under his arm, and he is on his way out the door. As he comes to the drawing room near the front door he peers in and says to the son, "How is it going with the plague today? How many was it this week? . . . Oh, that is splendid! I'm delighted to hear it. I'm on my way to the courts to have a game!" Would such an one as this ever be able to enter into the fellowship of the father and the son?

Or perhaps you meet another man, not nearly so frivolous and flippant as the first. He is dressed in a three-piece suit. His umbrella is under his arm. You find that he is on his way to the Board of Trade. "Well, you know, business has to go on even in the most difficult of times, and in times like these it is possible to make a good profit if one keeps his eyes open and his nose to the grind." He, too, stops by the drawing room, tips his hat to the father and son and says, "Glad to hear that the work is going well. I left a check on the table in the hallway to help continue the work. How is that poor soul there doing? My, he does look bad. But I must run along now. Business first." Can such a person enter into that mystery of fellowship between the father and the son? That will remain ever as alien to him as to someone from another planet.

The means and meaning of Sunday

Are you hungry for the sort of fellowship in Spurgeon's story? It does not begin with deciding to join up with the Son and his Father in their grand crusade. That would only be a works righteousness, without the soul depth of sanctification. Spurgeon saw that the belonging comes with feeling the soothing hands, of allowing the balm of the Physician to do its work, of convalescing in the house of God and getting to know intimately its layout and the ways of its triune Inhabitants, of growing to love the other servants of the house just because they are fellow survivors of the disease who also have been rescued from death on the streets.

That sort of relationship grows through a worship that flows like a river into the life of the individual and washes over all of the thoughts and doings of the week. And God established Sunday as one of the floodgates through which that river flows into our daily lives. The Word of God and the sacraments are special "means of grace" for God's empowering of our lives. Those means give Sunday's rest and communion special meaning as the Father's day of rest, the Son's day of redemption and resurrection, and the Holy Spirit's day of outpouring.

We remember the promise that there yet remains unto the children of God a Sabbath, a day of rest, the eternal rest that God has promised to all of those that trust in Him. So, Father, Son, and Holy Spirit—creation, resurrection, and eternal life—are symbolized in the concept of the Lord's Day, the Sabbath day.

Problems with knowing how to keep this day to the Lord are not new. In England, King James I, who commissioned the King James Bible, a few years later commissioned a book of sports. When this was published in 1618, to the consternation of many Christians, it encouraged all Englishmen to play sports on Sabbath afternoon. This was one of the final irritations that led a certain group of Christians to decide to leave the country altogether. The Pilgrims started departing the next year and in 1620 arrived in America.

It is interesting that, from the inception of America, the founders of our nation were concerned about the Lord's Day. The Pilgrims on the Mayflower were blown into Plymouth Harbor and landed on Clark's Island, across from the rock where they finally came ashore. When the storm lifted it was Sunday morning. They were delighted to see where they were. They had been at sea for months in crowded quarters. They were eager to rush across the bay, land, and get off the ship. They did not. Instead, the first thing they did was to honor the Sabbath day, to hold worship and praise God. On Monday morning they landed on Plymouth Rock.

In the early 1800s, some years after the founding of the United States, a wave of anti-Sabbath feeling swept the country, including the government. Someone got the idea of speeding the mails by operating on Sunday, and the law was passed that the postmaster would be replaced at any post office that was closed on Sunday. The Christians of Philadelphia were incensed at this action, and the city government voted to wage civil disobedience against what they considered an attack on their First Amendment freedoms. When the mail coach approached Philadelphia the driver found that a huge chain had been locked in place across the highway. All roads leading to the city were closed every Sabbath in defiance. Interesting, isn't it, that to this day the U.S. Postal Service is one of the few enterprises that does not operate on Sundays?

We see the turning of the Lord's Day into a frivolous day, forgetting that it is the *day of the Lord*, a day for worship and rejoicing in the Lord. The Sabbath should be different from other days. It shouldn't be simply given over to secular sports and business and work. We should not be rushing about, trying to get as much of the secular world in us as possible. What we pour into our Sabbath spills over into the rest of the week. The fourth commandment says we are not to work on the Sabbath; we are to cease our secular work for the week, and we are to turn our thoughts heavenward. Those who turn away from the Sabbath find their lives becoming more and more secularized, and their thoughts less and less stayed about the Lord.

The Sabbath should be a "day of rest and gladness," as one hymn-writer puts it, and not a day of solemnity and sadness. In the past some Christians have been guilty of taking all the joy from it. Older people have told me that in childhood their Sabbath reading material was restricted to the Bible and theological books. I recall reading that a few centuries back a Scotsman was arrested for smiling on the Sabbath day! In the early church at one point it was considered improper to kneel while praying on Sunday. One could only stand in prayer on that day. That is not the dominant feeling of most in the early church, though. The *Didache*, a manual for teaching Christians in the early second century, saw the importance of joyful, thankful worship. Notice also the importance set on getting ready for worship by getting interpersonal reconciliations in order first:

And on the Lord's own day gather yourselves together and break bread and give thanks, first confessing your transgressions, that your sacrifice may be pure. And let no man, having his dispute with his fellow, join your assembly until they have been reconciled, that your sacrifice may not be defiled; for this sacrifice it is that was spoken of by the Lord; In every place and at every time offer me a pure sacrifice; for I am a great king, saith the Lord, and my name is wonderful among the nations.

To observe the Sabbath properly we need to prepare ourselves for it. The *Didache's* instruction stressed one element Jesus said was important—so important that he said to leave the sacrifice on the altar and be reconciled (Matthew 5:24). Another issue involved in preparation is especially important today. In Old Testament times the day before the Sabbath was called "the day of preparation." You cannot observe the Sabbath without preparation. We need to purchase what needs to be purchased on the day of preparation, and not on the Lord's Day. Buying and selling was one of the reasons that God took the Hebrew people away into Babylonian captivity. In our great-grandparents' day Saturday was the special day of baking and cooking, so that little food preparation would be needed on Sunday. In many homes it gave a specially festive air to the day of preparation. The modern version of that practice often is going to a restaurant after church. That adds pressure to restaurant owners to take away the Sabbath day of their employees. More than one Christian store owner has complained that it is almost impossible to stay closed on Sundays, partly because of losing all of the Christian customers who do their shopping after church.

In giving to us the Sabbath, God has given to us a greater life. A medical study by Johns Hopkins Medical School found that men who attend church regularly have about one-half the chance of dying with a heart attack as those who do not. In the statistics 500 out of 100,000 who attend church regularly die with heart attacks; 900 out of 100,000 who do not attend church regularly die from heart attacks. If you stretch a rubber band but never let it relax, eventually it will lose its elasticity. And that is the way the human body reacts. The Sabbath day, properly exercised, adds a joy break to the cycle of life, a time of focusing off of self and onto those things for which we are created—to glorify God and to enjoy him. Little wonder the time of worship is also good for us.

The call of "Save Our Sunday" may seem a lost cause. Certainly Christians would not want to be so punctilious about it as were the Jews Jesus condemned for their lack of balance. The Jews observed 1521 laws covering every conceivable thing that might or might not be done on the Sabbath. A woman keeping those laws would not look in a mirror on the Sabbath because she might see a gray hair and be tempted to pull it out. Should she do so she would be carrying a burden. Such humorous laws were less funny to Jesus when he saw these hypocritical people refusing his right to heal. They were more worried about whether his disciples ate some grain from the field than they were to worship God in Spirit and in truth. As the *Westminster Confession* makes clear, the purpose of the Sabbath is the purpose of all of life—worship and fellowship—the floodgate through which enjoyment of God enters into all the week's life.

For those who perform works of necessity on Sunday, and for those who see no option but to fulfil employment demands on that day, the blessing of the Sabbath may still be found at other times. But this way is full of temptation to turn aside. And for those Christians who exemplify the Jews and fret about when the Sabbath will be over so they could get on with their lives, the blessing missed is costly. A great many earn the epitaph on a tombstone in France:

> "He was born a man,
> and died a grocer."

I can think of few sorrier ways for anyone to be remembered, but especially children of God in Jesus Christ, who are made to glorify and enjoy.

In that one day of God-centeredness, reminds the *Westminster Confession*, we find that all of our worship does indeed belong to God, that the pattern is God's to direct, and that the Mediator who truly leads each God-centered worship experience is Jesus Christ. The hours we spend communicating with fellow believers and our God in prayer, preaching, song, and sacrament bring us closest to what will be the highlight of heaven. For this reason if for no other, Sunday is a day saved for eternity. It is the holy cessation, the day for which we should long through the rest of the week. It has lost that place in our society. But the Sabbath is not kept in a society. It is kept in a heart—a heart saved for eternity.

The epitome of a Sabbath-keeper today is found in the beautiful story of Eric Liddell, the hero of the movie *Chariots of Fire*, who did one thing that has made him forever famous: He refused to run an Olympic race on Sunday. God blessed his stand. When he ran the alternative 400-meter race the next day he won the gold medal, although this was not his distance.

Another peculiarity in the story of Liddell tells us that his feelings about worship and the Sabbath were an extension of his view of life. Other runners were mystified by Liddell's unique sprinting style. He never looked where he was going. Instead, he burst from the starting gates and around the lane with his eyes fixed upward at the sky. When another runner tripped into his lane in one big race there was a terrible collision because Liddell had no thought of anyone being in his path. He flung himself forword as if there were no tomorrow and looked straight to the sky where his tomorrow lay. When the Japanese invaded China and interned missionary Liddell in a prison camp he exhausted himself in service until a disease took his life. The man whose courage stood until the last was strengthened by a cycle of life that revolved around looking skyward to glorify God and to enjoy him forever. The Sabbath lifted his eyes to eternity.

What makes relationships whole in Christ?

A lawful oath is a part of religious worship, wherein, upon just occasion, the person swearing solemnly calleth God to witness what he asserteth or promiseth; and to judge him according to the truth or falsehood of what he sweareth. . . . It is the duty of the people to pray for magistrates, to honor their persons, to pay them tribute and other dues, to obey their lawful commands, and to be subject to their authority, for conscience' sake. . . . Marriage was ordained for the mutual help of husband and wife; for the increase of mankind with a legitimate issue, and of the Church with an holy seed; and for preventing of uncleanness.
[Westminster Confession of Faith, chapters 22 to 24]

21

Sand in the Shoes

We now run together pieces of three chapters of the *Westminster Confession of Faith*. Chapter 22 covers lawful oaths and vows, chapter 23 the civil magistrate, and chapter 24, marriage and divorce. A common thread runs through this section, as the writers of the *Confession* summarize all that the Scriptures say about relationships among people. We might have added the sections on the church (chapters 25 and 26), but those have some special considerations we will want to look at. These brief statements do not seem as edifying as other parts of the Westminster documents, with reason: Since the fall, interpersonal relations have woven a web of pain. To deal with it all requires either an encyclopedia or a shopping list.

Issues related to the Christian and government have received some discussion above, so now we will focus on marriage as the most intricate part of the relationship web, keeping in mind that some principles apply to obligations with other people and even with government. The closer you get to the marriage covenant, the more you see that it is both a unique bond, and the template for other bonds. Martin Luther said that when he looked at the command to love his neighbor as himself he thought first of Katie Luther. She was, after all, his closest neighbor.

The law of love

It strikes me that the *Confession* most clearly says two things about relationships with our neighbors (those as close as a spouse and as far off as an opponent in political or philosophical warfare). One teaching is that our relationships relate to worship. How we treat others reflects how we treat

> *Let love be without dissimulation [deception]. Abhor that which is evil; cleave to that which is good. Be kindly affectioned one to another with brotherly love; in honour preferring one another.*
> [Romans 12:9–10]

God. Jesus said this in his answer about the greatest commandment of the law:

> Thou shalt love the Lord thy God with all thy heart, and with all thy soul, and with all thy mind. This is the first and great commandment. And the second is like unto it, Thou shalt love thy neighbour as thyself. [Matthew 22:37–39]

According to Matthew 6:12, 14–15, even God's forgiveness of us depends on how we forgive others.

The second teaching is that relationships do not come easy. Sinful people are selfish. We try to weasel out of obligations, and obligations are involved in relationships, whether an obligation to pray for my enemy, to obey my ruler, or to love my wife sacrificially. The *Westminster Confession* chapter on marriage makes the interesting statement about divorce: Human corruption is such that we are "apt to study arguments, unduly to put asunder those whom God hath joined together in marriage." In other words, we usually come up with an excuse to justify breaking obligations that become too much work. Things haven't changed all that much since the 1640s.

Human nature hasn't changed, but society certainly has. The great Roman Empire began as a lowly nation with strong moral values but grew steadily in strength and power until its might eclipsed the greatest grandeur ever achieved by Babylon, Assyria, or Egypt. Many books have been written on that subject, but one reason often overlooked is that for the first 500 years of Rome's existence there was recorded one divorce. Then, at the zenith of its glory, its people became decadent and they relaxed this extraordinary value placed on stable families. In the first century it was said that Roman women of the upper class changed husbands as often as they changed hairstyles. Waves of dissolution crashed upon the Empire as her foundation gave way. Finally hordes of barbarians from the north moved in to finish off a society that already had died within. There were other reasons for the fall of Rome, but few historians would deny that family disintegration was a major influence.

After the Puritan population began growing in America, even though not all the immigrants were Puritans or even Christians, the average number of divorces was one-third of one divorce per year. This was true when the colonial population reached 70,000. By the mid-1700s the divorce rate had climbed to one in 500 marriages. By 1812 there was one divorce for every 110 marriages. This slow climb continued until World War II. A book published during the war claimed that society was relaxing its attitudes toward marriage, and the author predicted an alarming increase in the number of divorces that bode ill for the future of American society. In the year that he wrote, divorces in the U.S. could be counted in the tens of thousands. His worst fears came to pass: There were 395,000 divorces in 1959. By 1965 the annual rate was 479,000. By 1977 the number of divorces had grown to over 1 million a year and in 1979 to 1.8 million a year. Today, depending on the part of the country, the number of divorces equals or exceeds one-half the number of marriages. This doesn't include the number of short-term live-in relationships that begin and end at the whim of the participants. The worst disaster has befallen the black family, which in the urban impoverished areas has virtually ceased to exist. More than two-thirds of all black children today are born into one-parent homes. Families receiving support through welfare, especially Aid to Families with Dependent Children (AFDC), cannot even afford to remain married. They qualify for benefits only if the father is missing. This is a tragic commentary of terrifying proportions. The attitude toward marriage relationships in particular, and all other relationships as a result, makes the standards of the *Westminster Confession* seem unreachable. I would also suggest one statistic that to me is most devastating in its implications: The divorce rate among professing Christians is only slightly lower than that for the surrounding society in any given area.

Innumerable books, classes, and counseling programs have been designed to help troubled marriages. Some are extremely good, but most are like the ambulance at the bottom of the cliff after the car has gone off the road and over the side of the mountain. Surely the church and the Word of God have something to say to those who have made a wreck of their marriages. Divorce is not the unpardonable sin. The grace of God is real. But instead of becoming the ambulances and hearses at the bottom, wouldn't it be better to build a safety rail around the top of the cliff to prevent tragedies? We need to realize what God thinks about the dissolution of the family unit, when men do separate what God has joined together. "I hate divorce," says the LORD God of Israel (Malachi 2:16 NIV).

The law God gave to Old Testament Israel makes two specific statements about marriage and divorce, in Deuteronomy 22 and 24. The former deals with a married person caught in the act of adultery. The penalty for adultery was death. When the Romans took away from the Jews the power of capital punishment, it was recognized that adultery destroyed the marital bond and laid grounds for divorce. Everyone agreed on this, but were there other grounds? Moses says in Deuteronomy 24 that a husband could put away his wife if he found "some uncleanness" in her. That is rather vague, so the Jewish teachers of the law sought to interpret this allowance, developing two schools of thought. The teacher Shammai led the strict interpretation that only uncleanness of a gross character would be grounds for a divorce. Another teacher, Hillel, guided the party that believed anything unseemly "in the eyes of the husband" would be a grounds. It was said that if a husband was not pleased with the way his wife cooked his eggs or combed her hair he could give her a writing of divorcement and put her away. Hillel is much more famous than Shammai. The *Westminster Confession* statement about human corruption reveals the secret of Hillel's popularity.

The Pharisees tried to pit Christ against one or the other of these schools, thinking to divide Jesus' followers. But Christ was never competing in a personality contest. He ignored the views of both Hillel and Shammai and went back beyond the Mosaic law to the purpose of marriage itself:

> Have ye not read, that he which made them at the beginning made them male and female, and said, For this cause shall a man leave father and mother, and shall cleave to his wife: and they twain shall be one flesh? Wherefore they are no more twain, but one flesh. What therefore God hath joined together, let not man put asunder. [Matthew 19:4–6]

Inherent in Christ's response is the implication that marriage is not a fifty-fifty partnership. It is not a true partnership at all, though that is a helpful metaphor. Marriage is a relationship—the closest relationship that any two people can know in this world. A husband and wife are one flesh. In this statement Jesus offered the secret to a happy marriage and the challenge to make a marriage work in an unfriendly culture: To men Jesus says, "Your wife is you"; to women he says, "Your husband is you." Two have become one flesh.

The sand of criticism and disinterest

Too often the marriage partnership suffers from the same woe as did a man who walked across the North American continent on foot. When he got to California, reporters questioned him about his travels. He was asked if he had ever felt that he wouldn't make it. "Yes, many times," he replied.

What had almost defeated him? Well, it wasn't the traffic of the big cities or the screeching of brakes and honking of horns. It wasn't even the interminable prairie of the Midwest that seemed to stretch on and on forever, nor the blazing sun over the hot Western desert. It wasn't even the snow-capped Rocky Mountains.

"What almost defeated me over and over again was the sand in my shoes."

It is this unheralded, seldom-discussed sand in the shoes that underlies some of the more spectacular reasons for marital failure. Much of this "sand in the shoes" is the abrasive sand of criticism, building up self by tearing down another in ever so small ways. Each grain seems insignificant, but they soon collect in very uncomfortable places.

This problem has its source in the parent-child relationship. A baby is born and lies in its crib, kicking its legs, waving its arms, and crying out for its parents. It is doing the one thing that comes naturally to every baby—seeking attention and looking for recognition. Soon the little one learns to talk: "Mommy, look! Look, Daddy! It's a rabbit! I drew it myself! Isn't it good, Daddy?" The child is expressing a need for acceptance and recognition that will be expressed over and over again throughout life. Is there really a basic difference between a child holding up a crayon picture, a college student laboring into the night for all A's, or Napoleon marching on Waterloo? The quest is for recognition, the search for acceptance by others.

But instead of acceptance little Johnny comes toddling out of the kitchen with his orangeade and it goes splat over the carpet. Then, like all Gaul, Johnny is divided into three parts: "You've done it again! How many times have I told you? Every time you pick up something you drop it. You are a numskull! Haven't you any sense at all? How are you ever going to get through school? You'll never amount to anything!" If a guest had spilled that drink mother would have dismissed it with the wave of a hand: "Oh, it's nothing at all. I'll just wipe it up later. I do it all the time myself."

By the time Johnny and Mary grow up, their feet have been worn to a bloody pulp by the sand in their shoes. But they hope to find a loving, soothing, comforting, accepting partner who will heal the wounds. They want someone who will see something worthwhile in them, because they may still suspect that there is something in them that is lovable. At last they find just such a person. They get married, and suddenly in alarm make the sad discovery that their partner is not so perfect as they thought. This person has some good points, but those bad points have got to go. Now one or both newlyweds makes the colossal mistake of supposing that the best way to magnify the good and get rid of the bad is to tell their spouse about the bad ones. If the husband or wife is told often and loudly enough, surely he or she will correct them and become ideal. Unfortunately, it seldom occurs to anyone to magnify the good points before all the world and let the bad points take care of themselves. If it ever did, the bad would likely shrivel away from lack of nurture.

Instead, the day comes when the husband or wife just suddenly isn't there any longer. "What does my husband see in that woman? She's older and uglier than I am. She must be blinder, too, if she thinks there is something nice about him! Can that woman who has run off with my husband be that dumb? And why would he leave me for her?"

While having lunch in a restaurant I noticed a couple sitting at the next table. They were not yet 35 years old, but they looked like they had been married for about 275 years. They never said one word to each other during the hour that I sat there and had lunch. Their chins were down on the table, and they looked like misery incarnate. I wondered what had brought this fine looking young couple to this abject state. After lots of years of counseling I suspect it was something like this:

"Honey, how do you like my new rose bush? It's blooming now. Aren't those roses beautiful?" But instead of sharing her enthusiasm he makes a grunting assent and wanders off. After a few encounters she realizes that the man who had a great fondness for roses when they were engaged now doesn't have any interest whatsoever in them or the time and energy she has spent growing them.

During the game of the week the scene changes: "Did you see that pass? Wow, 95 yards and in for a touchdown!"

"Yeah; but can't you do anything but sit there all day and watch football?"

Then the wife wants to share the beautiful poem she has found in a book.

"Poetry! I can't stand poetry. Why can't they write so you can understand what they're talking about?"

"I thought you liked poetry. You used to send me those . . ."

"Oh, I copied them off greeting cards."

Scratch roses. Scratch football. Scratch poetry. Scratch philosophy. Soon mealtimes become very quiet. Everything that either of them is really interested in has been put down by the other, verbally, by tone of voice, inference, sarcasm, rejection, or disinterested attitude. Their interests are boring. They are not worthwhile. They are unworthy of interest or importance. How foolish can we be that we create our own misery and then sit back and lament the sand in the shoes. The wise husband or wife realizes that a marriage license should be a hunting license, a license to seek virtue and goodness.

Whatsoever things are true, whatsoever things are honest, whatsoever things are just, whatsoever things are pure, whatsoever things are lovely, whatsoever things are of good report; if there be any virtue, and if there be any praise, think on these things. [Philippians 4:8]

If you want whole relationships with your spouse, your children, your boss, your best friend, your worst enemy, your brother or sister in Christ, that practical advice is the best place to start. Pour out the sand of devaluing the other person, the abrasive criticism and the thoughtless disinterest. Wives, what does your husband like that you could not care less about? Husbands, what does your wife like that you can't stand? The marriage covenant obligation demands that you learn enough about those interests to be able to support your partner and make him or her feel worthwhile. You may be amazed to find out that there really is something valuable in that interest, but the important thing is to communicate that you care.

The sand of unforgiveness

Another sandbox in a relationship is unforgiveness. Forgiveness is absolutely vital to wholeness in a sinful world, for we each have lots of occasions when we need to forgive—and more times when we need to be forgiven. Forgiveness in Christian living is not an option. No obligation more clearly connects with what God has done for us and expects us to mirror with one another. God forgave when it was neither expedient nor easy. If I avoid this aspect of loving neighbor as self I stand face-to-face with a bleeding figure writhing on a cross in my place.

But they and our fathers dealt proudly, and hardened their necks, and hearkened not to thy commandments, And refused to obey, neither were mindful of thy wonders that thou didst among them; but hardened their necks, and in their rebellion appointed a captain to return to their bondage: but thou art a God ready to pardon, gracious and merciful, slow to anger, and of great kindness, and forsookest them not. [Nehemiah 9:16–17]

For if, when we were enemies, we were reconciled to God by the death of his Son, much more, being reconciled, we shall be saved by his life. [Romans 5:10]

Who hath delivered us from the power of darkness, and hath translated us into the kingdom of his dear Son: in whom we have redemption through his blood, even the forgiveness of sins. [Colossians 1:13–14]

If we confess our sins, he is faithful and just to forgive us our sins, and to cleanse us from all unrighteousness. [1 John 1:9]

And we are compelled by the blood of Christ to go and do likewise.

After this manner therefore pray ye: Our Father which art in heaven, Hallowed be thy name. . . . And forgive us our debts, as we forgive our debtors. . . . For if ye forgive men their trespasses, your heavenly Father will also forgive you: But if ye forgive not men their trespasses, neither will your Father forgive your trespasses. [Matthew 6:9–15]

Judge not, and ye shall not be judged: condemn not, and ye shall not be condemned: forgive, and ye shall be forgiven. [Luke 6:37; see also Matthew 7:1]

And be ye kind one to another, tenderhearted, forgiving one another, even as God for Christ's sake hath forgiven you. [Ephesians 4:32]

Like many of the Lord's commands, this one is good for me. I need to forgive, for I need to be forgiven. This need exists in any human-to-human relationship, the closer the relationship the greater the need. In the marriage relationship I need to forgive, and I need to be forgiven, on a number of different levels. It is part of loving my closest neighbor as myself. In fact, according to Genesis, it *is* loving myself, if a husband and wife are one flesh.

The forgiving process may become complicated. People sometimes have trouble loving and forgiving others because they have the same difficulty with themselves. If we are Christians, of course, this should never be. We stand forgiven on the blood of Jesus Christ, and we have no right to withhold what God has personally given. In reality our neuroses and defense mechanisms can still get in the way, so that we do not feel forgiven, perhaps do not even wish to forgive ourselves for some reason, and so lack the desire to love and forgive others. "The heart is deceitful above all things, and desperately wicked: who can know it?" says God through the Prophet Jeremiah (17:9).

Thankfully, One does understand it, and it is his Spirit within us that empowers us to love the unlovely—even in ourselves. Forgiveness of others begins in self-awareness, of laying out our fears and feelings before the Lord, admitting our weakness, and asking his help. It may be that we have to begin by confessing to the Lord that we do not feel forgiving, do not feel forgiven, even though emotionally we know that we must forgive and are forgiven. If you go through these bitterly conflicting emotions, confess them and begin praying with all your heart for the one toward whom you feel them. Pray confessing that this love must come from the will and not from the emotions. Pray for that person's blessing, admitting that at the moment you don't really want it. If you do this you will begin to change. You cannot pray for someone, laying aside pretense, and remain an enemy. Jeremiah 17:14 goes on to make a wonderful promise, even in the midst of a deceitful heart: "Heal me, O LORD, and I shall be healed; save me, and I shall be saved: for thou art my praise." If you have broken relationships with anyone, and especially with your wife, the first step toward forgiveness and wholeness comes with praising God. He is the Source of wholeness, and when I center my thoughts on him I take them off the hurt and accept his healing touch.

Something else must be said about forgiving in that most intimate of relationships, the marriage. It is possible to forgive and love the adulterer, or a violent physical or sexual abuser, even when it is proper to end the marriage. God does not call a wife or a husband to undergo personal danger and torment and harm to children. The Bible allows but never *demands* that we divorce the marriage partner who commits adultery. Marriages can survive betrayal in glorious victory. The man or woman who allows a spouse to continue in ongoing or multiple adultery, however, should seek qualified Christian counsel, for the reason may have less to do with love than some unhealthy dependence. Still, the spouse who does have biblical grounds and seeks divorce does not have grounds for continual bitterness and hatred. That is neither personally healthy nor sanctifying, and it certainly does not honor God.

Forgiveness and judging

Thankfully, most of the needs for forgiveness are not so extreme, and so forgiveness is more a matter of sitting down by the way to empty the shoes of a little sand. I would not make light of these routine forgivenesses, for they are vitally important to keeping a marriage on track. The old movie platitude notwithstanding, "Love means saying you are sorry," and meaning it. And love means accepting that apology when it is given, even if the habit that seems so obnoxious doesn't disappear overnight. The wise wife or husband looks for the best in a spouse, realistically admits and discusses the flaws but stresses that acceptance and love transcends bad habits and mistakes and weaknesses. This is the pattern of forgiveness God shows to us, and we act most like our Father when we model his forgiveness: "Yet now hath he reconciled In the body of his flesh through death, to present you holy and unblameable and unreproveable in his sight" (Colossians 1:21b-22).

Suppose your husband has a serious problem with forgetting to pick up his clothes from the middle of the floor. Suppose your wife simply cannot brush her teeth without leaving a glob of toothpaste in the sink. How does one deal with these small but real annoyances without the critical spirit that henpecks and pours sand in the shoes? These flaws can shift the focus of the relationship until one no longer sees the good points. The glaring faults seem designed by the boorish spouse to make your life miserable. It should be such a simple thing for your spouse to change, but no matter how many times you remind, criticize, and harp, the actions seem to continue. In fact the husband or wife now becomes more sullen and defensive. Perhaps the one behavior changes. He begins to pick up his clothes. But a new tension, almost a power struggle for control, has begun.

A law of relationships is at work that someone will become whatever you say he or she is. The child who is called worthless and a failure will unconsciously meet that expectation. A child with the same level of intelligence and native ability which is continually encouraged and seen as worthwhile will tend to rise to the level of the confidence that has been expressed. Similarly, if a wife is continually disregarded and told she is a lazy slob who lies around the house all day, then what she does is obviously unappreciated. In fact, she will likely come to agree with that assessment and lose the drive to manage the home and children well. Why should she? The husband who is told he is a bum and will never amount to anything will fill that expectation. This is one of the reasons why all the great "wars on poverty" have only deepened the cycle of failure. The recipients are tagged, perceived, and labeled to be failures who will perpetually live on the dole. It is one reason successful rehabilitation will never be achieved within the prison system. The institutionalized individual almost inevitably comes to identify himself or herself with the Department of Corrections number they carry.

The Scriptures speak plainly about these matters, though we have tended to think the instruction idealistic. Jesus said:

> Judge not, that ye be not judged. For with what judgment ye judge, ye shall be judged: and with what measure ye mete, it shall be measured to you again. [Matthew 7:1–2]

Many believe he really did not mean *that* or they feel that somehow we can escape the inevitable consequences of the laws involved there. However, in the physical world we have been told that for every action there is an equal and opposite reaction. Jesus tells us that the same thing exists in the moral and spiritual realms. The Greek words might better be translated, "Do not continually be judging. Do not make this the way of your life." One of the problems of denying forgiveness and fault-finding is that, just as you blind yourself to your spouse's good points, so you blind your spouse to your own good points. I defy you to continually express what is wrong with your spouse and then expect him or her to deepen in love and admiration for you. Soon both of you will see nothing good, and you will sit before some marriage counselor as Mr. and Mrs. Frankenstein in one another's eyes.

Carrying one another's burdens

Christ is the Friend of sinners. The accuser is the Devil. In relationships we can mirror the love of God's forgiveness in Christ or the judgmental accusations of Satan. Certainly we can find and express fault with someone. Jesus was talking about habitual fault-finding of anyone, and especially that person with whom we are one flesh or our children. Paul gives a wise perspective in Galatians 6:1–2. Though spoken to the church it applies well to the marriage and all relationships with Christians. In fact, it is the obligation of relationships in Christ:

> Brethren, if a man be overtaken in a fault, ye which are spiritual, restore such an one in the spirit of meekness; considering thyself, lest thou also be tempted. Bear ye one another's burdens, and so fulfil the law of Christ.

This means that, instead of pecking away at faults, we go to the person in a spirit of meekness, after first considering our own weaknesses, and faults, and spiritual relationship with

God. We go not to demolish but to restore—actually to help the person carry the burden of that habit or fault, or some underlying issue that may be beneath the outward problem. Criticism must be approached as one approaches a dangerous explosive, with fear and trepidation. And it must never be used without accompanying notices of what is good, meaningful, and worthwhile in the person's life. The goal must be to fulfil the law of Christ, the goal of self-sacrificing, supportive love.

I am certain you will enrich your marriage, and remove the painful sand from the shoes of your life together, by putting Galatians 6:1 into practice in the context of Philippians 4:8. The secret is to look for the good in the other person, always striving to think about what is true, noble, right, pure, lovely, admirable, excellent, and praiseworthy in the life of another. What would happen if you took time to sit down with your spouse and participate or learn about something that he or she enjoys and is good at? What would happen if you sought opportunities to celebrate some little victory in his or her life or took a moment to pray with your spouse especially about some tension or problem? I am certain you would enrich your own marriage. You would bless your home, your children, your grandchildren. Love would blossom in your home. And on a different level those same techniques will bless your friends, coworkers, and even the person you can't stand.

The following quotation is excerpted from a poem from the most prolific author of all time: "anonymous." Maybe a reader will identify its original author. I have cherished its truths, and I hope you will be able to sign your name to both sides of its story, and thus fulfil the obligation of the law of love for neighbor as for self:

> I love you,
> Not only for what you are,
> But for what I am
> When I am with you.
>
> I love you,
> Not only for what

You have made of yourself,
But for what
You are making of me.

I love you,
for putting your hand
Into my heaped-up heart
And passing over
All the foolish, weak things
That you can't help
Dimly seeing there,
And for drawing out
Into the Light
All the beautiful belongings
that no one else had looked
Quite far enough to find.

I love you,
Because you are helping me
To make of the lumber
Of my life
Not a tavern
But a temple;
Out of the works
Of my every day
Not a reproach
But a song.

What makes relationships whole in Christ?

The catholic or universal Church, which is invisible, consists of the whole number of the elect, that have been, are, or shall be gathered into one, under Christ the head thereof; and is the spouse, the body, the fullness of him that filleth all in all.
[Westminster Confession of Faith, chapter 25]

22

Holy, Catholic Church

A little boy was busily building something out in the backyard. Observing the activity, his father went out to discover what was taking place and asked, "What are you building, son?"

"Shh! Shh! I'm building a church and we must be very quiet."

Eager to encourage this sense of reverence in his son, the father bent down and whispered, "And just why must we be so quiet in church, son?"

"Because all the people are asleep," came the whispered reply.

The New England Puritans knew how to deal with sleepers. Ushers were equipped with long poles. To the end of the pole was affixed a long and very sharp needle. John Wesley also was adept at handling sleepy congregations. One day he looked down from the pulpit at a snoozing man and stopped right in the middle of his sentence. Silence pervaded the room. Then Wesley cried out, "FIRE! FIRE!" The slumbering man leaped to his feet in surprise and asked, "Where?" Wesley answered, "In hell, man, for those who sleep under the gospel."

Building his church

I am not all that bothered that some sleep in church; my concern is that more sleep in bed because they don't bother to come at all, even among those who call themselves

Christians. One Lutheran minister listed in his bulletin some reasons "Why I don't go to the movies:

1. My parents made me go when I was a child.
2. No one speaks to me when I am there.
3. Because they always ask for money.
4. Because the manager never visits me at home.
5. Because the people who do go don't live according to what the movies teach."

And there came unto me one of the seven angels which had the seven vials full of the seven last plagues, and talked with me, saying, Come hither, I will shew thee the bride, the Lamb's wife.
[Revelation 21:9]

In spite of all the criticism, much of it as ridiculous as this, the church has continued to grow. Jesus guaranteed that the gates of hell would not prevail against it. He said, "I will build my church." He gave us the first lesson in church building while teaching his circle of disciples one day. He began with a question, "Who do people say the Son of Man is?" There were some popular and very complimentary answers to that question, for Jesus was loved by all except the religious leaders:

Some say that thou art John the Baptist: some, Elias; and others, Jeremias, or one of the prophets. He saith unto them, But whom say ye that I am? And Simon Peter answered and said, Thou art the Christ, the Son of the living God. [Matthew 16:14–16]

Jesus built his church, not upon the foundation of those who said and thought nice things about him, but upon the rock of the profession of faith that Peter first made that Jesus Christ is the divine Redeemer, Savior and Lord. That true church of Jesus Christ continues to grow. To watch television or read most secular media publications, one would suppose that the church has ceased to exist or is hopelessly fossilized and led by contemptible sexual perverts and social misfits. In fact, if you add up all the attendance figures from every game of professional sports played throughout the year in the United States and Canada, you will not come close to the total number of people who attend church. The church is the largest institution that has ever existed. More than 1.35 billion today profess faith in Christ at least nominally, and at the present rate of growth that number will reach 5 billion in another century if the Lord does not return. The church today is growing faster than the rate of population growth. That growth is not apparent to us because the historic denominations in the historically Christian West have overwhelmingly turned from the historic faith, and they are declining in membership. In the third world the number who share Peter's confession and gather into the universal body of Christ is growing at a phenomenal rate.

The purpose of the church

Despite the growth and all that Scripture says about this wondrous organization and its members, a lot of misunderstanding and misinformation exists about the church. Those reasons the minister came up with for not going to church bring to mind the basic question of why we *should* go to church. Surely we can worship God by ourselves, without a fancy building, a piano or organ, a preacher, and a lot of people. Yes, we can, but will we? Even in the first-century church, some were trying to follow Christ without the gathering of his people. The writer of the Book of Hebrews cautioned us not to follow their example. Why? Because we need to encourage one another (Hebrews 10:25). As sinful human beings we need to be encouraged and strengthened. We need to be chastened and disciplined. We need teaching and fellowship. We need to be responsible for and to other brothers and sisters. We need to be prepared for works of service. We need to be matured so we will no longer be tossed back and forth by the waves and blown here and there by every wind of teaching (Ephesians 4:14–16).

All of these are purposes of the church, but not the greatest purpose. The purpose of the church is to proclaim that Jesus is Lord. God could do all of his works by other means. But he has chosen to endow the bride of Christ with the greatest of all tasks, the commission of calling all the world to praise him forever.

This purpose empowers Evangelism Explosion and other movements that seek to invite the whole world to faith in Jesus Christ. I believe the church has the greatest purpose of any institution in all the world—a cosmic purpose established under cosmic authority. Jesus said:

> All power is given unto me in heaven and in earth. Go ye therefore, and teach all nations, baptizing them in the name of the Father, and of the Son, and of the Holy Ghost: Teaching them to observe all things whatsoever I have commanded you: and, lo, I am with you alway, even unto the end of the world. [Matthew 28:18b–20]

It is the purpose of the church to say that "Jesus is Lord" by the way we live and worship before him. But we can't adequately say that Jesus is Lord if we stay cooped up in our little Christian ghetto. Charles Van Engen makes this point well in a book entitled *God's Missionary People: Rethinking the Purpose of the Local Church*. At one point he relates that to say "Jesus is Lord" means "Jesus is Lord of the world." The church can only do that if it is going out into the world. Writes Van Engen:

> The Church of Jesus Christ exists when people confess with their mouth and believe in their heart that Jesus is Lord— Lord of the Church, of all people, and of all creation. Through this confession the Church emerges to become what it is, the missionary fellowship of disciples of the Lord Jesus Christ.

Only in the church are we endowed with the authority of God and the promise of Christ's presence to the end of the age. We are called to go into all the world and preach the gospel to all creation (Mark 16:15). Ours is not the work of saving the world or righting all wrongs. Ours is the job to be Christ's ambassadors, agents of reconciliation.

Holy and catholic, visible and invisible

The essential information we need to understand about the church is given to us in chapters 25 and 26 of the *Westminster Confession of Faith*, of which we have copied the theme quotation for this chapter. From those two chapters we can develop a list of statements about what the church is and is not:

The catholic church

A lot of confusion has arisen among Protestants when they repeat in the *Apostles' Creed* that they believe in "a holy catholic church." The word *catholic* comes from two Greek words, *kata*, meaning "according to," and *holios*, meaning "the whole." *Catholic* means "according to the whole" or "universal." This universality distinguishes the church from the boundaries of our own parochial denominations. Some Christians who suppose that the church is no larger than their own rigid confession are going to be utterly amazed to count God's people when they get to heaven. Christians who understand Scripture should plan to throw away the labels and get to know folks from every communion who have trusted in Jesus Christ, who have repented of their sins, and who have received him as Lord and Savior.

The one Head of the church

Jesus Christ is the Lord of the church. In fact the Bible uses the beautiful analogy of Christ as our Husband, and we his bride, made chaste and pure—holy. The church is holy because it is called out of the world and set apart unto

God. The word *holy* has two meanings in Scripture: (1) set aside for the worship and service of God; (2) cleansed and purified. Those who are truly part of the church find that their hearts are being sanctified and cleansed as they are prepared for the day when they shall bear no spot or blemish. The church is a long way from being perfect, but it is in the process of being cleansed by its Head. Human leaders are only servants in that process. There is room for only one true Head, and that is the Bridegroom.

The fulness of the Lord

The *Confession* says that the church "is the fulness of him who fills everything in every way." What does that mean? Colossians 1:16–20 makes an important connection between the being of God, the work of Christ, and the being of God's people:

> For by him were all things created. . . . And he is before all things, and by him all things consist. And he is the head of the body, the church: who is the beginning, the firstborn from the dead; that in all things he might have the preeminence. For it pleased the Father that in him should all fulness dwell; and, having made peace through the blood of his cross, by him to reconcile all things unto himself; by him, I say, whether they be things in earth, or things in heaven.

Paul writes that Christ's death and resurrection are an extension of his work as God, a work that began in creation, continued in God's providential control of creation, and climaxed in the work on the cross. Through the atonement God is reconciling all creation under Jesus Christ as God. That reconciliation preeminently includes bringing people into God's kingdom under Christ's headship—by way of the church. The church represents all the human race before God. The church is, says Peter, quoting the Old Testament description of Israel, a royal priesthood and a holy nation of people belonging to God (1 Peter 2:5). The church is a priesthood that represents the human race before God.

The fulness of Christ makes us responsible as salt and light, witness and intercessor before the Father. Christ sits in power and authority and glory in heaven and no longer visibly stands in the marketplace of humankind. Instead he has given to the world a Holy Spirit-empowered body to be his ambassador. We are the visible sign of Christ's kingship. That surely makes the church the most important institution that has ever existed for the good of the world. We are to stand as Jesus would stand if he were here. We will stand this watch on the ramparts until he comes to relieve us.

Inclusive and exclusive

"The church is the body of those who profess the true religion, together with their children." That statement makes a couple of points that have become fairly unpopular. First, we may be an inclusive body in urging all the world to be reconciled to God (see 2 Corinthians 5:11–21), but we are quite exclusive in demanding that our body only includes those who repent and place their faith in Jesus Christ as the Son of God, born of a virgin, suffered under Pontius Pilate, crucified, dead, buried, and arisen to sit at the right hand of God in power. The church is a body built upon a confession. Our belief has content. We teach that only one way takes sinful human beings to God.

Second, the church extends beyond those who fully understand and accept that true religion in that it takes in our children. We stand in a covenantal relationship that includes those too young to make a faith commitment on their own. They are holy through their parents. At some point they will have to make that commitment for themselves, but meanwhile they enjoy the nurture of God's family. For this reason a congregation shoulders much of the burden of praying for, guiding, and modeling Christ before the children of fellow members. No Christian is childless.

The ministry of the Word

God uses the church to gather and perfect the saints. We have the ministry of the Word of God. We have the ministry of the sacraments of baptism and the Lord's Supper. That means, among other things, that we are ministers to others, we are called to gather saints in evangelism and help disciple them, and we are also among those being gathered and discipled. In the church the Christian works both sides of the work of ministry. God gave us in Christ apostles, prophets, evangelists, pastors, and teachers (Ephesians 4:11) as we have needed them to disciple believers and win the lost. According to the *Confession*, God "doth by his own presence and Spirit, according to his promise, make them effectual thereunto." The church is a tool God uses to work his grace in the world and in my individual heart.

The invisible church

The true church is not the same as the organized church, but organization still is God's directive for us. This is to say that there exists a *visible* and an *invisible* body of Christ. The *Larger Catechism* sets the distinguishing marks of the visible, organized church, and the invisible, organic church.

What is the visible church? The visible church is a society made up of all such as in all ages and places of the world do profess the true religion, and of their children.

What is the invisible church? The invisible church is the whole number of the elect that have been, are, or shall be gathered into one under Christ the head.

When God led about 2 million descendants of Jacob out of Egypt he slowly organized them under judges, teachers, priests, clans, and families. At the end of the forty years in the wilderness the people were further organized into an army and, then into provinces and cities as they made a place for themselves in the land. This was a visibly organized people, called out from the rest of the nations as holy before him. In a real sense this was a visible church, organized around goals of praise, worship, and sanctified life. Membership in the visible body was not restricted to the direct descendents of Abraham, for Scripture records that many other people besides the Hebrews joined the Exodus. They too wanted to be free from bondage and they could see the miraculous ways in which God was blessing this people. At no time does Moses distinguish between the ethnic descendants of the Patriarchs and these recent converts. Israel was not a racial designation, but a faith designation identified by a visible structure.

There also was a visible sign of membership that identified both the Jews and their children. Before going into the promised land all of the males were circumcised. This was a seal of the visible covenant relationship. If some Israelite couple wanted to skip this part of the initiation or got a little squeamish about cutting the foreskin from their infant boy, they would have to leave the community. If one of the non-Jews who had accompanied Israel for the last forty years had said, "I shared the desert with you, but this is too much for me," he and all his family would have been excluded from the covenant people. Visible signs were vastly important to the visible community of God. They sealed both the men and the women, the boys and the girls to the covenant promises God had made.

Yet Paul explains in Romans 2 and 1 Corinthians 3 that being part of the visible was never enough. Most Israelites had settled for the visible, without "circumcising their hearts" before God. There was no invisible, committed faith behind the outward organization for these people. As a result, "But with many of them God was not well pleased: for they were overthrown in the wilderness" (1 Corinthians 10:5). The outward realities are only meaningful if the inward realities match.

> For circumcision verily profiteth, if thou keep the law: but if thou be a breaker of the law, thy circumcision is made uncircumcision. Therefore if the uncircumcision keep the

righteousness of the law, shall not his uncircumcision be counted for circumcision? And shall not uncircumcision which is by nature, if it fulfil the law, judge thee, who by the letter and circumcision dost transgress the law? For he is not a Jew, which is one outwardly; neither is that circumcision, which is outward in the flesh: But he is a Jew, which is one inwardly; and circumcision is that of the heart, in the spirit, and not in the letter. [Romans 2:25–29a]

Anyone who has read ahead in Paul's Epistle to the Romans knows where this argument is headed. No one has kept the law! So is there no invisible, true church, behind the visibly organized one? No, there is one, only because of God's grace.

The invisible church is "the whole number of elect, that have been, are, or shall be gathered together into one." The invisible church now living in the world consists of all those truly called by God and justified by faith. When this body gathers for worship, along with those who are not saved, the church becomes visible. The visible church may or may not have a building, but it has some sort of organization, human direction, and gathering point for worship, teaching, fellowship, and praise. Those of us who lead the visible church should desire to become as close as possible to the invisible church, but we will never be exactly the same as the gathering of the born-again.

This dramatically differentiates the church to which I belong from every other sort of organization with which I may affiliate. A person's name may be on a church roll. The person may be baptized and partake of the sacrament of the Lord's Supper. The person may act as a deacon, elder, preacher, or attain some other high post. But unless the person is a part of the invisible church of Christ that person is not truly a member of the Body of Christ. Only those who are truly born anew are in the only church that counts. Therefore, we had better not be satisfied with the mere externalities of religion. Religion is a matter of the heart, a transformation of the soul only the Spirit of God can bring about. All those who place their trust in Christ for salvation, and all those who abandon all trust in their own goodness and acknowledge their sinfulness, receive the blessed gift of life eternal from the pierced hands of Christ.

The imperfect body

Even the purest churches are subject to mixture and error. As the saying goes, if you ever find the perfect church, whatever you do, don't join it. You will surely mess it up. The reason for these studies is that I am convinced there is a set of teachings that corresponds closely with the truth God has revealed in Scripture. If I didn't think that, I would change what I believe until I did find such teachings. I am not so foolish as to believe, however, that I have things all figured out or that the Westminster Assembly or the reformers or the early church fathers had it all figured out. All theologians are human, and we all are sinful. Only God has the corner on truth. Still, we have undergone times in the history of the church when truth was a rare commodity, and the teaching available had degenerated until they were synagogues of Satan. One such time is now, and Christians must be wary that they part company from a congregation that refuses to submit to Scripture. That doesn't mean everyone must agree about what the Bible teaches. It does mean the Bible must be regarded as the Word of God.

A community of saints

Continuing our list of the basic teachings about the church we turn to what the *Confession* says in chapter 26, "Of the Communion of Saints." Its central point is that all of the saints of God are united to Christ and to one another by the Holy Spirit and by faith.

Sinners and saints

The word *saint* comes from the word *sanctify* and means to be cleansed or set aside to God. The *communion of the saints* does not refer to any fellowship of super-Christians that have achieved a gold medal in the Olympics of faith. The saints talked about in the Bible are not due any special adoration. They are simply we who are redeemed. The church is a *koinonia* fellowship of saints—a kind of fellowship unique to the Christian community. The Bible identifies *koinonia* as a fellowship bound into nothing less than a new race of people. Scripture recognizes many families of peoples who are loosely tied by common ancestry, culture, or skin color. The Bible teaches that these families have become alienated from one another by sin's depravity. But Scripture only recognizes the existence of two "races," and these two are the people who are God's and the people who are Satan's. All those who are God's are brothers and sisters in Christ.

As you walk into the church building's sanctuary where you hold membership, look around for a moment. Do you see brothers and sisters with whom you will spend eternity? If you are in a church where not everyone is familiar to you, get to know some of your relatives you haven't met before. Is there someone you have chosen to ignore for some reason? Be brutally honest with yourself and ask if you are turned off by some unworthy prejudice against a brother or sister—perhaps his or her clothing or background, or accent, or reputation, or skin color. You need not be best friends with every other person in the church. Those who study such things say our circle of friends in a church can exceed no more than thirty. But neither should prejudices of any sort cut us off from fellowship with the larger body. Make a special point to pray for those about whom you have negative feelings of any kind. Also, when those feelings are caused by a bitter, broken relationship, we have a special responsibility to God to be reconciled to brothers and sisters.

One of the great preachers of the past, John Jowett, wrote that the church is vastly impoverished because so little communion is exercised. We need to hear from the mature saints, those who have struggled in their own spiritual lives and who have seen victory. We need to hear how they escaped the snare, how they captured a fortified hill in their lives, how they comforted their hearts at the grave by the side of the way.

What about those who have grown old in Christ? What delicacies of insight can be shared by the aged pilgrims? Have they seen the glimmer of the golden city? Do they yearn to be with those they have loved? What can we learn from their many years? What about the young pilgrims? How are they faring? What can we do to strengthen their arms? We need to be tapped and shared in the fellowship of the saints. What are the things to be tapped and shared?

Unity in love

Every relationship should be built upon a common ground. We need to share some commonality. The Westminster framers said that our vertical fellowship with Christ communes with him "in his graces, sufferings, death, resurrection, and glory." Those are the things we hold in common with God in Jesus Christ. Think about that thought. The only things we have in common with God are those very things he has given to us. We have already likened this unity of fellowship to the relationship of a dying person rescued from the street with his loving benefactor (see pp. 377–79). The rescuer in Charles Spurgeon's story was rich and powerful; his life and experiences had nothing at all in common with those of the plague victims he saved. But out of the rescue and the victim's response there could grow a bond of fellowship.

That is the vertical fellowship with God; the horizontal fellowship is that of the shared experiences of the rescued. The *Confession* speaks of a unity of love in which believers share God's gifts and graces with one another. They also share in the common duties God has given them to do, including the duty to build one another up. Their fellowship is described as being on two levels:

1. shared experiences as inner people in whom the Spirit dwells;
2. shared experiences as outward people who live for one another's mutual good.

Intertwining lives

It is by their very profession in Christ that saints are bound to one another. *Koinonia* is not an optional but an indispensable part of Christian life in worship and mutual edification. It is the responsibility of the church that Christians also relieve each other in need, according to the abilities of the fellow believers to do so. And the *Confession* specifies that this responsibility to help one another is not solely in operation within a local family of believers. As God gives opportunity, serving fellowship extends its helping hand to "all those who, in every place, call upon the name of the Lord Jesus." Thus, evangelistic missions to neighborhoods and nations is not the church's only responsibility under the Great Commission mandate. Raising up a world witness includes enabling and encouraging believers in other places.

What communion is not

As with so many Christian doctrines, the propensity of people to extend them into areas God never intended always is a danger. The Westminster Assembly addressed two dangers related to the communion of saints that still come up occasionally today:

> This communion which the saints have with Christ, doth not make them in anywise partakers of the substance of his Godhead, or to be equal with Christ in any respect: either of which to affirm is impious and blasphemous. Nor doth their communion one with another, as saints, take away or infringe the title or property which each man hath in his goods and possessions.

Does the communion between the Christian and God make the Christian in some way akin to God himself? Some cults have said so. Mormons at the root of their theology, for example, hold to a God who is quite human-like in appetites and abilities. It is their goal to attain in afterlife to that sort of godhood, so that we (male Mormons, anyway) and God will meet and fellowship as equals. The whole point of liberal Christian theology takes another tack in tying our fellowship to a Christ who is no more God than are we. We can enjoy mystical union with this historical Jesus, and so become no more than we already are (see p. 260).

The other error that often has crept into the church is that of a Christian form of communism. These idealistic communities have never achieved success for long, and at least a few of them, including the Oneida Community in the 1800s and the recent followers of David Koresh, shared even sexual intimacy with one another. One of the standard lines of the modern cult has been to force all members to renounce their families and devote themselves body and soul and finances to the fellowship. Some say that this is what the early church did in Jerusalem, which is decidedly not true. In Acts 4:36–37 Barnabas sold a field and gave it to the community treasury. He sold one field, not all that he had. In Acts 5, Ananias and Sapphira are condemned by Peter, not for withholding some of their wealth, but for lying about what they had given in order to try to gain the applause of others.

The Bible counsels to openly give of our substance for the welfare of our brothers and sisters. We are never counseled to drop out of society's economy, impoverish ourselves, and submerge ourselves in the *koinonia* of the body. *Koinonia*, like becoming one flesh in marriage, celebrates our individuality and empowers us as individual believers before God.

Other pictures of the church

The Bible uses the pictures of a body, a family, a race, and a nation or kingdom to describe *koinonia*. Other pictures also describe this fellowship.

1. We are *joint heirs* with Jesus Christ and the inheritors of all things.
2. We are the *hoi pistoi, the believers* in the living God.
3. We are *disciples or learners*, the *mathetēs*. From Christ we learn our worldview, our values, our, hope, faith, and love.
4. We are a *fellowship of slaves*. The word sometimes is translated "servant," but the meaning in Roman culture was that of a slave in bonds, the lowest level of servitude found in the Roman world. Paul delighted to call himself the "bond slave of Jesus Christ."
5. We are a *community of witnesses*. The Greek word *martys* is the origin of our word *martyr.* Originally it simply meant to proclaim one's faith, but it came to mean to witness by giving one's life in the arena. What a oneness is created among those who put their lives on the line as they boldly witness for the living Christ. In Scripture the word *witness* can refer to a legal sense of giving testimony, to an eyewitness declaration of fact, to what is confessed, and to dying for those facts. We are witnesses in all those senses to something that is breathtakingly important to the world, the greatest event in all of history.
6. We are the *branches* and Christ is the Vine. As a fellowship we draw sustenance from our Source.
7. We are the *walking dead*. We were dead. Then we were crucified with Christ and raised with him to glory. Now we are dead to the things of the world.
8. We are *soldiers of Christ*. No one who has ever served on the front lines in war does not understand the special bonds of fellowship forged in a foxhole.

The dynamics of relationships in Christ are almost indescribable, even through these and other pictures. Nothing quite like it exists in other religions, but I have seen this mystical union around the world. I recall sitting on an airplane next to a young mother. We politely exchanged a few strained pleasantries between strangers, then got around to spiritual things. I discovered that she had accepted Christ two years before. Our conversation then unfolded easily as we found we shared an understanding about everything that mattered. We were of one mind and one heart about a world-and-life view.

We were the church.

What does the future hold in Christ?

What benefits do believers receive from Christ at death?
The souls of believers are at their death made perfect in holiness, and do immediately pass into glory; and their bodies, being still united to Christ, do rest in their graves till the resurrection.

What benefits do believers receive from Christ at the resurrection?
At the resurrection, believers being raised up in glory, shall be openly acknowledged and acquitted in the day of judgment, and made perfectly blessed in the full enjoying of God to all eternity.
[Westminster Shorter Catechism, questions 37, 38]

23

"I Will Not Be Shaken"

As John Knox lay dying, those around the bed of the great transformer of Scotland wondered if his magnificent faith had seen him through to his end. "Hast thou hope?" they asked. Not a word did he speak in response. Knox simply lifted his finger upward and breathed his last.

As these words are written a number of Branch Davidian followers await their hope—the reincarnation of David Koresh, whose self-proclaimed messiahship went up in flames with 80 followers in the Waco, Texas, tragedy.

Here are two reactions to the problem of hope. Is either founded on a rock? I believe only one Source of hope exists today, the same Source Knox and countless others have found in their darkest hours. "Find rest, O my soul, in God alone," advises King David, the transformer of ancient Israel, "Truly my soul waiteth upon God: from him cometh my salvation. He only is my rock and my salvation; he is my defence; I shall not be greatly moved [or shaken]."

What a statement to make: In the midst of life's greatest challenges, in the midst of their own foolish sins, in the midst of impossible situations, in the midst of dying agonies, Knox and David were transformers because they were transformed people. They were transformed people because their hope was built upon the Rock of their salvation.

Living transcendently

As we conclude our tour through Scripture by way of the *Westminster Confession of Faith* and *Larger* and *Shorter* catechisms we have left some subjects untouched and exhausted none of the rich veins of truth in these documents. But we have sought a pattern for believing and living as transformed, transforming people, and now we come to the bottom line: If God is the God of the Bible, then we need only point upward to find the rest for our soul. If God has made a way of salvation in Jesus Christ and his will for our lives is good and satisfying, we have hope. If our chief end

> *And I saw a new heaven and a new earth: for the first heaven and the first earth were passed away; and there was no more sea.*
> [Revelation 21:1]

for eternity is to glorify God and to enjoy him forever, we have hope. In fact, come what may, no other people on earth have such a reason for hope.

To hope is to live transcendently. Hope is a confidence in something bigger than existential circumstances. This doesn't mean the person who hopes lives in a fantasy view of reality or trusts in a David-Koreshly confidence without foundation. The apostle Paul understood the realities quite well, yet he hoped in the Rock of salvation.

Paul saw that in the gospel is a world transforming power able to charge people with righteousness, and lack of righteousness produces hopelessness:

For I am not ashamed of the gospel of Christ: for it is the power of God unto salvation to every one that believeth; to the Jew first, and also to the Greek. For therein is the righteousness of God revealed from faith to faith: as it is written, The just shall live by faith. [Romans 1:16–17]

He saw life's sufferings as life-transforming experiences in Christ:

Therefore being justified by faith, we have peace with God through our Lord Jesus Christ: By whom also we have access by faith into this grace wherein we stand, and rejoice in hope of the glory of God. And not only so, but we glory in tribulations also: knowing that tribulation worketh patience; And patience, experience; and experience, hope: And hope maketh not ashamed; because the love of God is shed abroad in our hearts by the Holy Ghost which is given unto us. [Romans 5:1–5]

He saw in the world's traumas a future of transforming redemption in Christ:

The Spirit itself beareth witness with our spirit, that we are the children of God: And if children, then heirs; heirs of God, and joint-heirs with Christ; if so be that we suffer with him, that we may be also glorified together. . . . For we know that the whole creation groaneth and travaileth in pain together until now. And not only they, but ourselves also, which have the firstfruits of the Spirit, even we ourselves groan within ourselves, waiting for the adoption, to wit, the redemption of our body. For we are saved by hope: but hope that is seen is not hope: for what a man seeth, why doth he yet hope for? But if we hope for that we see not, then do we with patience wait for it. [Romans 8:16–17, 22–25]

In the midst of a generation that was filled with anxieties over the cold war and the nuclear sword of Damocles that hung above humanity's head, I remember sitting in a classroom at Columbia Theological Seminary listening to Dr. Manford George Gutzke, professor of Bible. He was talking about current events of the time and made a most startling statement: "They say they are going to blow up the world. Well, let them blow it up. Who needs it anyway?"

I thought, "What a bold and audacious thing for anyone to say." Gutzke believed in life that transformed situations because it pointed to a larger reality.

We live, now as when Gutzke made that statement, in a time of great fear. Two generations have grown up, married, and borne children under the threat of a thermonuclear war. That threat of global annihilation seems somewhat abated with the fall of communism, but many of the missiles are lying about in the hands of even less stable governments than that of the USSR. There are world leaders who partake in hatreds so intense that they would delight to wipe out millions of enemies with one well-placed strike. And even without nuclear capability, some of them have managed to kill hundreds, thousands, and in one African nation recently, perhaps 100,000.

Hope and fear

Hope can be hard to come by in a society that has turned away from God. A recently published study by the Annie E. Casey Foundation studied statistics in every state, finding, among other things, that in the period from 1985 to 1991 the murder rate for teenagers doubled, most killed by other teenagers. Record numbers also dropped out of school or had babies out of wedlock. The report concluded that young people in the United States, especially in the impoverished areas, live without hope for the future. Their hopelessness becomes a self-fulfilling prophecy. Without the incentive to think they can succeed, they follow their parents' track into welfare dependence, the men fathering another generation like themselves and abandoning the mothers to raise the family alone. Staggering social problems defy solutions here and around the world. There is no possibility of transforming hope unless something bigger than the problems exists.

Every generation has experienced hopelessness. For one example, in England and later in the United States during the worst abuses of the Industrial Revolution, unimaginable poverty degraded the lives of millions of people. I recall seeing a letter a wealthy German businessman received from his bank when the German mark was devalued in 1924. This man had millions of marks in the bank, but the letter informed him that they had no coins small enough to represent his account; therefore they were closing it as empty. The same thing happened in China in 1946. Certainly it could happen again. We have no basis for confidence that we will not by next week face an empty bank account in an economically devastated economy. In fact, given the level of sin in our society, it would seem only just that we should.

Then we come to Jesus, and he tells us as he did those disciples who were terrified by their circumstances and his power, "Fear not!" In the upper room as he faced the cross he told the disciples to not let their hearts be troubled—not to fear. The reason they were not to fear was not that the situation was about to improve. It most decidedly was not. The reason for their confidence was that "in my Father's house are many mansions: if it were not so, I would have told you. I go to prepare a place for you. And if I go and prepare a place for you, I will come again, and receive you unto myself; that where I am, there ye may be also" (John 14:2–3).

The *Westminster Shorter Catechism* looks at what Christ was going to prepare and summarizes it as the benefits we believers receive at death:

> What benefits do believers receive from Christ at death?
>
> The souls of believers are at their death made perfect in holiness, and do immediately pass into glory; and their bodies, being still united to Christ, do rest in their graves till the resurrection.

What a marvelous hope is thus unfolded. The apostle John, in the last two chapters of his great Revelation, pulls the curtains aside for a few moments to reveal some glimpses of those many mansions:

And I saw a new heaven and a new earth: for the first heaven and the first earth were passed away; and there was no more sea. And I John saw the holy city, new Jerusalem, coming down from God out of heaven, prepared as a bride adorned for her husband. And I heard a great voice out of heaven saying, Behold, the tabernacle of God is with men, and he will dwell with them, and they shall be his people, and God himself shall be with them, and be their God. And God shall wipe away all tears from their eyes; and there shall be no more death, neither sorrow, nor crying, neither shall there be any more pain: for the former things are passed away. [Revelation 21:1–4; compare Isaiah 65:17–25]

If the world blows up, its passing away will usher in a day without death and mourning and with God. Are such marvelous pictures as are painted by John to be taken literally or are they just symbols? In those final chapters of the Revelation John takes the most magnificent and matchless beauties known and paints with them a picture of the Holy City, New Jerusalem. If this is a mere symbolic representation of the greater reality, then it is beyond the ability of human tongue and speech to declare.

How glorious must that new heaven and new earth be. On a transparent crystalline morning, where the sunlight beams brightly and everything seems to be more alive, when there is a slight chill and yet a warmth from the sun, the wonder of the world seems impossible to surpass. How could anyone improve on such a day? And yet the finest earth day shall be as nothing, for "Eye hath not seen, nor ear heard, neither have entered into the heart of man, the things which God hath prepared for them that love him. But God hath revealed them unto us by his Spirit" (1 Corinthians 2:9–10a).

Our hope for now

In God's presence

God will create a new heaven and a new earth as the final abode of the redeemed, a new creation for his beloved. Even now he reveals it to us by his Spirit. What revelation by his Spirit? Certainly the Spirit's work in Scripture gives us some revealed information about the glories of this planned honeymoon cottage to be built by the Bridegroom for the bride. I suspect, however, that Paul here speaks of the Holy Spirit himself, for the truly great thing about our future glory is that we will be *with* God, to glorify him and to enjoy him forever. And in the Holy Spirit we now have Immanuel, "God with us" in a spiritually tangible sense. In the Holy Spirit the Christian experiences heaven. In the Spirit hope is something future we can only dimly see and not yet experience—but in the Spirit hope also is sealed to confidence we now *know*. This is the view of eternity we do not have to wait to see.

In God's glory

What else do we know about the future state of the Christian? One of the first things John tells us is that the New Jerusalem will experience the light of the glory of God, and its light will be as a transparent jasper stone. The average jasper is opaque, but there are some, about which the apostle speaks, that were clear as crystal, either blue or green. There will be no need for sun or moon, whether literally or figuratively, for the glory and brightness of God shall light it. Without night there will be no need for artificial light.

In God's renewed body

How then shall we sleep? Why should we? We no longer will be in the wearying city of humanity, with its fallen, wearing-out bodies. In the city of God, why should there be weariness? Energy will never flag; enthusiasm will never dampen; a perfect body will know no limitations. There will be no more death nor sorrow nor sadness nor pain. For many, I am sure, that in itself will mean heaven. Many have not known a day without acute pain. What leaping and running for joy there will be for you who now limp along or coast in a wheelchair. No more pain in the knees, or hips, or back, or neck, or head. I think of intensely crippled Christians I have seen die, knowing that the moment their last breath was over they could turn soul somersaults like an energy-bursting, young cheerleader.

In God's renewed worship

Without the barriers between us and God of sinful bodies and guilty consciences, no steeples will dot the skyline of the Holy City. No temple or church building will be needed, for the Lamb and the Lord God Almighty are the temple. There we shall see the face of God and live—and that forever. You will not need to meditate in your heart on God. You may talk with the living Christ or the Father as a beloved, accepted spouse and child.

In God's renewed society

This new world will draw its sustaining force from God. A river of life will flow from the throne of God and the Lamb, watering the tree of life and the fruits of twelve great crops. And the tree will be for the healing of the nations. All that our hopeless society sees in the world today is sick and degraded. The world's societies seem to be represented in John's revelation of heaven, but there they will be whole and fruitful. Human society will be restored to God's original vision.

But John tells us there will be no more sea. I think that John may be saying something symbolic and significant. The "sea" in his circumstances, and in the lives of the ancients was not a place of amusement and joy. It was a place of mystery and death. Except for the bravest sailors in the most advanced nautical peoples, the Phoenicians for example, ships were never sailed beyond sight of land. There was no compass, nor charts, and the shallows were not marked. Few wished to risk their lives upon the sea.

The sea meant separation in John's life. He had been banished to the Island of Patmos and could not reach out to those he loved except by letter and prayer. Patmos is a rugged, mountainous island, and the traditional spot where John wrote is in a cave high above the coastline. From this secluded retreat one can look far out to sea, overwhelmed by aloneness and separation. He could watch the different color shadings of the waters as they broiled into angry waves with the coming of a storm. Far away lived his friends and children in the Lord. Oh, that the sea might be removed, that he might join those he loved. In the holy city Christ showed him it was clear that no longer would there be barriers—either physical or emotional. There would be no more sea.

In God's renewed identification

A marvelous directory names the residents of that city of God. Just knowing it exists gives me the same conviction it gave Paul "that neither death, nor life, nor angels, nor principalities, nor powers, nor things present, nor things to come, nor height, nor depth, nor any other creature, shall be able to separate us from the love of God, which is in Christ Jesus our Lord" (Romans 8:38–39). This directory is the Lamb's Book of Life. In it are inscribed all the names of those who have trusted in Christ, the Lamb of God who has taken away the sin of the world. God's grace is so great that that book is larger than any earthly telephone directory, for it contains the names of untold millions of people God chose to be saved before the foundation of the earth, the names of those for whom Christ died.

This is the register of the people who need not be shaken by the situations of today. We are shaken only when we have forgotten who we are. Paul wrote the victorious Epistle to the Philippians while in chains, a situation that would bring some of us to the depths. Paul surely had times of depression. Second Timothy describes a low point for the apostle. Yet even at that moment he was not shaken from his faith. In Philippians he sees his imprisonment encouraging others to speak out courageously (1:14). He knows that not all who preach have the purest of motives, but at least they are preaching the Word of God (vv. 15–18). But whatever happened, Paul said, would "turn to my salvation through your prayer, and the supply of the Spirit of Jesus Christ, according to my earnest expectation and my hope, that in nothing I shall be ashamed, but that with all boldness, as always, so now also Christ shall be magnified in my body, whether it be by life, or by death" (vv. 19–20). Notice that his hope in himself was not complete, for he hoped that he not be shaken—that he remain courageous. His hope in God was fully confident: "For to me to live is Christ, and to die is gain" (v. 21).

In his dark night of the soul, when all seemed to have left him, Paul could say with continuing confidence:

> I have fought a good fight, I have finished my course, I have kept the faith: Henceforth there is laid up for me a crown of righteousness, which the Lord, the righteous judge, shall give me at that day: and not to me only, but unto all them also that love his appearing. [2 Timothy 4:7–8]

The dark side of glory

Not everyone has the ground that Paul did for his confidence. All the while we glory in the salvation of those for whom Christ died we realize that most people have good reason to be without hope in the world. Those beautiful images John saw are not for them. In fact, their lives are so cut off from God that to stand in his presence would not be beautiful at all, but condemnation itself.

While referring to the "glory of his mercy in the eternal salvation of the elect," the *Westminster Confession* considers the darker side of glory: John's vision of hopeless eternal damnation of those who are wicked and disobedient. Is this stress the result of the fact that the Westminster writers were joyless doom-sayers who missed the message of God's grace? Anyone who has followed their catalog of praise through these books knows that isn't the case. Rather, they understand that those with hope must do more than sing the song of the redeemed. That day will come, and it has now come for those men who toiled over these words so long ago. It is not yet that time for us. The fact is too clear that most of the world remains without hope and under the power of Satan. A day is coming. God has already circled it on his calendar, "when he will judge the world in righteousness by Jesus Christ." In that day the rebellious angels will be finally and irrevocably judged and cast in hell. And every man and woman who has ever lived will see the videotape of life examined with the intense scrutiny of a holy, righteous Judge. Everything we have done will be unveiled for all to see. That thought should make each of us feel a bit hopeless. The question will be whether our lives will be covered by Christ's blood. Only those who can hide under the atoning blood of Christ will be saved from joining the fate of Satan and his angels.

People say, "Well, I believe that we have our hell right here on earth." There is a certain sense in which they are right. The Bible teaches that we have a foretaste of our inheritance in this world. We get a little preview of coming attractions—the basis for hope or hopelessness. However, the foretaste of hell is only a foretaste, what Scripture describes as an "earnest" on our inheritance. When you put earnest money down on a piece of property you are promising that more will come.

The reality of the intermediate state

Two important realities must be assessed concerning the redeemed hope and contrasting unredeemed hopelessness in which people must live. First, we need to understand something of what happens at death. Second, we need to know something of the last judgment we face. Drawing together what Scripture says of the state of the person after death and the resurrection of the dead, the *Westminster Confession* presents the following propositions.

Continuing consciousness

First, at death the human body turns to dust, but the soul, which is immortal, lives on. The intermediate state is one of continued conscious existence. The Bible knows of no soul sleep, no eternal rest, no purgatory, no etherland where one has a second chance, certainly no sinking into oblivion, which is the great non-Christian hope. The dust returns to the ground it came from, says Ecclesiastes 12:7, and the spirit returns to God.

We have a partial view of this state in the transfiguration of Jesus in Matthew 17, Mark 9, and Luke 9. Peter, James, and John accompany Jesus up onto a high mountain to pray. Their prayer time, however, was interrupted by the unveiled glory of Christ and the appearance of the spirits of Elijah and Moses. These two Old Testament saints had not been sleeping. They were aware of what was going on in the plan of salvation by which they themselves would be saved. They were able to discuss, we assume with understanding, the coming passion of Christ. This must have been a particularly meaningful moment for Moses, who had not been allowed to set foot in the promised land with the children of Israel, but died and was buried by God on Mount Nebo across the Jordan River. With Elijah he now visited the land of his dreams.

Jesus gives us other indications of the high level of consciousness after death. In Luke 16 he tells a vivid story of the rich man and the beggar named Lazarus who died and lived on—Lazarus in the restoring comfort of heaven and the rich man in the torment of hell.

As Jesus hung on the cross he looked over at a fellow sufferer and promised him that *that very day* they would meet in another place. When the Romans broke the thief's legs, and he slowly suffocated from the pressure on his chest, he suddenly found himself no longer pierced through and bleeding. At that moment of joyous consciousness on the other side of the passage into death, that man found Jesus, who had gone ahead of him. That very night their spiritual bodies shared together glorious fellowship at the feasting table of God, even as Christ's body lay in a new tomb and the thief's shattered remains were heaved into the common pit grave of criminals. The thief was present as Christ appeared before the Father and laid the final perfect sacrifice for sin before him. Memories of that day's intense pain—his screams under the flogging whip, the searing spasms as the nails were driven through his wrists, and the unimaginable pain of each fight for breath—all those memories eased away, replaced by the glory of the redeemed. The day that had begun in hopelessness ended in unveiled glory.

Purpose in death

Second, as the thief learned, the soul of the righteous is received by God and stands in God's presence. For the Christian, to be absent from the body is to be at home with the Lord—death swallowed up by life. That is our purpose in death:

> For we know that if our earthly house of this tabernacle were dissolved, we have a building of God, an house not made with hands, eternal in the heavens. For in this we groan, earnestly desiring to be clothed upon with our house which is from heaven: if so be that being clothed we shall not be found naked . . . , that mortality might be swallowed up of life. Now he that hath wrought us for the selfsame thing is God, who also hath given unto us the earnest of the Spirit. [2 Corinthians 5:1–5]

Since this is the state of the situation, Paul remarks in Philippians 1:23 that he is torn between wishing to live to serve God and wishing to die to be with God. He adds that to die and be with Christ is the far superior option. The *Confession* summarizes Scripture in saying: "The souls of the righteous, being then made perfect in holiness, are received into the highest heavens, where they behold the face of God in light and glory, waiting for the full redemption of their bodies."

Third, the souls of the wicked are immediately separated from God in hell, where they also wait for the final judgment of their rebellion. The clearest indication of this again rests on Jesus' story of the rich man, a story not told as a parable, symbol, or metaphor, but to describe a time and place in historical reality. References to "sleep" in death, on the other hand, are couched in metaphor language. I believe that language mostly relates to the Bible's description of the physical body. It has been incorrectly interpreted by some to refer to the intermediate state of the soul.

Daniel 12:2 tells us that "many of them that sleep in the dust of the earth shall awake, some to everlasting life, and some to shame and everlasting contempt." Scripture invariably connects the dust of the earth with the physical body. Jude 6 describes the rebellious angels as being chained in darkness awaiting judgment. Since we know these demons still have a degree of activity in the affairs of earth, we must conclude that their darkness is the same sin-clouded consciousness of rebellion that the Bible identifies with evil. Those without Christ in the intermediate state are likely living in the same darkness that obscured Christ during their lifetime on earth.

C. S. Lewis's book *The Great Divorce* tells the fanciful story of a busload of souls from hell who go on holiday to heaven. The point Lewis makes is that, as bad as things may be in hell, those who reject God in life would act no differently in death. They would not want to live in heaven if given the choice. Their vision of God is no brighter now than it was then. Not even the rich man in Jesus' story asks to cross the great divide.

Fourth, a day is coming that will shake the world to its roots, a day when the soul and a renewed physical body will unite once again. God did not intend for us to live as disembodied souls, and at the day of resurrection that division of body and spirit will be removed. This great event will accompany the return of Christ and the final judgment of the world and its inhabitants. This area of Christian doctrine called *eschatology* is only alluded to in the *Westminster Confession* and requires a discussion far beyond the scope of this look at life in the presence of God. Worthy Christians read the Bible with far different interpretations, and I think God only intends to make four eschatological points clear in Scripture:

1. A final day of resurrection and of judgment is coming.
2. God's people should be watching for the Lord's return at all times and evangelizing the world as if the opportunity will end tonight.
3. We are to live today as if that full return has happened. We are to have the values of a fully restored kingdom of God.
4. All people will be judged in a great assize, those who are covered by the blood of Christ and those who are not.

The *Confession* says in chapter 33:

As Christ would have us to be certainly persuaded that there shall be a day of judgment, both to deter all men from sin, and for the greater consolation of the godly in their adversity: so will he have the day unknown to men, that they may shake off all carnal security and be always watchful, because they know not at what hour the Lord will come; and may be ever prepared to say, "Come, Lord Jesus, come quickly. Amen."

That applies to Christians as well as unbelievers. We should all shake off carnal security so we will not be shaken at the judgment. The standard maxim of church work is that 20 percent of the people do 80 percent of the work. There is an indication then, that 80 percent of the people (plus some of the 20 percent who are trying to accumulate points with God) have an improper understanding of the lordship of Christ. They will stand before Christ, and some of them will be amazed when he says, "Go away, I don't see your name in the Lamb's Book of Life, and I don't recognize your face. We have never met."

Others who do know Christ but have never given him an ounce more of their life than was required, will see their lives blistered under the heat of his gaze. We learn from Scripture, especially from 1 Corinthians 3, that believers will be judged for their fruits. Their punishment for sin will be covered by the blood of Christ, but their life's product—whether they produced the fruit of the Spirit as submissive servants of the King—will be lost. Paul describes our fruit as contributing materials to a building, which will one day be put to the torch by God. Some materials won't burn; they will stand the test: Diamonds, rubies, sapphires, and emeralds of love to the Master will glow with the heat of purified sacrifice. We can't understand exactly what those treasures will mean in the economy of heaven, but we do know their value will be eternal and great. We will hear those words of blessing: "Well done, good and faithful servant."

But 1 Corinthians 3 also describes other materials in our building—wood, hay, straw. In the intense fire of judgment, how long will those last? Those whose love for Christ is so listless that they plan to just get by will see all that they regarded as meaningful burned away. Says Paul, "he shall suffer loss: but he himself shall be saved; yet so as by fire."

To stand unshaken before God

It is delightful to think of all the beauties and majesty and the wonder that God has prepared for those that trust in his Son. The *Shorter Catechism* says that believers at the resurrection will be raised up in glory, found righteous before God in the day of judgment, and "made perfectly blessed in the full enjoying of God."

But my heart is filled with great heaviness that some whose names are written on the roll of the church congregation I pastor have not repented nor turned from the way of the world and the flesh and the devil. They have never embraced Jesus Christ as their own Savior and Lord. They may have taken a vow in front of a congregation in which they were solemnly asked: "Do you, in sincerity, love the Lord Jesus Christ?" They may have answered, "I do." Yet they delude themselves. Their sincere love is with the world and its pleasures. One early church father said that such people "lick the world." This world is their candy—their joy and crown. Their thoughts and energies are given to it. Their citizenship is not in heaven. Their thoughts do not dwell with Christ there. For those people, and for those who have not yet even pretended to love Christ, God has both good and grim news that comes straight from the throne room of heaven:

> I am Alpha and Omega, the beginning and the end. I will give unto him that is athirst of the fountain of the water of life freely. He that overcometh shall inherit all things; and I will be his God, and he shall be my son. But the fearful, and unbelieving, and the abominable, and murderers, and whoremongers, and sorcerers, and idolaters, and all liars, shall have their part in the lake which burneth with fire and brimstone: which is the second death. [Revelation 21:6b–8]

The point of return or no-return

As we conclude exploring the heights and depths of what we believe about God, about salvation, and about our ultimate purpose, I pray that you have been strengthened in your understanding and your awe of the real God, *Alpha* and *Omega*, Beginning and End, Father, Son, and Holy Spirit, Creator and Redeemer. I hope you now feel the challenge to give your life to him more fully, that you know a little more of what it means to glorify God and to enjoy him forever. I also ask whether you are in fact ready to face that great day when all things will be revealed and all justice done. Have you passed days or weeks or months, or years, with more thoughts about where you will spend your two-week vacation next summer than where you will spend the next two billion trillion eons of centuries? It will either be in the paradise of God, or the pain and condign punishment of hell.

Do you know for sure that your name is written there? If you do not, then I would urge you to make sure. You do not know when that last moment of choice will come. Whenever Christ will return, the fragility of life means your point of no return may be today.

To come to Jesus Christ, to embrace him as Savior and Lord, to trust him as your Substitute who died in your place, to enthrone him as Lord and King of your soul. Those are the things that make life worth living and satisfying. They also are the foundation stones on which you can stand and not be shaken, no matter what circumstance arises.

The Westminster *pattern*

24

Transforming Truths

It is no compliment to be called a "puritan." The epithet depicts a dour prude, without joy or a living faith. That is just about as inaccurate a description of the historic Puritans as can be imagined. In fact, Sir Thomas More, an opponent of the Puritans in England, charged that the Protestant was one who was "dronke of the new must [wine] of lewd lightnes of minde and vayne gladnesse of harte."

Such a description might well apply to one who has been transformed by God and is being continually conformed to God's will by the presence of the Holy Spirit within. Each of us is transformed more and more as we learn to glorify God and to enjoy him forever. If that is "lewd lightnes of minde and vayne gladnesse of harte," then our world and our churches need it. Whatever you think of being a puritan, I hope these books drawing on the Puritan *Westminster Confession of Faith* and the *Larger* and *Shorter* catechisms have lightened and enlightened your mind about the glory of God, the thrill of his mercy in Christ, and the satisfying life found in following his perfect will. Such gladness of heart is hardly vain.

Since these documents are not commonly familiar, and they are well worth reading in total, it seems appropriate to collect at least excerpts as a reference. Space does not permit extensive quotations from the *Confession of Faith* itself, so I include only snippets from its chapters. Most of the selec-

442

tions that follow are from the catechisms, in general following the sequence of the *Shorter Catechism*, since its answers offer the most precise and easy-to-remember explanations of Christian doctrine I have ever heard. In fact, we have two groups of questions and answers because the Westminster framers intended the *Shorter Catechism* to be memorized by children and the *Larger Catechism* by adults. That is embarrassing to some of us who pride ourselves on know-

> *Wherefore seeing we also are compassed about with so great a cloud of witnesses, let us lay aside every weight, and the sin which doth so easily beset us, and let us run with patience the race that is set before us, looking unto Jesus the author and finisher of our faith; who for the joy that was set before him endured the cross, despising the shame, and is set down at the right hand of the throne of God.*
> [Hebrews 12:1–2]

ing the children's answers. We ministers will be especially chagrined. The Westminster divines believed ministers should memorize both sets, and commit to mind the *Confession* as well.

While memorizing some of these answers should not take the place of learning Scripture, I suggest that you will enrich your mind if you know, or at least become familiar with, the questions and answers that follow. Most are taken from the first half of the two documents, covering what we should believe concerning God. The section on the ten commandments is from the second half of the *Shorter Catechism*, concerning the duty God requires of us.

The headings refer to the "quest questions" used throughout these chapters.

Who am I?

Shorter Catechism 1. What is the chief end of man? Man's chief end is to glorify God, and to enjoy him forever.

How can I know any ultimate truth for certain?

S. C. 2. What rule hath God given to direct us how we may glorify and enjoy him? The word of God, which is contained in the Scriptures of the Old and New Testaments, is the only rule to direct us how we may glorify and enjoy him.

Larger Catechism 4. How doth it appear that the Scriptures are the word of God? The Scriptures manifest themselves to be the word of God, by their majesty and purity; by the consent of all the parts, and the scope of the whole, which is to give all glory to God; by their light and power to convince and convert sinners, to comfort and build up believers unto salvation: but the Spirit of God bearing witness by and with the Scriptures in the heart of man, is alone able fully to persuade it that they are the very word of God.

S. C. 3. What do the Scriptures principally teach? The Scriptures principally teach what man is to believe concerning God, and what duty God requires of man.

Confession, chapter 1. The authority of the holy Scripture, for which it ought to be believed and obeyed, dependeth not upon the testimony of any man or church, but wholly upon God (who is truth itself), the Author thereof; and therefore it is to be received because it is the word of God. . . . The whole counsel of God, concerning all things necessary for his own glory, man's salvation, faith, and life, is either expressly set down in Scripture, or by good and necessary consequence may be deduced from Scripture. . . . All things in Scripture are not alike plain in themselves, nor alike clear unto all; yet those things which are necessary to be known, believed, and observed, for salvation, are so clearly propounded and opened in some place of Scripture or other, that not only the learned, but the unlearned, in a due use of the ordinary means, may attain unto a sufficient understanding of them.

Is there a Source of ultimate truth?

L. C. 2. How doth it appear that there is a God? The very light of nature in man, and the works of God, declare plainly that there is a God; but his word and Spirit only do sufficiently and effectually reveal him unto men for their salvation.

Who or What is the Source of ultimate truth?

S. C. 4. What is God? God is a Spirit, infinite, eternal, and unchangeable, in his being, wisdom, power, holiness, justice, goodness, and truth.

S. C. 5. Are there more Gods than one? There is but One only, the living and true God.

S. C. 6. How many persons are there in the Godhead? There are three persons in the Godhead; the Father, the Son, and the Holy Ghost; and these three are one God, the same in substance, equal in power and glory.

L. C. 10. What are the personal properties of the three persons in the Godhead? It is proper to the Father to beget the Son, and to the Son to be begotten of the Father, and to the Holy Ghost to proceed from the Father and the Son from all eternity.

L. C. 11. How doth it appear that the Son and the Holy Ghost are God equal with the Father? The scriptures manifest that the Son and the Holy Ghost are God equal with the Father, ascribing unto them such names, attributes, works, and worship, as are proper to God only.

Is anyone in control out there?

S. C. 7. What are the decrees of God? The decrees of God are, his eternal purpose, according to the counsel of his will, whereby, for his own glory, he hath foreordained whatsoever comes to pass.

L. C. 18. What are God's works of providence? God's works of providence are his most holy, wise, and powerful preserving and governing all his creatures; ordering them, and all their actions, to his own glory.

S. C. 8. How doth God execute his decrees? God executeth his decrees in the works of creation and providence.

S. C. 9. What is the work of creation? The work of creation is, God's making all things of nothing, by the word of his power, in the space of six days, and all very good.

S. C. 10. How did God create man? God created man male and female, after his own image, in knowledge, righteousness, and holiness, with dominion over the creatures.

S. C. 11. What are God's works of providence? God's works of providence are, his most holy, wise, and powerful preserving and governing all his creatures and all their actions.

S. C. 12. What special act of providence did God exercise towards man in the estate wherein he was created? When God had created man, he entered into a covenant of life with him, upon condition of perfect obedience; forbidding him to eat of the tree of the knowledge of good and evil, upon the pain of death.

Confession, chapter 5. The almighty power, unsearchable wisdom, and infinite goodness of God so far manifest themselves in his providence that it extendeth itself even to the first fall, and all other sins of angels and men, and that not by a bare permission, but such as hath joined with it a most wise and powerful bounding, and otherwise ordering and governing of them, in a manifold dispensation, to his only holy ends; yet so as the sinfulness thereof proceedeth only from the creature, and not from God; who, being most holy and righteous, neither is nor can be the author or approver of sin.

If there is a good God, why . . . ?

S. C. 13. Did our first parents continue in the estate wherein they were created? Our first parents, being left to the freedom of their own will, fell from the estate wherein they were created, by sinning against God.

S. C. 14. What is sin? Sin is any want of conformity unto, or transgression of, the law of God.

S. C. 15. What was the sin whereby our first parents fell from the estate wherein they were created? The sin whereby our first parents fell from the estate wherein they were created, was their eating the forbidden fruit.

S. C. 16. Did all mankind fall in Adam's first transgression? The covenant being made with Adam, not only for himself, but for his posterity; all mankind, descending from him by ordinary generation, sinned in him, and fell with him, in his first transgression.

S. C. 17. Into what estate did the fall bring mankind? The fall brought mankind into an estate of sin and misery.

S. C. 18. Wherein consists the sinfulness of that estate whereinto man fell? The sinfulness of that estate whereinto man fell, consists in the guilt of Adam's first sin, the want of original righteousness, and the corruption of his whole nature, which is commonly called Original Sin; together with all actual transgressions which proceed from it.

S. C. 19. What is the misery of that estate whereinto man fell? All mankind by their fall lost communion with God, are under his wrath and curse, and so made liable to all miseries in this life, to death itself, and to the pains of hell forever.

L. C. 27. What misery did the fall bring upon mankind? The fall brought upon mankind the loss of communion with God, his displeasure and curse; so as we are by nature children of wrath, bond slaves to Satan, and justly liable to all punishments in this world, and that which is to come.

L. C. 28. What are the punishments of sin in this world? The punishments of sin in this world are either inward, as blindness of mind, a reprobate sense, strong delusions, hardness of heart, horror of conscience, and vile affections; or outward, as the curse of God upon the creatures for our sakes, and all other evils that befall us in our bodies, names, estates, relations, and employments, together with death itself.

L. C. 29. What are the punishments of sin in the world to come? The punishments of sin in the world to come, are everlasting separation from the comfortable presence of God, and most grievous torments in soul and body, without intermission, in hell-fire forever.

S. C. 20. Did God leave all mankind to perish in the estate of sin and misery? God having, out of his mere good pleasure, from all eternity, elected some to everlasting life, did enter into a covenant of grace to deliver them out of the estate of sin and misery, and to bring them into an estate of salvation by a Redeemer.

How did Jesus Christ make a way to God?

L. C. 31. With whom was the covenant of grace made? The covenant of grace was made with Christ as the second Adam, and in him with all the elect as his seed.

L. C. 32. How is the grace of God manifested in the second covenant [of grace]? The grace of God is manifested in the second covenant, in that he freely provideth and offereth to sinners a Mediator, and life and salvation by him; and requiring faith as the condition to interest them in him, promiseth and giveth his Holy Spirit to all his elect, to work in them that faith, with all other saving graces, and to enable them unto all holy obedience, as the evidence of the truth of their faith and thankfulness to God, and as the way which he hath appointed them to salvation.

L. C. 34. How was the covenant of grace administered under the Old Testament? The covenant of grace was administered under the Old Testament, by promises, prophecies, sacrifices, circumcision, the Passover, and other types and ordinances, which did all fore-signify Christ then to come, and were for that time sufficient to build up the elect in faith in the promised Messiah, by whom they then had full remission of sin, and eternal salvation.

L. C. 35. How is the covenant of grace administered under the New Testament? Under the New Testament, when Christ the substance was exhibited, the same covenant of grace was and still is to be administered in the preaching of the word, and the administration of the sacraments of baptism and the Lord's supper; in which grace and salvation are held forth in more fulness, evidence, and efficacy, to all nations.

S. C. 21. Who is the Redeemer of God's elect? The only Redeemer of God's elect is the Lord Jesus Christ, who, being the eternal Son of God, became man, and so was, and continueth to be, God and man in two distinct natures, and one person, forever.

L. C. 38. Why was it requisite that the Mediator should be God? It was requisite that the Mediator should be God, that he might sustain and keep the human nature from sinking under the infinite wrath of God, and the power of death, give worth and efficacy to his sufferings, obedience, and intercession; and to satisfy God's justice, procure his favor, purchase a peculiar people, give his Spirit to them, conquer all their enemies, and bring them to everlasting salvation.

L. C. 39. Why was it requisite that the Mediator should be man? It was requisite that the Mediator should be man, that he might advance our nature, perform obedience to the law, suffer and make intercession for us in our nature, have a fellow-feeling of our infirmities; that we might receive the adoption of sons, and have comfort and access with boldness unto the throne of grace.

L. C. 40. Why was it requisite that the Mediator should be God and man in one person? It was requisite that the Mediator, who was to reconcile God and man, should himself be both God and man, and this in one person, that the proper works of each nature might be accepted of God for us, and relied on by us, as the works of the whole person.

S. C. 22. How did Christ, being the Son of God, become man? Christ, the Son of God, became man, by taking to himself a true body, and a reasonable soul, being conceived by the power of the Holy Ghost, in the womb of the Virgin Mary, and born of her, yet without sin.

S. C. 23. What offices doth Christ execute as our Redeemer? Christ as our Redeemer, executeth the offices of a prophet, of a priest, and of a king, both in his estate of humiliation and exaltation.

S. C. 24. How doth Christ execute the office of a prophet? Christ executeth the office of a prophet, in revealing to us, by his word and Spirit, the will of God for our salvation.

S. C. 25. How doth Christ execute the office of a priest? Christ executeth the office of a priest, in his once offering up of himself a sacrifice to satisfy divine justice, and reconcile us to God, and in making continual intercession for us.

S. C. 26. How doth Christ execute the office of a king? Christ executeth the office of a king, in subduing us to himself, in ruling and defending us, and in restraining and conquering all his and our enemies.

S. C. 27. Wherein did Christ's humiliation consist? Christ's humiliation consisted in his being born, and that in a low condition, made under the law, undergoing the miseries of this life, the wrath of God, and the cursed death of the cross; in being buried, and continuing under the power of death for a time.

S. C. 28. Wherein consisteth Christ's exaltation? Christ's exaltation consisteth in his rising again from the dead on the third day, in ascending up into heaven, in sitting at the right hand of God the Father, and in coming to judge the world at the last day.

How can someone come to Christ?

S. C. 29. How are we made partakers of the redemption purchased by Christ? We are made partakers of the redemption purchased by Christ, by the effectual application of it to us by his Holy Spirit.

S. C. 30. How doth the Spirit apply to us the redemption purchased by Christ? The Spirit applieth to us the redemption purchased by Christ, by working faith in us, and thereby uniting us to Christ in our effectual calling.

L. C. 66. What is that union which the elect have with Christ? The union which the elect have with Christ is the work of God's grace, whereby they are spiritually and mystically, yet really and inseparably, joined to Christ as their head and husband; which is done in their effectual calling.

S. C. 31. What is effectual calling? Effectual calling is the work of God's Spirit, whereby, convincing us of our sin and misery, enlightening our minds in the knowledge of Christ, and renewing our wills, he doth persuade and enable us to embrace Jesus Christ, freely offered to us in the gospel.

Confession, chapter 7. Man by his fall having made himself incapable of life by that covenant, the Lord was pleased to make a second, commonly called the covenant of grace: wherein he freely offered unto sinners life and salvation by Jesus Christ, requiring of them faith in him that they may be saved, and promising to give unto all those that are ordained unto life his Holy Spirit, to make them willing and able to believe. . . . Under the gospel, when Christ the substance was exhibited, the ordinances in which this covenant is dispensed are the preaching of the word and the administration of the sacraments of Baptism and the Lord's Supper; which, though fewer in number, and administered with more simplicity and less outward glory [than the Old Testament sacrifices and rituals], yet in them is held forth in more fullness, evidence, and spiritual efficacy, to all nations, both Jews and Gentiles; and is called the New Testament. There are not, therefore, two covenants of grace differing in substance, but one and the same under various dispensations. [In other words, both Old Testament and New Testament believers must be saved in the same way—through justification by faith in the atoning death of Christ. See also chapter 11: "The justification of believers under the Old Testament was, in all these respects, one and the same with the justification of believers under the New Testament."]

What do we do about guilt?

S. C. 32. What benefits do they that are effectually called partake of in this life? They that are effectually called do in this life partake of justification, adoption, and sanctification, and the several benefits which in this life do either accompany or flow from them.

S. C. 33. What is justification? Justification is an act of God's free grace, wherein he pardoneth all our sins, and accepteth us as righteous in his sight, only for the righteousness of Christ imputed to us, and received by faith alone.

What does it mean that Christians are adopted?

S. C. 34. What is adoption? Adoption is an act of God's free grace, whereby we are received into the number, and have a right to all the privileges of the sons of God.

Confession, chapter 12. All those that are justified God vouchsafeth, in and for his only Son Jesus Christ, to make partakers of the grace of adoption; by which they are taken into the number, and enjoy the liberties and privileges of the children of God; have his name put upon them; receive the Spirit of adoption; have access to the throne of grace with boldness; are enabled to cry, *Abba* Father; are pitied, protected, provided for, and chastened by him as by a father; yet never cast off, but sealed to the day of redemption, and inherit the promises, as heirs of everlasting salvation.

What is a sanctified life?

S. C. 35. What is sanctification? Sanctification is the work of God's free grace, whereby we are renewed in the whole man after the image of God, and are enabled more and more to die unto sin, and live unto righteousness.

S. C. 36. What are the benefits which in this life do accompany or flow from justification, adoption, and sanctification? The benefits which in this life do accompany or flow from justification, adoption, and sanctification, are, assurance of God's love, peace of conscience, joy in the Holy Ghost, increase of grace, and perseverance therein to the end.

Confession, chapter 16. Good works are only such as God hath commanded in his holy Word, and no such as, without the warrant thereof, are devised by men out of blind zeal, or upon any pretense of good intention. These good works, done in obedience to God's commandments, are the fruits and evidences of a true and lively faith; and by them believers manifest their thankfulness, strengthen their assurance, edify their brethren, adorn the profession of the gospel, stop the mouths of the adversaries, and glorify God, whose workmanship they are, created in Christ Jesus thereunto, that, having their fruit unto holiness, they may have the end, eternal life.

What is saving faith?

S. C. 86. What is faith in Jesus Christ? Faith in Jesus Christ is a saving grace, whereby we receive and rest upon him alone for salvation, as he is offered to us in the gospel.

Confession, chapter 14. The grace of faith, whereby the elect are enabled to believe to the saving of their souls, is the work of the Spirit of Christ in their hearts, and is ordinarily wrought by the ministry of the Word; by which also, and by the administration of the sacraments and prayer, it is increased and strengthened. By this faith a Christian believeth to be true whatsoever is revealed in the Word, for the authority of God himself speaking therein; and acteth differently upon that which each particular passage thereof containeth; yielding obedience to the commands, trembling at the threatenings, and embracing the promises of God for this life and that which is to come. But the principal acts of saving faith are accepting, receiving, and resting upon Christ alone for justification, sanctification, and eternal life, by virtue of the covenant of grace.

What does it mean to repent?

S. C. 87. What is repentance unto life? Repentance unto life is a saving grace, whereby a sinner, out of a true sense of his sin, and apprehension of the mercy of God in Christ, doth, with grief and hatred of his sin, turn from it unto God, with full purpose of, and endeavor after, new obedience.

Confession, chapter 15. Although repentance be not to be rested in as any satisfaction for sin, or any cause of the pardon thereof, which is the act of God's free grace in Christ; yet is it of such necessity to all sinners that none may expect pardon without it. As there is no sin so small but it deserves damnation, so there is no sin so great that it can bring damnation upon those who truly repent. Men ought not to content themselves with a general repentance, but it is every man's duty to endeavor to repent of his particular sins particularly. As every man is bound to make private confession of his sins to God, praying for the pardon thereof, upon which, and the forsaking of them, he shall find mercy; so he that scandalizeth his brother, or the Church of Christ, ought to be willing, by a private or public confession and sorrow for his sin, to declare his repentance to those that are offended, who are thereupon to be reconciled to him, and in love to receive him.

What assurances does the Christian have in death?

L. C. 85. Death, being the wages of sin, why are not the righteous delivered from death, seeing all their sins are forgiven in Christ? The righteous shall be delivered from death itself at the last day, and even in death are delivered from the sting and curse of it; so that, although they die, yet it is out of God's love, to free them perfectly from sin and misery, and to make them capable of further communion with Christ, in glory, which they then enter upon.

S. C. 37. What benefits do believers receive from Christ at death? The souls of believers are at their death made perfect in holiness, and do immediately pass into glory; and their bodies, being still united to Christ, do rest in their graves, till the resurrection.

L. C. 79. May not true believers, by reason of their imperfections, and the many temptations and sins they are overtaken with, fall away from the state of grace? True believers, by reason of the unchangeable love of God, and his decree and covenant to give them perseverance, their inseparable union with Christ, his continual intercession for them, and the Spirit and seed of God abiding in them, can neither totally nor finally fall away from the state of grace, but are kept by the power of God through faith unto salvation.

L. C. 81. Are all true believers at all times assured of their present being in the estate of grace, and that they shall be saved? Assurance of grace and salvation not being of the essence of faith, true believers may wait long before they obtain it; and, after the enjoyment thereof, may have it weakened and intermitted, through manifold distempers, sins, temptations, and desertions; yet are they never left without such a presence and support of the Spirit of God as keeps them from sinking into utter despair.

Confession, chapter 17. They whom God accepteth in his Beloved, effectually called and sanctified by his Spirit, can neither totally nor finally fall away from the state of grace; but shall certainly persevere therein to the end. . . . Nevertheless they may, through the temptations of Satan and of the world, the prevalency of corruption remaining in them, and the neglect of the means of their preservation, fall into grievous sins; and for a time continue therein; whereby they incur God's displeasure, and grieve his Holy Spirit; come to be deprived of some measure of their graces and comforts; have their hearts hardened, and their consciences wounded; hurt and scandalize others, and bring temporal judgments upon themselves.

What makes an ethical standard "Christian"?

S. C. 42. What is the sum of the ten commandments? The sum of the ten commandments is, To love the Lord our God with all our heart, with all our soul, with all our strength, and with all our mind; and our neighbor as ourselves.

S. C. 46. What is required in the first commandment? The first commandment requireth us to know and acknowledge God to be the only true God, and our God; and to worship and glorify him accordingly.

S. C. 47. What is forbidden in the first commandment? The first commandment forbiddeth the denying, or not worshiping and glorifying the true God as God, and our God, and the giving of that worship and glory to any other, which is due to him alone.

S. C. 50. What is required in the second commandment? The second commandment requireth the receiving, observing, and keeping pure and entire, all such religious worship and ordinances as God hath appointed in his word.

S. C. 51. What is forbidden in the second commandment? The second commandment forbiddeth the worshiping of God by images, or any other way not appointed in his word.

S. C. 54. What is required in the third commandment? The third commandment requireth the holy and reverend use of God's names, titles, attributes, ordinances, word, and works.

S. C. 55. What is forbidden in the third commandment? The third commandment forbiddeth all profaning or abusing of anything whereby God maketh himself known.

S. C. 58. What is required in the fourth commandment? The fourth commandment requireth the keeping holy to God such set times as he hath appointed in his word; expressly one whole day in seven, to be a holy sabbath to himself.

S. C. 61. What is forbidden in the fourth commandment? The fourth commandment forbiddeth the omission or careless performance of the duties required, and the profaning the day by idleness, or doing that which is in itself sinful, or by unnecessary thoughts, words, or works, about our worldly employments or recreations.

S. C. 64. What is required in the fifth commandment? The fifth commandment requireth the preserving the honor, and performing the duties, belonging to everyone in their several places and relations, as superiors, inferiors, or equals.

S. C. 65. What is forbidden in the fifth commandment? The fifth commandment forbiddeth the neglecting of, or doing anything against, the honor and duty which belongeth to everyone in their several places and relations.

S. C. 68. What is required in the sixth commandment? The sixth commandment requireth all lawful endeavors to preserve our own life, and the life of others.

S. C. 69. What is forbidden in the sixth commandment? The sixth commandment forbiddeth the taking away of our own life, or the life of our neighbor unjustly, or whatsoever tendeth thereunto.

S. C. 71. What is required in the seventh commandment? The seventh commandment requireth the preservation of our own and our neighbor's chastity, in heart, speech, and behavior.

S. C. 72. What is forbidden in the seventh commandment? The seventh commandment forbiddeth all unchaste thoughts, words, and actions.

S. C. 74. What is required in the eighth commandment? The eighth commandment requireth the lawful procuring and furthering the wealth and outward estate of ourselves and others.

S. C. 75. What is forbidden in the eighth commandment? The eighth commandment forbiddeth whatsoever doth or may unjustly hinder our own or our neighbor's wealth or outward estate.

S. C. 77. What is required in the ninth commandment? The ninth commandment requireth the maintaining and promoting of truth between man and man, and of our own and our neighbor's good name, especially in witness-bearing.

S. C. 78. What is forbidden in the ninth commandment? The ninth commandment forbiddeth whatsoever is prejudicial to truth, or injurious to our own or our neighbor's good name.

S. C. 80. What is required in the tenth commandment? The tenth commandment requireth full contentment with our own condition, with a right and charitable frame of spirit toward our neighbor, and all that is his.

S. C. 81. What is forbidden in the tenth commandment? The tenth commandment forbiddeth all discontentment with our own estate, envying or grieving at the good of our neighbor, and all inordinate motions and affections to anything that is his.

S. C. 82. Is any man able perfectly to keep the commandments of God? No mere man since the fall is able in this life perfectly to keep the commandments of God, but doth break them in thought, word, and deed.

S. C. 85. What doth God require of us, that we may escape his wrath and curse due to us for sin? To escape the wrath and curse of God due to us for sin, God requireth of us faith in Jesus Christ, repentance unto life, with the diligent use of all the outward means whereby Christ communicateth to us the benefits of redemption.

How is life made free in Christ?

Confession, chapter 20. The liberty which Christ hath purchased for believers under the gospel consists in their freedom from the guilt of sin, the condemning wrath of God, the curse of the moral law; and in their being delivered from this present evil world, bondage to Satan, and dominion of sin, from the evil of afflictions, the sting of death, the victory of the grave, and everlasting damnation; as also in their free access to God, and their yielding obedience unto him, not out of slavish fear, but a child-like love and a willing mind. . . . God alone is Lord of the conscience, and hath left it free from the doctrines and commandments of men which are in any thing contrary to his Word, or beside it in matters of faith or worship. . . . They who, upon pretense of Christian liberty, do practice any sin, or cherish any lust, do thereby destroy the end of Christian liberty; which is, that, being delivered out of the hands of our enemies, we might serve the Lord without fear, in holiness and righteousness before him, all the days of our life.

How is life made rich in Christ?

Confession, chapter 21. The light of nature showeth that there is a God, who hath lordship and sovereignty over all; is good, and doeth good unto all; and is therefore to be feared, loved, praised, called upon, trusted in, and served with all the heart, and with all the soul, and with all the might. But the acceptable way of worshiping the true God is instituted by himself, and so limited by his own revealed will, that he may not be worshiped according to the imaginations and devices of men, or the suggestions of Satan, under any visible representation or any other way not prescribed in the Holy Scripture. . . . This Sabbath is then kept holy unto the Lord, when men, after a due preparing of their hearts, and ordering of their common affairs beforehand, do not only observe an holy rest all the day from their own works, words, and thoughts, about their worldly employments and recreations; but also are taken up the whole time in the public and private exercises of his worship, and in the duties of necessity and mercy.

What makes relationships whole in Christ?

L. C. 62. What is the visible church? The visible church is a society made up of all such as in all ages and places of the world do profess the true religion, and of their children.

L. C. 64. What is the invisible church? The invisible church is the whole number of the elect that have been, are, or shall be gathered into one under Christ the head.

Confession, chapter 24. Marriage was ordained for the mutual help of husband and wife; for the increase of mankind with a legitimate issue, and of the Church with an holy seed; and for preventing of uncleanness. . . . Although the corruption of man be such as is apt to study arguments, unduly to put asunder those whom God hath joined together in marriage; yet nothing but adultery, or such wilful desertion as can no way be remedied by the Church or civil magistrate, is cause sufficient.

Confession, chapter 25. The catholic or universal Church, which is invisible, consists of the whole number of the elect, that have been, are, or shall be gathered into one, under Christ the head thereof; and is the spouse, the body, the fulness of him that filleth all in all.

Confession, chapter 26. All saints that are united to Jesus Christ their head, by his Spirit and by faith, have fellowship with him in his graces, sufferings, death, resurrection, and glory: and being united to one another in love, they have communion in each other's gifts and graces, and are obliged to the performance of such duties, public and private, as do conduce to their mutual good, both in the inward and outward man.

What does the future hold in Christ?

L. C. 86. What is the communion in glory with Christ, which the members of the invisible church enjoy immediately after death? The communion in glory with Christ, which the members of the invisible church enjoy immediately after death, is, in that their souls are then made perfect in holiness, and received into the highest heavens, where they behold the face of God in light and glory, waiting for the full redemption of their bodies, which even in death continue united to Christ, and rest in their graves as in their beds, till at the return of Christ they be again united to their souls. Whereas the souls of the wicked are at their death cast into hell, where they remain in torments and utter darkness, and their bodies kept in their graves, as in their prisons, till the resurrection and judgment of the great day.

L. C. 87. What are we to believe concerning the resurrection? We are to believe, that at the last time there shall be a resurrection of the dead, both of the just and unjust; when they that are then found alive shall in a moment be changed; and the self-same bodies of the dead which were laid in the grave, being then again united to their souls forever, shall be raised up by the power of Christ. The bodies of the just, by the Spirit of Christ, and by virtue of his resurrection as their head, shall be raised in power, spiritual, incorruptible, and made like to his glorious body; and the bodies of the wicked shall be raised up in dishonor by him, as an offended judge.

L. C. 88. What shall follow after the resurrection? After the resurrection of the just and the unjust shall follow the final judgment of angels and men. That all may watch and pray and be ready for the coming of the Lord, the day and hour whereof no man knoweth.

S. C. 38. What benefits do believers receive from Christ at the resurrection? At the resurrection, believers being raised up in glory, shall be openly acknowledged and acquitted in the day of judgment, and made perfectly blessed in the full enjoying of God to all eternity.

Scripture Index

Genesis
1:1	75, 102
1:26–27	102
1:26–31	145
1:27–2:25	224
1:28	124, 143, 360
1:31	88, 122, 143
2:2–3	146
2:17	128
2:18–25	146
2:19–20	145
3:7–13	147
3:14–15	149–50
3:14–24	147–48
3:16–17	174
3:22	102
3:22–24	131
6:6	81
8:20–9:17	82
9:5–6	329
11:7	102
12–21	269–70
14	176
15:6	204
15:8–21	78–79
18:19	195
22	270–71

Exodus
3:14	95
4:11	121
9:16–17	140
9:22–26	134
10:21–23	134
15:11	84
19:6a	338
20:2–17	334–35
20:8–10	371
20:13	329
20:19	335
34:7	167

Leviticus
11:44a	252
24:17	329

Numbers
6:24	103
11:17, 25	103
23:19–20	78
35:16–31	329

Deuteronomy
6:4–5	93, 107
6:10–12	118–19
18:15, 18–19	176
18:22	43
19:19b–21	341
22	389
24	389, 390

Joshua
10:11	134
10:12–14	134

1 Samuel
2:2	84
2:6–8	138
15:29	78, 81

2 Samuel
23:2–3	103

1 Kings
8:27–28	79
17:1	134
18:41–45	134

1 Chronicles
16:25	122, 123

2 Chronicles
5:13	88
6:18–19	79
6:26–27	134
30:8	188

Nehemiah
9:5	80
9:6b	121
9:16–17	394

Job
3:17–19	293
9:2b	205
9:11	76
14:4	198
15:20–26	208
18:5–14	208
21:23–26	293
34:17–19	86–87
34:23–28	86–87
34:24	138
42: 5–6	73–74

Psalm
1:3	267
2:2–6	140
2:6	178
8	31
19	62
19:1–2	60, 62
31:14–15a	127
31:19	88
32:3–4	211
33:11	81
37:23	246
38:5–6, 10–11	209
45:6–7	102
49:16–17	293
51	279
51:4	151
51:5–6, 10, 17	278–79
51:10	192
52:9	88
75:6–7	138
90:12	296
100:3	136
100:5	88
102:19, 21–22	180
103: 17	81
104:24, 28b	122
104:30	103
106	88
106:13–15	119
106:38	329
110:1	102
110:4	177
113:7–9	138
116:15	303

Proverbs
127:1–2	130–31
130:3–4	204
139:7–8	76
139:13–14	121
145	88
148:5–6	122

13:15	153, 155
14:12	21, 23–24
16:9	138
19:21	138
19:29	329
21:1	140
22:2	121
28:17	329

Ecclesiastes
1:2	311
1:15	312
3:14	81
5:10–11	313
7:28	313
8:8a	293
8:14	313
12	313
12:7	433
12:13	314

Isaiah
4:3–6	46
4:10	137
6:3	85, 103
6:5	74
6:8	102
7:14	102
9:6–7	102–3
11:3b–5	181
13:20	51
14:26–27	138
23	46
29:29	329
38:18	293
38:7–8	134
40:21–22, 26, 28	120–21

44:3	331	26:12	46	4:17	280	9:47–48	226
45:22–24	136	28:23	46	5:16	251	10:18	87–88
46: 8–10	127	33:11b	199	5:17	337	13:13	300
48:12–15	52	35:5–6	329	5:22	329	14:36	310
51:9	52	35:34, 9	47	5:28	253	16:15	408
53:11	204	37:24	179	5:38–39, 41–42	340		
53:12	177			5:45	88		

Daniel

55:1, 3a	187, 188, 189–90	12	435	5:48	250, 349	**Luke**	
		2:18–19	122	6:9–15	395	1:32–33	179
56:6–7	180	2:23b	194	6:12, 14–15	387	2:11	181
58:13–14	375			6:21	126	4:14–21	176
59:3–7	329			6:24	251	6:36	250
61:1	176	**Joel**		7:1	395	6:37	395
61:1–2	357	2:32	180	7:1–2	399	7:48–49	103
62:11	181			7:1–5	329	8:1	176
63:10–11	103			7:11	88	8:13	247
65:17–25	427	**Amos**		7:13–14	226	9	433
66:1–2	121–22	4:12b–13	111	8:33–34	248	12:8	104
				10:20	104	13:1–3	281
				10:29	133	15:7	281

Jeremiah

		Jonah		11:5	176	15:11–32	281
1:5	195	3:4, 10	81	11:29	253	16	433
2:5	129			12:1–13	372	16:19–31	435
4:4	188			12:8	372	18:7–8	86
6:16	310	**Micah**		13	247	22:42	310
6:30	190	1:5–6	46–47	13:56–58	248	23:40–43	434
7:9–10	329	6:6–8	310	14:22–27	134	23:42–43	295
10:23	136	6:8	149	15:19–20	329	23:44–45	134
17:9	396			15:30–31	134	24:19	176
17:9–10	317, 321			16:13–16	405	24:47–48	281
17:14	396	**Nahum**		17	433		
23:5	178–79	1:2–3	188	19:4–6	390		
23:5–6	103	1:7	88	21:11	176	**John**	
24:9	46	1:8, 14	48–49	22:10–13	217	1:1	104
27:36	46	2:5–6	48	22:14	190	1:12	227, 228
29:21	46	3:1	329	22:37–39	329, 387	1:14	104, 167
31:3b	167	3:13	48	23:35	329	1:18	76
33:11	88	3:17	49	24:13	300	1:49	178–79
35:17	46			24:20	372	2:23–25	248
47:4	46	**Habakkuk**		24:35	81	3	182–83
49:9–10	47–48	1:13	245, 167	25:31–33, 46	226	3:3b	170
49:17–18	47	2:13	129–30	25:31–46	329	3:14–15	183
50:13, 39	50–51			25:34	157	3:16	14, 183, 188
51:26	50			25:41b	214		
51:42–43	51–52	**Zechariah**		26:39	310	3:36	226
51:58	50	6:12b–13	177	28:18	103	4:19	176
				28:18b–20	157, 407	4:21–24	180
		Malachi		28:19	105	4:23–24	14, 76, 344
Ezekiel		2:16	389	28:19–20	188		
16:49	329	3:6	81			4:42	181
18:20a, 21, 30b–32	280			**Mark**		5:24	246
		Matthew		1:14	176	6:37	190
18:23, 32	82	2:1–2, 9	134	3:11	248	6:37, 39–40	246
18:4	86	2:5–6	179	4:35–41	134	6:44	195
25:13	47	3:7–8	280	8:35	33	6:65	195
26:4, 5, 12, 14	44–46	3:15	249	8:35–37	77	8:36	198, 357
26:7	45	3:16–17	105	9	433	8:44a	227
						8:58	104
						9:4	301

10:10	245	3:10–12	150	3	412, 437	4:11–13	251
10:27–30	246–47	3:11	224			4:14–16	407
10:35	53	3:21–24	213	3:16	104	4:24	250
10:36–38	104	3:21–5:21	204	4:7	195	4:32	250, 395
11:25–26	291, 292	3:23	166, 213	5:7	344	5:1–2a	250
11:35	292	3:25–26	87	5:9–13	340	6:10–17	278
14:2–3	426	4:24	215–16	6:20	137	6:14	284
14:6	89	5:1–2	218	8	367	6:16	268
14:11	106	5:1–5	424	8:6	122		
14:15, 23	246	5:10	395	10:5	413	**Philippians**	
15:1, 4–6	244	5:12–19	150	10:31	29	1:11b	252
15:26	104, 105	5:20	348	11:29–30	245	1:14–21	431
16:13	89	6:15–16	325	15:55–57	294	1:21a	282
17:3	105	6:20, 22	137			1:21–24	295
17:17	36, 53, 89	6:23	215	**2 Corinthians**		1:23	434
		7	15	3:17	353	1:29	195, 216
17:19	249	7–8	195	3:18	251	2:9–11	136–37
18:33–37	178–79	7:25–8:2	207	5:1–5	294, 434	2:13	192
18:37–38	88	7:7	347	5:6–8	295	2:14–15	250
19:30	347	7:7–24	207	5:11–21	193, 410	3:10–11	11, 73
20:28	104	8:5–8	195	5:17	184	4:8	394, 400
21:15	211	8:15b	234	5:17–18a	171		
		8:15–17a	223	5:21	167	**Colossians**	
Acts		8:15–25	31	6:17–18	228	1:13–14	395
		8:16	77	9:6–8	29–30	1:18–20	409
2:37–38	274–75	8:16–17, 22–25	424	10:17	198	1:21b–22	397
2:39	191	8:18–21	123	11:23–33	282	1:22	249
3:22	176	8:19–23	155	13:9	249	1:28	249
3:36–37	418	8:28–30	194			3:8	329
4:36–37	418	8:29, 38–39	247	**Galatians**			
5	418	8:30	189, 190	1:6–9	355	**1 Thessalonians**	
5:1–11	245	8:32	88	3:10–14	349	3:13	249
5:3–4	104	8:33–34	203, 214, 239	3:28	358	1:4–5a	192
7:37	176			4:6	105	4:14	77
7:48–50	76	8:38–39	430	5:1	357	5:20	43
14:17	88	9	195	5:13	358	5:23	249
15:12–18	180	9:8	227	6:1–2	399, 400		
16:31	168, 267	9:19	199			**2 Thessalonians**	
17:28	74	9:25	194	**Ephesians**		1:11	88, 192
		10:9	216	1:3–14	30	2	336
Romans		10:12–13	180	1:4	157	2:11–12	190–91
		10:17	191	1:4–6	224	2:13	191
1:14	282	11:29	300	1:7	215		
1:16–17	423–24	11:36	29, 143	1:9	199	**1 Timothy**	
1:18–20	57–58, 59	11:7–8	190	2:10	137, 252	4:4	122
1:18–23	115	12:1–2	31, 253, 279	2:1–2	227		
1:18–32	206			2:1–10	224–25	**2 Timothy**	
1:21	224	12:9–10	387	2:8	195	2:15	259
1:24	129	14	367	2:8–10	248	3:16	249
1:28	60, 69	14:2–4	329	2:8–9	166, 216, 257, 267	3:16–17	16, 37, 38, 40
1:30	329	14:9–12	136	2:9	264	3:1–5	309
2	412			3:20	137	4:7–8	431
2:1–3	329	**1 Corinthians**		4:11	411		
2:5–8	188	2:9	31, 297				
2:15	347	2:9–10a	427				
2:25–29a	413	2:16	251				
3:10	213						

Hebrews

1	104
1:1	261
1:2–3	123
4:9–10	374
5:5–10	177
5:9–10	249
6:17–18	81
6:19–20	177
7:15–28	177
9:11–14, 24	177
10:15	105
10:25	407
12	31
12:1–2	15, 443
12:4–13	219
12:14	252
12:22–24	294
12:28–29	137, 245

James

1:2–4	250

1:2–5	262
1:13	79
1:17	88
1:22–27	267
2:10–11	214
2:14–17	251
2:14–25	267
2:18–26	248
4:1–2, 11, 12	329

1 Peter

1:9	77
1:18–21	158
2:5	410
2:9a	338
2:12	251
3:18	105

2 Peter

1:3	88
1:19–21	38, 40
3:14	250

1 John

1:8b	213
1:9	214, 395
2:1	177
2:9–11	329
2:15b–17	252
3:15	329
4:12	250
4:14	181

Jude

6	435
18	329

Revelation

1:5b–6	338
1:8	80
1:17–18	80
1:20	373
2:4–5	284, 285
2:5	287, 340
2:7b	288

3:2–3, 16	340
4:8	85
5:9	224
5:9–13	31
9:7–9	134
13:8	158
14:13	295
21:1	156, 174, 423
21:1–4	427
21:5	162, 123, 174
21:6b–8	438
21:8	329
21:9	405
22:15	329

Subject index

A Narrative of Surprising Conversions (Edwards), 277–78

Abba, 221, 223, 233, 234, 235, 316

Abel, 294

ability, human, 196, 197–98, 330

abortion, 111–12, 113, 322, 328, 364–65

Abraham, 78–79, 119, 176, 204, 269–71, 227, 232, 412

absolute dependence, 98, 278, 281, 288

absolutes, 152, 205, 319–31, 335, 346, 358, 361

abuse in family, 206, 207, 233, 309

acceptance, desire for, 391–94, 398. *See also* justification.

accepting Christ, 258, 263–71

access to God, 218, 234, 373–74, 424, 450

actions, ethical, 322, 327–28

actual guilt. *See* guilt.

Adam and Eve, 124, 145–46, 148, 151, 173, 187, 224, 228–29, 231, 318, 371, 376

adaptation, 67, 68

Adonai Yahweh, 73

adoption, 26, 31, 30, 155, 178, 194, 221–35, 257, 264, 282, 298, 316, 330, 415, 424, 450, 452–53

adultery, 151, 335, 339–40, 347, 389–90, 397

affections, 211, 278, 276, 284, 285, 309

afflictions, freedom from, 356

Aid to Families with Dependent Children (AFDC), 389

AIDS. *See* HIV.

alcoholic, 164

Alexander the Great, 45, 50, 52

algae, 65

"all things new." *See* re-creation.

Allah, 39

Alpha and *Omega*, 73, 80

Alpha and the Omega, Christ as, 438

altruism, 313, 323, 325–26

ambassador for Christ, 158, 193, 196–97, 407, 410

American Atheist Society, 117

American Museum of Natural History, 114

Amiens, 142

amino acids, 66–67

amorality, 153, 319

Amos, 176

analogies for Trinity, 93–94

Ananias and Sapphira, 245, 418

Ancient of Days, 73

angels, 31, 77, 104, 128, 131, 135, 156, 214, 226, 249, 294, 355, 359, 370, 432

anger, divine, 29, 78, 227, 245, 302, 344, 351, 356; human, 29, 192, 207, 208, 218, 238, 302, 347

Animal Farm, 358

annoyances in marriage, 397–98

anointed one. *See* Messiah.

anorexia, 207

antinomianism, 325, 336, 337

anxiety, 208

apathy, 152

Apostles' Creed, 408

Aquinas, Thomas, 84

archeology, 38–39, 49, 51, 52, 337

arianism, 101

ark of the covenant, 85, 177

Arminianism, 195–96, 197, 198, 300

Arminius, Jacob, 196

armor of God, 278, 284, 285, 288

Arndt, W. F., 42

arts, 124, 158, 361

ascension, 94, 106

Ashurbanipal, 49

assurance in Christ, 192, 265, 266, 268, 302–3, 456

Assyria, 48–49, 81–82, 388

astrology, 97, 143, 262

astronomy, 61–62

atheism, 95, 97, 100, 116–17, 118, 123, 144, 298, 323, 346

atmosphere, 63, 64

atomic theory, 61, 62

atonement, 10, 14, 85, 86, 87, 99, 105, 106, 136, 148, 156–58, 150, 155–56, 157–58, 161, 167, 174, 175, 177, 178, 179, 182, 183, 184, 189, 193, 203, 204, 207, 211, 214, 215–18, 221, 225, 227, 229, 230, 237, 240, 242, 246, 249, 264, 270–71, 274, 277, 294, 297, 299, 302, 310, 311, 316, 318, 337, 344, 345, 346–47, 351, 355–56, 394–95, 410, 416, 430, 434, 436, 443, 450

attacks on Scripture, 96, 259, 260

Augustine, 195

Austria-Hungary Empire, 142

authority, in family, 342; of God, 334, 335, 407; of Jesus, 157; of Scripture, 13, 21–22, 23, 30–31, 35–54, 73, 96, 99, 128, 129, 135, 136, 258, 259

autonomy, 197, 198–199
awakenings. *See* revivals.
awareness of sin, 277, 278, 280, 281, 312, 347

Babylon, 44–45, 48, 49–52, 388
Babylonian captivity, 382
baptism. *See* sacraments.
Baptists, Danbury, 363
Barnabas, church father, 373; in Acts, 418
Barnum, P. T., 298
Barth, Karl, 98–100
Barthianism. *See* neo-orthodoxy.
Bartimaeus, 175
Bathsheba, 211
Bavinck, Herman, 203
Before the Face of God (Sproul), 144
Belgian Congo, 307
belief, 9–13, 32, 167–68, 182, 183, 184, 201, 204, 215, 226, 247, 248, 255, 258, 263–64, 267, 291, 321, 367, 423
Belleau Wood, 142
belt of truth, 278, 284, 285, 288
Bentham, Jeremy, 324
Bethlehem, 222
betrayal, forgiving, 397
Bill of Rights, 364
biology, 32
bitterness, 192, 396–97
black family, 389
Blanshard, Paul, 361
blessings of God, 28–30, 31, 88, 139, 284, 330
blindness, spiritual, 33–34, 37, 57–60, 69–70, 115–16, 182, 188, 190, 277, 357
blood cells, 66
blood of Jesus Christ. *See* atonement.
blue laws, 370, 371
boasting. *See* pride.
body, human, 294, 428–29, 433; of Christ, 251, 414, 419
Boettner, Loraine, 105
bondage to sin, 129, 133, 137, 188, 196, 198, 199, 217, 348, 356
Bonhoeffer, Dietrich, 211

Born Again (Colson), 171
born again. *See* regeneration.
boy with a demonic spirit, 9–10
brain, 68, 205
Brainerd, David, 298
Branch Davidians, 12, 177, 178, 422
Brave New World (Huxley), 116
Bres, Guido de, 131–32, 135
bride of Christ, 403, 405, 409, 427, 428
Bridegroom. *See* bride of Christ.
bridge, missing, 256–57
"broadly evangelical," 172
brokenness, 278–79, 285, 288
brotherhood of humanity, 222, 226–27, 229–31
Bryan, William Jennings, 114
Buddhism, 39, 43, 97, 164
Bulgaria, 142
Bundy, Ted, 154
Bunyan, John, 348
Burckhardt's Travels in Syria (Burckhardt), 47–48
Burckhardt, John L., 47–48
burden-bearing, 390, 399–400
Buswell, J. Oliver, 100
butterfly, 170–71, 184

cabin of doubt, 12, 58, 62, 66, 69
Cadillac over the cliff, 156–57, 158
California, 364–65
call of God, 169, 180, 185, 186–200, 201, 298, 300; external, 188, 190, 199, 280; inward, 26, 189, 190, 191–93, 201, 224, 237, 240, 246, 263–64, 308, 311, 357–58, 413, 451
Calvin, John, 74, 94, 195, 203
Calvinism, 195–96, 300
Camus, Albert, 33
Canaan, 176
cancer, 301
capital punishment, 43, 329, 339, 389–90
capitalism, 116

carbon dioxide, atmospheric, 64
Carey, William, 283
Casey, Annie E., 425
caterpillar, 170–71, 181, 184
catholic church. *See* church.
causation, 62, 133
cell structure, 66–67
centering on God, 376
ceremonial law, 337, 338, 344–45
certainty of eternal life, 290, 298–99
Chalcedon, Council of, 92–93
Chambers, Whitaker, 66
chance, 61–62, 63, 126, 132
character of God, 78–79, 83
Chariots of Fire, 384
charismatic renewal, 172, 299
Charles I, 24
Charles II, 356, 359
chastisement. *See* punishment.
cheap grace, 86, 211
Chesterfield, Lord, 33–34
Chicago, 164, 202–3
chief end of man. *See* purpose, for life.
child, of God, 124, 155, 178, 181–82, 184, 200, 221–35, 276, 310, 330, 336, 380, 384, 424; of Satan, 229; of wrath, 29. *See also* adoption; Father, God as.
childbirth, 147
children under covenant, 410–11, 412
Children's Catechism, 79
children, 158, 341–42, 375, 385
China, 283, 364, 384, 426
choice human. *See* free, will.
Christ, as Branch, 177, 178; as Bridegroom, 285, 403, 405, 409, 427, 428; as Creator, 180; as Defender, 179; as Finisher of faith, 443; as Head of the church, 169, 179–80, 411; as Heir, 169, 180–81; as Judge, 169, 180–81, 203, 214, 215; as Lamb, 158, 429, 430; as King, 169, 136–37, 175, 178–79, 181, 410, 450; as

Liberator, 297, 367; as Lord, 184, 189, 310, 374, 439; as Lord of Sabbath, 372; as Passover, 344; as Physician, 211, 287; as Priest, 169, 175, 176–78, 179, 181, 215, 249; as Prophet, 169, 175, 176, 179, 181, 450; as Pursuer, 189, 193, 197–98, 200; as Re-creator, 122–24; as resurrection, 291, 292; as second Adam, 150, 188, 448; as Servant, 179, 180, 231; as Shepherd, 179; as Son of Man, 226; as Vine, 243, 419; as Word, 167; assurance in, 268; conformity to, 249, 250–51, 253; denial of, 210; eternality of, 178, 179; faith in, 297; fellowship with, 416; gifts of, 330; grace of, 30; holiness of, 214, 243; hope in, 263; humanity of, 106, 449; humiliation of, 450–51; identification with, 193, 231, 424, 430–31; intercession of, 449; law of, 372, 399; miracles of, 174–75; need for, 347, 348–49; obedience of, 215, 249, 449; perfect life of, 204; power of, 137, 164, 181, 248; presence of, 426, 434; prophecies concerning, 44; unity in, 415, 416–17, 421, 426, 427, 455; will of, 442. *See also* atonement; death, of Christ; deity of Christ; lordship of Christ; mediator; resurrection of Christ; return of Christ; righteousness, of Christ; salvation in Christ; Savior, Christ as.

Christian, as branch, 419; as called, 169; as child of God, 31, 155; as glorified, 169; as justified, 169; as redeemed, 169; as reflection, 251; as seed, 169; confidence of, 131, 132; death of, 294–95, 302–3; duty, 339, 417, 443, 457–58; ethic, 321, 328–31; failures of, 301; faith, 258–71, 295; fearful, 290–91, 299; holiness, 216, 228, 237, 245–48, 249, 279, 421, 426, 427; Holy Spirit in, 106; hope, 299; ideals, 193; judgment of, 301, 437; law and, 336–50; liberty, 354–67, 370, 459; lifestyle, 245, 317–19, 336, 339, 345–46, 357, 367, 372, 374, 385–401, 417–19; living, 241, 249–52, 253, 282–83, 300; obedience, 245, 290, 291; power to live, 330; principles, 358; psychology, 212–13; righteousness of, 250; Science, 142; security, 246–48; sin in, 206, 216, 244, 248, 273, 399–400. *See also* sanctification.

Christology, 92–93

church, 26, 403–20, as bride of Christ, 403, 405, 409, 427, 428; as family, 419; as holy nation, 179–80, 338, 410, 419; attendance in, 406; community, 299; confrontation with state, 362–66; discipline, 26, 339–41; early, 245, 274, 309, 372, 381–82; false teachers in, 336; families in, 344, 389; foundation of, 405–6; government, 56–57; holiness of, 339–41, 409; Holy Spirit in, 410, 415, 417; humanism in, 362; inclusive, 410; indebtedness of, 283; immorality in, 339; invisible, 411–14, 460, 461; leaders in, 411, 412, 413; legalism in, 213; love in, 339; membership, 182, 257; ministry of, 411; need of, 252; nurture in, 411; organic, 411; organized, 411, 412; playing at, 287–88; purpose of, 409; salvation through, 299; social care in, 342–44, under Christ, 169, 179–80, 411; unity of, 403, 408–11, 414–19; universal, 180, 403; view of Scripture, 367; visible, 411, 412, 413, 460, 461; weakness in, 198, 279–80, 309, 320, 367, 414; work of, 249–50. *See also* fruitfulness, Christian; witness to world.

Church of Scotland, 25

Church, Richard, 32

circumcision, 318, 412–13, 449

citizenship, 228–29, 308, 338–39, 340, 363–66, 385

city of God, 427–30

civil, disobedience, 381; law, 337, 338–39; liberty, 356; religion, 357

Clark, Gordon, 328

cleansing, 214, 264

Clement of Alexandria, 373

clinging to Christ, 218, 266

Clock maker, God as, 95

co-heirs with Christ, 221–35, 419, 424. *See also* adoption; family, church as.

Cohen, Mickey, 192

colleges, 172

colonial America, 388

Colson, Charles, 171

Columbia Theological Seminary, 424

commandments of God. *See* law of God.

commitment to Christ, 248

communion with God, 151, 155, 158, 318, 414. *See also* sacraments.

communism, 66, 324, 346, 358, 418, 425

compass, inner, 23

compassion. *See* mercy.

complexity of nature, 62, 68

Concept of God, The (Nash), 83–84

conception, 327

condemnation, 155, 188, 190–91, 203, 204, 207, 214, 215, 216, 246, 318, 319, 333, 336, 349, 351, 355, 356, 395, 431–32

condescension, 231

conduct, principles, 320
conduit, faith as, 267–68
confession, of faith, 173, 248, 407–8, 410, 416; of guilt, 183, 184, 214, 215, 217, 382, 395, 396, 397, 455
confidence, in God, 131, 132, 290–91, 295, 423; in Scriptures, 259–60
conformity, to Christ, 249, 250–51, 253; to law, 347
Confucius, 39, 43, 179
connectedness, 244, 245, 248, 253, 330, 376–79, 383–84. *See also* fellowship, with God.
conscience, 26, 205–11, 277–78, 280, 281, 357; liberty of, 355, 356
consequences of actions, 154–56, 188, 218–19, 243, 245, 326, 322, 327, 330, 399
consistency of Scripture, 38, 261
Constance, Council of, 302
Constantine, 372, 373
Constitution, U.S., 357, 358, 363–64, 366
construction, Christian under, 242, 249, 250
contentment, 312
contradictions in Scripture, 38, 41–42, 84
Cooke, Harold, 114
Coral Ridge Presbyterian Church, 36, 153
corruption, 151, 243–44, 277, 292, 424
cosmological argument, 60–62
cosmos. *See* universe.
Cosmos (Sagan), 79
counseling, 210, 397
courage, 431
courts, 212, 242, 339, 364, 365
covenant, 26; children in, 410–11, 412; marriage, 394, 397, 339; nation, 318; new, 294; of grace, 148, 149–50, 155, 157–58, 169, 173–74, 180, 181, 188, 223, 224–25, 258, 263, 318, 339, 448, 451–52; of life, 141, 144–46, 148, 149, 151, 173–74, 187,

223, 224, 318, 333, 446; people, 412–13; relationship, 213, 267; with Noah, 82
coveting, 253, 335, 347
creation, 26, 106, 109, 120–23, 173, 200, 224, 374; belief in, 32, 99, 142, 365–66, evidence of, 37–38, 57, 59, 60–69; goodness of, 143–44, 145, 148; hope of, 155–56, 424; new, 428; preservation of, 132–35, 155–56, 187; revelation of God in, 37–38, 74, 88, 144, 170, 200, 445; stewardship, 124; wonder of, 20
creation ordinances, 371
creativity, 88, 344–45
Creator. *See* creation.
credo belief, 10–13
creeds, 13, 16–17, 162, 308. See also *Westminster Confession of Faith*; *Westminster catechisms*.
crime, 119, 151, 192, 204, 212, 214, 364–65, 425. *See also* criminal law.
criminal law, 337, 338, 339–41. *See also* crime.
crisis, of conscience, 276, 277–79, 280, 281, 302, 309, 319–20, 423; theology of. *See* neo-orthodoxy.
criticism, 391–94, 397–98
Cromwell, Oliver, 24
cross, fellowship in, 193
crossroads, 310
crucifixion. *See* atonement.
Ctesias, 48
cults, 12–13, 92, 101, 117, 172–73, 418
cultural mandate, 124, 145–46, 147–48, 157, 187, 360, 361
culture, 22, 23, 124, 131, 179, 309–10
curse of law, 289, 317, 349, 351, 356
cut-flower syndrome, 319, 328, 330, 331
Cyaxares, 48
cycle, of devotion, 374–75, 380, 383; of failure, 398
cynicism, 89, 143

"daddy," 235
danger of rebellion, 276
Darius III, 45
darkness, 134, 176, 183, 184, 208, 224, 395, 435
Darrow, Clarence, 113–14
Darwin, Charles, 32, 115
David, 60, 62, 151, 174, 178, 179, 192, 209, 211, 278–79, 422
Day of Atonement, 85, 177, 344
day of Sabbath, 369, 372–74
Dead Sea scrolls, 53
death, 76–77, 150, 256, 351, 421–39; fear of, 290–91, 299; for sin, 86–87, 141, 150, 183, 184, 188, 215, 218, 224, 227, 280, 315, 318–19, 447, 448; of Christ, 14, 158, 161, 167, 174, 177, 178, 189, 193, 203, 215, 237, 264, 274, 316, 410; denial of, 296; power of, 10, 289–303, 325, 356, 455, 461–62; separation of, 292; to sin, 241, 420; way of, 21, 23, 33–34; sting of, 293–94, 295, 299, 302, 303, 351, 455, 459. *See also* capital punishment; slavery, to sin and death.
debtor to God, 281, 282–84
decay, bondage to, 155
deceit of heart, 317, 396
Declaration of Independence, 358
declaration of righteousness, 216
decrees of God, 26, 446
deeds. *See* actions, ethical.
Defender, Christ as, 179
Definition of Chalcedon, 92–93
degeneration, 156–57, 229, 319–20. *See also* depravity.
degradation, 151, 170, 195, 343, 360, 426. *See also* depravity.
deism, 92, 95–96, 98, 99, 363
deity of Christ, 12, 14, 99, 100, 102–3, 103–4, 123, 158, 167, 169, 174, 189, 248, 260, 264, 271, 274, 410, 449

delight in God, 375
deliverance, 180, 289, 299
delusion of sin, 190–91, 217, 278, 438
democracy, 142, 357
demons, 77, 210, 248. *See also* angels; Satan.
demonstration of love, 240
denial, of Christ, 210; of death, 295–96; of sin, 205, 210
denominations, 171
dependence. *See* absolute dependence.
depravity, 57–60, 69, 142–57, 150, 152–55, 170, 206, 207, 213, 224, 228–29, 277–79, 279–80, 317, 387–88, 390
depression, 208, 209, 218, 248, 291, 301, 431
DeShazer, Jacob, 163–64, 168
design of creation, 60–69, 133, 135, 137, 317
desire, for God, 192, 193; human, 311
devotion, cycle of, 374, 380, 383
dialectical theology. *See* neo-orthodoxy.
"Dialogue Between Men of Living Faiths," 97–98
Didache, 381–82
dimensions of faith, 264
Diodorus Siculus, 48
direction of God, 233, 266, 315, 336, 411
dirtiness of sin, 206, 210, 218, 276
discernment, 262
discipleship, 124, 301, 411, 407, 419
discouragement, 398
dis-ease of sin, 206
disintegration of family, 388–89
disinterest, 392–93
Disney, Walt, 146–47
disobedience, 207, 215, 227
divine nature, 232
divorce, 341, 366, 386–90, 397, 375
Dixon, Jeane, 43–44
Dobson, James, 154

Does the Bible Contradict Itself? (Arndt), 42
Dogmatics in Outline (Barth), 100
dogmatism, 21
Doolittle, Jimmy, 163
doubt, 301, 302, 303
Doyle, Arthur Conan, 202
drugs, 192, 207
Du Maurier, George, 32
Dunkirk, 142
Dunphy, John J., 362
duty, Christian, 314, 315, 318, 333, 385, 387–89, 417, 443, 444, 457–58
dynamic (modal) monarchianism, 94

Eagle, God as, 95
ear, 66
Earhart, Amelia, 23
early church, 245, 274, 309, 372, 381–82
earth, 134; new, 423, 427, 428; science, 62–65
Eastern philosophy, 12, 143
Ecclesiastes, 311–14
economic devastation, 426
Eddy, Mary Baker, 142
Eden, 145, 156, 360, 371
Edom, 47–48
education, 124, 113–14, 361–62, 365, 366
Edwards, Jonathan, 277, 280, 281
effectual call, 189–200, 201, 237, 240, 246, 263–64, 451. *See also* call of God; Holy Spirit.
egoism, 323–24
egolatry, 309
Egypt, 52, 270, 337, 338, 388
Einstein, 61
El, 102
election, 106, 189, 193, 214–15, 224, 246, 249, 255, 403, 411, 413, 448–49, 460
electrons, 62
El Elyon, 73
Elihu, 86
Elijah, 302, 433
Elohim, God as, 102
El Shaddai, 73

Elutheras, 360
Elwell, Walter, 103
Emmaus, 373
emotional, acceptance, 264; belief, 248; faith, 267; needs, 146, 148; response to Scripture, 99
emotionalism, 12, 13, 14, 97, 98, 100, 106, 172, 191, 197, 247, 300, 312
emotions, 23, 96, 199, 211, 218, 258, 275, 278, 396, 397
end, and means, 322–23, 326; of the world, 180
enemy, love for, 396–97
England, 358, 380, 426
English Civil War, 17, 24–25, 309, 356
enjoying God, 19, 27, 28–30, 31, 37, 73, 120, 124, 130, 157, 158, 162, 173, 187, 224, 244, 245, 257–58, 293, 294, 310, 314, 316, 331, 359, 361, 370, 374, 383–84, 421, 423, 427, 428, 437, 442, 444
enlightened mind, 185, 192
enlightened selfishness. *See* egoism.
Enlightenment, 12, 43, 95, 96, 152
Enoch, 302
environment, 64–65, 145, 147
Ephesians, 284–85, 286, 287
Ephesus, 284
Equal Rights Amendment (ERA), 364–65
error, 92, 94, 56–57, 172
eschatology, 57, 436
estate of sin and misery. *See* sin, state of.
eternal life, 31, 33, 105, 137, 167, 173, 183, 184, 197, 198, 215, 221, 224, 234, 246, 258, 263, 267, 282, 290, 291, 294, 297, 298–99, 303, 375, 380, 384, 414, 421, 427, 453. *See also* heaven.
eternality, of Christ, 178, 179; of God, 73, 75, 76, 79–80, 97, 120, 129, 144, 148, 445; of matter and energy, 79–80
ethics, 15, 308, 316–31, 367, 320–28, 354, 358

eugenics, 324

Euphrates River, 51, 52

euthanasia, 113, 322, 366

evangelicals, 172

Evangelism Explosion, 165–68, 110, 191, 218, 290

evangelism, 110, 124, 157, 158, 163, 193, 197, 198–99, 199–200, 251, 281, 283–84, 406, 411, 444

evangelists, 411

evangelization, 436

"Everybody's doing it!" ethic, 328

evidence, in creation, 37–38, 57, 59, 60–69; for existence of God, 58–59, 69–70, 200; for inspiration, 38–54, 58

evil, 139, 151, 183, 318, 347, 351, 387; cost of, 151, 152–55; freedom from, 356; problem of, 128, 132, 133, 143, 144–57, 281; purging, 341

evolution, 31–33, 63, 67, 68, 76, 98–99, 110, 113–16, 120, 133, 172, 323, 325–26

evolutionary worldview. *See* naturalistic worldview.

exaltation of Christ, 136–37, 177, 215, 226, 410, 424, 433, 443, 450, 451

excellence, 87–88

excommunication, 339, 340

existential awareness of nonbeing, 208

existentialism, 326

expectations of others, 398

external call. *See* call of God, external.

external morality, 264

extra-sensory perception, 97

"eye for an eye" law, 340–41

eyes, 67–68

Ezekiel, prophecies of, 44–45, 46, 47

failure, 218

failure in marriage, 391–97

fairness of God, 152, 154, 230

faith, 100, 166, 167–68, 201, 203, 204–5, 216; as bridge,

265; as freeway, 265; boasting in, 197; content of, 13; counterfeit, 275; dead, 267; empowering, 258; evolution as, 31–33; expressed through love, 318–19; focus of, 266–67; gift of, 195, 255; in Christ, 297, 298, 410; laws regarding, 356; living by, 295; nurturing, 268; of Abraham, 269; of unbelief, 61, 68–69; pillars of, 56–57; recumbent, 265–67, 269, 295; rejection of, 300; repentance and, 273–77; righteousness by, 87, 213; saving, 255–71, 454, 455; shallow, 247; source of, 263; stepping out in, 307; testing of, 250; through Word, 191; transforming, 442; unity in, 415; victorious, 268, 422; without submission, 248; worship in, 376. *See also* justification.

faith-healing, 172

faithfulness, 282; of God, 214; to Scripture, 290

fall, effects of, 26, 195, 203, 206, 213, 218, 223, 277, 279–80, 292, 301, 303, 317, 318, 319, 356, 360, 376, 386, 387–88, 424, 429; of humanity, 99, 128, 130–31, 133, 147–49, 157, 162, 170, 173–74, 185, 188, 190, 193, 196, 224, 228–29, 447

false, faith, 275; teachers, 336; testimony, 335

fallen nature. *See* depravity; fall.

falling from grace. *See* security.

family, 375; abuse, 206, 207, 397; church as, 419; institution of, 371; law, 337, 338, 341–42; protection of, 344; relationships, 323; stability, 388; worship, 376

Fantasia (Disney), 146

"fatal flaw" of faith, 144

fatalism, 32–33, 128–29, 139

fate, 126, 127, 129

Father, God as, 94, 95, 100, 106, 124, 144, 173, 178, 226–27, 228, 229–31, 233, 245, 297, 316, 330, 376, 452–53

"Father's Eyes" (Grant), 232–33

fear, 208, 212, 302, 303, 359, 425; of death, 290–96, 299; of God, 307–8, 311, 318, 334, 335, 459, 460; of the Lord, 245, 252, 258; slavery to, 223

"feel-good" ethics, 326

fellowship, 285, 382, 383, 384, 406; of church, 376, 413, 415–17; with Christ, 303, 416; with God, 187, 146, 148, 224, 245, 288, 370, 374, 376–79, 455; with others, 146, 148

Fiddler on the Roof, 127

Fields, W. C., 297

final state, 292

fingers of God, 300

finished plan of salvation, 346–47

Finney, Charles, 196–97, 198–99

fire, God as consuming, 137

First, Amendment, 362–66, 381; Great Awakening, 277

First love, 284

"five words," 165–68

Flanders fields, 142

flesh. *See* worldliness.

Fletcher, Joseph, 320

Flew, Anthony, 144

flood, 81–82

focus of faith, 266–67

follow, call to, 139

food chain, 64

forbearance of God, 154

"force," God as. *See* pantheism.

foreknowledge of God. *See* omniscience of God.

foresight of God. *See* omniscience of God.

forgetting God, 118–19

forgiveness. *See* mercy.
Fort Lauderdale, Florida, 308
Fortress, God as, 422
foster parents, 231–32
foundation for faith, 264, 267
free, gift of heaven, 166; will, 26, 83, 127, 128–29, 134–35, 138–40, 185, 187, 188, 196, 198–99, 300, 447
freedom, 146, 176, 203; from evil, 356; from death, 289, 299; from law, 349; from sin, 137, 155; 197, 198, 216, 218–19, 237, 286, 294, 303, 330, 338, 351; in Christ, 297, 355–56; of God, 79, 83–84, 137–40
French Revolution, 61, 95
Freud, 205
fruit of guilt, 207–11
fruitfulness, Christian, 124, 243–44, 252, 285, 295, 437, 453
frustration, 156; at sin, 207; of creation, 155–56
Fuchida, Mitsuo, 164, 168
fudge grace, 238–41
fugitive from God, 186
fulfillment of law, 337–38
fundamentalists, 172
Fundamentals, The, 172
futility. *See* worthlessness.
future, God's knowledge of, 83

Gabriel, angel, 39–40
Gadarene demoniacs, 248
galaxies, movement of, 62
gambling, 366
Gardener, God as, 144, 243
garment of grace, 243, 252
"Gateway to the West," 56
genealogies, 178
generation, 156
genetic code, 127, 134, 232–33
genocide, 323, 324, 425
Gentiles, 82
German theology, 95–96
Germany, 324, 426
Gershenfeld, 213
Gerstner, John, 217
gifts of God, 88, 195–96, 201, 206, 215, 216, 218, 225,

231–34, 248, 251, 257, 300, 330, 346, 411, 424. *See also* Holy Spirit.
Gillespie, George, 75
Gingrich, F. W., 42
Gish, Duane, 114
giving to God, 418–19
glorification, 169, 185, 190, 194, 199, 218, 303, 421, 424, 426, 427, 428
glorifying God, 19, 31, 37, 73, 120, 124, 130, 157, 158, 162, 173, 187, 224, 245, 257–58, 293, 294, 310, 314, 316, 359, 361, 370, 374, 383–84, 423, 428, 442, 444, 457
glory, 193–94, of Christ, 123, 198, 289, 410, 424, 433; of God, 29–30, 60, 123, 136–37, 143, 144, 166, 213, 218, 226, 230, 251, 428, 437, 442
goals of sanctification, 249–52
God, 26, 166–67; acceptance by, 299; access to, 218, 450; Almighty, 73; anger of, 302, 344, 356; as Clock maker, 95; as consuming fire, 245; as Creator, 122, 230, 245; as Father of Light, 297; as Fortress, 422; as holy, 120; as Master Architect, 319; as power, 120; as Protector, 88; as Restorer, 88; as Rock, 422, 423; as Salvation, 422; as Spirit, 75–78; as Trinity, 78, 91, 92–107; 120; as truth, 120; as victim of sin, 155; attributes of, 31, 37, 72–74, 74–89; authority over creation, 133–35, 334, 335, 407, 446; blessings of, 88; call of, 186–200, 298, 300, 357–58; character of, 83; children of, 178, 221–35; constancy of, 132; direction of, 266, 336, 411; doctrine of, 55, 56–57; eternality of, 75, 76, 79–80, 97, 120, 129, 144, 148, 445; evidence for, 69–70; fairness of, 230; faithfulness of, 214; family

of, 229; fatherhood of, 30, 124, 178, 226–27, 229–31, 233, 245, 316, 330, 452–53; fellowship with, 245; fingers of, 300; foreknowledge of, 131; forgiveness of, 214; freedom of, 79, 83–84; glory of, 9, 10, 143, 144, 166, 213, 218, 230, 416, 442; grace of, 88, 206, 218, 413, 416, 417, 424, 430; hand of, 246, 299, 300, 311; hope in, 218; image of, 446; immensity of, 76, 78; imminence of, 78, 79; immutability of, 76, 80–82, 445; incomprehensibility of, 120–21, 132, 135; infinity of, 75, 76, 78–79, 120, 129, 144, 148, 445; intimacy with, 244; invisibility of, 76, 144; judgment of, 228, 242, 294, 299, 317, 339; law of, 212, 215, 273, 389, 309, 311, 314, 345, 424, 447; most High, 73; name of, 73, 88, 95; natures of, 94; pain of, 292, 301, 446; passions of, 76, 77–78; peace with, 218; perfection of, 76, 79, 230, 245; pity of, 234; plan of, 196, 301, 224–25; purpose of, 80, 81, 242, 317; rebellion against, 290; relationship with, 14; righteousness of, 81, 129, 149, 273, 367, 424; unchangeability of, 75, 80–82, 129, 148, 299, 445; unity of, 76; views of, 95–101; weakness in, 144–45, 312; works of, 88, 446; wrath of, 57. *See also* Christ; gifts of God; goodness, of God; holiness, of God; Holy Spirit; justice of God; kingdom, of God; love, of God; omnipotence of God; omnipresence of God; omniscience of God; plan of God; promises of God; providence; revelation, of God; sovereignty of God; transcendence of God; will, of God.

God, the Atom and the Universe (Reid), 61

"God-Breathed." *See* inspiration of Scripture.

God-centeredness, 15, 384

godlessness, 58, 59–60

God's Missionary People (Van Engen), 407

God's plan of salvation, 136–37

gold in Christian life, 240, 253

golden rule, 182–83

good, advice, 345, 346; and evil, 97; news, 14, 345, 357; works, 26, 137, 182–83, 185, 192, 197, 206, 217, 218, 248, 249, 251–52, 257, 264–65, 267, 299, 330, 350. *See also* self-righteousness.

"good enough," 164

Good Morning America, 153

goodness, of creation, 143; of God, 37, 75, 82, 87–88, 120, 122, 125, 128–29, 132, 144–45, 148, 307–8, 310, 445

Gordon, A. J., 264–65

Gordon, Ernest, 119

gospel, 14, 32, 170, 176, 180, 196, 197, 203, 240, 274, 283–84, 348–49, 351; accepting, 264; adding to, 355–56; call of the, 190; perverting, 355–56; power, 192, 345; rejection of, 58

gospel of grace, 325

Gospels, 260

gossip, 192, 339–40

Gould, Stephen Jay, 120

governing of creation. *See* providence.

government, 26, 158, 337, 338–41, 358, 363, 380–81, 385, 386. *See also* civil law.

grace, cheap, 211; covenant of, 148, 149–50, 169, 173–74, 174, 180, 181, 188, 223, 224–25, 257, 258, 263, 318, 339, 448, 451–52; God's, 88, 154, 155–56, 166, 185, 190, 199, 201, 203, 204, 206, 213,

214, 217, 218–19, 221, 231, 238–41, 241, 267, 273, 281, 290–91, 313, 316, 319, 325, 345, 349, 413, 416, 417, 424, 430; irresistible, 191–93, 224; means of, 255, 299; works of, 451–53; transforming, 278. *See also* justification.

Graham, Billy, 191

Grant, Amy, 232

gratitude. *See* thankfulness.

gravity, 63

Great Commission, 124, 157, 158, 407, 417

Great Divorce, The (Lewis), 435

"great faith," 268

Great Physician, 211

greatest good for the greatest number, 145, 149, 324

Greece, 45

greed, 126, 309

Greek Grammar in Light of Historical Research (Robinson), 42

grief, 292, 301, 427

grieving Spirit, 248

groaning of creation, 156

ground for hope, 290–91, 299

growth, spiritual, 11, 247, 248, 265, 367, 406

guilt, 211–14; actual, 166, 204, 205, 206, 207, 218, 231, 242–34, 336, 347, 351, 447; confession of, 217; feelings, 202–3, 205–7, 210, 277–79, 313, 327, 357; freedom from, 356; fruit of, 207–11; neurotic, 206; removing, 212–16; types of, 206–7; ultimate, 206

Gutzke, Manford George, 424–25

Haeckl, Ernst, 115

hail, 134

hand of God, 246, 299, 300, 311

hanging gardens of Babylon, 49

Haran, 269

hardened heart, 190

hatred, 396–97

Hawley, Robert C., 361–62

headship, 148, 169, 179–80

healing, 134, 139, 175, 213; of relationships, 396–97

health, trusting Christ for, 266–67

heart attacks, 382–83

heart, deceitfulness of, 317; of flesh, 185, 193; of stone, 185, 193, 197; renewal, 191–93, 237, 240; sinful, 129; spiritual, 189

heaven, 166, 167, 234, 275, 290, 294, 299, 384, 427, 429, 433, 437, 455, 462; new, 423, 427, 428. *See also* eternal life.

heavens, 60, 61–62

"heaviness," 84–85

hedonism, 28

Heidelberg Catechism, 132

Heir, Christ as, 169, 180–81. *See also* co-heirs with Christ.

hell, 86, 174, 188, 214, 226, 247, 290, 298, 299, 311, 312, 351, 356, 432, 433, 435, 439, 447, 448, 461, 462

Henry, Patrick, 352–54, 355, 359, 362

Heraclius, 48–49

Herberg, Will, 319–20

heresy. *See* error.

Herodotus, 50, 51

Hesperopithecus haroldcookii, 114

high priest, 85, 177

higher criticism of Scripture, 96, 102

Hillel, 390

Hinduism, 39, 96

Hiroshima, 142

historical accuracy of Bible, 38–39

history, 83, 99–100, 131, 133, 134, 308, 357, 358; of Christianity, 57; of the Bible, 39

Hitler, Adolf, 100, 297

HIV, 28, 153–54

holiness, Christian, 137, 192,

228, 237, 241–50, 252, 253, 279, 359, 421, 426, 427, 435, 453; human, 120, 232; of Christ, 214, 243; of church, 339–41, 409; of God, 57, 58, 74, 75, 79, 82, 84–85, 120, 129, 133, 148, 149, 151, 162, 203, 206, 215, 230, 243, 244, 245, 252, 276, 280, 295, 334–35, 337, 339, 347, 366–67, 445, 459; of Sabbath, 371

Holiness churches, 172

holocaust, 324

holy of holies, 85, 177

Holy Spirit, coming of, 373, 374, 380; deity of, 78, 94, 100, 103, 104–5, 317, 428; direction from, 233; filling with, 330; firstfruits of, 155; freedom in, 360; gifts of, 56, 232–33, 346, 448; grieving, 248; in Christ, 176, 357; in Christian, 234, 237, 251, 253, 317, 330, 353, 396, 424, 442; in church, 410, 415, 417; in gospel, 192; joy in, 286; law of, 207; neo-orthodox view of, 99; things of, 124; transforming power of, 10; work of, 30, 40, 54, 80, 106, 135, 144, 172, 173, 176, 182, 185, 189, 190, 191–93, 199, 221, 223, 224, 225, 249, 253, 255, 257, 258, 263–64, 264–65, 268, 274, 300–1, 308, 319, 330–31, 414, 424, 428, 445; worship of, 376

home schools, 365

homosexuality, 21–22, 113, 172, 364–65, 366

honoring others, 385, 387

hope in God, 217, 218, 263, 277, 290–91, 293, 297–98, 299, 422–39, 424

hopeless, 188, 347, 348, 359, 423, 425, 431–32

horoscope, 43, 97, 261–62

Hosea, 176

hospital, 242

"Hound of Heaven" (Thompson), 186–87, 193, 197–98, 200

House, of Commons, England's, 25; of Lords, England's, 25

house of prayer, 180

How Should We Then Live? (Schaeffer), 14

Human Values in the Classroom (Hawley), 361

human beings, 14, 76–77, 120, 145, 147, 211, 435; fallenness, 292, 301, 303, 317, 424, 429; mind, 93–95, 96, 132, 150, 152, 224, 258; nature, 155; perspective, 311–13; rights, 95, 366

human inability. *See* inability.

humanism, 12, 14, 131, 143, 149, 173, 198, 213, 227, 312, 352, 358, 361, 361–66

Humanist magazine, 361, 362

humanity, fallenness, 318, 319

Hume, David, 98

humility, 310, 337, 344; before God, 149, 150; of Christ, 136

Hus, Jan, 301–2

husband, 341–42, 385

Huxley, Aldous, 116; Julian, 110, 116; Thomas, 110

"I AM THAT I AM," 95

idealism, German, 96

ideals, Christian, 193

identification with Christ, 193, 231, 249, 250, 424, 430–31

idolatry, 126, 129, 269, 284, 309, 334, 344, 357, 457

image of God, 120, 148, 155, 241, 329, 446

imaging, 97

Immanuel, 428

imminence of God, 78, 79, 96–100, 122

immorality in the church, 339

immortality, desire for, 130–31

immutability of God, 76, 80–82

imputation, 151, 201, 203, 204, 241, 243

inability, 60, 151, 155, 156, 166, 195–96, 197–98, 199, 278, 349

incarnation, 99, 105, 222, 161, 167

inclusiveness of church, 410

incomprehensibility of God, 94, 120–21, 132, 135. *See also* knowledge; transcendence of God.

independence from England, 352–54

India, 283

Industrial Revolution, 426

infallibility of the Bible, 40, 54

infanticide, 366

infinity, of God, 75, 76, 78–79, 96, 99, 120, 129, 144, 148, 445; of creation, 61–62

influences, 134

Ingersoll, Robert, 298

inheritance, 233–34

inner person, 278

Inspiration and Authority of the Bible, The (Warfield), 40

inspiration of Scripture, 38–54, 58, 40, 176

Institutes of the Christian Religion (Calvin), 74

insufficiency. *See* inability.

intellect, 11–12, 258

intellectual assent, 167–68, 248, 257, 258, 263, 264, 266, 267, 275

intercession, 177, 178, 191, 215, 233, 344, 410

interest in Christ's blood, 215

intermediate state, 292, 432–34

internal call. *See* call of God, inward.

Interpreter, 348

interpreting Scripture, 259, 261

intimacy with God, 194, 233, 244, 286, 295

Invisible God, 73, 76, 144

invisible church. *See* church, invisible.

invitation of gospel, 188, 190

irresistible grace. *See* call of God, inward.

Isaac, 119, 270–71

Isaiah, prophecies of, 44, 46, 51, 74, 102, 120–21, 176, 178, 204

Ishmael, 270

Islam, 39–40

Israel, nation of, 82, 85,

118–19, 177, 180, 183, 232, 318, 334, 337, 338, 339, 341, 342, 343, 389, 410, 412–13, 422, 433
Iwo Jima, 142

Jackson, Mississippi, 256
Jacob, 119, 179, 232
James, 9, 433
James I, 380
Japan, 384
Jaycees, 343
Jeans, James Hopwood, 62
Jefferson, Thomas, 363, 364, 365–66
Jehovah as name of God, 234
Jehovah's Witnesses, 234
Jennifer, 235
Jeremiah, 46, 47–48, 50–52, 103, 176, 310
Jerusalem, 46–47, 175, 176–77, 180, 248, 271, 294, 372, 418; new, 427, 428
Jesus, as Christ, 357, 406–7; as "good teacher," 88; as Lord, 193; as Savior, 193; as second Adam, 79; as Son of man, 183; as way, truth, and life, 182; atonement of, 78–79; authority of, 157; birth of, 450; claims of, 41; deity of, 80, 92, 183; healings by, 9–10; Holy Spirit from, 106; infinity of, 79; limitations of, 83; law and, 337; lordship of, 136–38, miracles of, 134; neo-orthodox view of, 99; prophecy and, 178; Son of God, 178; transfiguration of, 9; weeping, 292. *See also* Christ.
Job, 73–74, 86
John, apostle, 9, 104, 246, 373, 427, 430, 431, 433
John the Baptist, 280
Johns Hopkins Medical School, 382–83
Jonah, 81–82
Jordan River, 433
Joseph, 178
Joshua, 337
Jowett, John, 416

joy, 180, 297–98, 381–82; loss of, 265
Judah, 178
Judas, 10
Judeo-Christian ethic, 365–66, 367
Judge, Christ as, 169, 180–81, 203, 226, 299, 317, 339; God as, 242, 294; human, 329, 340, 395, 397–99, 397–99
judgment, 86–87, 134, 135, 154, 181, 183, 190–91, 204, 206, 214, 230, 301, 437; final, 26, 292, 308, 421, 431–32, 435, 436, 461–62
judgment-justice-justification model, 213, 214
Julian the Apostate, 50
Jupiter, 63
justice of God, 29, 75, 82, 86–87, 120, 125, 129, 132, 148, 149, 150, 162, 166–67, 178, 181, 199, 204, 214, 225, 310, 313, 319, 445
justification, 26, 105, 150, 155, 169, 174, 185, 190, 194, 199, 201, 203–19, 221, 225, 227, 229, 231, 235, 241, 243, 244, 252, 255, 257, 258, 263, 264, 267, 274, 276, 281, 290, 295, 298, 299, 300, 312, 316, 318, 319, 333, 336, 349, 350, 413, 424, 448–50, 452, 453
Justin Martyr, 373

Kagawa, 284
Kant, Immanuel, 95–96, 98
keeping Sabbath. *See* Sabbath.
Kennedy, John F., 233; John, Jr., 233
Kentucky, 366
kindness, 192
King, Christ as, 95, 136–37, 169, 175, 176–79, 180, 181, 410, 450; God as, 31, 41, 230, 233, 217–18, 366, 382
King James Version, 234
kingdom, of God, 31, 137, 139, 157–58, 161, 170, 178–79, 182, 217–18, 226, 227, 228, 230, 231, 280, 295, 299, 366, 382, 395; of priests, 338

kings, God's rule over, 135–36
Kinsey Report, 328
Kipling, Rudyard, 32
Kitty Hawk, North Carolina, 222
Knowing God (Packer), 41
knowledge, human, 11, 14, 37–38, 72–75, 76, 120, 132, 135, 139, 170, 232, 257, 312; of sin, 347. *See also* omniscience of God.
Knox, John, 422, 423
koinonia, 415–17
Kojiki, 39
Korean awakening, 281
Koresh, David, 418, 422, 423
Kuiper, R. B., 279

labels, 171–73
Lamb, Christ as, 429, 430
Lamb's Book of Life, 234, 430, 437
Lange, Hermann, 297
Laplace, Pierre-Simon, 61
Larger Catechism. See Westminster, *catechisms.*
last days, 309
law of God, 26, 31, 166, 177, 179, 180, 181, 258, 269, 315, 317–19; as power of sin, 195, 207, 294; Christ and, 372; curse of, 356; fulfillment of, 337–38; gospel and, 212, 242–43, 345–50, 355–56, 370, 413; guilt of, 212–16; hopelessness in, 347; marriage in, 389–90; of love, 387–91, 399–400; of Spirit, 207; purposes of, 229, 333–50; rebellion to, 347–48; respect for, 273, 314, 335; restraint in, 341, 319; Sabbath, 383
"Lawful Oaths and Vows, Of," 26, 385–86
lawful power, 359
lawlessness, 336. *See also* rebellion, against God.
laws of nature, 76, 134
Lazarus, 174, 198, 292, 301
leaders, 337, 342, 413; duty to, 385, 387

leap in the dark, 36, 98, 258
Lear, Norman, 335–36, 346
Lebanon, 172
legal strivings, 277–79, 280, 281
legalism, 206, 213
legislating morality, 365
Lessing, Gotthold Ephraim, 96
Lewis, C. S., 72–73, 435
liability for punishment, 204, 214, 215, 277, 212–16, 218, 242–44, 252
liberalism, 98–99, 142, 418
liberation, 165, 176, 203, 221, 237, 286, 303, 330, 337, 349, 356, 357, 367. *See also* freedom, in Christ.
liberty, 141, 187, 351–67, 357; Christian, 26, 354–67
"liberty or death" speech, 352–54, 360
Liddell, Eric, 384
life, 141, 144–46, 183; affections, 283–85; control of, 311; covenant of, 148, 149, 173–74, 187, 223, 224, 318; in Christ, 291, 268; in God, 308; new, 191–92, 245; passages, 173, 292; purpose of, 296; source of, 121, 122, 319; value of, 111–14, 328–29; victorious, 310. *See* eternal life.
lifestyle, Christian, 249–52, 253, 300, 317–19, 374–84, 385–401, 417–19. *See* sanctification.
lifting up a spouse, 400
Light, Christ as, 183, 184, 251; of God's glory, 428
lightning, 64
"Li'l Abner," 209
limited God, 128–29
limpet, 266
Lincoln, Abraham, 47, 359
Lion, the Witch, and the Wardrobe, The (Lewis), 72
living sacrifices, 279, 316–31
Livingstone, David, 283
loans, 342–43
logic, 96, 259
London, 24, 202, 283
Lord of the church, 408

Lord's day. *See* Sabbath.
Lord's Supper. *See* sacraments.
lordship of Christ, 13, 136–38, 158, 173, 184, 193, 204, 218, 228, 247, 248, 251, 263, 264, 275, 290, 291, 301, 374, 407–8, 409, 436–37
losing salvation. *See* security.
Lot, 270
lottery, 126
love, 14, 164, 179, 215, 216, 299, 350; Christian, 117–18, 199, 240–41, 250; debt of, 281, 282–84; for Christ, 13, 211, 247, 284–88; for enemies, 396–97; for God, 15, 30, 31, 87, 88, 146, 165, 167, 168, 188, 192, 194, 200, 245, 281, 284, 291, 318, 329, 338, 374, 387; for others, 318, 325–26, 327, 329, 338, 358, 372, 386–401, 417, 418–19, 461; for self, 309; for spouse, 386; for world, 252; in church, 339; of God, 10, 87, 88, 106, 167, 175, 194, 235, 289, 301, 303, 311, 394, 424; law of, 387–91, 399–400; parental, 224; power of, 343–44; sacrificially, 387–91; unity of, 417
Lucifer, 128
lust, 237, 252, 347
Luther, Katie, 386; Martin, 203, 204, 281, 360, 386
Lutheran, 300
lying, 347, 418

Macedonia, 45
Madison, James, 366
mail delivery, Sabbath, 380–81
mainline churches, 172
majesty of Christ, 177
Malachi, 176
malnourishment, spiritual, 165, 309
manic-depression, 210
manuscripts of Scripture, 39
marriage, 26, 27–28, 58, 141, 146, 148, 153, 158, 285, 323, 341, 366, 385, 386, 388, 390, 397, 460

Mars, 63
martyrdom, 111, 131–32, 297, 302, 419
Marvin, David, 117–18, 123
mass of earth, 63
materialism, 28–29, 61, 79–80, 118–19, 335
mathematics, 61, 62
Matthews, L. Harrison, 32
maturity, 192
Mayflower, 380
meaning. *See* purpose, for life.
meaninglessness, 319
means, of grace, 255, 380, 444; of salvation, 198–99; of sanctification, 253; to ends, 113
Medes, 48, 50
media, 153, 361, 406
mediator, 26, 148, 169, 173, 174, 176, 177, 178, 179, 181, 215, 278; 281, 294, 337, 376, 384, 424, 448
Mediterranean Sea, 45–46, 267
Melchizedek, 176–77, 178
Menninger, Karl, 202–3, 205
mental institution study, 205
mercy, of God, 15, 86, 125, 129, 131, 149, 151, 154, 166–68, 195, 199, 201–19, 224, 265, 273, 276, 281–82, 345, 349–50, 431, 442, 455; human, 29, 150, 250, 265, 310, 325–26, 339, 342–44, 372, 387, 394–99
mercy killing. *See* euthanasia.
message of shame, 118, 123
Messiah, 102–3, 175, 178, 179, 180, 274, 357; false, 179
metamorphosis. *See* re-creation; regeneration.
metaphors describing God, 94–95
metaphysical knowledge, 96
Micah, prophecies of, 46–47
Michelangelo, 298
Mignan's Travels (Mignan), 52
Mill, John Stuart, 324
mind, human, 12, 192, 195, 276–77, 317; lightness of, 442; of Christ, 251
miracles, 9–10, 134, 248
missions, 417

modalism, 100
"moderate" theology, 22
modernism, 98, 173, 299
"modernity," 113
Moody, Dwight L., 298
moon, 63–64
moral absolutes. *See* absolutes.
moral, law, 260, 315; reasoning, 58, 98, 112–13, 152–55, 320, 366
morality, 217, 257; legislating, 365
More, Thomas, 442
Mormonism, 418
Morris, Henry M., 68–69
Morton, T. Ralph, 321
mortuary, 295–96
Mosaic law. *See* law of God.
Moscow Book Fair, 116–17
Moses, 95, 118, 174, 183, 334, 335, 337, 390, 433
motivation seminars, 97
motive in ethics, 322
motives, 326–27, 329
Mount Moriah, 270–71; Nebo, 433; Seir, 47–48; Zion, 294
Mowrer, O. Hobart, 209
Muhammad, 39, 43, 179
murder, 151, 324, 328–29, 330, 335, 347, 425
Murray, John, 366–67
Muslims, 105–6, 172, 210
mutual respect and honor, 342
mystical union, 418, 420
mysticism, 97, 99–100
myth, Bible as, 58

Nabopolassar, 48
Nahum, prophecies of, 48
name of the LORD, 179–80, 231, 334
Narramore, S. Bruce, 206, 211
Nash, Ron, 83–84
nation of God, 179–80, 338, 410, 419
National Press Club, 335
nations, 135–36, 178, 179, 224, 329, 358, 366, 382, 429
natural selection, 67
naturalistic worldview, 110–24
nature, 38, 131, 135

natures of Christ, 92–93, 94
Nazareth, 248
Nazism, 358
Nebuchadnezzar, 44–45, 46
need, for Christ, 189, 347, 348–49; for Savior, 207; for Sabbath, 374; ; human, 230, 235; to forgive, 395–96
neighbor, love for. *See* love, for others.
neo-orthodoxy, 12, 99–100
Nero, 322
Nettleton, Asahel, 281
neurosis, 205, 209, 210, 211, 213–14, 218, 396
neurotic guilt, 206–7
neutrality, 163
New Age movement, 58, 69, 97, 174, 192
New Hebrides, 266
New Testament symposium, 260
newness. *See* re-creation; regeneration.
Newtonian physics, 61
Nicodemus, 161, 181–83, 184
Niebuhr, H. Richard, 320–21
Nietzsche, Friedrich, 32
Nightingale, Florence, 284, 322
nihilism, 143, 312
Nihongi, 39
Nineveh, 48–49, 81–82
nitrogen cycle, 64
Noah, 174, 280
non-negotiables, 355, 356, 359, 366–67
nonbeing, 208
nonreason, 97, 98, 100
Noonan, Frederick, 23
Normandy, 142
North American Man/Boy Love Association (NAMBLA), 113
Northern Ireland, 172
nuclear threat, 425
nurture in the church, 411

O'Hair, Madalyn Murray, 117
oaths, 385, 386
obedience, 141, 149, 150, 158, 175, 179, 184, 200, 201, 215, 224, 245, 248, 249–52, 253,

258, 262, 264, 270, 282–84, 290, 291; of Christ, 150, 231, 249, 311, 315, 319, 325, 330, 336, 338, 407
objective guilt. *See* guilt.
obligations, 387
oceans, 63–64
old age, 291, 416
Old Testament, 337–45, 389, 409, 449; believers, 175, 293, 382; prophecies, 44–52, 176; prophets, 178; view of Trinity, 101–3
omnipotence of God, 10, 31, 37, 41, 58, 73–74, 75, 78–79, 82, 83, 84, 120–21, 125, 128–29, 132, 133–35, 139, 144–45, 148, 162, 185, 204, 245, 302–3, 445, 446
omnipresence of God, 76, 77, 78, 79, 96, 177, 180, 218, 248, 266, 316, 317, 344, 374, 407, 408, 427, 428, 462
omniscience of God, 31, 75, 76, 82–83, 96, 120, 122, 125, 129, 133, 134, 135, 139, 140, 144–45, 148, 149, 188, 193–94, 245, 248, 311, 445, 446
one flesh, 390–91, 395
one-parent homes, 389
Oneida Community, 418
open hand, principle of, 28–30, 339, 343
oppression, 87, 151, 218, 219, 357, 360
optimism, 143
ordo salutis, 225
organic church. *See* church, invisible.
organized church, 411, 412
Origin of Species (Darwin), 32, 115, 116
origin of the universe, 79–80, 110
original, righteousness, 151; sin, 150–52, 218, 447
Orwell, George, 358–59
Osborn, Henry Fairfield, 68, 114
"Other," God as, 95–100
others, love for, 318, 325–26, 327, 329

Ottoman Empire, 142
oughts, 196
oxygen, 64–67
ozone layer, 64–65

Packer, J. I., 41
paganism, 346
pain, 206–12, 213, 291, 292, 302, 303, 427, 429
Paine, Thomas, 298
Pakistan, 209
paleontology, 114
pantheism, 80, 95, 96–100, 133
paradise, 145, 226, 288, 295
paradox, 99, 100
pardon, 201, 203, 204, 241, 282
parents, 311, 334, 341–42, 365, 391–92
Paris Museum, 49
Parliament of England, 24, 25, 356
partnership, marriage not, 390; with God, 249, 252
passages, life, 292
passions of God, 76, 77–78
Passover, 344, 449
pastoral counseling, 213
pastors, 251, 411
paternalism, 230
patience, 192, 424
Patmos, 430
Paton, 266
pattern for worship, 376, 384
Paul, apostle, 11, 16, 204, 232, 282, 283, 284, 286, 322, 370, 423, 430–31
peace, 152, 164, 177, 319, 323; covenant of, 122; with God, 218, 263, 424
Pearl Harbor, 164
pedophilia, 113
penance, 209
penitence, 276, 274–75
Pentecost, 373
Pentecostals, 172
People for the American Way, 335
people of God, 409, 410
perfectibility of humanity, 142
perfecting of the saints. *See* sanctification.
perfection of God, 58, 74, 76,

79, 106, 182–83, 230, 348–49, 421, 426
persecution, 118, 282, 285
perseverance of the saints. *See* security.
Persia, 45, 50
persons of Trinity, 94
perspective, eternal, 232, 276, 298
persuasion, 198–99
perverting the gospel, 355–56
Peter. *See* Simon Peter.
Pharaoh, 140
Pharisees, 280
Philadelphia, 381
philanthropy, 325
Philippians, 430–31
philosophy, 208, 312, 323–24, 326, 335, 352, 361–62
Physician, Christ as, 287
physics, 79–80
physiology, 66–69
pierced by sin, 274–75
pietism, 360–61
piety, 182, 257
pilgrim quest, 15–17
Pilgrim's Progress, The, (Bunyan), 348
Pilgrims, 380
"pillar of religion, foremost," 203
pity of God, 234
plague illustration, 377–79
plan of God, 129, 132, 139, 157–58, 180, 181, 187, 196, 224, 301. *See also* purpose, of God.
plan of salvation. *See* salvation.
plankton, 64
Planned Parenthood, 324
plants, authority over, 145, 148
playing church, 287
pleasure, love of, 309
Plymouth Rock, 380
Pogo, 210
political correctness, 152
politics, 335, 361
polytheism, 95, 100–1
Pontius Pilate, 88–89, 410
pornography, 154, 328, 366
possession, Christian as, 30

post-, abortion syndrome, 28, 112; modern world, 309–10
poverty, 342–43, 389, 425–26
power of Christ, 11, 137, 181, 248; of Christian, 241; godliness; 309, 445; of gospel, 192, 349, 350, 423–24; of sin, 87, 219.
powerlessness. *See* inability.
pragmatism, 22, 326
praise, 107, 122, 132, 135, 145, 148, 218, 286, 338, 344, 374, 396, 413
prayer, 75, 84, 97–98, 100, 101, 106, 139, 158, 177, 191, 233, 248, 249, 255, 262, 269, 285, 337, 376, 384, 385, 387, 396, 415, 439; as means of sanctification, 253
preaching, 176, 177, 260–61, 269, 280, 346, 376, 384, 407, 431
predestination, 185, 189–200, 224, 225
prejudice, 415
preparation, for death, 292, 298; for worship, 382
prerogatives of authority, 137
presence of Christ, 426, 434. *See also* omnipresence of God.
preservation of creation, 133–35
presuppositions, 213, 259, 260, 267
pride, 29, 197, 217, 253, 277, 309, 349
priest, 148, 175; Christ as, 169, 175, 176–78, 179, 181, 249, 344, 450
priesthood, church as, 410
Prince Caspian (Lewis), 72–73
principles of worship, 375–76
prison, 384, 398
Prison Fellowship, 112–13
privileges of family of God, 231
"process" theology, 80
prodigal son, 230, 280–81
promises of God, 29–30, 78–79, 162, 180, 184, 188, 221, 223, 227, 234, 241, 246–47, 258, 265, 266, 269–71, 301, 315, 318, 330, 380, 407, 411

proof of the Bible, 36–54
prophecy in the Bible, 38, 40, 42–52, 151, 181, 259–61, 449; charismatic, 172
prophet, 102–3, 175, 176, 178, 179, 179–80; Christ as, 169, 175, 176, 179, 181, 450
prospector, 240
prosperity, danger of, 119
protection, 88, 342, 344
protest of abortion, 365
Protestantism, 195
providence, 26, 37–38, 106–7, 109, 121, 122, 125–40, 141, 157, 187, 200, 445, 446
psychiatry, 212, 213
psychology, 199, 205–7, 208, 209, 212–13
psychosomatic illness, 211
punishment, 155, 167, 204, 206, 207, 211–14, 218, 229, 230, 233, 245, 302, 330, 339, 340, 345. *See also* atonement.
purgatory, 290, 299, 433
Puritans, 266, 286, 296, 301, 388, 404, 442
purity of God. *See* holiness, of God.
purpose, for church, 406–8; for law, 337; for life, 11, 19, 24, 27, 30, 33, 37, 73, 110, 120, 157, 224, 245, 258, 293, 294, 296, 310, 311–14, 316, 359, 370, 383–84, 423, 444; for marriage, 390–91; of God, 62, 63, 80, 81, 169, 192, 194, 199, 242, 301, 317, 319, 446

quality of life, 319
quantum physics, 61, 62
quest for God, 10–11, 13, 14, 15–17, 20–21, 30–32, 89, 110, 162, 170, 310, 443
Qumran, 53
Qur'an, 39–40, 43

races, 178, 179; God's people as, 415, 418
radiation, 64–65
radical depravity. *See* depravity.

rain, 134
Rand, Ayn, 323
rape, 365
rationalism, 14, 95–96
rationality and faith, 12
Ray's Collection of Travels, 51
realization of sin, 183, 184
rebellion, 129, 151, 173, 187, 188; against God, 155, 183, 184, 195, 199, 206–7, 210, 224, 229, 244, 265, 276, 290, 317, 347–48, 357, 361, 394
rebirth. *See* re-creation, regeneration.
receiving Christ, 258, 263–71
reclamation, 231
reconciliation, 171, 178, 184, 193, 204, 282, 341, 382, 395, 397, 407, 410, 415–16
re-creation, 122–24, 137, 156, 161–68, 170–84, 174–75, 181–82, 183, 184, 192, 193, 216, 224–25, 229, 237, 264, 288, 317, 317–19, 428–31
recumbent faith, 265–67, 269, 295
redating Scripture, 42–43
redemption, 30, 154, 155–56, 158, 167, 169, 188, 203, 213, 221, 246, 329, 345, 346–47, 349, 356, 357, 380, 395, 424, 428, 430, 433, 436, 449–450; *See* atonement; salvation.
reflection of Christ's glory, 251
Reformation, 131, 203
regeneration, 105, 156, 157–58, 169, 170, 171, 172–75, 182, 183, 184, 216, 224–25, 229, 237, 264, 299, 414
rehabilitation in prison, 398
Reid, James, 61
Reimarus, Hermann Samuel, 96
reincarnation, 97, 422
rejection of God, 146, 150, 162, 175, 190–91, 196, 197, 224, 226, 438
relationships, 27–28, 145, 148, 192, 264, 279, 308, 375, 382, 385–401, 415–16, healing, 396–97
relative truth, 58, 222, 362

religion, 13, 98, 165, 179, 230, 257, 362, 376, 420
religious freedom, 24, 361, 362–66
"remember," 314
remembering first love, 286–88
renewed person, 241, 286–88
reordering, 258
repentance, 26, 86, 188, 192, 206–7, 230, 248, 247, 248, 257, 273–88, 275, 276, 280, 295, 344, 367, 410, 454–55. *See also* confession.
"repenting" of God, 81–82
reproduction, 67
requirements of God, 149, 150, 310
responsibility to one another, 417, 418–19
rest. *See* Sabbath.
restitution, 341
restoring power of God, 88, 229, 231, 399–400
restraint of law, 319
resurrection, of Christ, 98, 99, 104, 105, 106, 158, 161, 167, 184, 189, 203, 215–16, 264, 293–94, 369, 372–73, 410, 451; of humanity, 11, 14, 167, 291, 292, 374, 380, 424, 432, 435–37, 461–62
resurrection, day of. *See* Sabbath.
return of Christ, 181, 301, 226, 249, 259, 260–61, 308, 336, 372, 432
revelation, by Christ, 176; of God, 37–38, 39–41, 57, 59, 60–69, 94–95, 96, 99, 106, 132, 135, 158, 162, 173, 200, 206, 334, 428; of John, 373; in Scripture, 101, 197, 258, 261, 317, 329, 444–45, 334, 336, 424; new, 261
revenge, 340
revivals, 198, 225, 277–79, 281, 299, 336
Revivals of Religion (Finney), 198
rhythm of week, 146
rich man and Lazarus, 433, 435

rich young ruler, 192
right hand of God, 189
righteousness, by faith, 87, 203–5, 213, 227, 423–24, 435; crown of, 431; fruit of, 252; human, 74, 120, 148, 150, 151, 204, 231, 325, 359; of God, 81, 86–87, 129, 135, 149, 201, 203, 206, 273, 367; in Christ, 182–83, 216, 217, 248–52, 264, 294, 424; of Christ, 167, 179, 181, 203, 204, 213, 215, 217, 227, 229, 237, 241, 243, 249, 264, 276, 290–91, 294. *See also* good, works.
rights, 230, 231
river of life, 429
Robinson, A. T., 42
Rock, God as, 95, 422, 423
Roe v. Wade, 111
roles, sexual, 148
Roman Catholic Church, 172, 299
Roman Empire, 50, 388
Romania, 117–18, 123
Rousseau, Jean Jacques, 95
Rowell, E. A., 48
rule for living, law as, 336
rule of God. *See* providence.
Rule, Bible as, 35, 36–38
Russell, Bertrand, 32, 33
Russia, 117–18, 336, 346
Rutherford, Samuel, 286

Sabbath, 26, 141, 146, 148, 180, 286, 334, 339, 345, 369–84, 460
Sabellianism, 94, 100
sacraments, 26, 56, 182, 253, 255, 269, 275, 299, 376, 380, 384, 407, 411, 413, 449
sacrifice, 253, 344, 382, 449. *See also* atonement.
Sadducees, 280
safety, in Christ, 178, 266–67; of unbelief, 58, 59
Sagan, Carl, 61, 79
Salem, 176
salt and light, Christian as, 15, 357, 410
salvation, in Christ, 30, 106, 136–37, 154, 155–56, 161–68, 176, 178, 180, 181, 182–84, 185, 188, 189, 191, 217, 246, 264, 266–67, 271, 277, 295, 346, 395, 422, 423, 424; plan of, 14, 37–38, 173, 174, 183–84, 196, 316, 448–52; remembering, 283, 285, 346; requirements for, 257; through church, 299; through faith, 166; way of, 225. *See also* adoption; justification; security.
Samaria, 46–47
sanctification, 26, 36, 85, 105, 106, 149, 169, 180, 192, 216, 218, 230, 237–53, 257, 258, 263, 265, 267, 294, 298, 315, 316, 357–58, 367, 377–79, 411, 435, 444, 452, 453, 455
sand in relationships, 391–97
Sarah, 232, 270
Sargon, 49
Satan, 101, 149, 210, 214, 227, 228, 229, 247, 278, 307–8, 322, 331, 351, 356, 361, 399, 432, 447
satisfaction. *See* atonement.
Saturday as Sabbath. *See* day of Sabbath.
Saturday Review of Literature, 212
Saul, King, 209; of Tarsus, 168
Save Our Sunday organization, 370–71, 383
saving, faith, 26, 167–68, 248, 255–71, 455; graces, 237
Savior, Christ as, 13, 73, 86, 136–37, 166, 167, 169, 179–80, 184, 189, 193, 207, 218, 227, 228, 263–64, 290, 299, 310, 356, 357, 374, 439, 449, 451
Schaeffer, Francis, 14
schizophrenia, 209, 210
Schleiermacher, Friedrich, 98
Schoenberg, Arnold, 32
schools, 113–14, 119, 158
science, 12, 32, 39, 60–69, 83, 96, 113–14, 259, 361
Scopes, John, 113–14
scorning others, 329
Scotland, 422
Scripture, 25, 53–54, application of, 240, 262; as compass, 23; as truth, 237, 239, 258–60; attacks on, 96, 259, 260; authority of, 13, 21–23, 30–31, 35–54, 73, 96, 99, 128, 129, 135, 136, 258, 259, 260–62, 444; confidence in, 12–13, 259–60, 321; consistency of, 261; defining worship, 345; faith foundation in, 267; faithfulness to, 290; freedom in, 356; learning, 442; interpreting, 15–16, 225, 259, 261; means of grace, 185, 191, 248, 253, 334, 336, 424, 380; reading, 285, 299, 376; repentance in, 280–81; revelation by, 101, 132, 135, 176, 197, 258, 261, 317, 329, 367, 414, 444–45; rules for living, 444; teaching of, 195, 212, 227; Trinity in, 101–6; truth of, 12–13, 38, 39–41, 57, 61, 89, 162, 173, 265, 367; witness of, 54. *See also* Word.
sea, 156, 423, 427, 429–30
sealing by the Holy Spirit, 30
search and rescue mission, 179
Second Adam, Christ as, 79, 150, 188, 448
second causes, 133, 134, 136
second coming. *See* return of Christ.
Second Timothy, 431
secular ethics, 320–28
secular humanism. *See* humanism.
secularism, 32, 328
security, 26, 244, 246–48, 250, 290, 299, 300–3, 424, 443, 455, 456
self-, actualization, 12, 13, 27–28, 312–13; awareness, 198, 277–79, 295, 396, 415; centeredness, 146, 233, 264; control, 78, 309; deception, 213; denial, 325; destructive guilt, 206–7; discipline, 358;

substitutionary atonement. *See* atonement.
suffering, 151, 195, 209, 281, 297, 301; of Christ, 11, 249, 424, 450
sufficiency of Scripture, 162
suicide, 33, 207, 366, 375
summum bonum. See ultimate, good.
sun, 63, 134
Sunday as Sabbath. *See* day of Sabbath.
superficial faith, 277, 280
supernatural, 110–24, 199
suppression, 63, 68–69
Supreme Court, U.S., 112
survival of fittest, 113
swearing, 192
Sweden, 153
symmetry in creation, 62
synagogue, 373
Syria, modern, 51

Tahmisian, T. N., 115
Taoism, writings of, 39
Taylor, Hudson, 283
teachers, 251, 411
technology, 319, 323
teleological ethics, 322–26, 327
teleology, 62–63, 120
temple, 175, 176, 177, 344, 429
temporal faith, 167, 257, 266–67
temptation, 248
Ten Commandments, 182–83, 334–35, 366, 372, 443, 456–59, 318–19
Tertullian, 373
testimonies, dying, 296–98, 302
testing truth, 43, 259–60
Tetelestai, 161
Tevye, 127
thankfulness, 137, 158, 207, 224, 282, 283, 285, 344, 349–50, 381–82
theism, 95, 133
theocracy, 25, 337, 339, 341
theology, 14, 15, 76, 92, 93
theonomy, 337
theory of relativity, 61
Theos, 234
Thessalonians, 192

thief on cross, 295, 433–34
Thirty Years War, 152
Thomas, apostle, 104, 346, 373
Thomas, Cal, 335–36
Thompson, W. R., 114–15
Thornbury, George Walter, 32
threatenings in Scripture, 258
three-dimensional faith, 263–71
throne of God, 177, 429
"through" faith, 267–68
"Thus says the Lord . . . ," 41
tides, 63–64
Tigris River, 48
Tillich, Paul, 208
tilt of the earth, 63
time, 79–80
Timothy, 16
Tokyo, 284
tolerance, 152
tongues, speaking in, 172
Topical Analysis of the Bible (Elwell), 103
torment of guilt, 208
totalitarianism, 116, 358
traditions, religious, 22, 23
transcendence of God, 76, 78, 79, 84–85, 88, 95, 98, 99, 100, 121, 366–67
transcendent living, 423–25
transcendental meditation, 97
transfiguration, 433
transformed people, 205, 245, 276, 284, 414, 422, 423, 424
transforming, ethic, 316; faith, 257–58, 278, 442; gospel, 423–24; power, 200, 241, 302; truth, 14, 25–27, 36, 163, 165–68, 189, 198, 199, 235, 282, 196, 218, 291, 309
transgressor, way of, 151, 152–55
treason, 300
Treaty of Westphalia, 152
tree, of knowledge, 141; of life, 141, 288, 429
trials, 250
Trinity, 94, 100, 120, 144, 222, 233, 376, 445; belief in, 98, 105; creative power of, 144; God as, 78, 91, 92–107, 161, 173; roles of, 106–7;

scriptural teaching on, 101–6; unity of, 246
Trueblood, 319
trust in Christ, 127, 139, 146, 157, 167–68, 183, 188, 189, 204, 216, 257, 264, 345, 414; in God, 380, 384, 414
truth, 12, 14, 20–27, 35, 99, 299; growing in, 262; of God, 75, 78, 81, 82, 88–89, 120, 129, 148, 263, 347, 445; of Scripture, 96, 162, 239, 258, 260–62, 265, 444; relative, 222; suppression of, 22–25, 53–54, 57–60; transforming, 291; ultimate, 40, 182. *See also* belt of truth; Scripture.
Truths That Transform broadcasts, 36
turning from sin. *See* repentance.
Tyre, 44–46

ultimate, authority, 262, 206, 218; good, 145, 149–52, 323–24; source of reality, 95; truth, 20–27, 25–27, 152
ultraviolet rays, 64–65
"uncaused cause," 80
unchangeability of God, 75, 80–82, 120, 129, 148, 299, 445
"uncleanness" in wife, 390
understanding, human, 38, 135, 150, 185
union with Christ, 455
Unitarians, 105–6
United States, 426
unity, in Christ, 189; with Christ, 251, 358, 421, 426, 427; of the church, 411, 414–19; of creation, 61–62; false, 227; of God, 76, 91, 94, 246, 247, 445; in love, 417
universal call, 188–90, 199, 280. *See also* call of God.
universal church. *See* church, universal.
universalism, 223, 226–27, 230, 235

universe, 61–62, 79–80, 96, 133, 137, 187; God as. *See* pantheism.

University of Virginia, charter of, 365–66

unknowable God, 98, 99, 100

"unmoved mover," 80

unrighteousness. *See* wickedness.

Ur, 269

USSR, 425

utilitarianism, 113, 324–25

value, 325–26; of life, 120, 121, 328–29

values, clarification, 361–62; spiritual, 335–36; system, 320

Van Engen, Charles, 407

vanity. *See* worthlessness.

Vedic writings, 39

Venus, 63

vicarious atonement. *See* atonement.

Vicksburg, Mississippi, 256

victims of sin, 154–56

Victorian society, 206

victory in Christ, 184, 265, 288, 294, 299, 302, 310, 351; in relationships, 397

Vine, Christ as, 243

virgin birth, 98, 174, 189, 264, 410, 450

Virginia, 352

virtue, 217, 335

Virtue of Selfishness, The, (Rand), 323

visible Church, 180, 411, 412, 413, 460, 461

Volney's Travels (Volney), 47

Volney, Constantin, 47

Voltaire, 61, 95, 298

Vos, Geerhardus, 203

walk with God, 310, 375

walking on water, 134

wall of separation, 156, 162, 362–66

Warfield, Benjamin B., 40

wars, 98, 111, 142, 163–64, 358. *See also* by name.

Washington, George, 298

way of salvation, 150, 182

wealth, 266–67, 312–13

weather, 134

web of pain, 386

Webb, Robert, 228–29

wedding feast, 217

week, rhythm of, 146

welfare, 342–44, 398, 425

Wells, H. G., 128

Welsh awakening, 281

Wesley, Charles, 215; John, 404

"Western ape-man," 114

Western culture, 21, 118, 119, 143, 152, 230, 309–10, 319–20, 346, 352, 365

Westminster, Assembly, 16–17, 24–25, 74–75, 414, 417–18; *catechisms,* 16–17, 25, 27, 30, 36–37, 38, 75, 132–33, 141, 145–46, 150, 162, 176, 178, 179, 182, 203, 241, 289, 302, 308, 315, 316, 421, 423, 426–27, 437, 442–62; *Confession of Faith,* 16–17, 25–27, 53–54, 60, 76, 77–78, 109, 120–21, 125, 144, 152, 162, 150–51, 169, 180, 181, 185, 191–93, 192, 193, 201, 215, 221, 225, 231, 237, 247, 255, 258, 260, 268, 273, 276, 286, 301, 308, 330, 333, 336, 351, 356, 357, 359, 369, 383, 384, 385, 386, 387–88, 389, 390, 408, 409, 411, 414, 417, 423, 431, 432, 435, 436, 442–62

Whatever Became of Sin? (Menninger), 205

"whatever works" ethic, 326

Whitefield, George, 33–34

Why I Am Not a Christian (Russell), 32

"Why I don't go to the movies," 405

wickedness, 74, 86, 190–91, 277, 285, 293, 431, 435

wife, 341–42, 385

wilderness, 412

will, of Christ, 442, 307–14, 315, 318, 319, 333, 334, 336, 349, 423, 446; of God, 37, 41, 71, 78, 80, 83–84, 132, 133, 137–40, 155, 176, 189–90, 198, 199, 233, 246–47, 307–14, 315, 318, 319, 334, 336, 349, 423, 446; human, 192, 197, 199, 225, 240, 249, 258, 276, 277, 311, 330, 396; renewing of, 185, 193

Wilson, Robert Dick, 42

wisdom, 74, 296; of God, 37, 75, 82–83, 120, 122, 125, 129, 133, 144, 148, 311, 445; human, 232, 312

witness to world, 10, 153, 193, 199–200, 251, 269, 281, 339, 346, 360, 374–75, 410, 416, 419

Wizard of Oz, 312

Word, Christ as, 99, 167; ministry of, 249, 255, 268–69, 411. *See also* preaching.

work, blessing of, 145, 147–48, 381; on Sabbath, 383

workmanship, 137, 252, 453

works, covenant of, 318; righteousness, 29–30, 206, 276, 277, 346, 380

world, 224; witness to, 193, 251

World Council of Churches, 97–98

World War I, 98, 142, 164

World War II, 142, 163–64, 358, 388

world-infected church, 309

worldliness, 252–53, 286, 291, 300, 311, 438

worldviews, 110, 191–92, 264, 267, 308, 313, 325–26, 366

worship, 4, 13–14, 26, 106, 122, 126, 137, 146, 148, 158, 175, 179, 180, 248, 253, 279, 285, 286, 279, 308, 318, 334, 344–45, 356, 369, 371, 373, 374, 375–76, 381–82, 384, 385, 406, 413, 417, 456; relationships and, 387

worthlessness, 129–31, 150, 164–65, 168, 170, 188, 193–94, 210, 224, 311, 313, 325–26

wrath of God. *See* anger, divine.
Wright, Katherine, 222; Orville, 222; Wilbur, 222
"writings of the enlightened," 39

Wycliffe, John, 302
Wynkoff, David, 56–57

Yahweh, 234
young people without hope, 425

Zacchaeus, 174–75
Zagros Mountains, 48